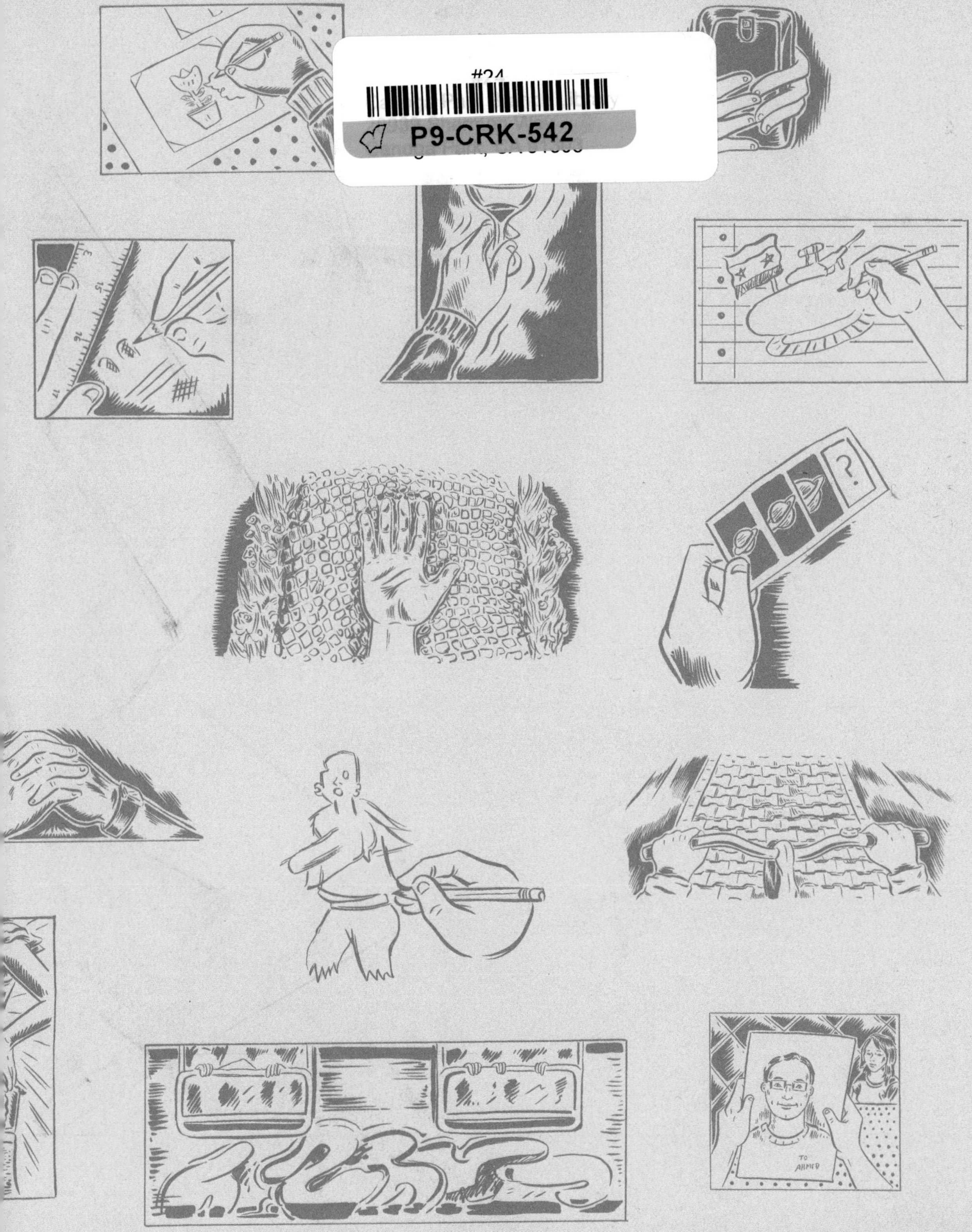
?
TO
AHMED

Supervising Editor: Gary Groth
Designer: Keeli McCarthy
Editor: Kristy Valenti
Production: Paul Baresh
Editorial Assistance: RJ Casey, Conrad Groth, Eric Huberty, Manon Hume,
Minna Lee, and Sara Podwall
Publicist: Jacq Cohen
Associate Publisher: Eric Reynolds
Publisher: Gary Groth

Fantagraphics Books, Inc. 7563 Lake City Way NE, Seattle, WA 98115
(800) 657-1100

www.fantagraphics.com

Follow us on Twitter @fantagraphics and on Facebook
at Facebook.com/Fantagraphics

ISBN: 978-1-68396-132-1
Library of Congress Control Number: 2018936469
First Edition: October 2018
Printed in China

DRAWN TO BERLIN

COMIC WORKSHOPS IN REFUGEE SHELTERS
AND OTHER STORIES FROM A NEW EUROPE

ALI FITZGERALD

FANTAGRAPHICS BOOKS

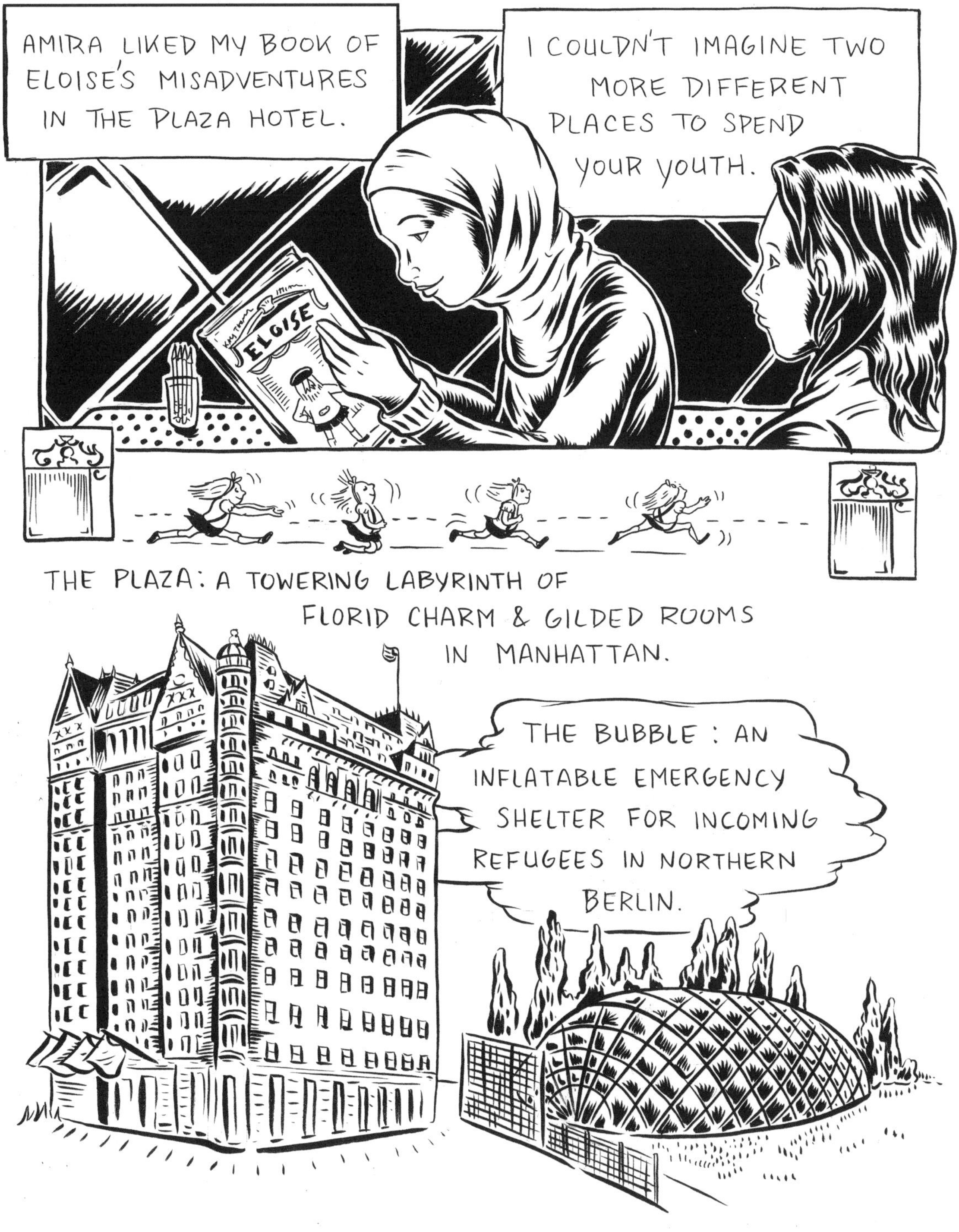
AMIRA LIKED MY BOOK OF ELOISE'S MISADVENTURES IN THE PLAZA HOTEL.
I COULDN'T IMAGINE TWO MORE DIFFERENT PLACES TO SPEND YOUR YOUTH.
ELOISE
THE PLAZA: A TOWERING LABYRINTH OF FLORID CHARM & GILDED ROOMS IN MANHATTAN.
THE BUBBLE: AN INFLATABLE EMERGENCY SHELTER FOR INCOMING REFUGEES IN NORTHERN BERLIN.

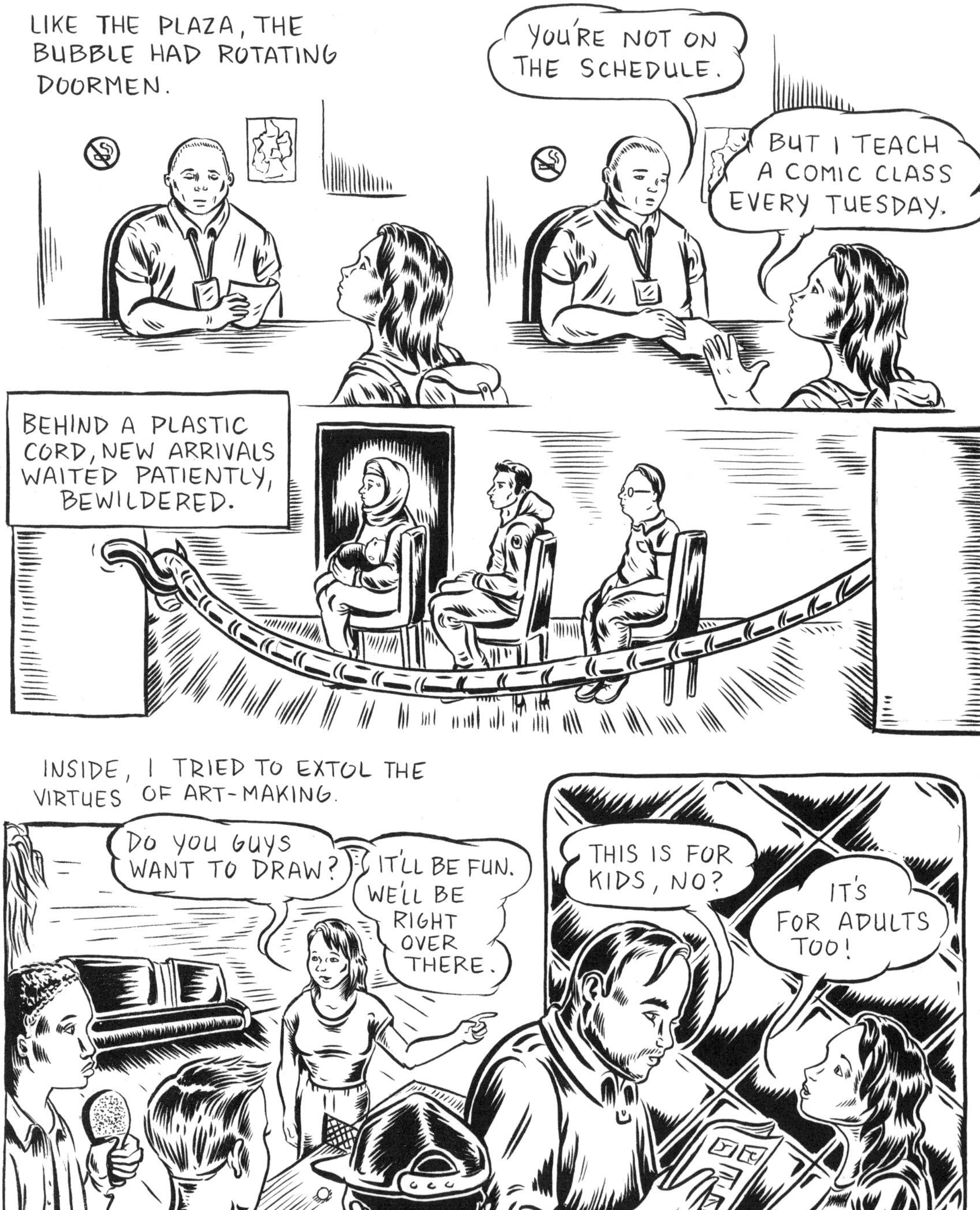
LIKE THE PLAZA, THE BUBBLE HAD ROTATING DOORMEN.
YOU'RE NOT ON THE SCHEDULE.
BUT I TEACH A COMIC CLASS EVERY TUESDAY.
BEHIND A PLASTIC CORD, NEW ARRIVALS WAITED PATIENTLY, BEWILDERED.
INSIDE, I TRIED TO EXTOL THE VIRTUES OF ART-MAKING.
DO YOU GUYS WANT TO DRAW?
IT'LL BE FUN. WE'LL BE RIGHT OVER THERE.
THIS IS FOR KIDS, NO?
IT'S FOR ADULTS TOO!

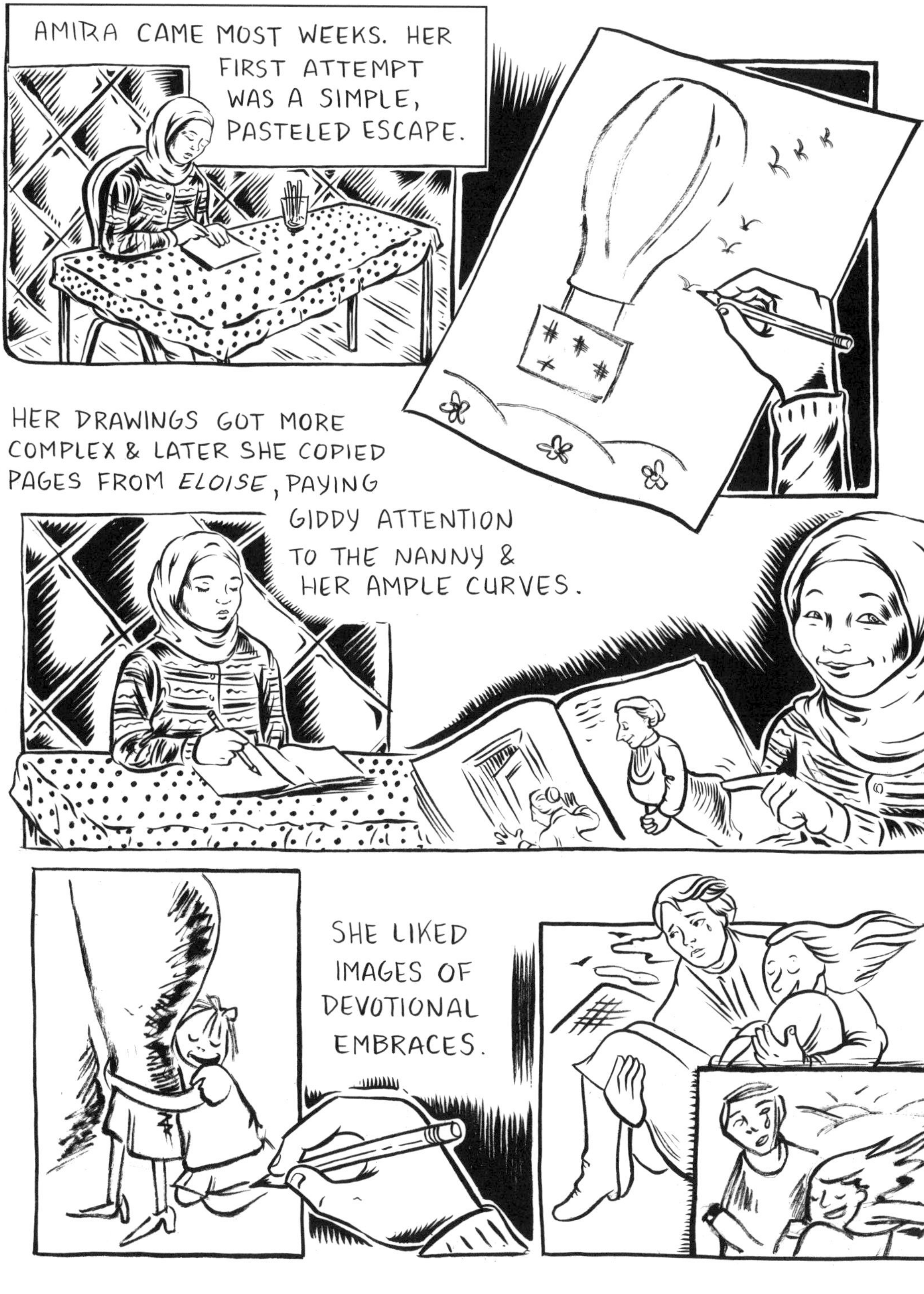
AMIRA CAME MOST WEEKS. HER FIRST ATTEMPT WAS A SIMPLE, PASTELED ESCAPE.
HER DRAWINGS GOT MORE COMPLEX & LATER SHE COPIED PAGES FROM *ELOISE*, PAYING GIDDY ATTENTION TO THE NANNY & HER AMPLE CURVES.
SHE LIKED IMAGES OF DEVOTIONAL EMBRACES.

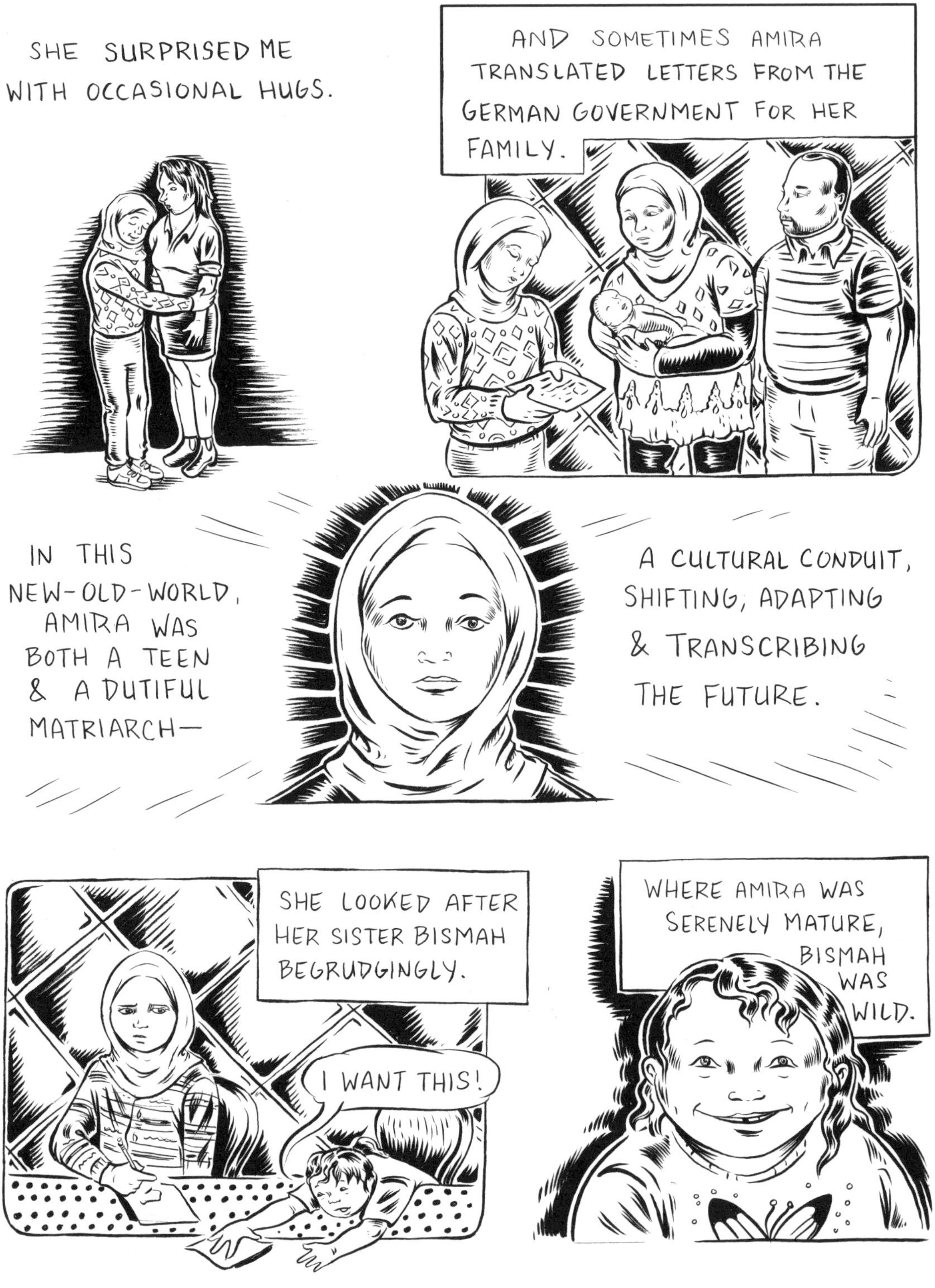
SHE SURPRISED ME WITH OCCASIONAL HUGS.
AND SOMETIMES AMIRA TRANSLATED LETTERS FROM THE GERMAN GOVERNMENT FOR HER FAMILY.
IN THIS NEW-OLD-WORLD, AMIRA WAS BOTH A TEEN & A DUTIFUL MATRIARCH—
A CULTURAL CONDUIT, SHIFTING, ADAPTING & TRANSCRIBING THE FUTURE.
SHE LOOKED AFTER HER SISTER BISMAH BEGRUDGINGLY.
I WANT THIS!
WHERE AMIRA WAS SERENELY MATURE, BISMAH WAS WILD.

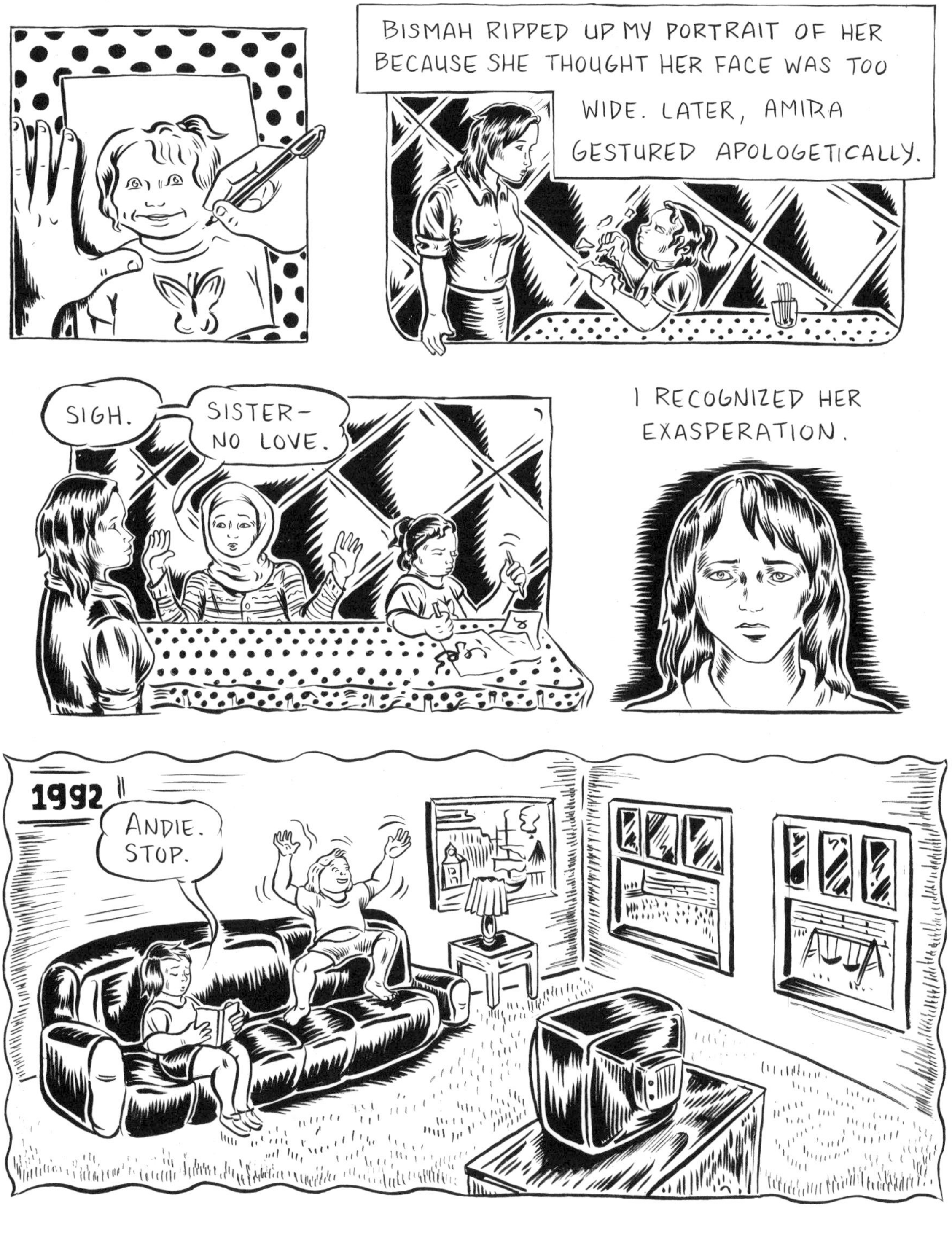
BISMAH RIPPED UP MY PORTRAIT OF HER BECAUSE SHE THOUGHT HER FACE WAS TOO WIDE. LATER, AMIRA GESTURED APOLOGETICALLY.
SIGH.
SISTER- NO LOVE.
I RECOGNIZED HER EXASPERATION.
1992
ANDIE. STOP.

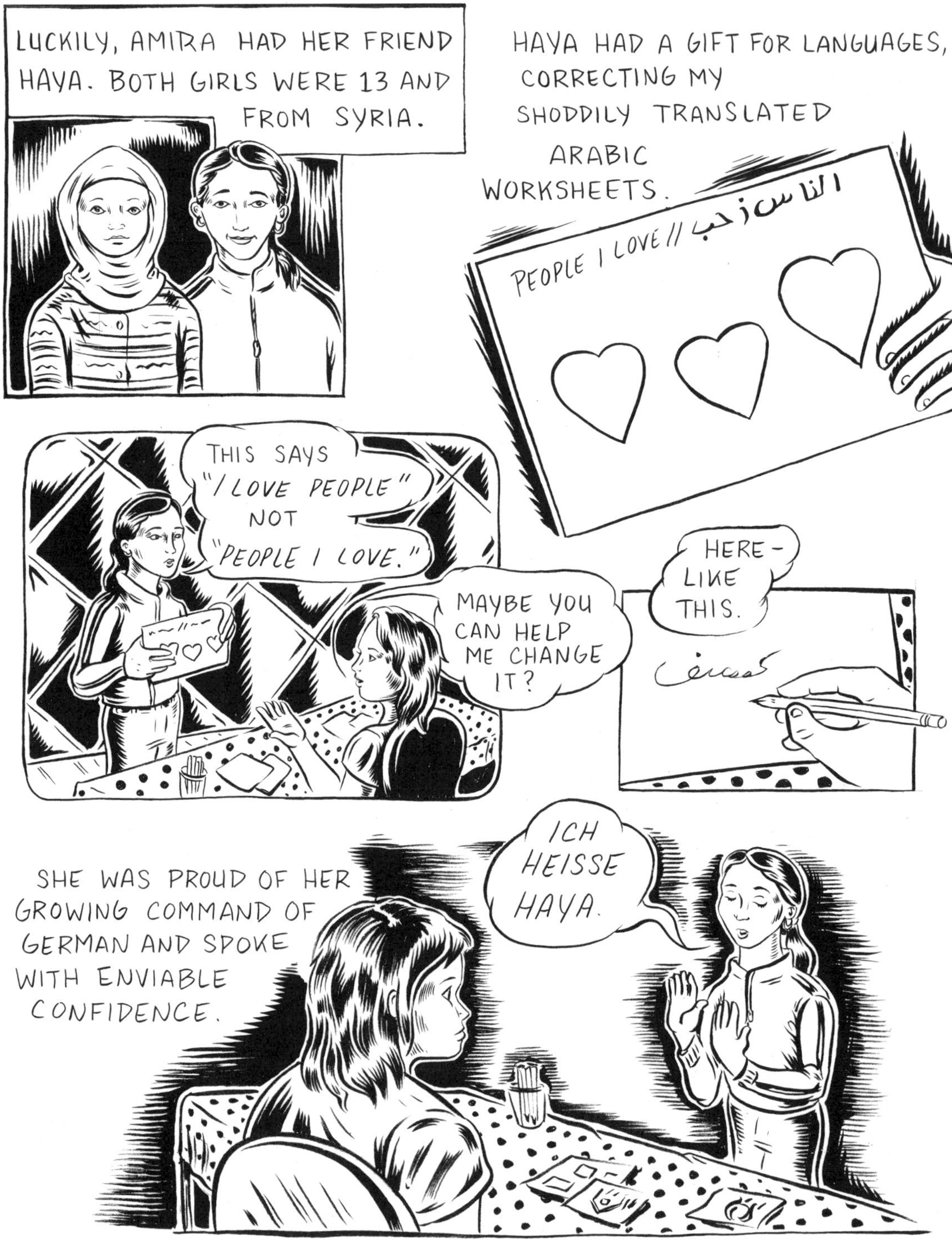
LUCKILY, AMIRA HAD HER FRIEND HAYA. BOTH GIRLS WERE 13 AND FROM SYRIA.
HAYA HAD A GIFT FOR LANGUAGES, CORRECTING MY SHODDILY TRANSLATED ARABIC WORKSHEETS.
PEOPLE I LOVE //
THIS SAYS "I LOVE PEOPLE" NOT "PEOPLE I LOVE."
MAYBE YOU CAN HELP ME CHANGE IT?
HERE- LIKE THIS.
SHE WAS PROUD OF HER GROWING COMMAND OF GERMAN AND SPOKE WITH ENVIABLE CONFIDENCE.
ICH HEISSE HAYA.

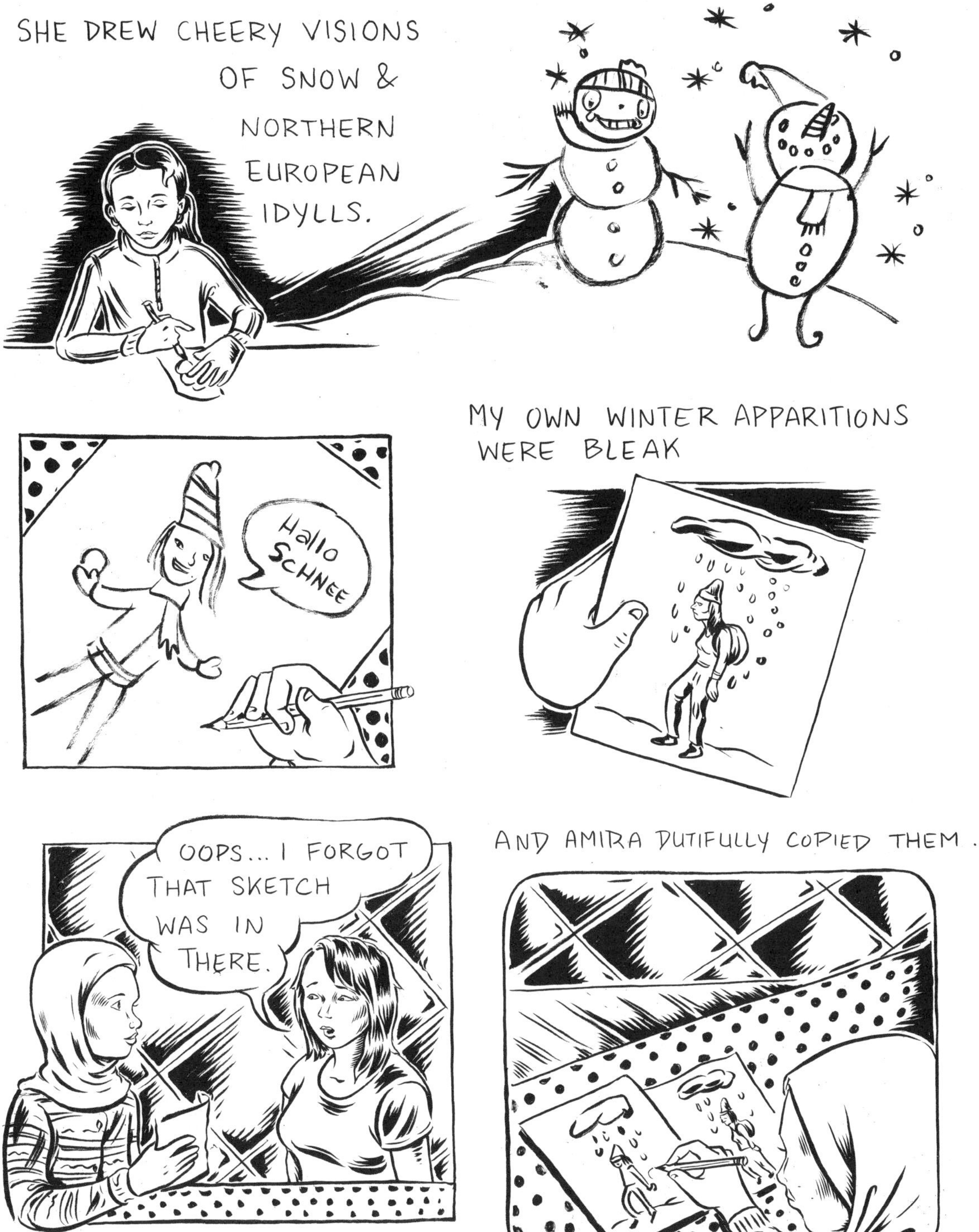
SHE DREW CHEERY VISIONS OF SNOW & NORTHERN EUROPEAN IDYLLS.
Hallo Schnee
MY OWN WINTER APPARITIONS WERE BLEAK
OOPS... I FORGOT THAT SKETCH WAS IN THERE.
AND AMIRA DUTIFULLY COPIED THEM.

I TAUGHT THEM FACIAL EXPRESSIONS USING A GENERIC, RUBBERY MAN.

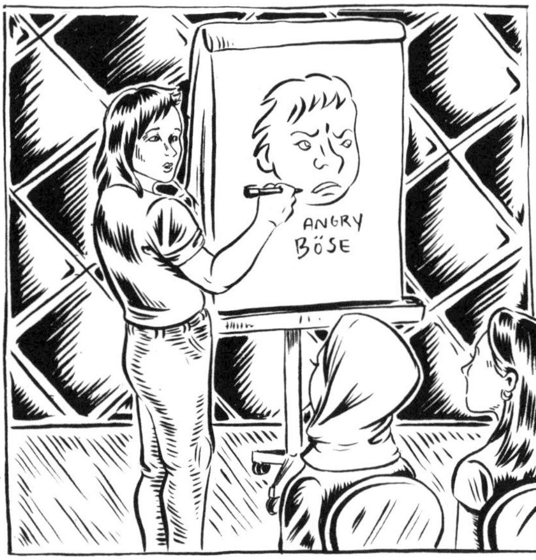
ANGRY
BÖSE

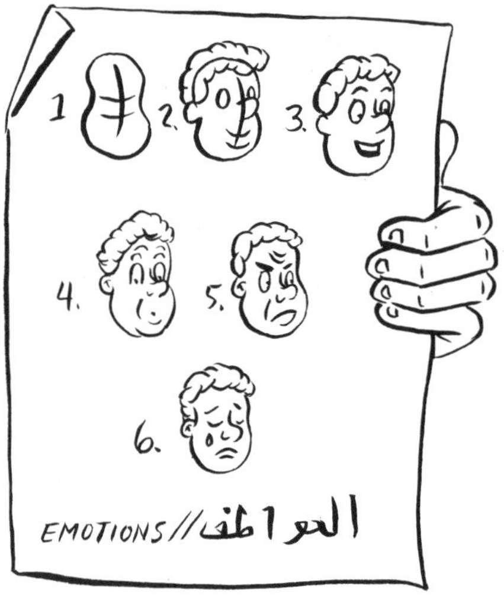
1
2.
3.
4.
5.
6.
EMOTIONS//العواطف

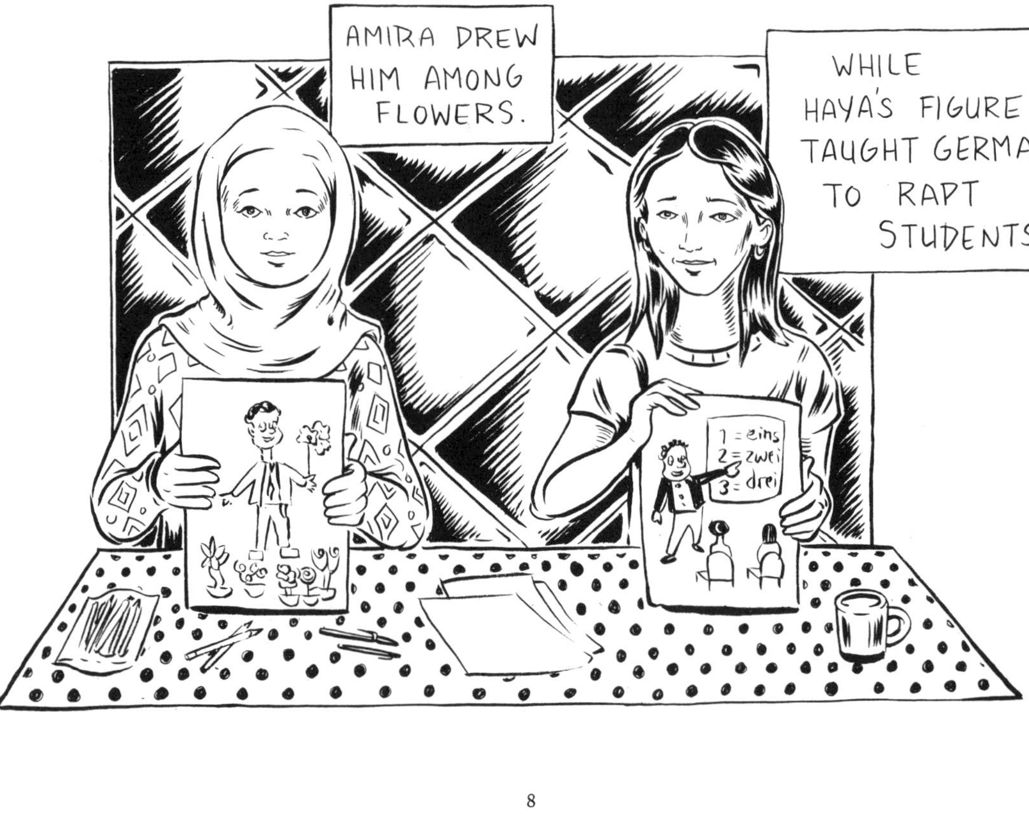
AMIRA DREW HIM AMONG FLOWERS.
WHILE HAYA'S FIGURE TAUGHT GERMAN TO RAPT STUDENTS.
1 = eins
2 = zwei
3 = drei

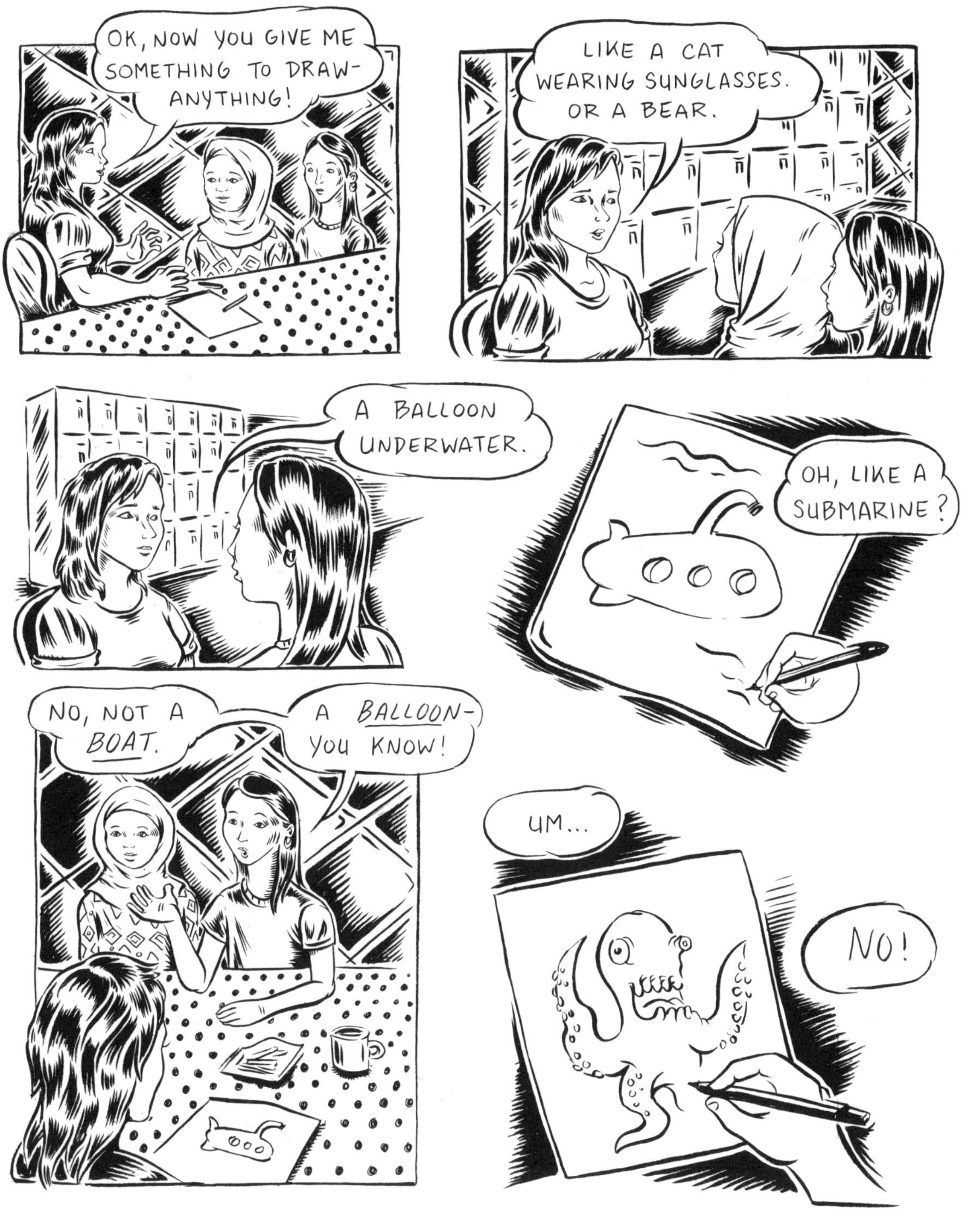
OK, NOW YOU GIVE ME SOMETHING TO DRAW- ANYTHING!
LIKE A CAT WEARING SUNGLASSES. OR A BEAR.
A BALLOON UNDERWATER.
OH, LIKE A SUBMARINE?
NO, NOT A BOAT.
A BALLOON- YOU KNOW!
UM...
NO!

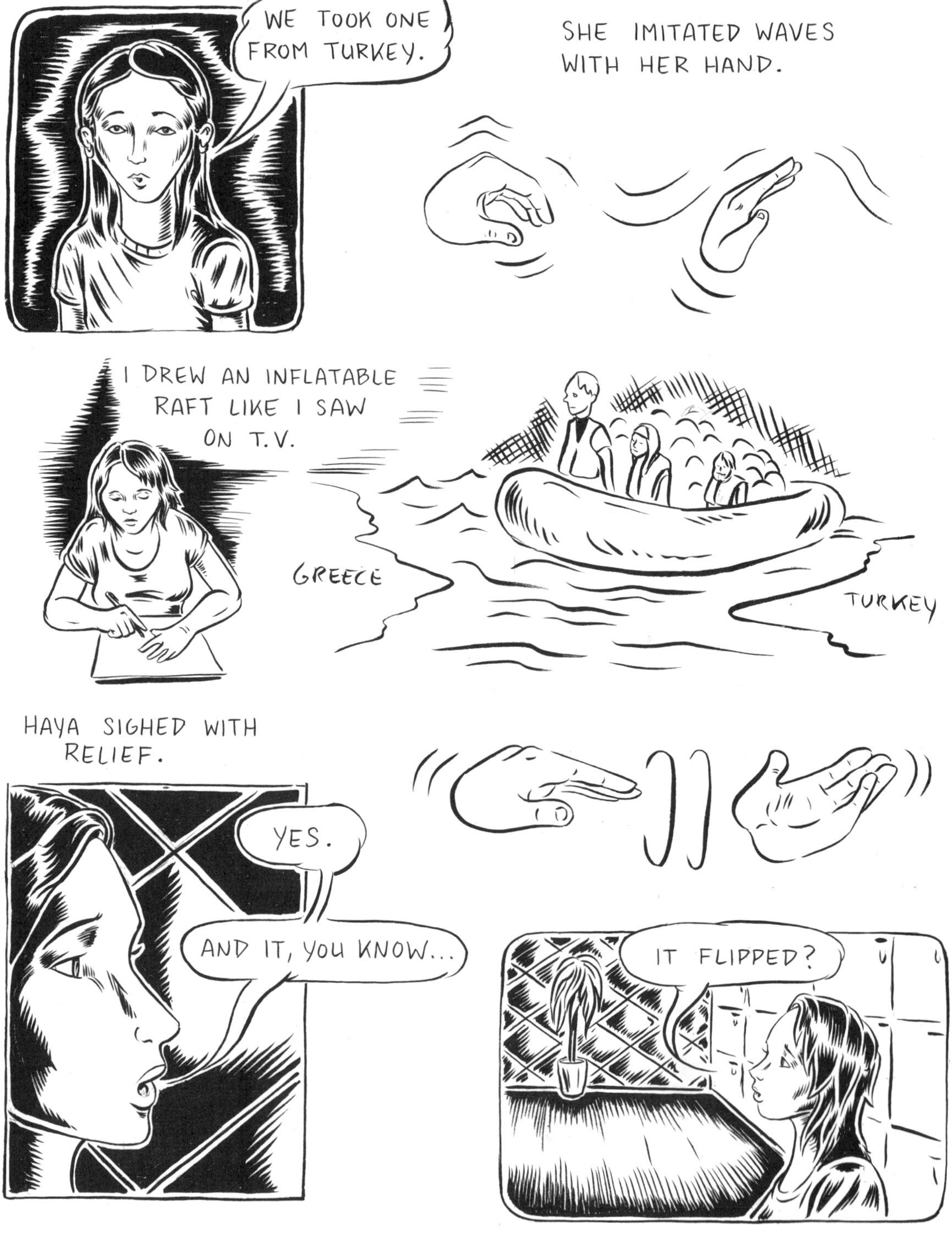
WE TOOK ONE FROM TURKEY.
SHE IMITATED WAVES WITH HER HAND.
I DREW AN INFLATABLE RAFT LIKE I SAW ON T.V.
GREECE
TURKEY
HAYA SIGHED WITH RELIEF.
YES.
AND IT, YOU KNOW...
IT FLIPPED?

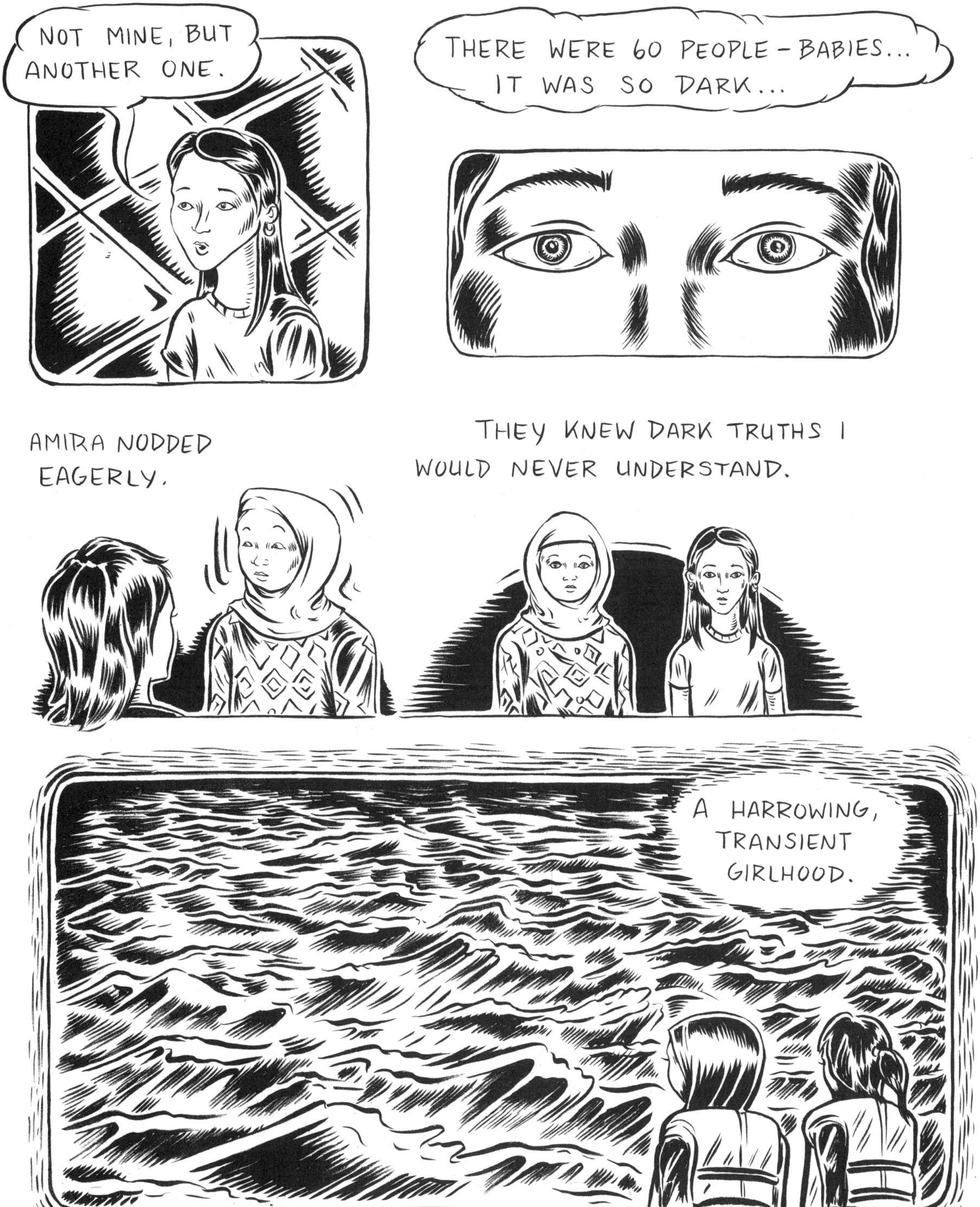
NOT MINE, BUT ANOTHER ONE.
THERE WERE 60 PEOPLE - BABIES... IT WAS SO DARK...
AMIRA NODDED EAGERLY.
THEY KNEW DARK TRUTHS I WOULD NEVER UNDERSTAND.
A HARROWING, TRANSIENT GIRLHOOD.

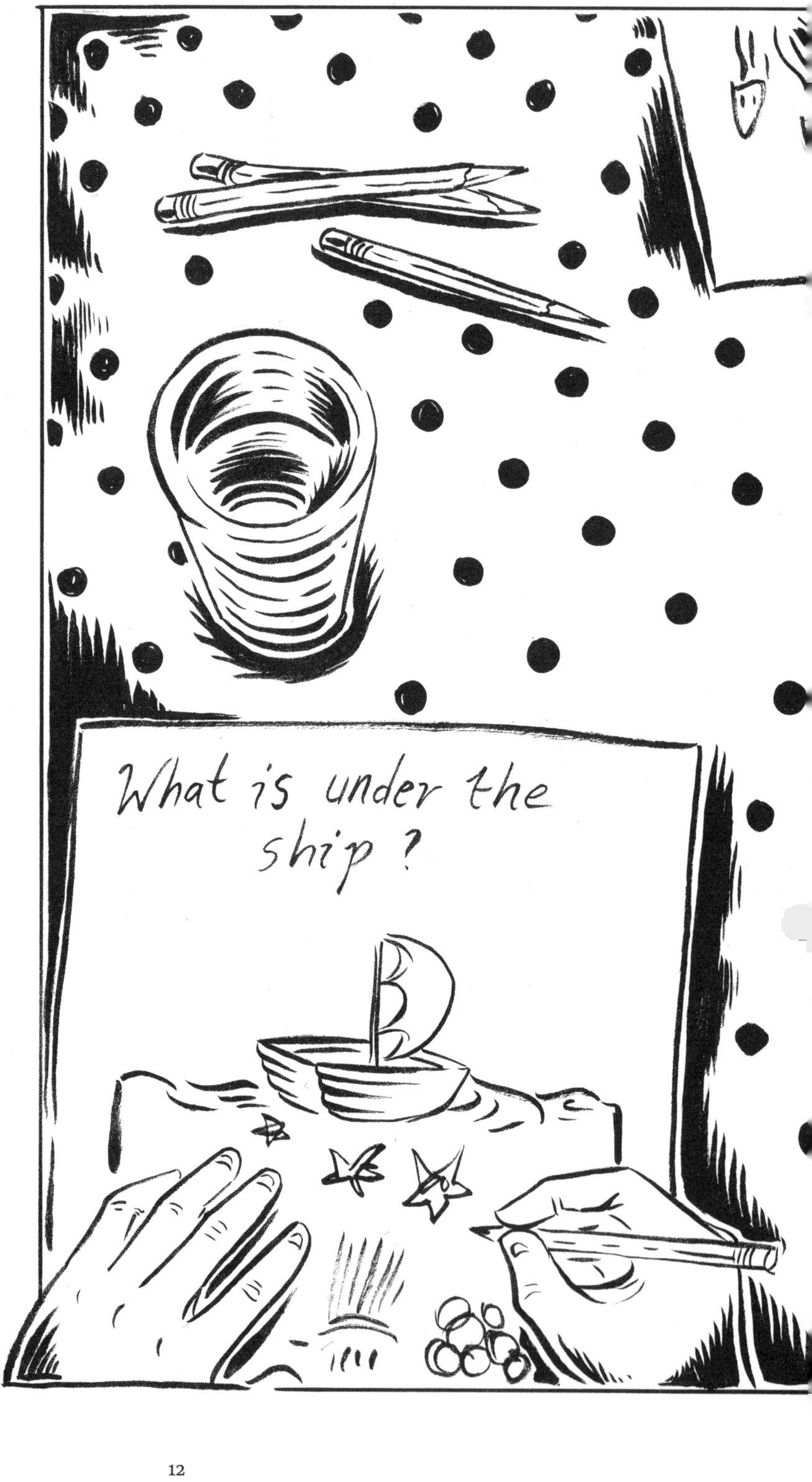
What is under the ship?

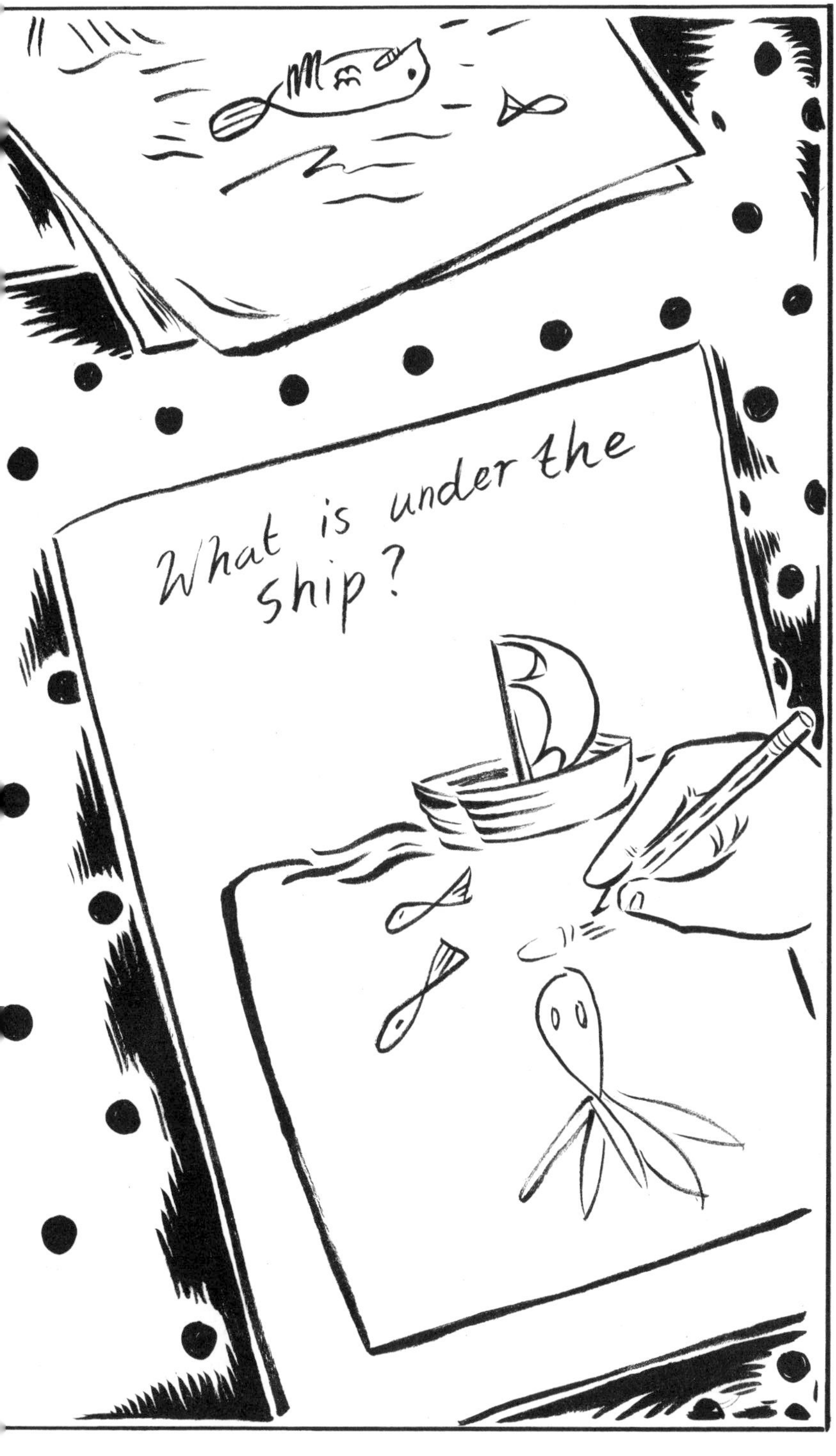
What is under the ship?

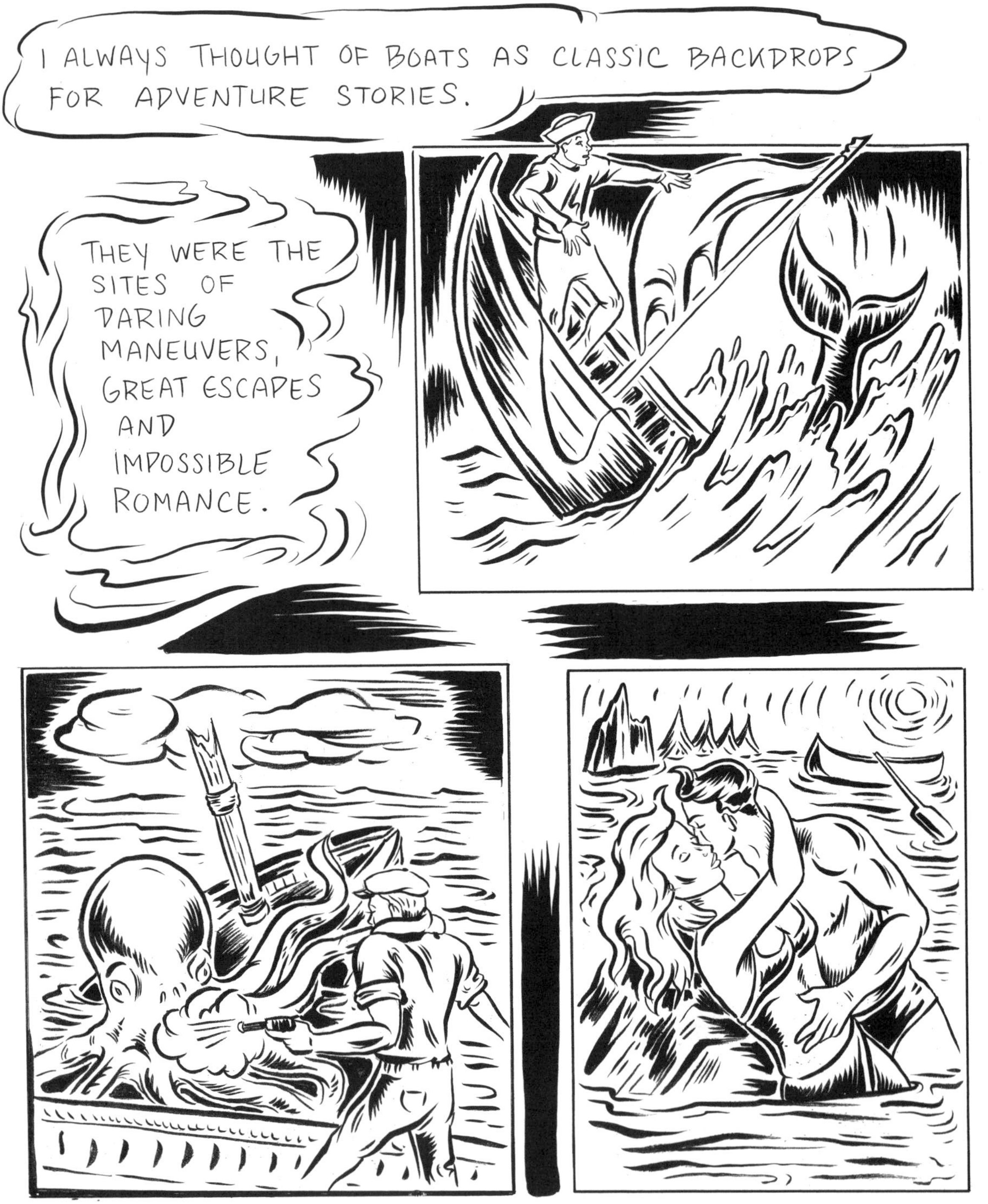
I ALWAYS THOUGHT OF BOATS AS CLASSIC BACKDROPS FOR ADVENTURE STORIES.
THEY WERE THE SITES OF DARING MANEUVERS, GREAT ESCAPES AND IMPOSSIBLE ROMANCE.

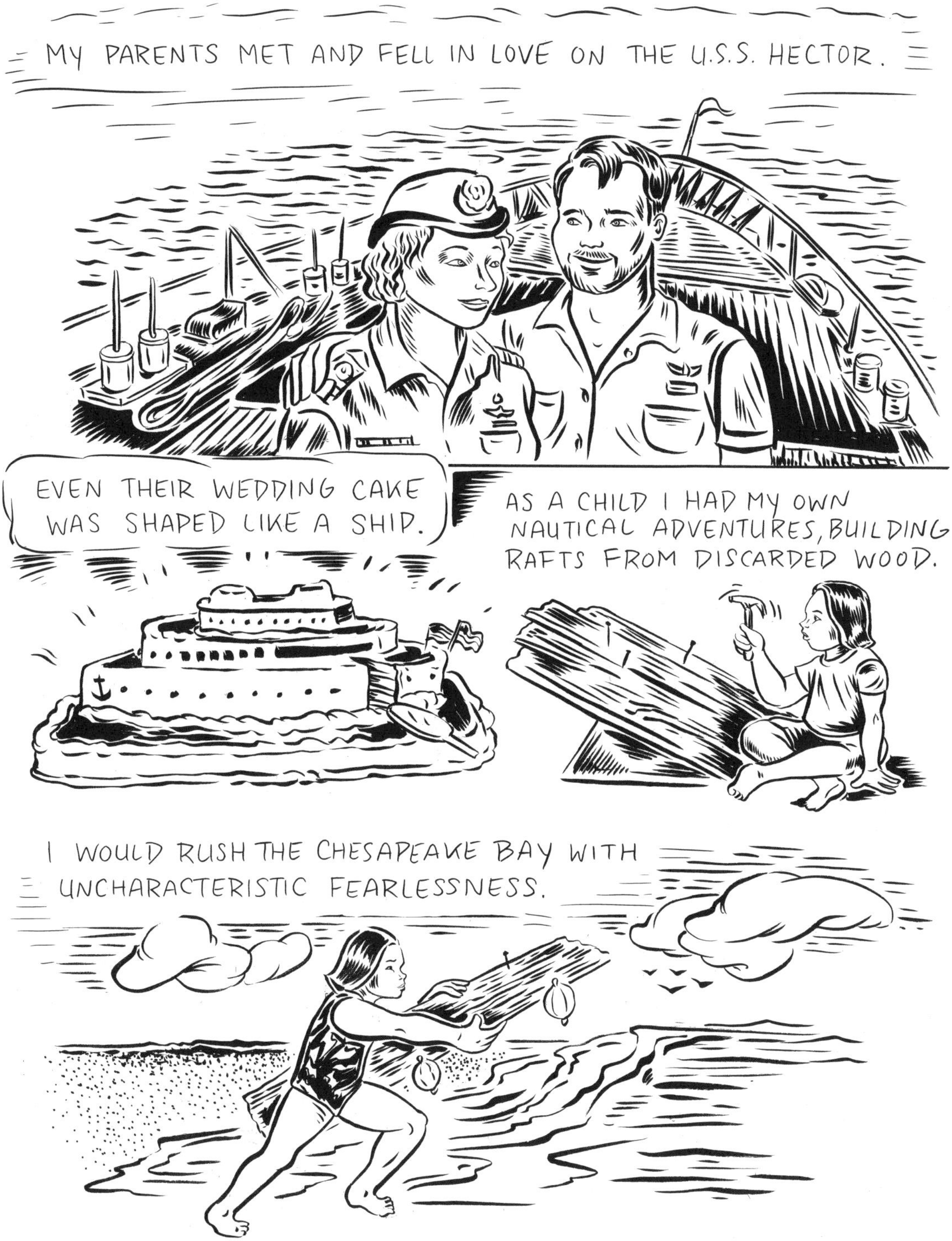

MY PARENTS MET AND FELL IN LOVE ON THE U.S.S. HECTOR.
EVEN THEIR WEDDING CAKE WAS SHAPED LIKE A SHIP.
AS A CHILD I HAD MY OWN NAUTICAL ADVENTURES, BUILDING RAFTS FROM DISCARDED WOOD.
I WOULD RUSH THE CHESAPEAKE BAY WITH UNCHARACTERISTIC FEARLESSNESS.

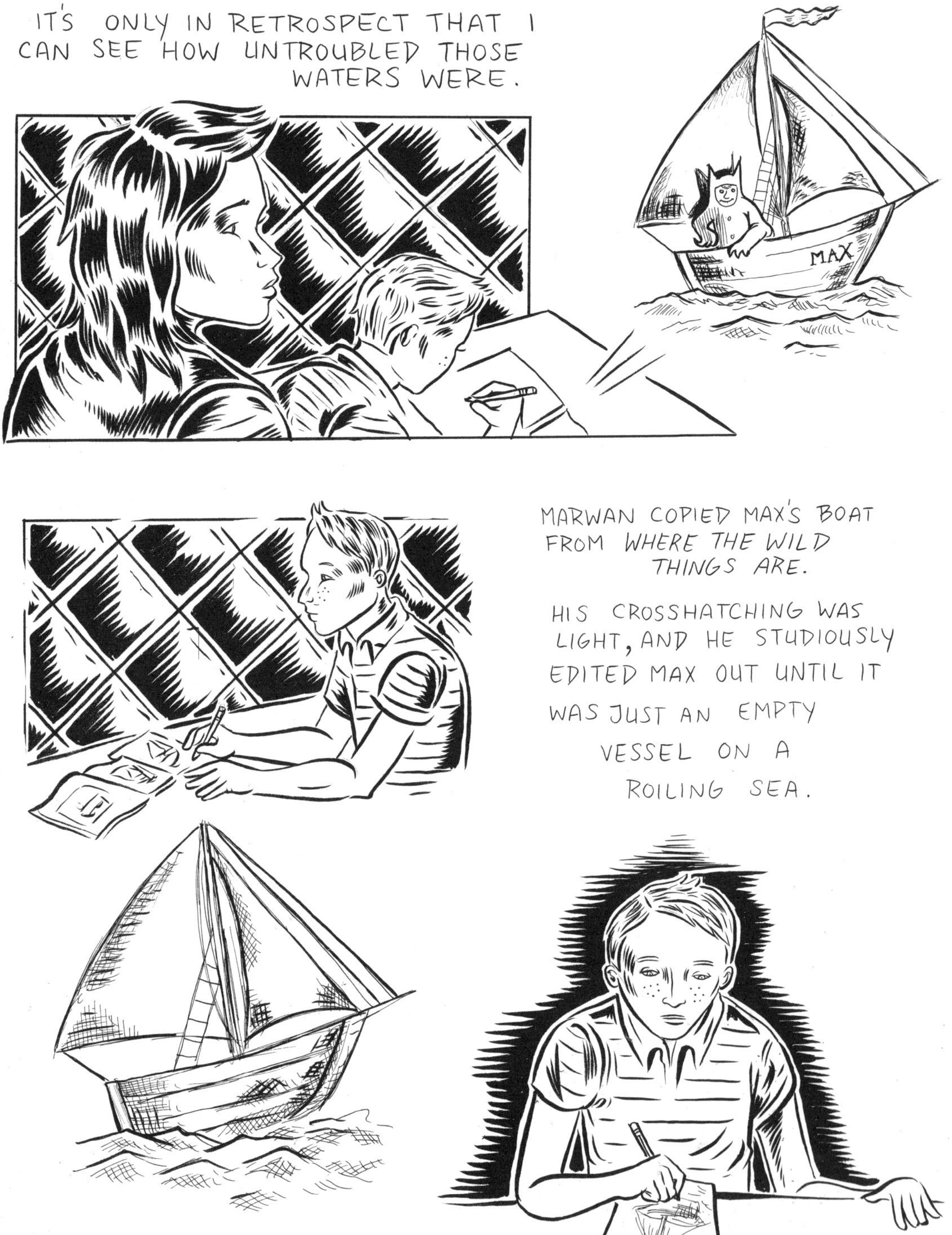
IT'S ONLY IN RETROSPECT THAT I CAN SEE HOW UNTROUBLED THOSE WATERS WERE.
MAX
MARWAN COPIED MAX'S BOAT FROM *WHERE THE WILD THINGS ARE.*
HIS CROSSHATCHING WAS LIGHT, AND HE STUDIOUSLY EDITED MAX OUT UNTIL IT WAS JUST AN EMPTY VESSEL ON A ROILING SEA.

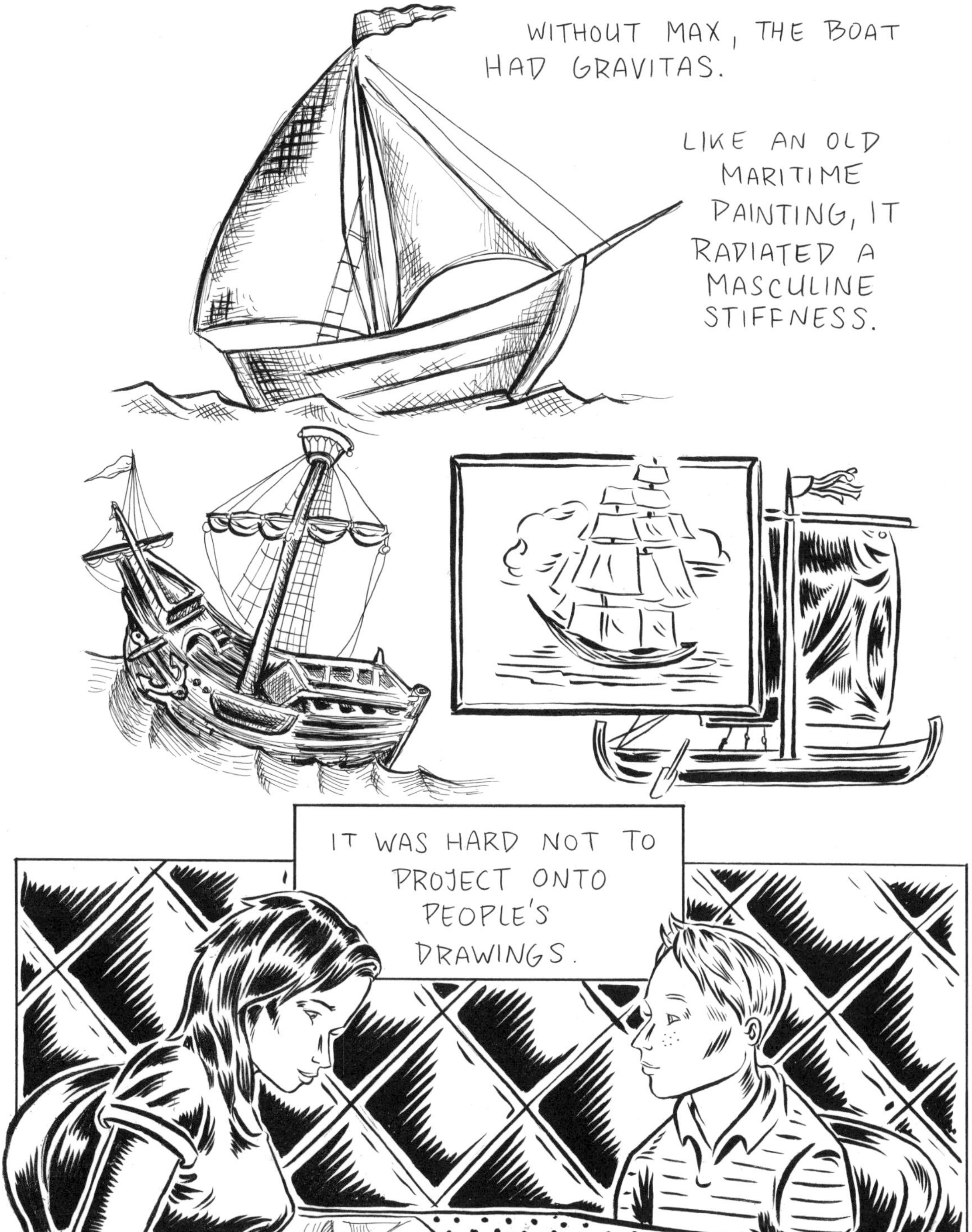
WITHOUT MAX, THE BOAT HAD GRAVITAS.
LIKE AN OLD MARITIME PAINTING, IT RADIATED A MASCULINE STIFFNESS.
IT WAS HARD NOT TO PROJECT ONTO PEOPLE'S DRAWINGS.

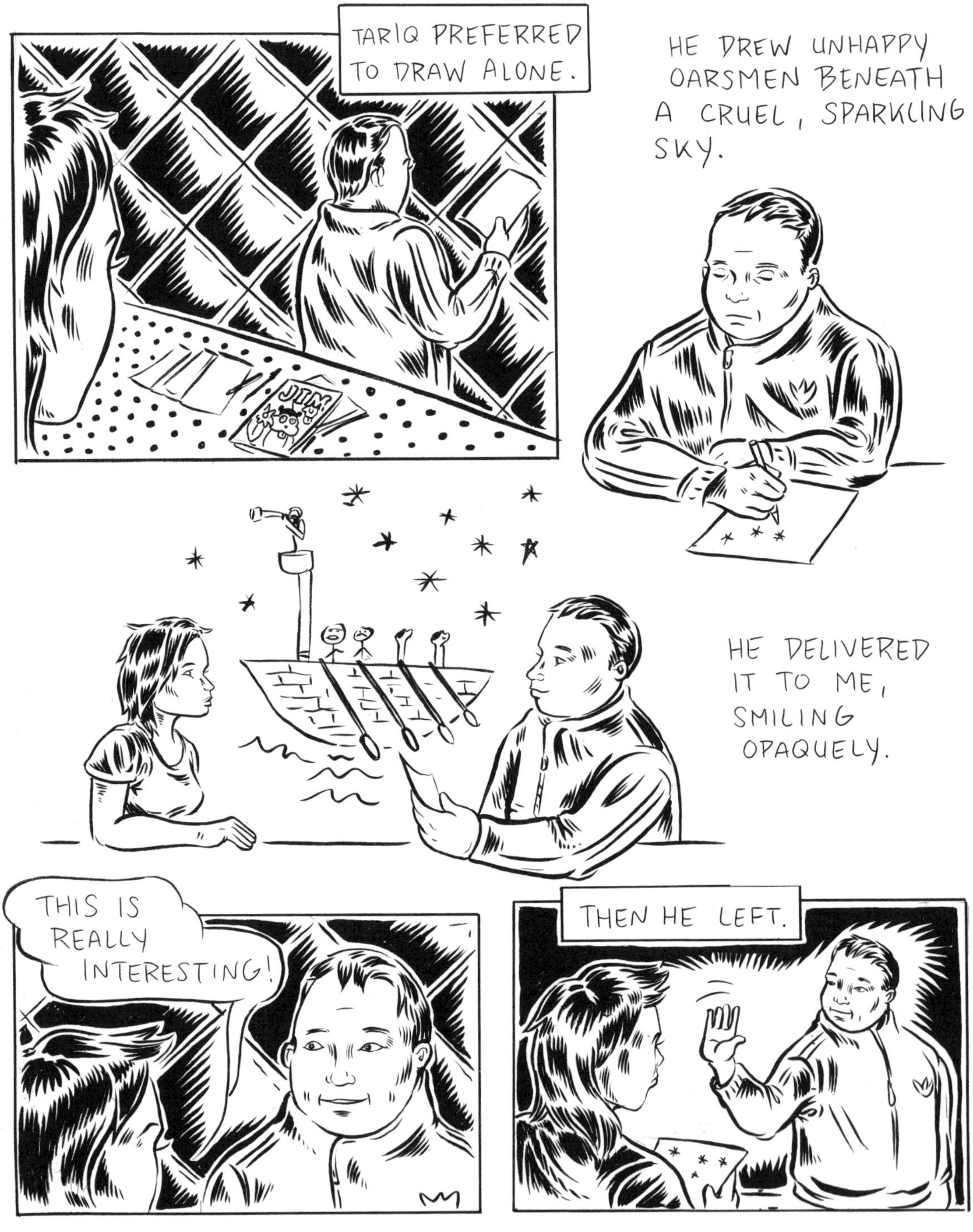
TARIQ PREFERRED TO DRAW ALONE.
HE DREW UNHAPPY OARSMEN BENEATH A CRUEL, SPARKLING SKY.
HE DELIVERED IT TO ME, SMILING OPAQUELY.
THIS IS REALLY INTERESTING!
THEN HE LEFT.

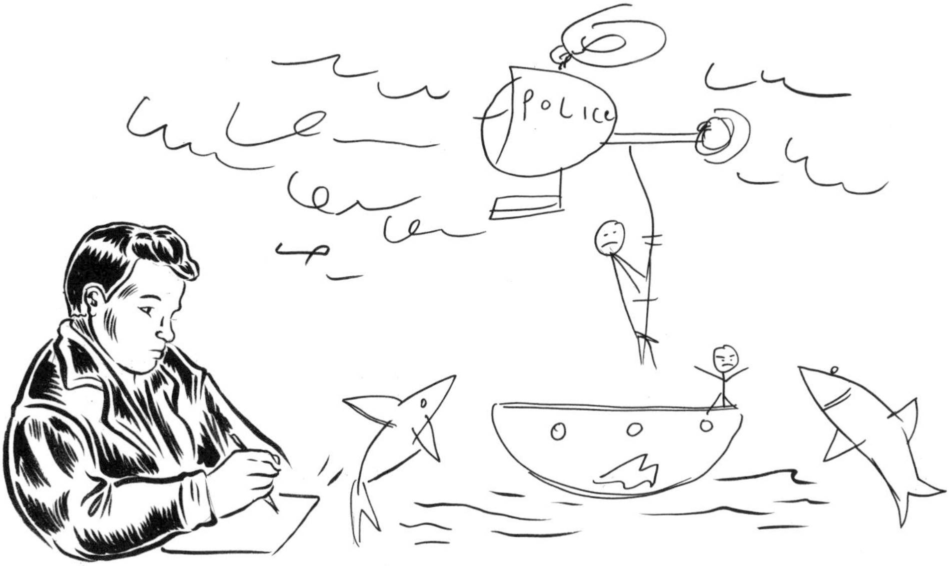
POLICE

A LOT OF SEASCAPES WERE RINGED BY FEARS.

OTHERS WERE IDYLLS, PLACID AND REMOTE.

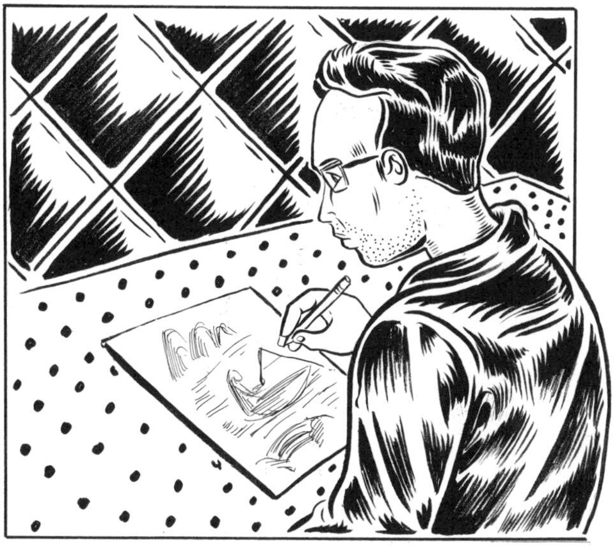

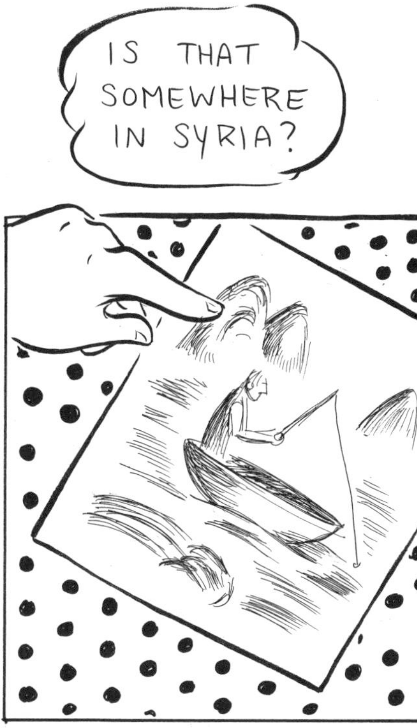
IS THAT SOMEWHERE IN SYRIA?

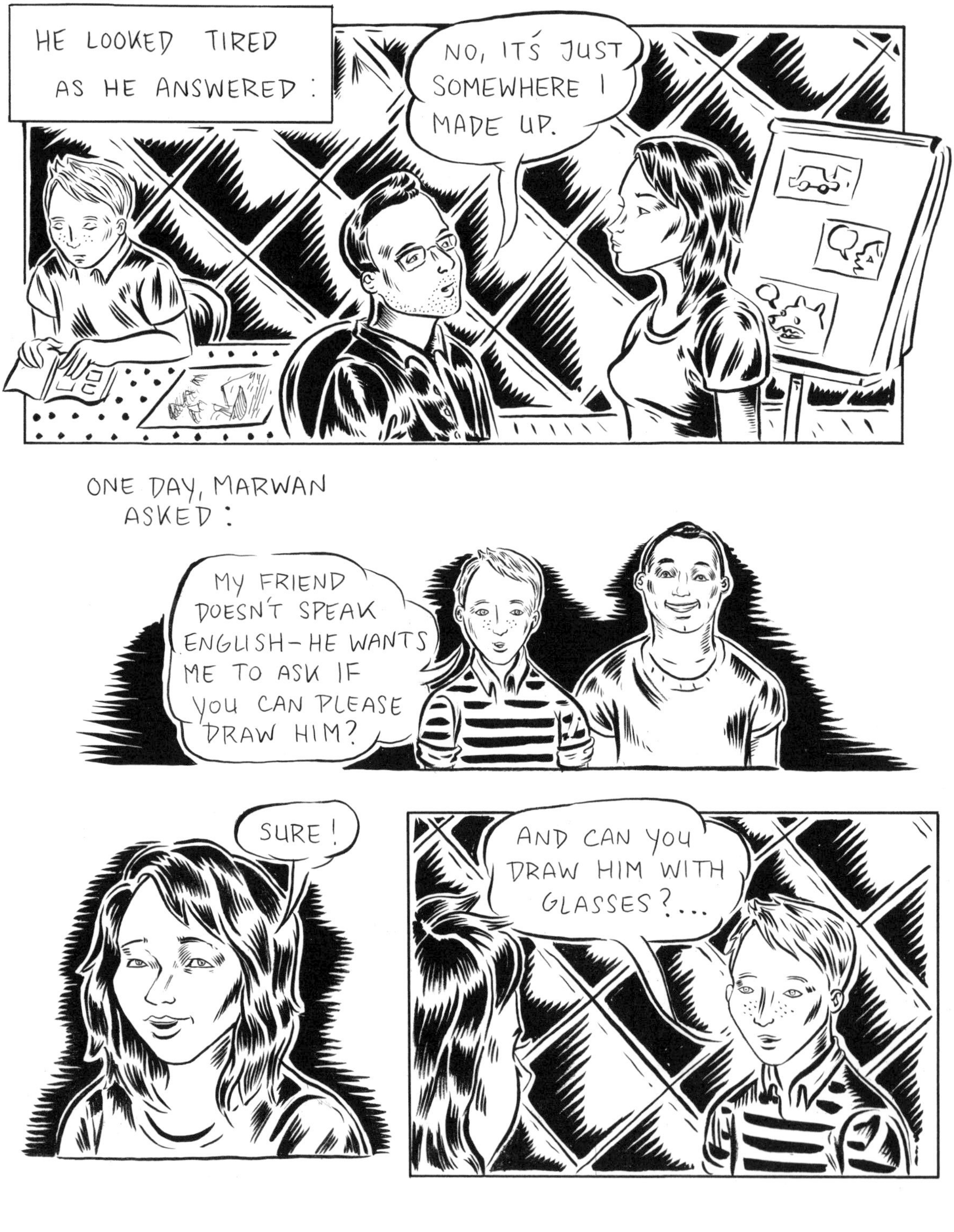
HE LOOKED TIRED AS HE ANSWERED:
NO, IT'S JUST SOMEWHERE I MADE UP.
ONE DAY, MARWAN ASKED:
MY FRIEND DOESN'T SPEAK ENGLISH–HE WANTS ME TO ASK IF YOU CAN PLEASE DRAW HIM?
SURE!
AND CAN YOU DRAW HIM WITH GLASSES?...

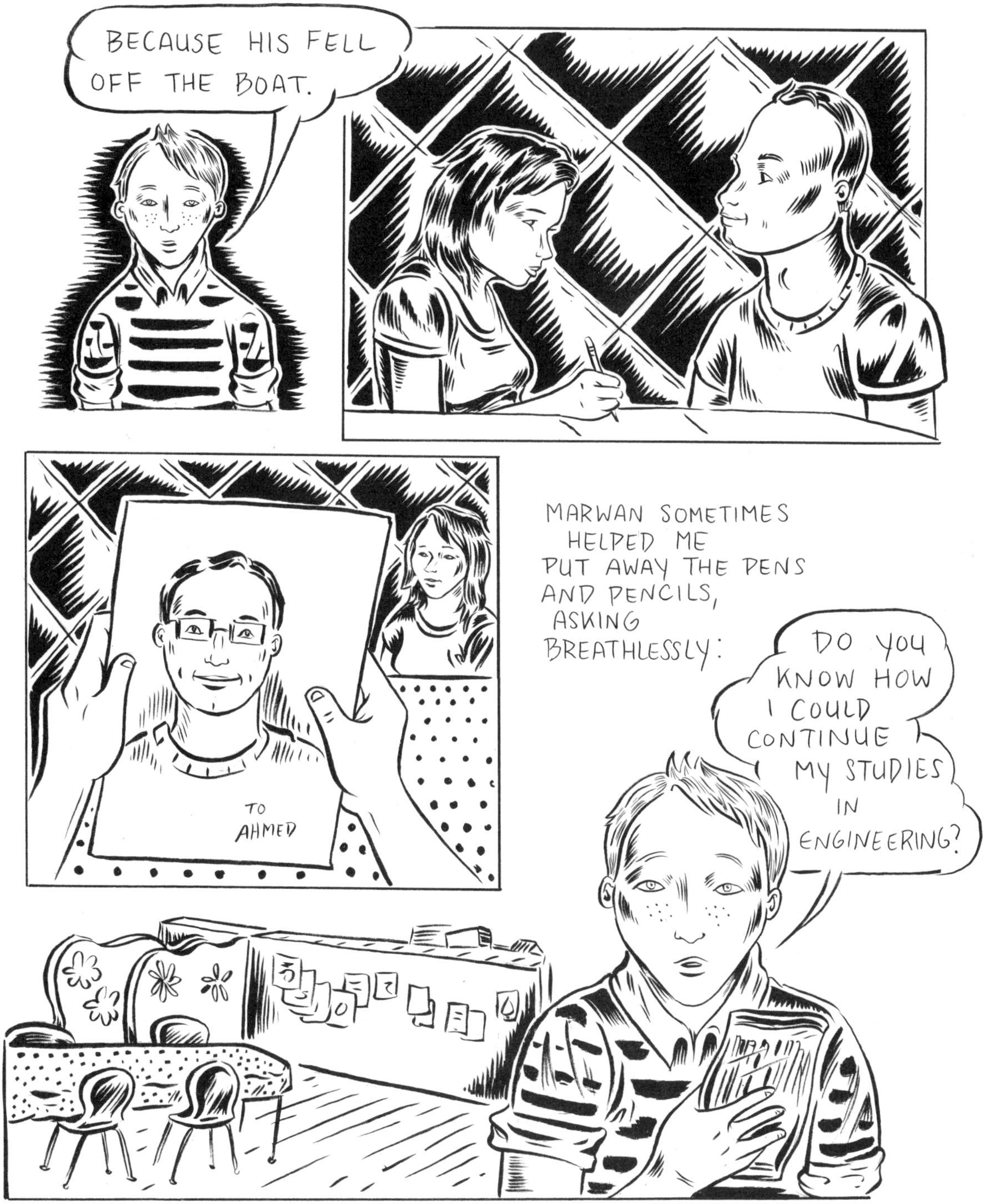
BECAUSE HIS FELL OFF THE BOAT.
TO AHMED
MARWAN SOMETIMES HELPED ME PUT AWAY THE PENS AND PENCILS, ASKING BREATHLESSLY:
DO YOU KNOW HOW I COULD CONTINUE MY STUDIES IN ENGINEERING?

I NEVER HAD A CONCRETE ANSWER.

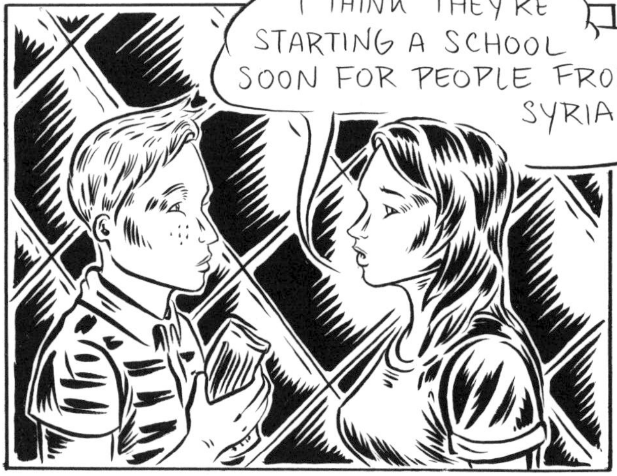
I THINK THEY'RE STARTING A SCHOOL SOON FOR PEOPLE FROM SYRIA...

I BROUGHT IN ARCHITECTURAL BOOKS BECAUSE MARWAN LIKED DRAWING CITYSCAPES.

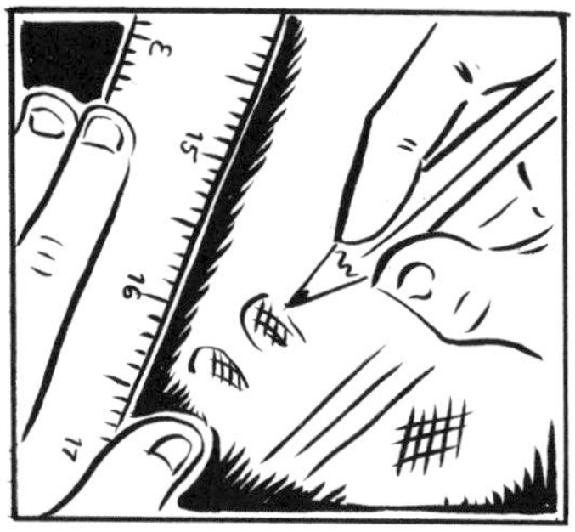

ONCE, HE DREW THE EIFFEL TOWER AND EXCLAIMED:

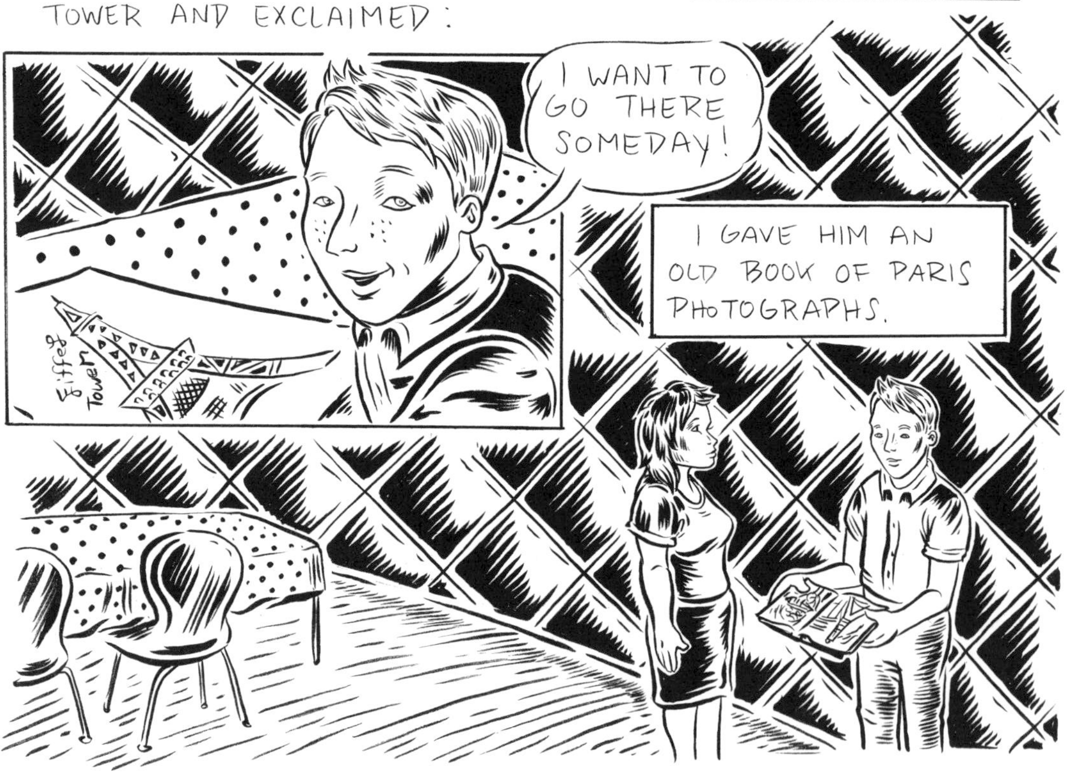
I WANT TO GO THERE SOMEDAY!
Eiffel Tower
I GAVE HIM AN OLD BOOK OF PARIS PHOTOGRAPHS.

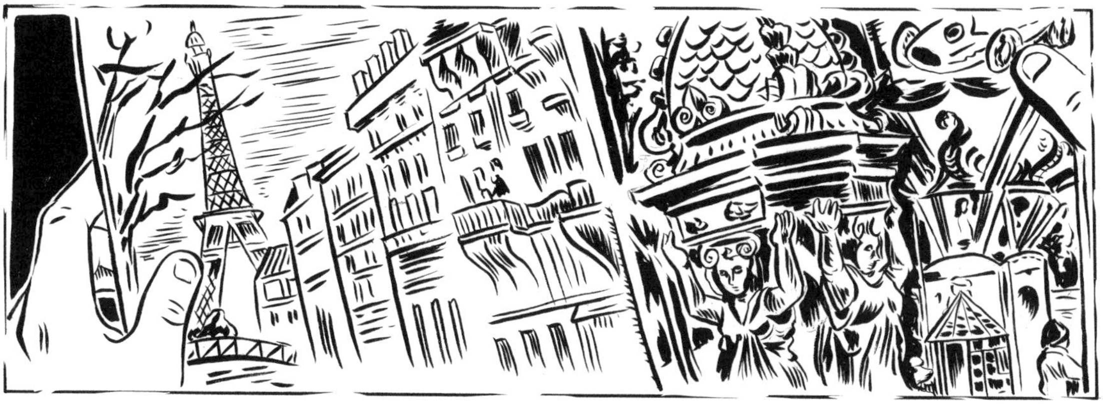

THE NEXT WEEK MARWAN WAS GONE AND I HAD FORGOTTEN TO GET HIS EMAIL.

THIS HAPPENED FREQUENTLY, BUT IT NEVER BECAME A BREEZY TRANSIENCE.

IT ALWAYS FELT LIKE LOSING A FRIEND.

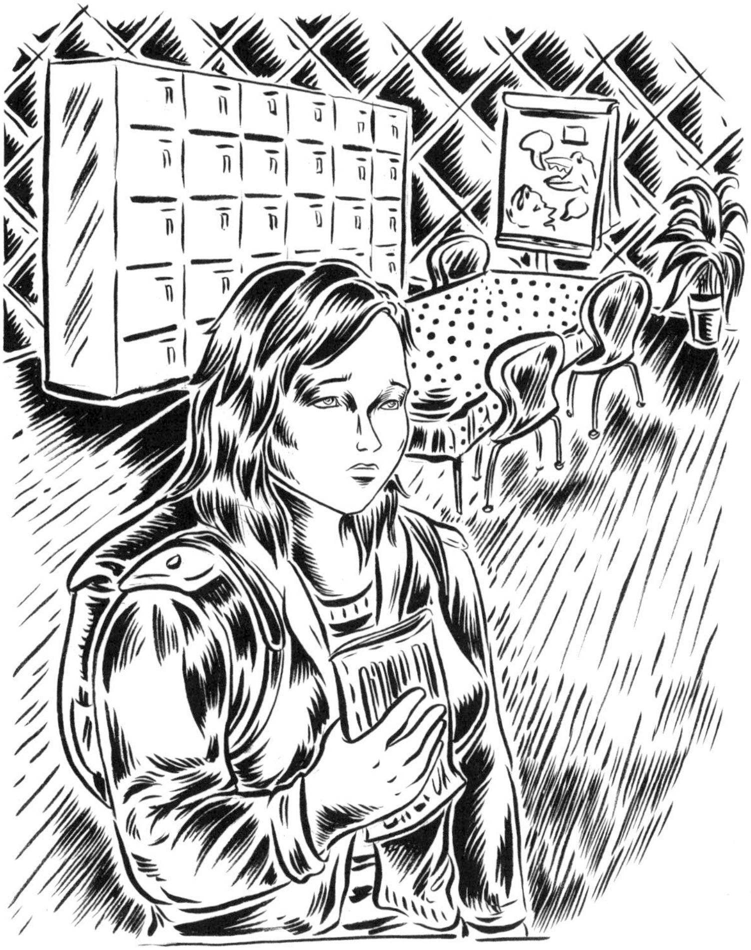

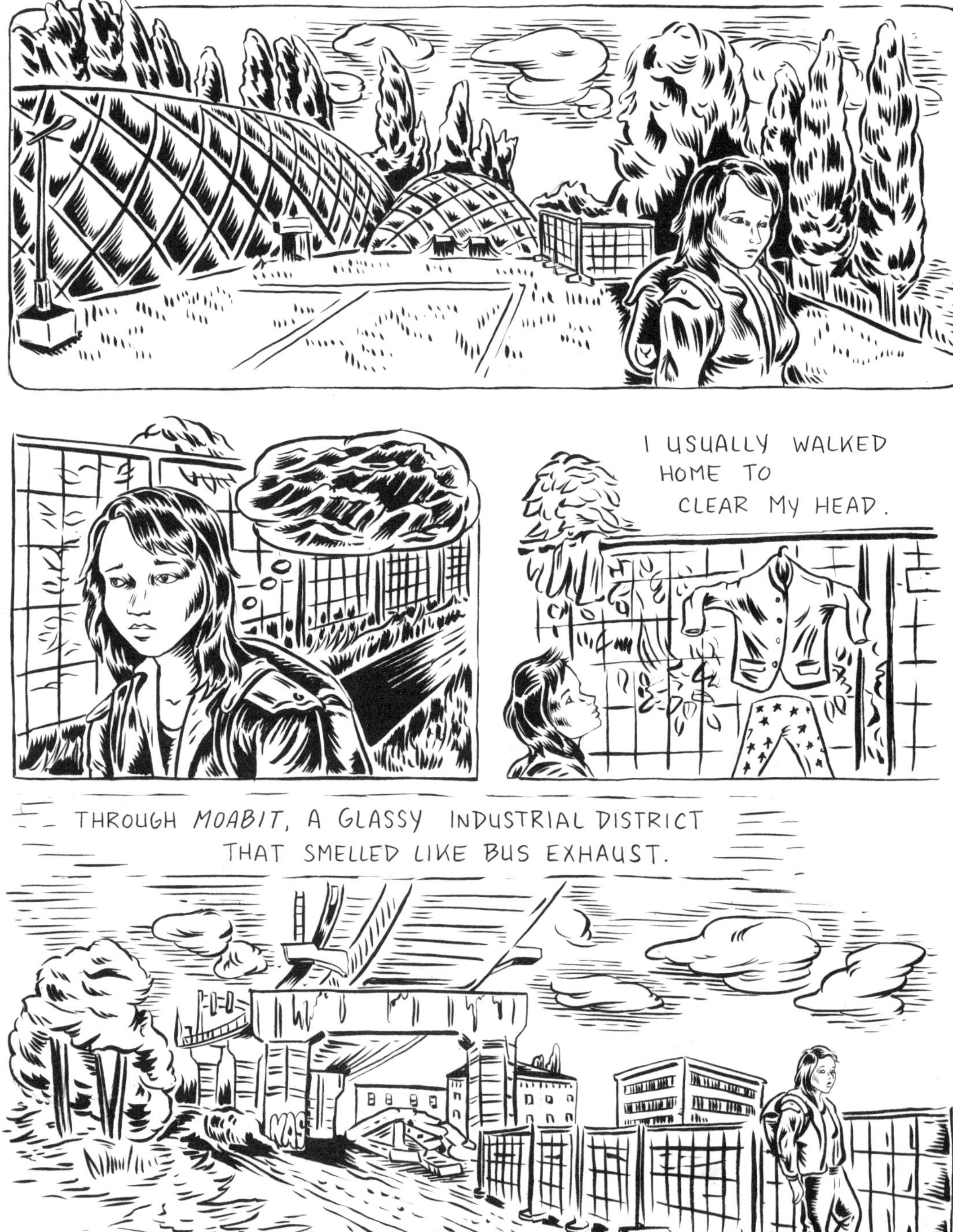
I USUALLY WALKED HOME TO CLEAR MY HEAD.
THROUGH *MOABIT*, A GLASSY INDUSTRIAL DISTRICT THAT SMELLED LIKE BUS EXHAUST.

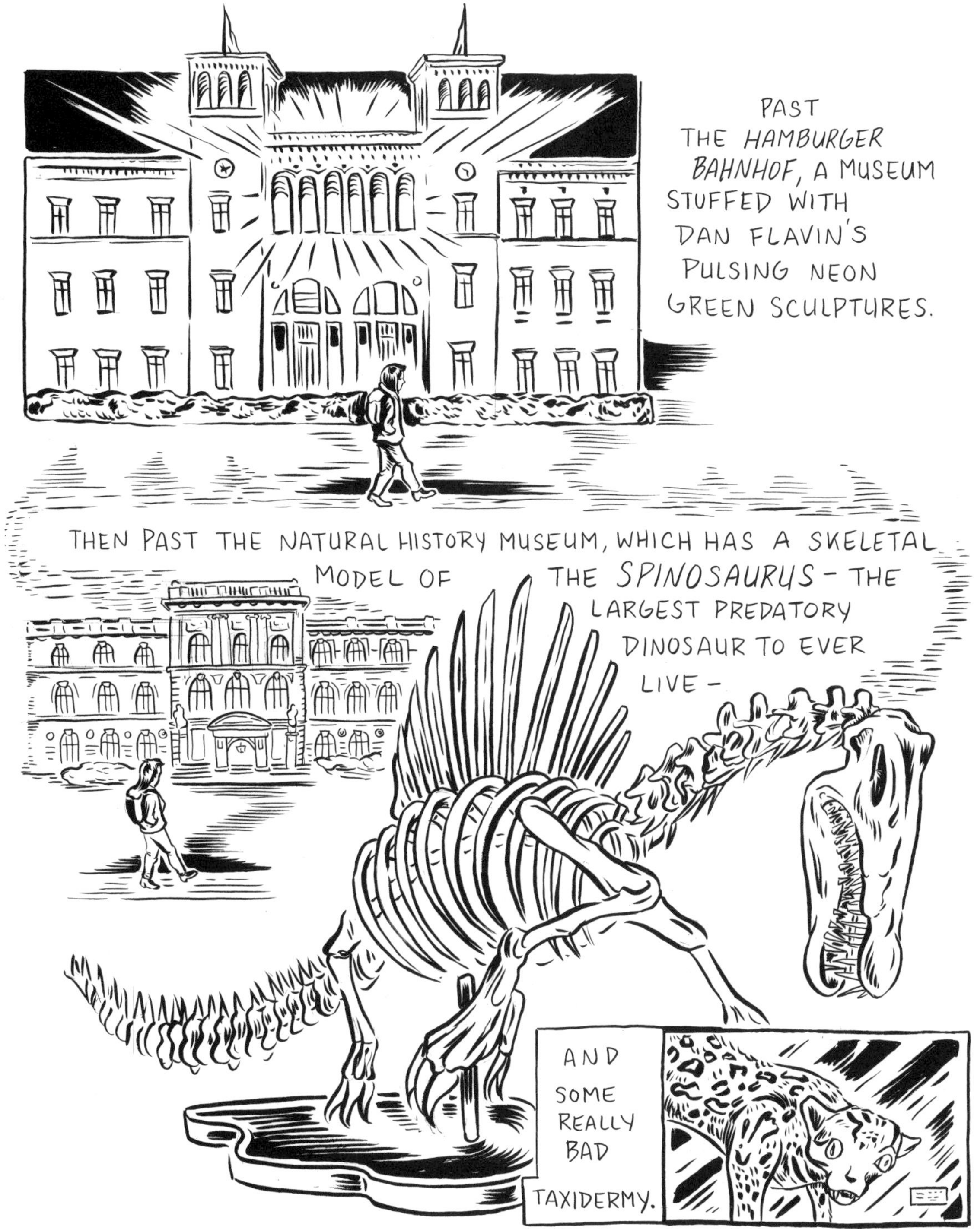
PAST THE *HAMBURGER BAHNHOF*, A MUSEUM STUFFED WITH DAN FLAVIN'S PULSING NEON GREEN SCULPTURES.
THEN PAST THE NATURAL HISTORY MUSEUM, WHICH HAS A SKELETAL MODEL OF THE *SPINOSAURUS* - THE LARGEST PREDATORY DINOSAUR TO EVER LIVE -
AND SOME REALLY BAD
TAXIDERMY.

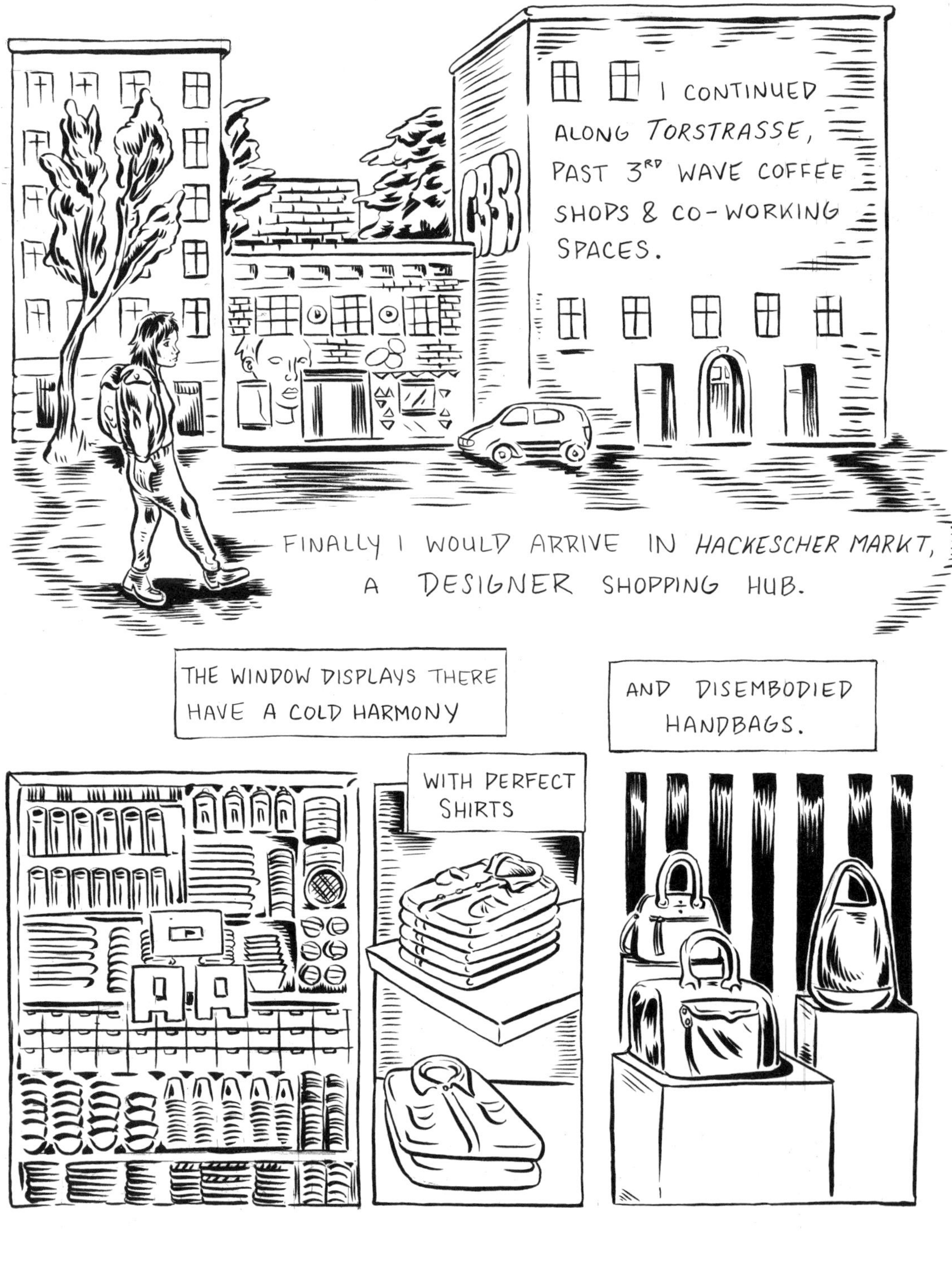
I CONTINUED ALONG TORSTRASSE, PAST 3RD WAVE COFFEE SHOPS & CO-WORKING SPACES.
FINALLY I WOULD ARRIVE IN HACKESCHER MARKT, A DESIGNER SHOPPING HUB.
THE WINDOW DISPLAYS THERE HAVE A COLD HARMONY
WITH PERFECT SHIRTS
AND DISEMBODIED HANDBAGS.

POLISHED STREET ART LINGERS IN COURTYARDS.

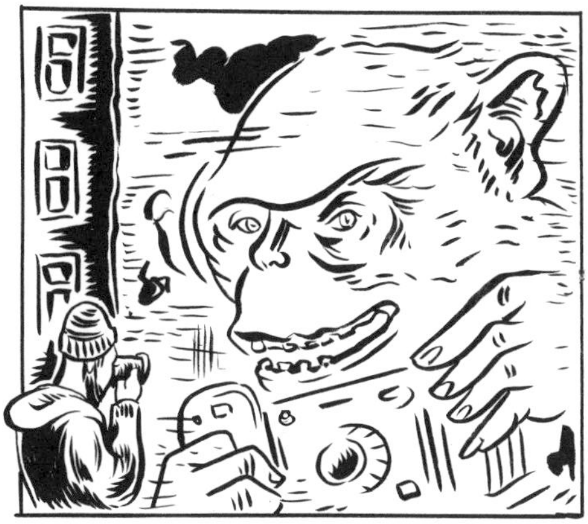

THERE ARE RARE FLASHES OF ART NOUVEAU, WHICH FEEL OUT OF SYNC WITH BUTCH, BRUTALIST BERLIN.

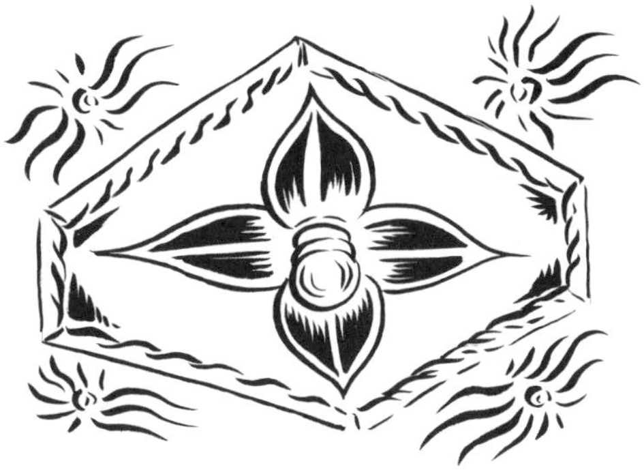

TOURISTS WEAR THE SMILING MASKS OF LEISURE.

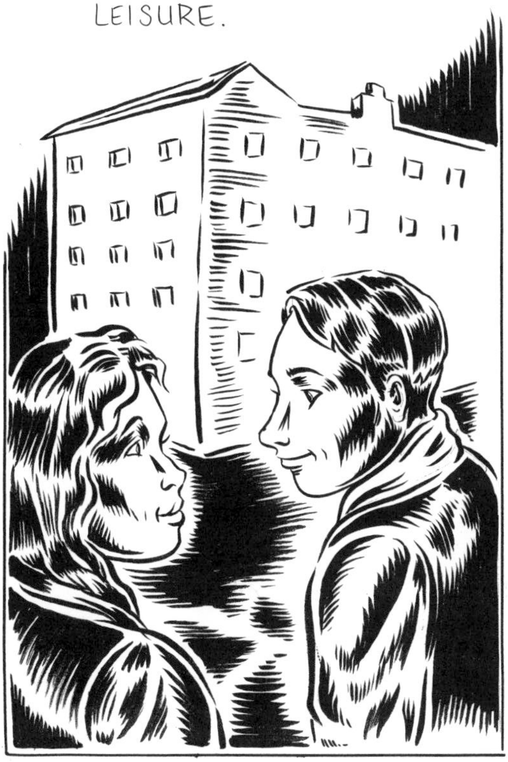

AND PEOPLE SPEAK ABOUT ART AND ITS RELEVANCE.

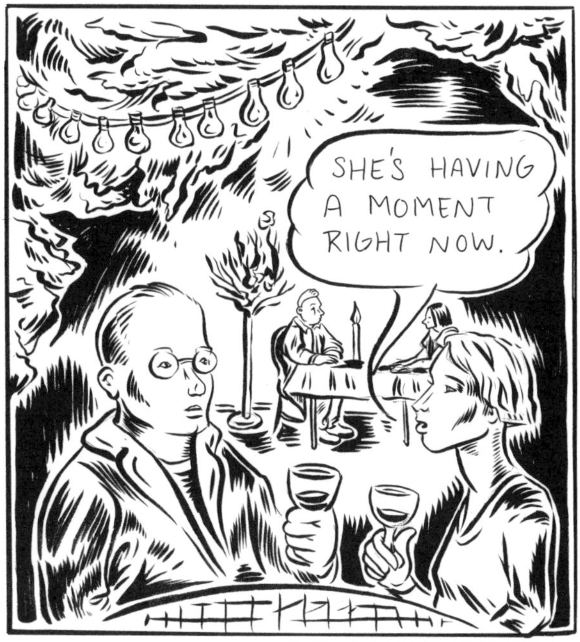
SHE'S HAVING A MOMENT RIGHT NOW.

BEFORE IT WAS AN ART OR SHOPPING HUB, THIS PART OF BERLIN WAS A THRIVING JEWISH QUARTER KNOWN AS THE SCHEUNENVIERTEL.

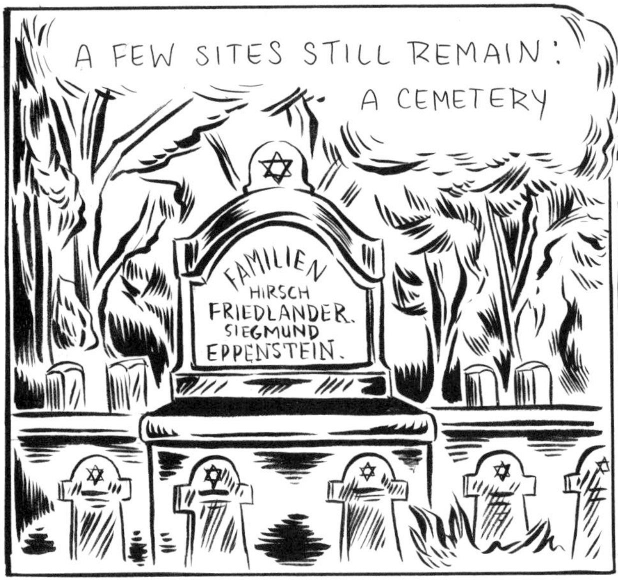
A FEW SITES STILL REMAIN:
A CEMETERY
FAMILIEN HIRSCH FRIEDLANDER. SIEGMUND EPPENSTEIN.

A RESTORED SYNAGOGUE

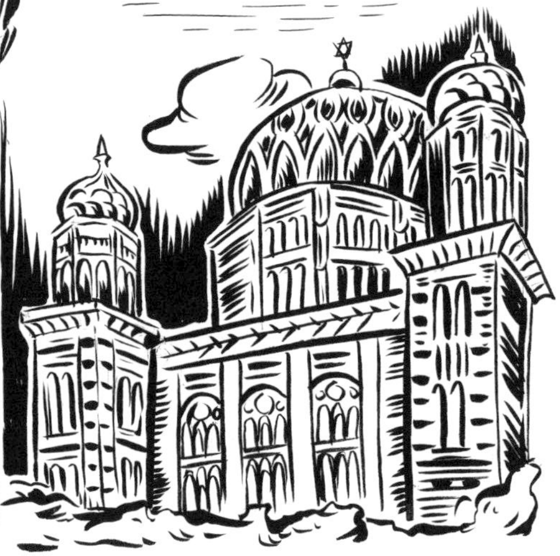

AND A JEWISH GIRLS' SCHOOL, WHICH WAS FORCIBLY SHUTTERED IN 1942, WHEN MOST OF THE STUDENTS AND TEACHERS WERE SENT TO DEATH CAMPS.

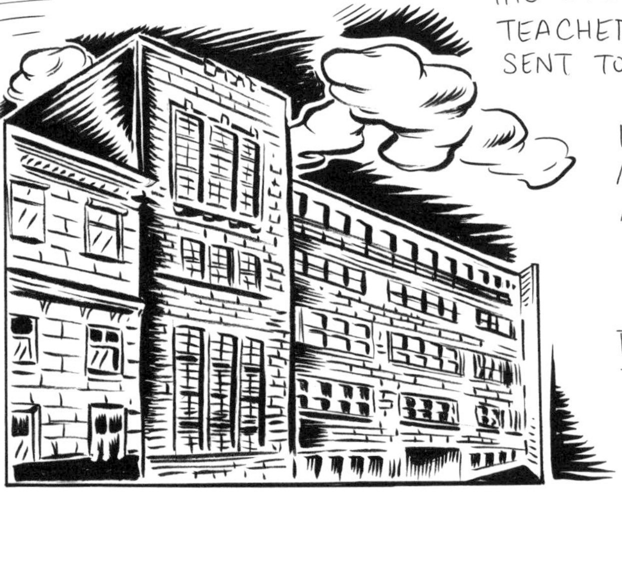

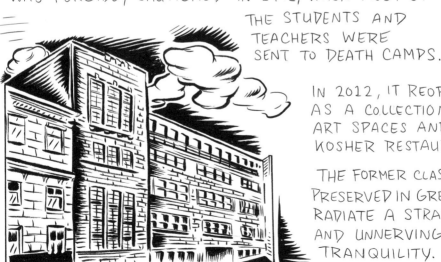

IN 2012, IT REOPENED AS A COLLECTION OF ART SPACES AND KOSHER RESTAURANTS.

THE FORMER CLASSROOMS, PRESERVED IN GREEN TILE, RADIATE A STRANGE AND UNNERVING TRANQUILITY.

PERIL OF THE EAST

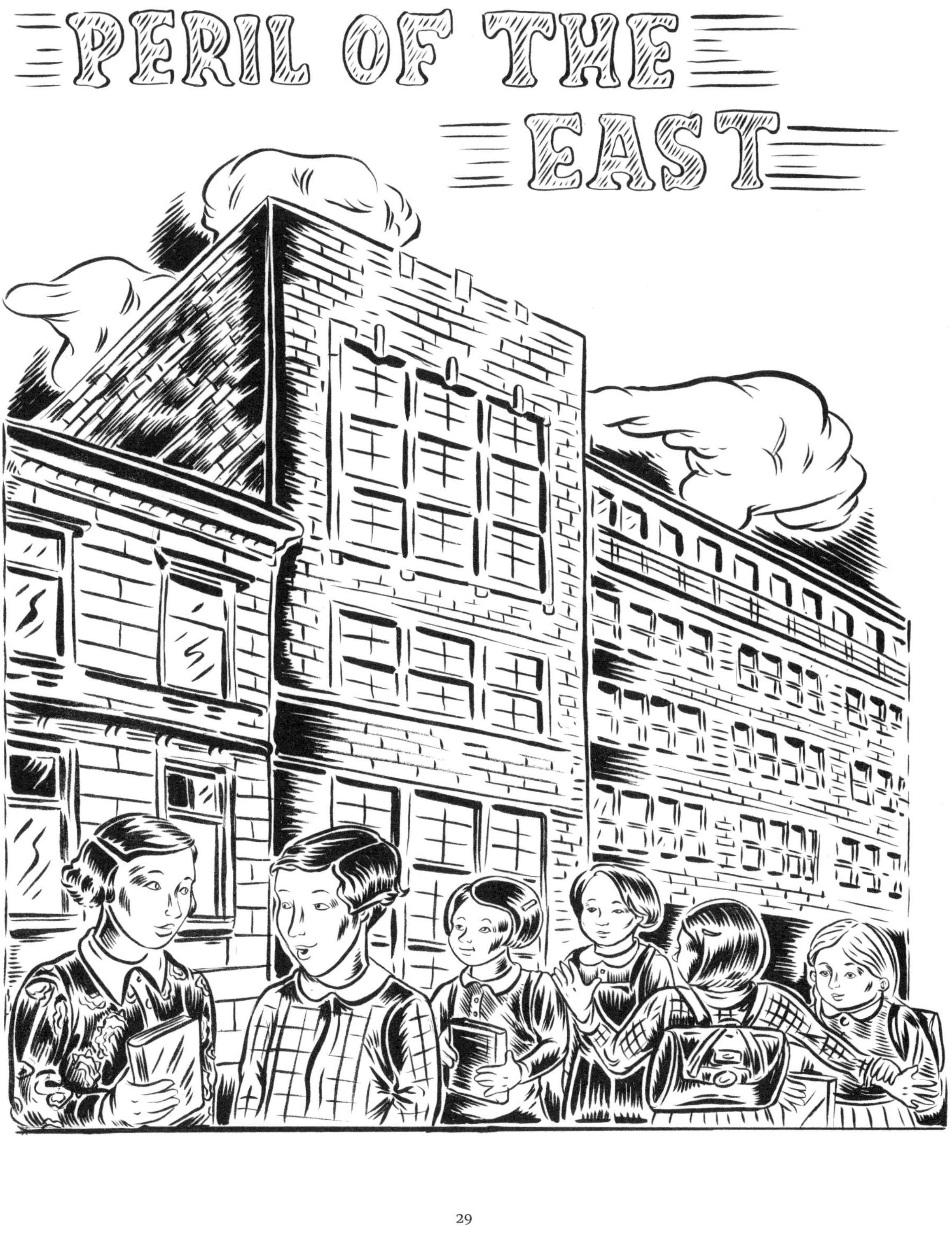

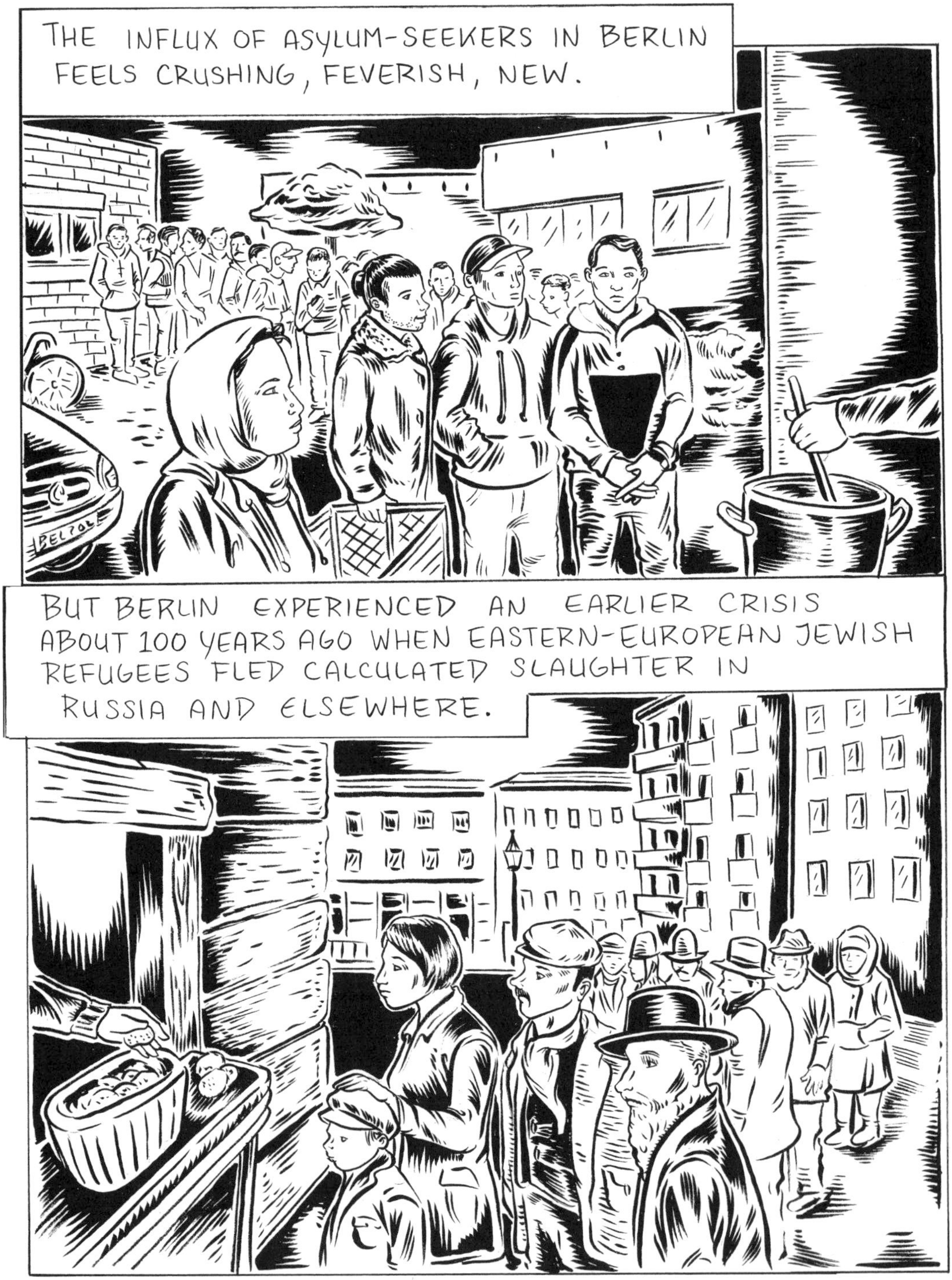
THE INFLUX OF ASYLUM-SEEKERS IN BERLIN FEELS CRUSHING, FEVERISH, NEW.
BUT BERLIN EXPERIENCED AN EARLIER CRISIS ABOUT 100 YEARS AGO WHEN EASTERN-EUROPEAN JEWISH REFUGEES FLED CALCULATED SLAUGHTER IN RUSSIA AND ELSEWHERE.

THE SCHEUNENVIERTEL OFFERED CHEAP TENEMENT HOUSES AND A SENSE OF RELATIVE SAFETY TO THOSE FLEEING POGROMS.

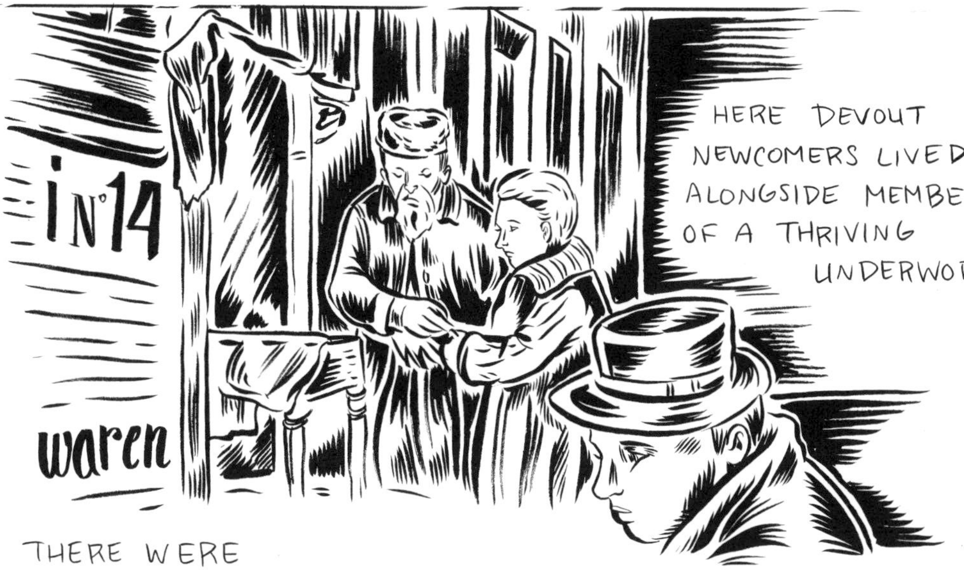
N°14
waren
HERE DEVOUT NEWCOMERS LIVED ALONGSIDE MEMBERS OF A THRIVING UNDERWORLD.

THERE WERE BLACK-MARKET OFFERINGS

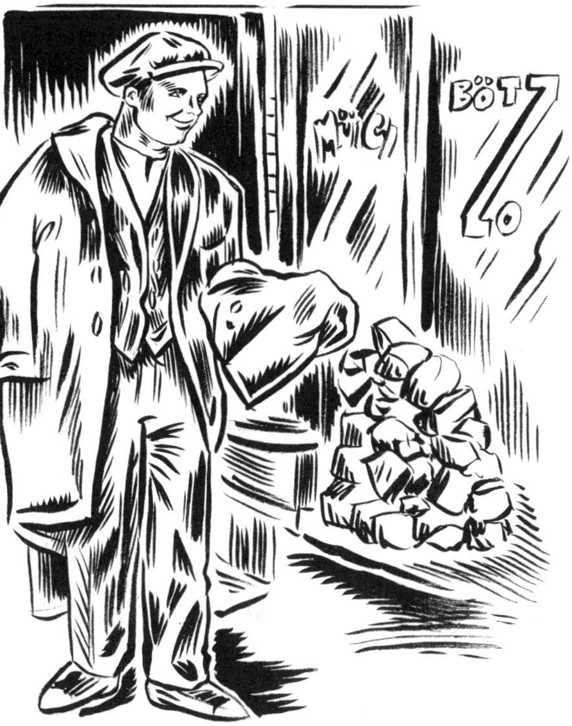

AND AN ASSORTMENT OF PLEASURE-CENTERS.

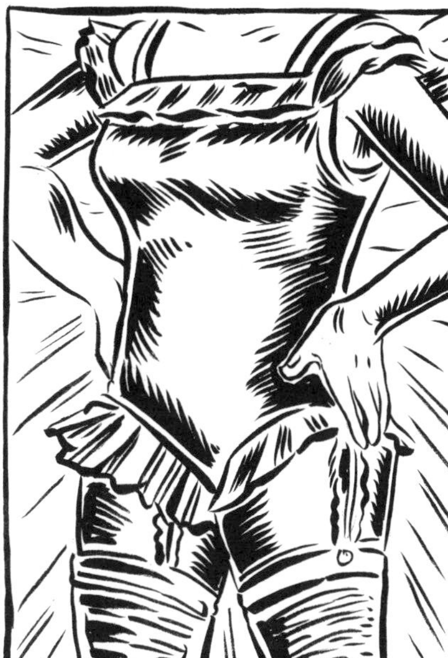

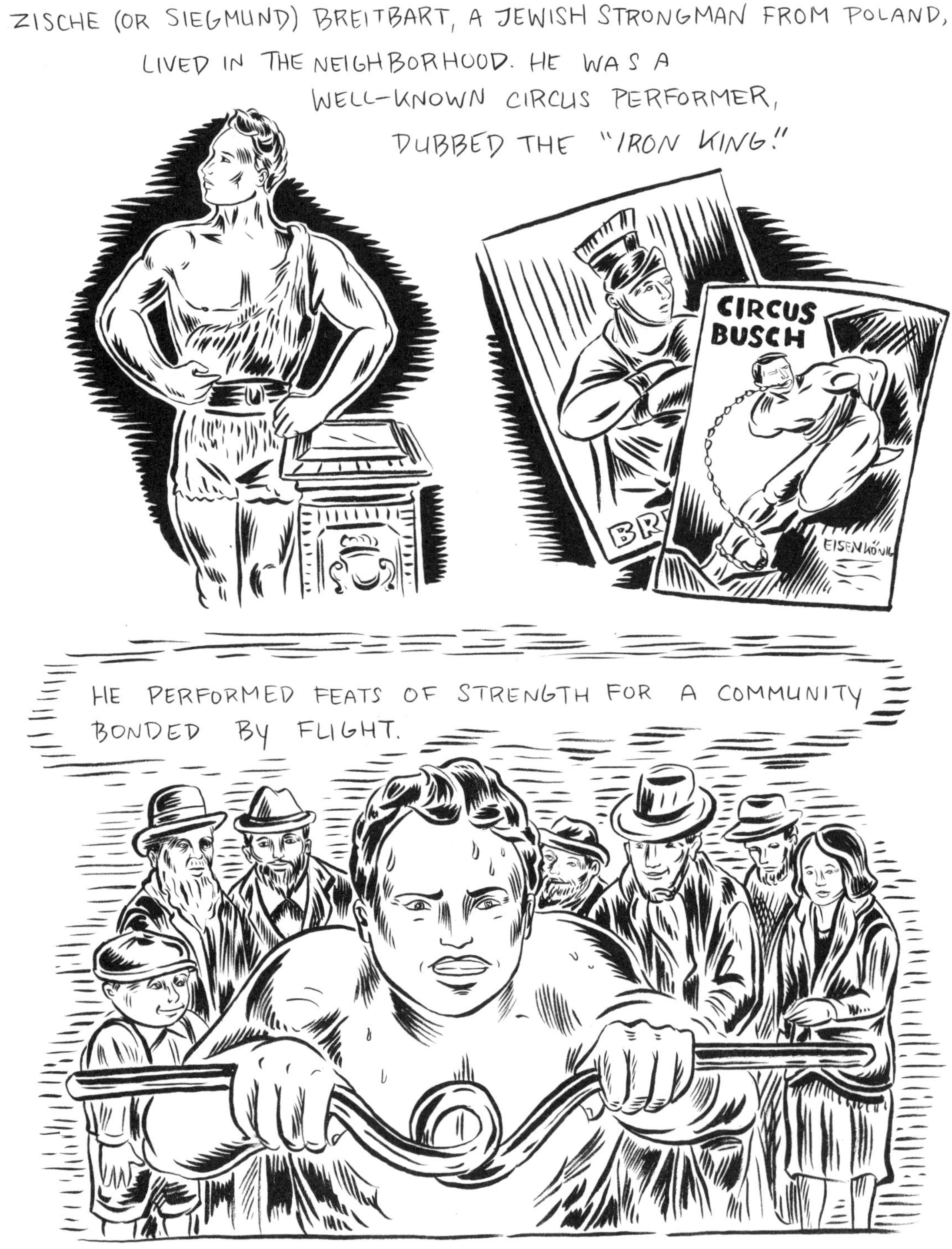
ZISCHE (OR SIEGMUND) BREITBART, A JEWISH STRONGMAN FROM POLAND, LIVED IN THE NEIGHBORHOOD. HE WAS A WELL-KNOWN CIRCUS PERFORMER, DUBBED THE "IRON KING!"
CIRCUS BUSCH
HE PERFORMED FEATS OF STRENGTH FOR A COMMUNITY BONDED BY FLIGHT.

IN 1920, JOURNALIST AND NOVELIST JOSEPH ROTH DOCUMENTED THE LIFE OF JEWISH REFUGEES IN THE SCHEUNENVIERTEL.

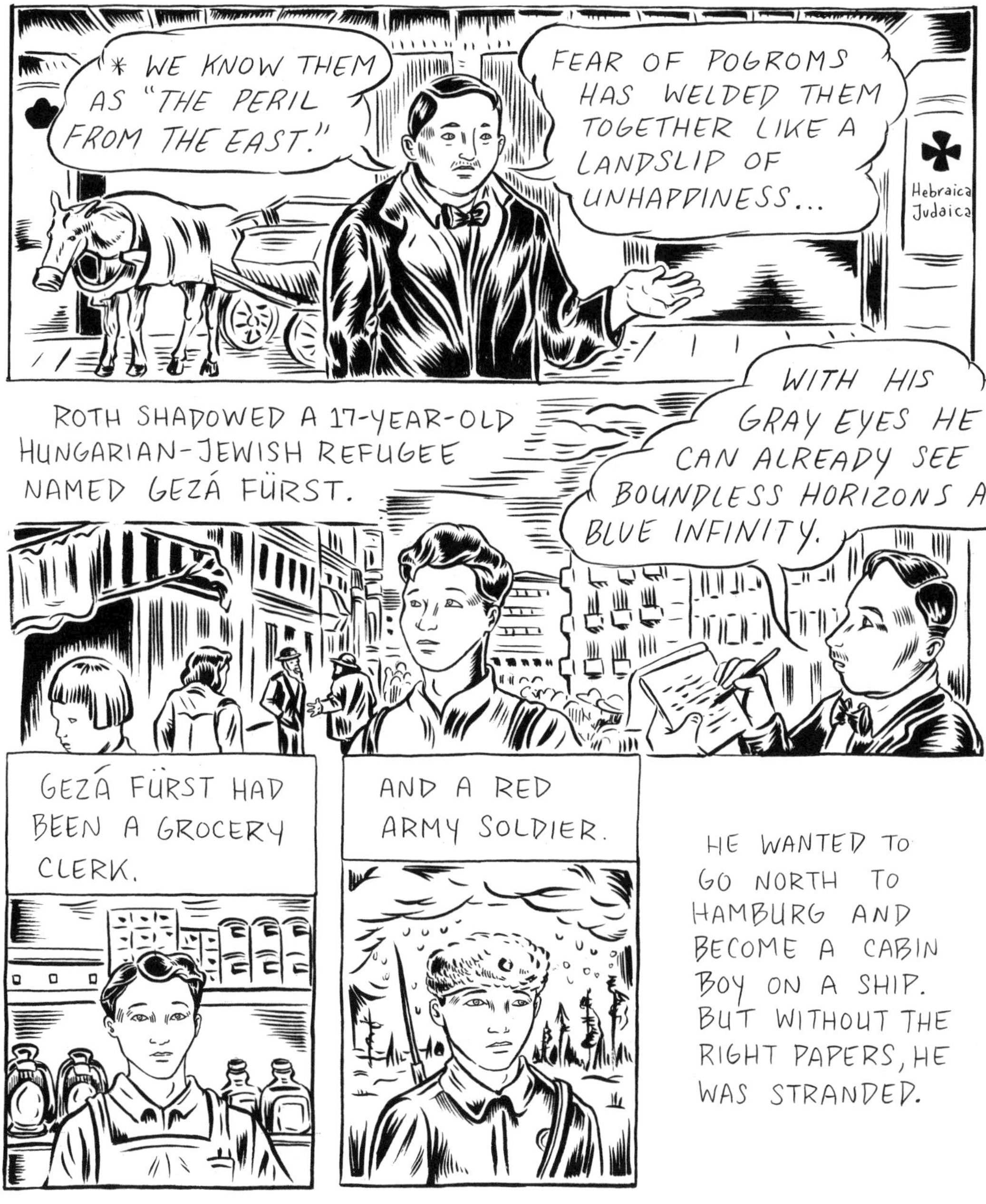
* WE KNOW THEM AS "THE PERIL FROM THE EAST."
FEAR OF POGROMS HAS WELDED THEM TOGETHER LIKE A LANDSLIP OF UNHAPPINESS...
Hebraica Judaica
ROTH SHADOWED A 17-YEAR-OLD HUNGARIAN-JEWISH REFUGEE NAMED GEZÁ FÜRST.
WITH HIS GRAY EYES HE CAN ALREADY SEE BOUNDLESS HORIZONS AND BLUE INFINITY.
GEZÁ FÜRST HAD BEEN A GROCERY CLERK.
AND A RED ARMY SOLDIER.
HE WANTED TO GO NORTH TO HAMBURG AND BECOME A CABIN BOY ON A SHIP. BUT WITHOUT THE RIGHT PAPERS, HE WAS STRANDED.

* FROM *WHAT I SAW: REPORTS FROM BERLIN 1920-1933*

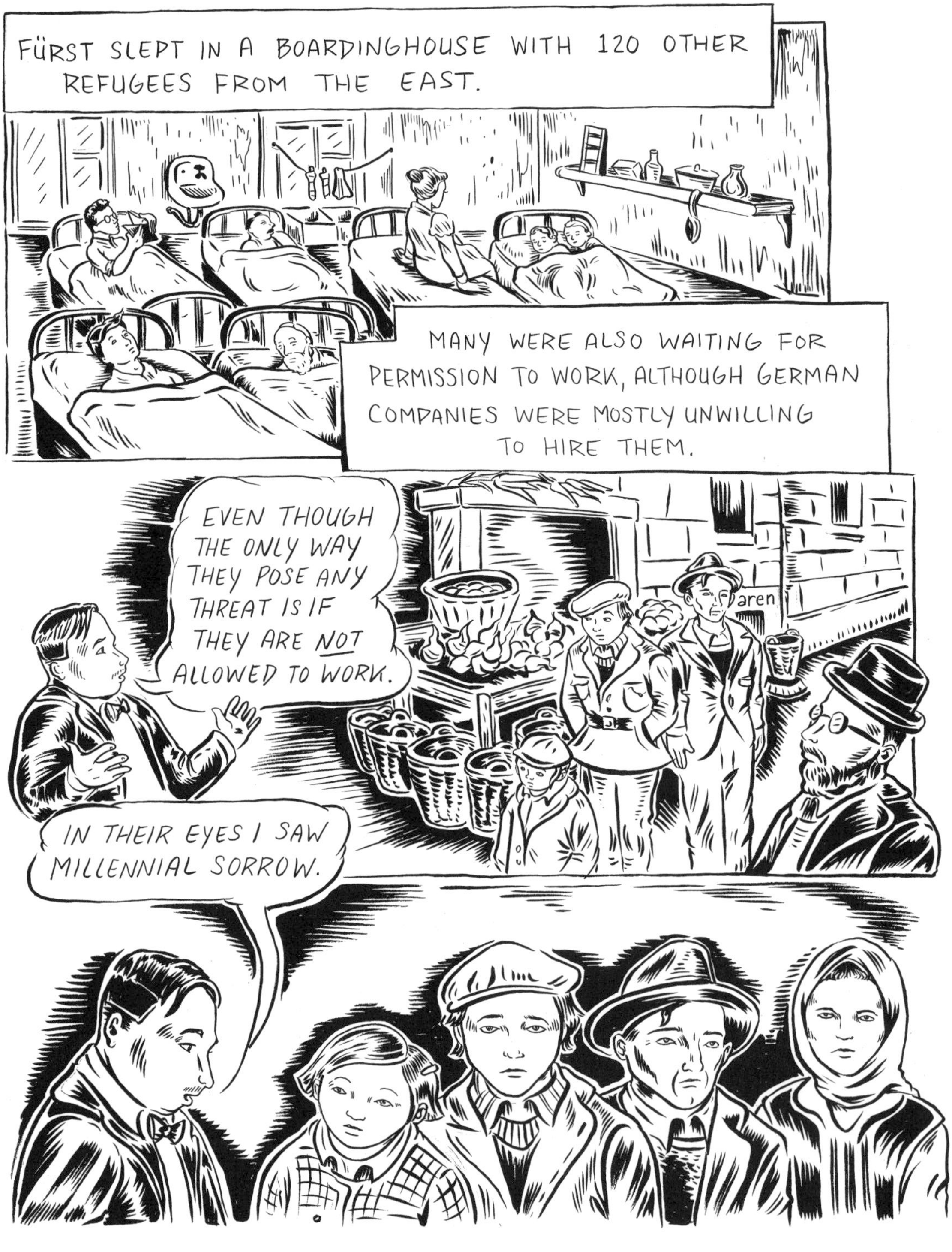
FÜRST SLEPT IN A BOARDINGHOUSE WITH 120 OTHER REFUGEES FROM THE EAST.
MANY WERE ALSO WAITING FOR PERMISSION TO WORK, ALTHOUGH GERMAN COMPANIES WERE MOSTLY UNWILLING TO HIRE THEM.
EVEN THOUGH THE ONLY WAY THEY POSE ANY THREAT IS IF THEY ARE NOT ALLOWED TO WORK.
aren
IN THEIR EYES I SAW MILLENNIAL SORROW.

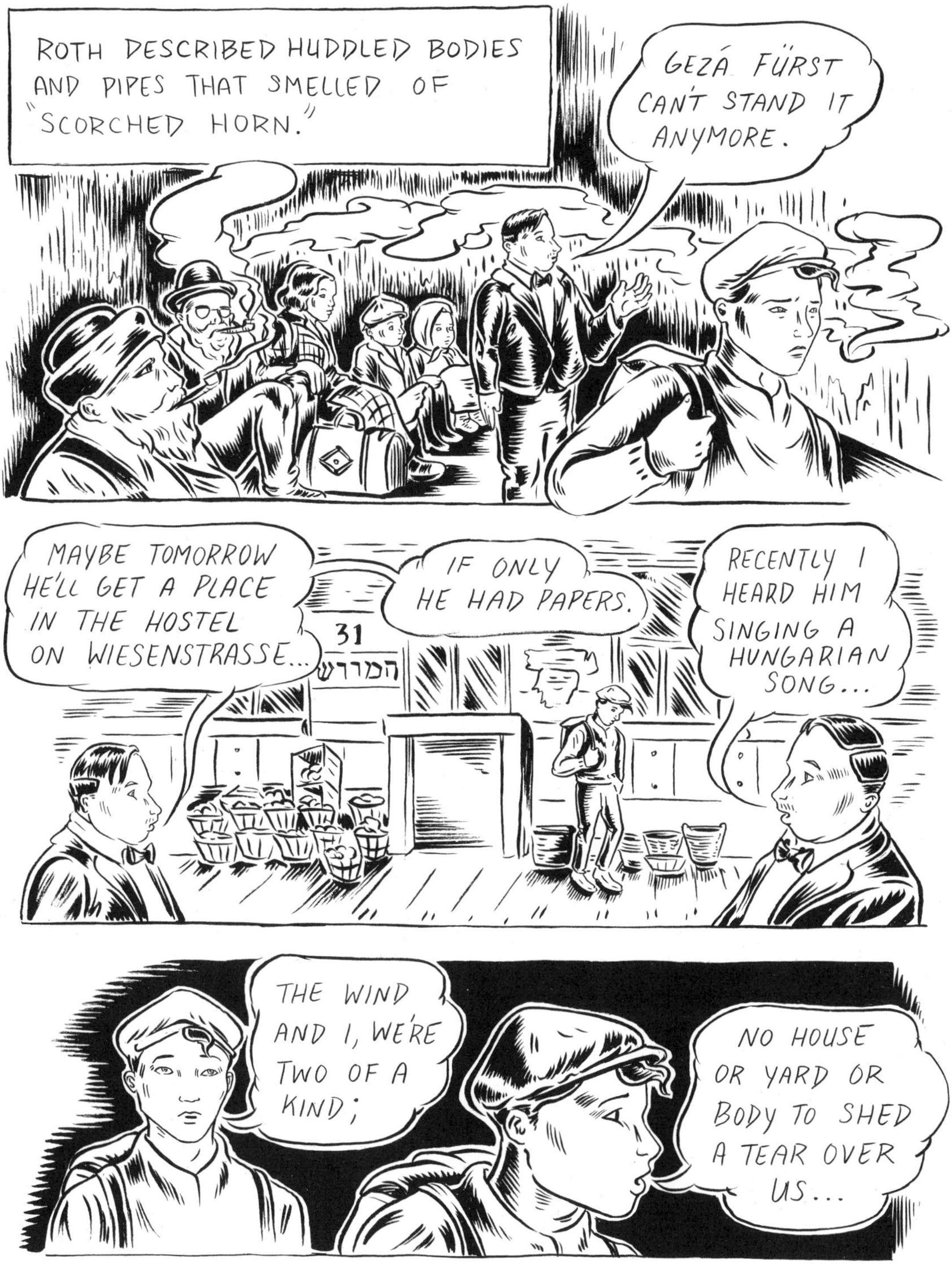
ROTH DESCRIBED HUDDLED BODIES AND PIPES THAT SMELLED OF "SCORCHED HORN."
GEZÁ FÜRST CAN'T STAND IT ANYMORE.
MAYBE TOMORROW HE'LL GET A PLACE IN THE HOSTEL ON WIESENSTRASSE...
IF ONLY HE HAD PAPERS.
31
המדרש
RECENTLY I HEARD HIM SINGING A HUNGARIAN SONG...
THE WIND AND I, WE'RE TWO OF A KIND;
NO HOUSE OR YARD OR BODY TO SHED A TEAR OVER US...

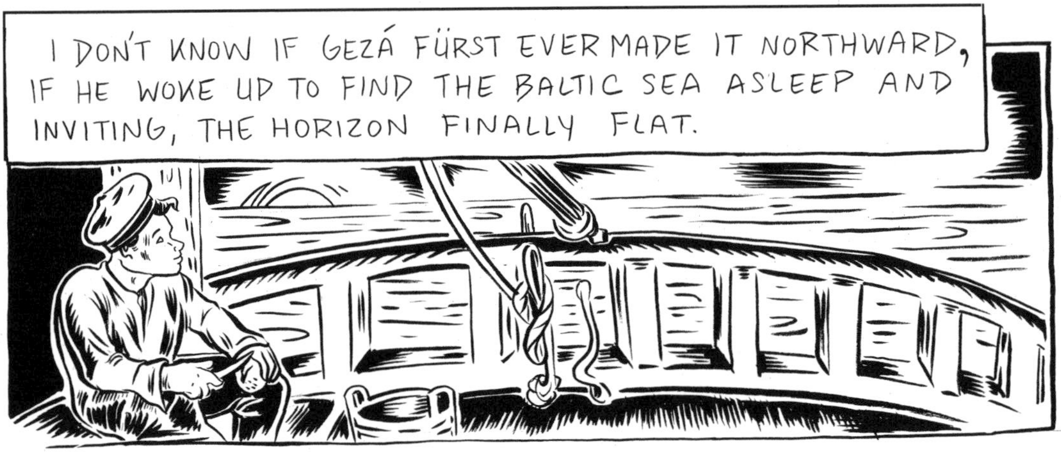
I DON'T KNOW IF GEZÁ FÜRST EVER MADE IT NORTHWARD, IF HE WOKE UP TO FIND THE BALTIC SEA ASLEEP AND INVITING, THE HORIZON FINALLY FLAT.

HOW LONG DID HE STAY IN THE EPHEMERAL SPACE OF THE *SCHEUNENVIERTEL*? DID HE LEAVE BEFORE *KRISTALLNACHT* IN 1933? WAS HE THERE IN 1935 WHEN GERMAN-JEWS WERE STRIPPED OF THEIR CITIZENSHIP? HE WOULD HAVE BEEN 32 THEN.

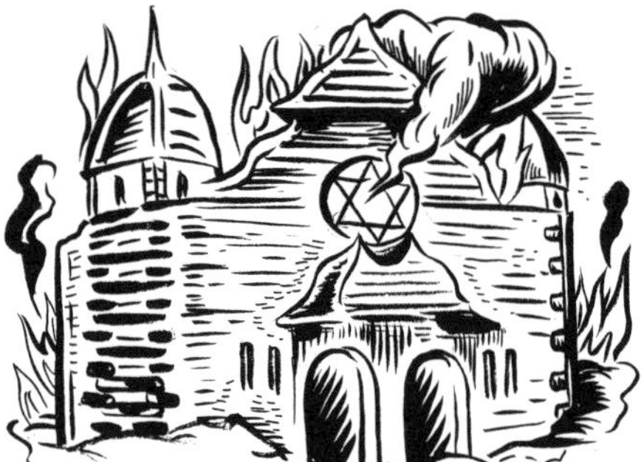

MAYBE HE MADE IT TO A NEW WORLD.

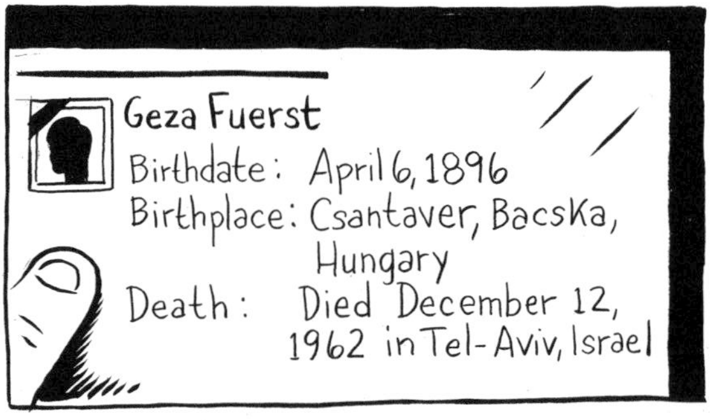
Geza Fuerst
Birthdate: April 6, 1896
Birthplace: Csantaver, Bacska, Hungary
Death: Died December 12, 1962 in Tel-Aviv, Israel

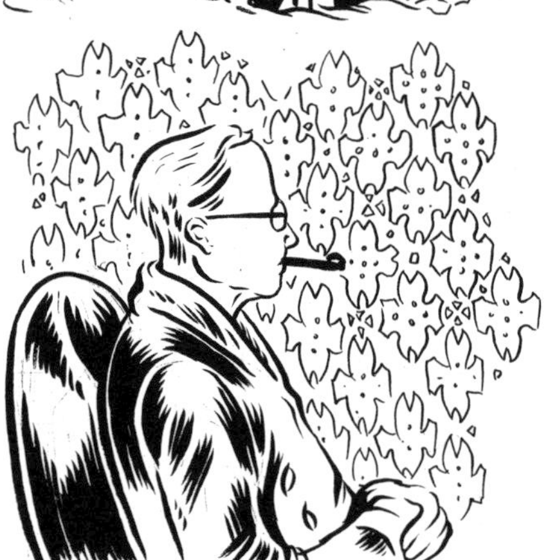

BUT WHAT INDIGNITIES DID HE SUFFER TO GET THERE?

WE'RE LEFT TO IMAGINE.

WANDERWEG

WAIT, YOU _WALKED_ FROM GREECE TO MACEDONIA?

YES.

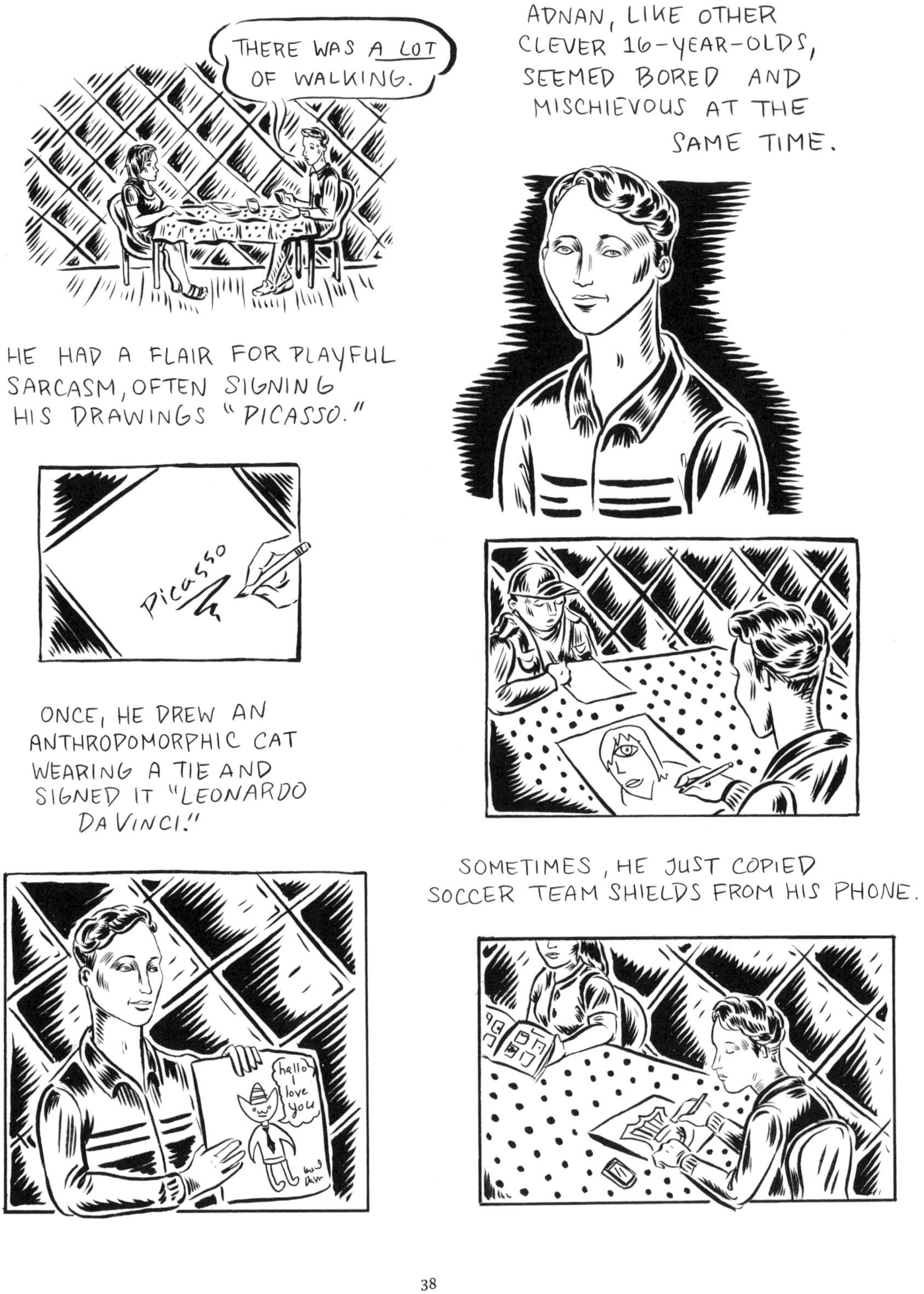
THERE WAS A LOT OF WALKING.
ADNAN, LIKE OTHER CLEVER 16-YEAR-OLDS, SEEMED BORED AND MISCHIEVOUS AT THE SAME TIME.
HE HAD A FLAIR FOR PLAYFUL SARCASM, OFTEN SIGNING HIS DRAWINGS "PICASSO."
Picasso
ONCE, HE DREW AN ANTHROPOMORPHIC CAT WEARING A TIE AND SIGNED IT "LEONARDO DA VINCI."
hallo I love you
SOMETIMES, HE JUST COPIED SOCCER TEAM SHIELDS FROM HIS PHONE.

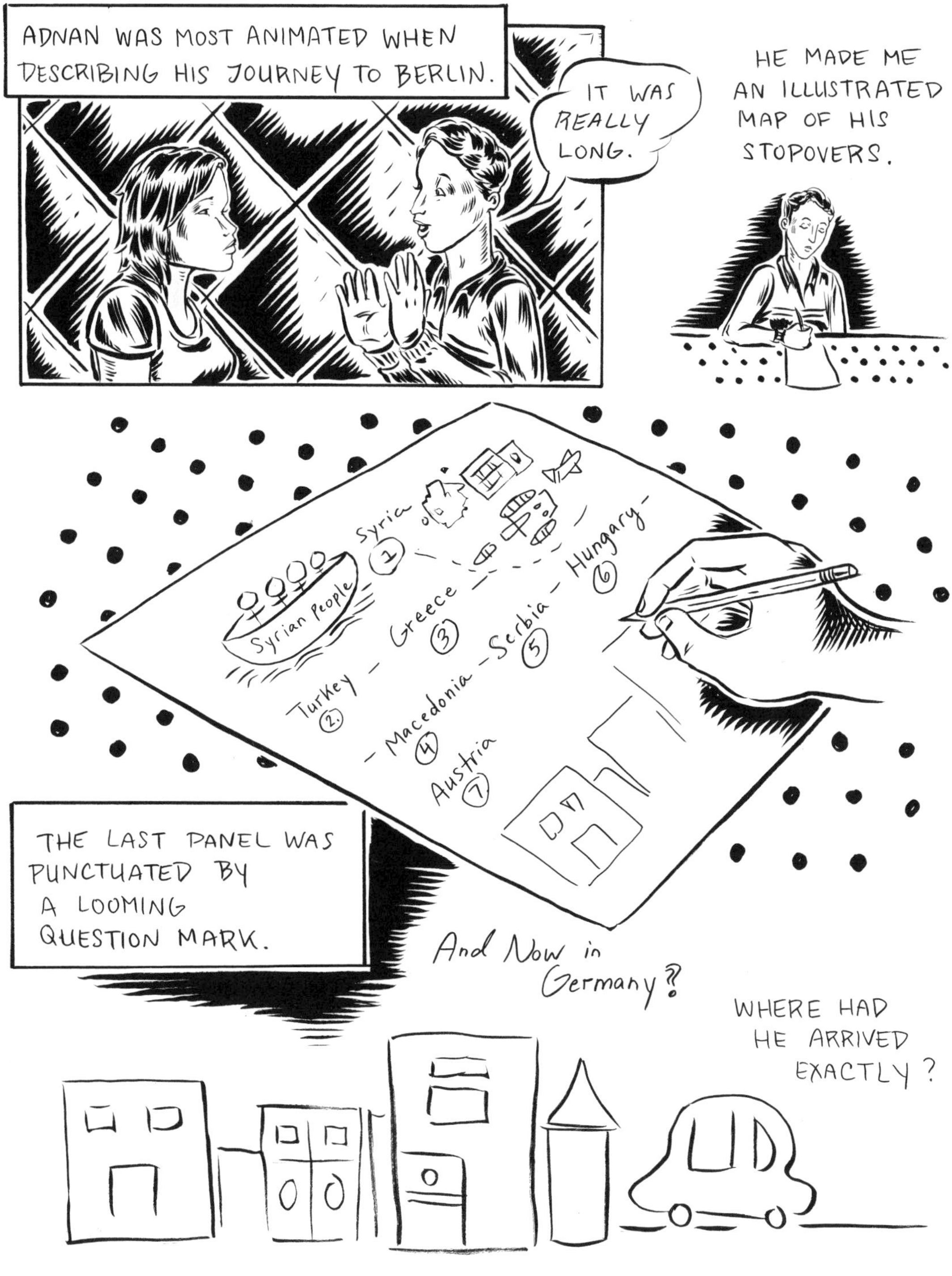
ADNAN WAS MOST ANIMATED WHEN DESCRIBING HIS JOURNEY TO BERLIN.
IT WAS REALLY LONG.
HE MADE ME AN ILLUSTRATED MAP OF HIS STOPOVERS.
Syria 1
Syrian People
Turkey 2.
Greece 3
Macedonia 4
Serbia 5
Hungary 6
Austria 7
THE LAST PANEL WAS PUNCTUATED BY A LOOMING QUESTION MARK.
And Now in Germany?
WHERE HAD HE ARRIVED EXACTLY?

A LOT OF PEOPLE AT THE SHELTER HAD TAKEN THE SAME
ROUTE: FLEEING SYRIA FOR THE TURKISH COAST

CROSSING THE TREACHEROUS AEGEAN AND
MEDITERRANEAN, LANDING
ON ISLANDS LIKE LESBOS AND KOS

WALKING TO THE MACEDONIAN BORDER

RIDING A TRAIN THROUGH UNKNOWN,
FURTIVE VALLEYS

SKIRTING THE SERBIAN FORESTS

FACING OFF WITH HUNGARIAN POLICE

TAKING THE TRAIN FROM BUDAPEST TO VIENNA

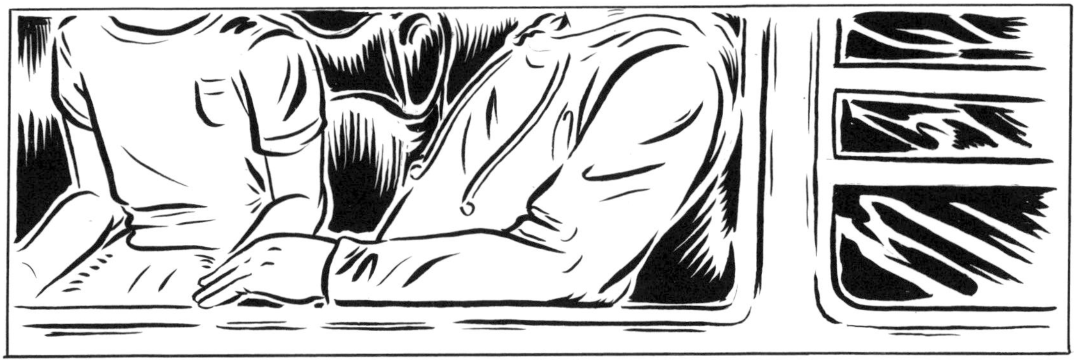

AND FINALLY ARRIVING IN BERLIN.

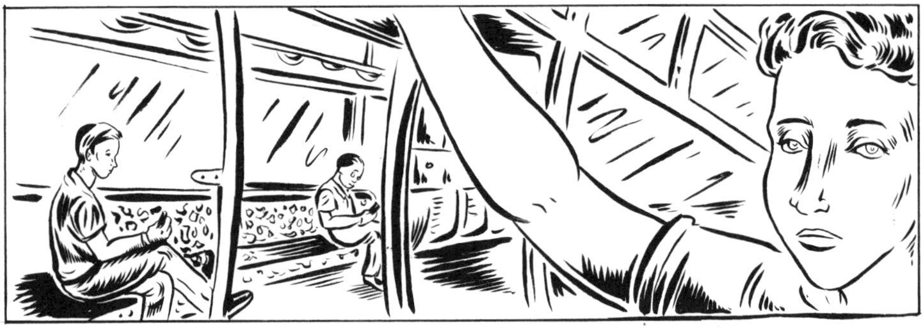

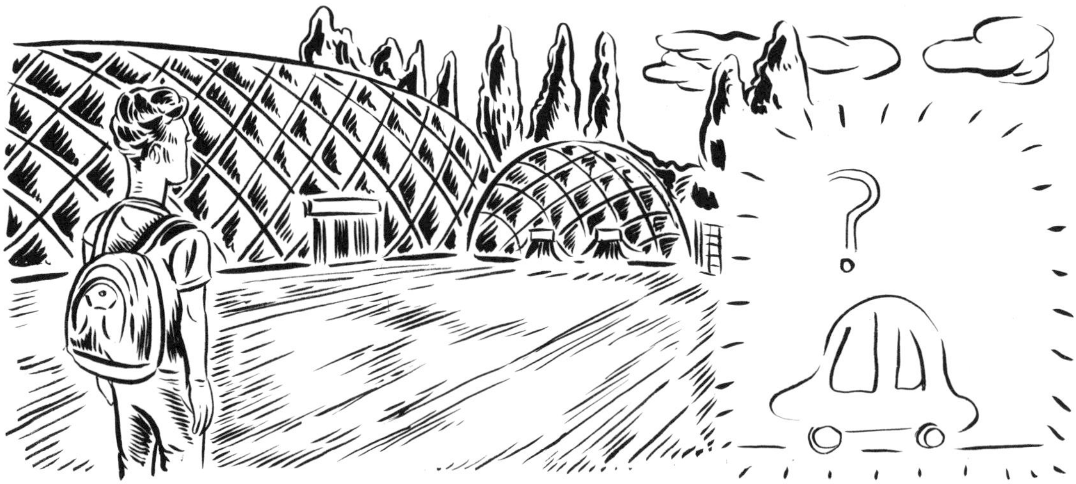

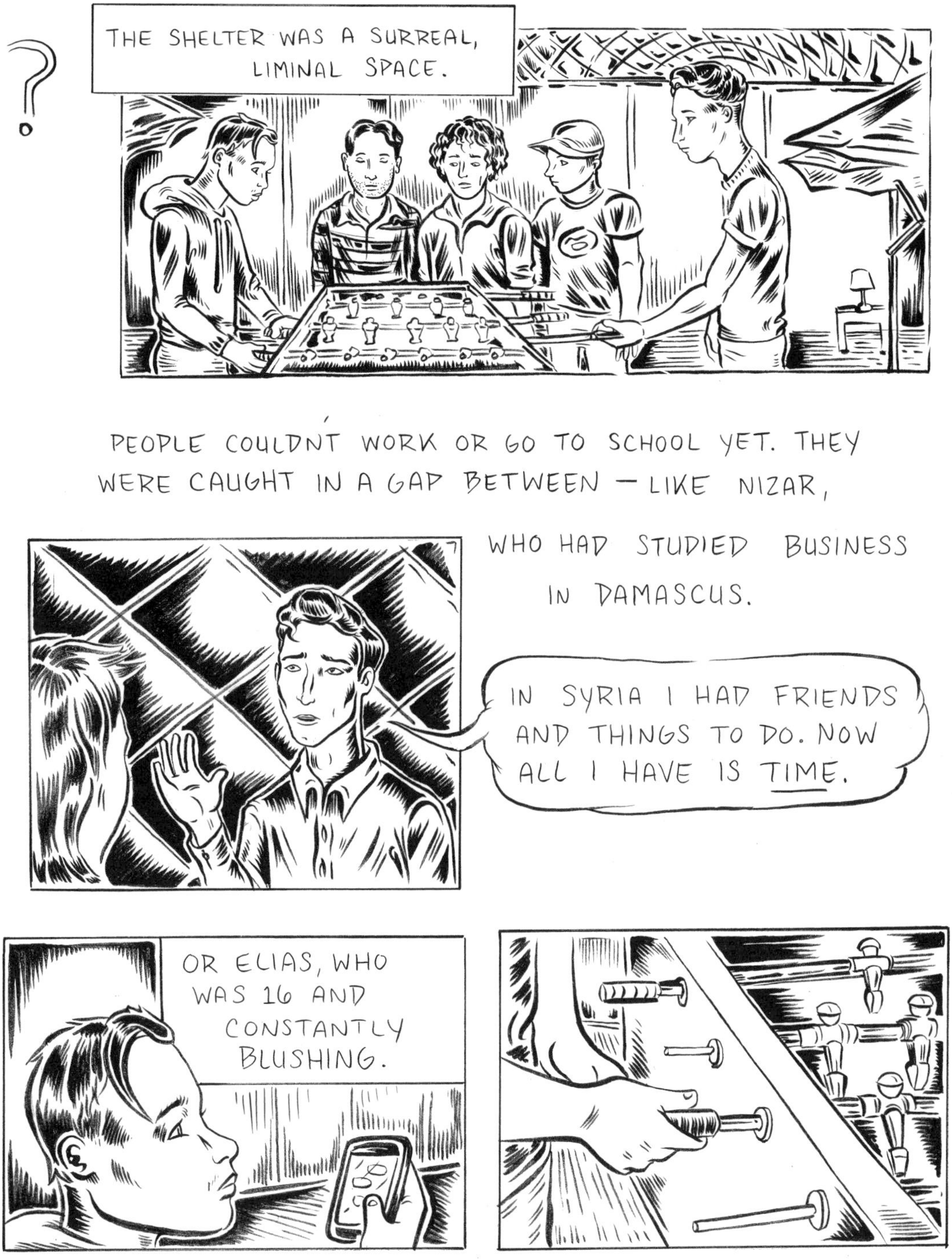
THE SHELTER WAS A SURREAL, LIMINAL SPACE.
PEOPLE COULDN'T WORK OR GO TO SCHOOL YET. THEY WERE CAUGHT IN A GAP BETWEEN — LIKE NIZAR,
WHO HAD STUDIED BUSINESS IN DAMASCUS.
IN SYRIA I HAD FRIENDS AND THINGS TO DO. NOW ALL I HAVE IS TIME.
OR ELIAS, WHO WAS 16 AND CONSTANTLY BLUSHING.

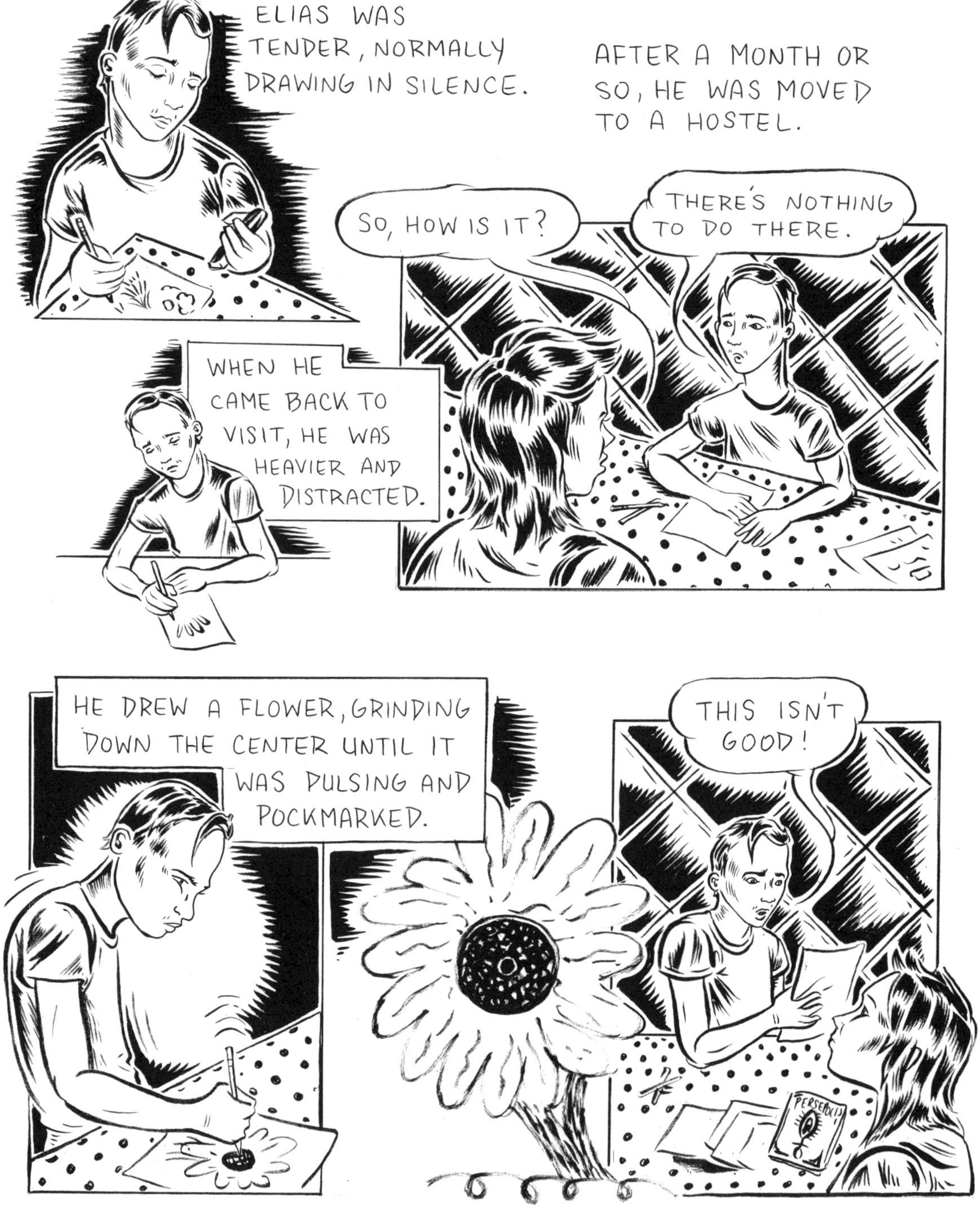
ELIAS WAS TENDER, NORMALLY DRAWING IN SILENCE.
AFTER A MONTH OR SO, HE WAS MOVED TO A HOSTEL.
SO, HOW IS IT?
THERE'S NOTHING TO DO THERE.
WHEN HE CAME BACK TO VISIT, HE WAS HEAVIER AND DISTRACTED.
HE DREW A FLOWER, GRINDING DOWN THE CENTER UNTIL IT WAS PULSING AND POCKMARKED.
THIS ISN'T GOOD!
PERSEPOLIS

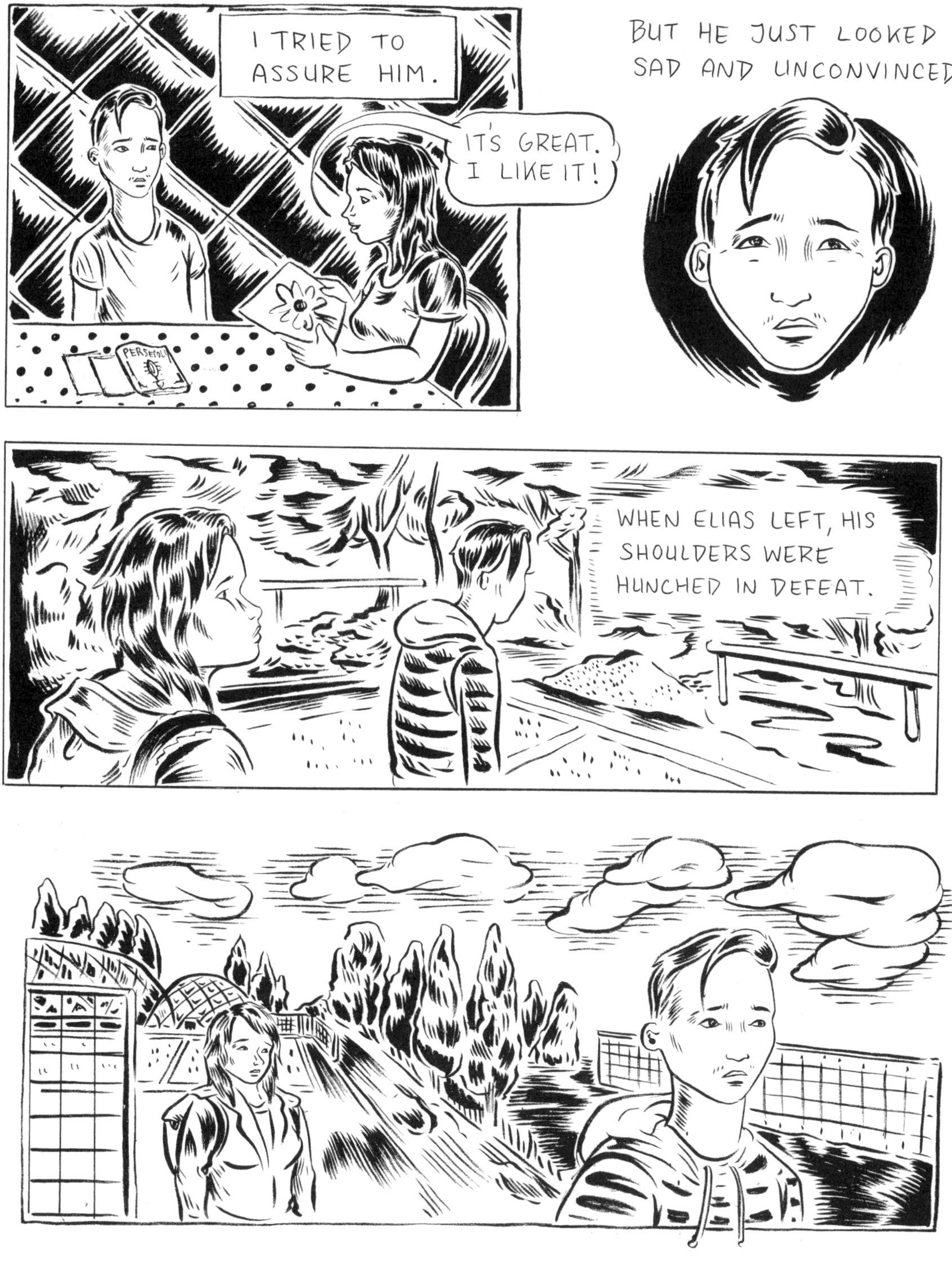
I TRIED TO ASSURE HIM.
IT'S GREAT. I LIKE IT!
BUT HE JUST LOOKED SAD AND UNCONVINCED.
WHEN ELIAS LEFT, HIS SHOULDERS WERE HUNCHED IN DEFEAT.

CHRISTOPHER ISHERWOOD WANTED TO WRITE A BOOK
ABOUT BERLIN CALLED *THE LOST.*

IT WOULD HAVE BEEN
A SPRAWLING EPIC
OF OTHERNESS.

BUT THERE WERE JUST TOO MANY
LONELY PEOPLE, AND HE COULDN'T
FIGURE OUT HOW TO CONNECT
THEM ALL.

ELIAS, ADNAN AND THE OTHERS WERE STUCK IN A DEFLATING ASYLUM PROCESS.

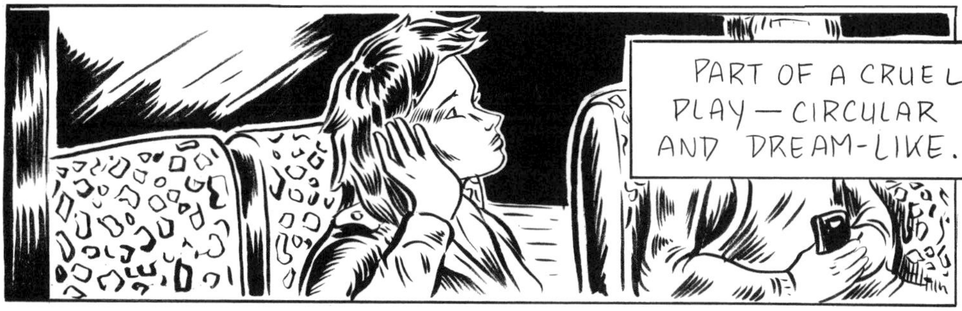
PART OF A CRUEL PLAY — CIRCULAR AND DREAM-LIKE.

the curse of time

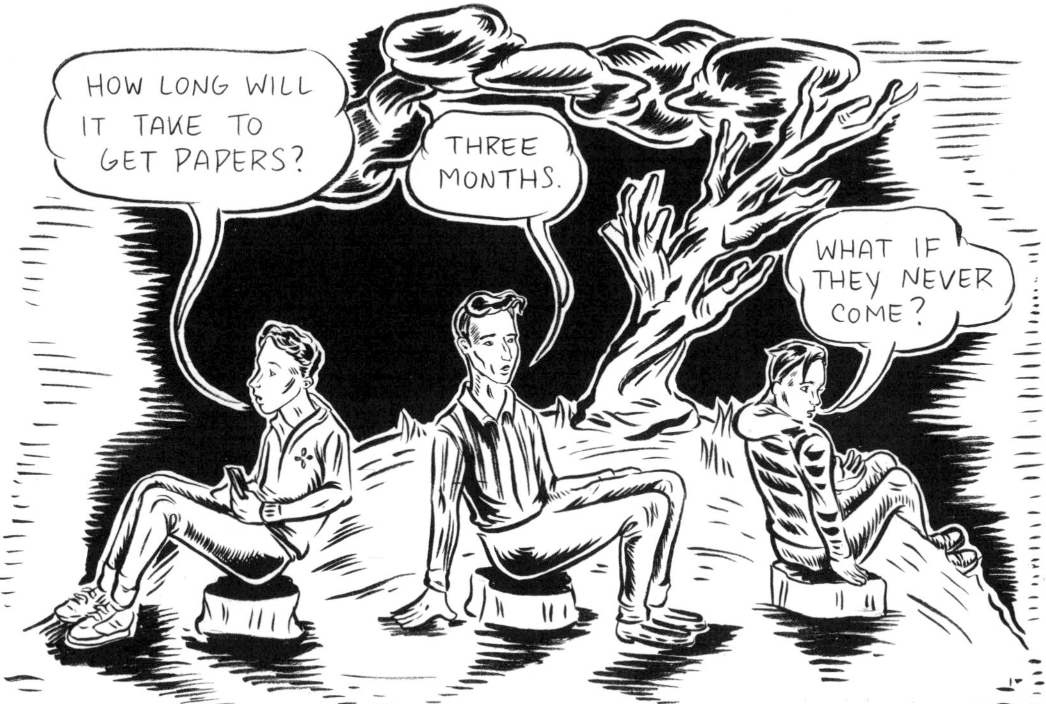
HOW LONG WILL IT TAKE TO GET PAPERS?
THREE MONTHS.
WHAT IF THEY NEVER COME?

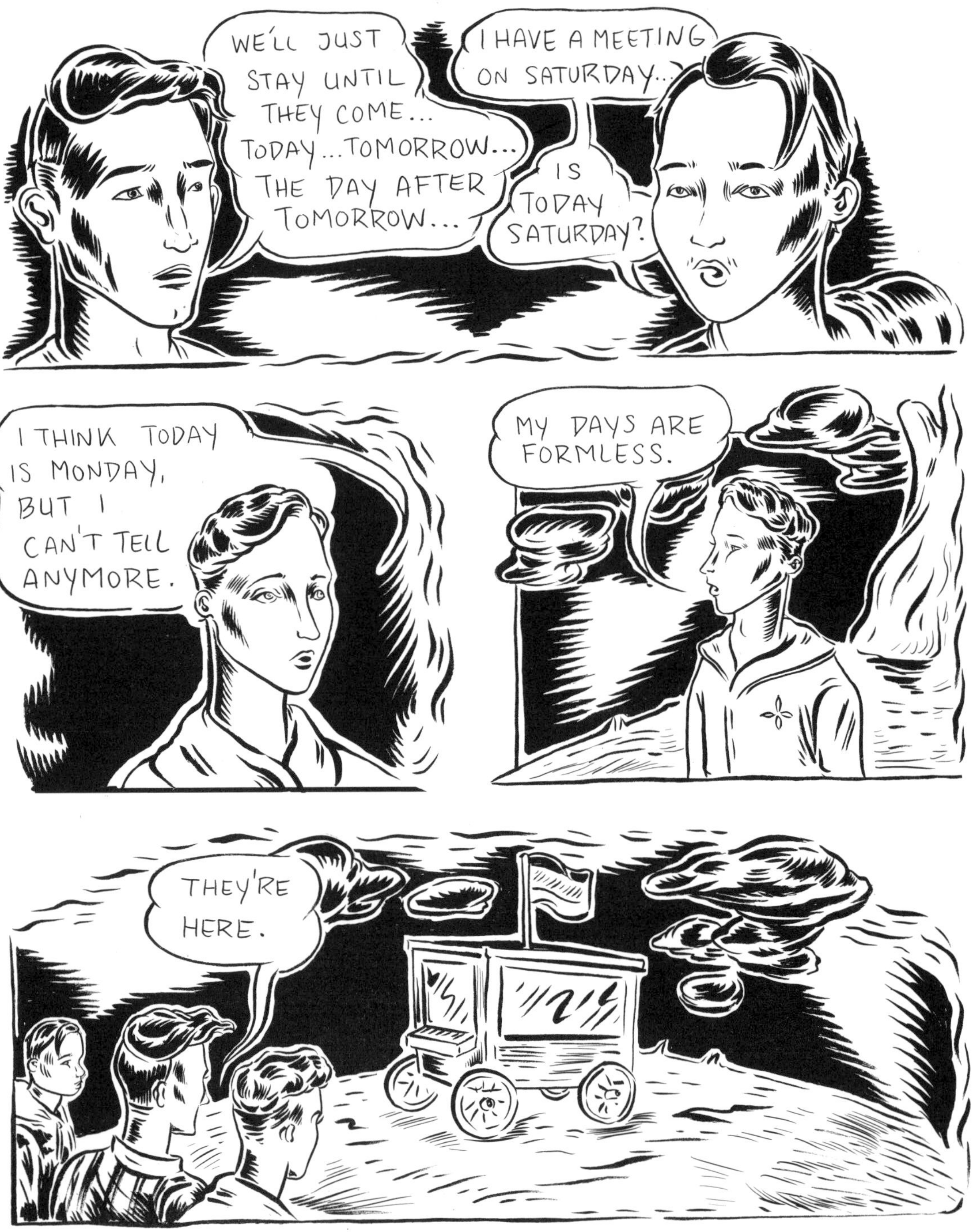
WE'LL JUST STAY UNTIL THEY COME... TODAY...TOMORROW... THE DAY AFTER TOMORROW...
I HAVE A MEETING ON SATURDAY...
IS TODAY SATURDAY?
I THINK TODAY IS MONDAY, BUT I CAN'T TELL ANYMORE.
MY DAYS ARE FORMLESS.
THEY'RE HERE.

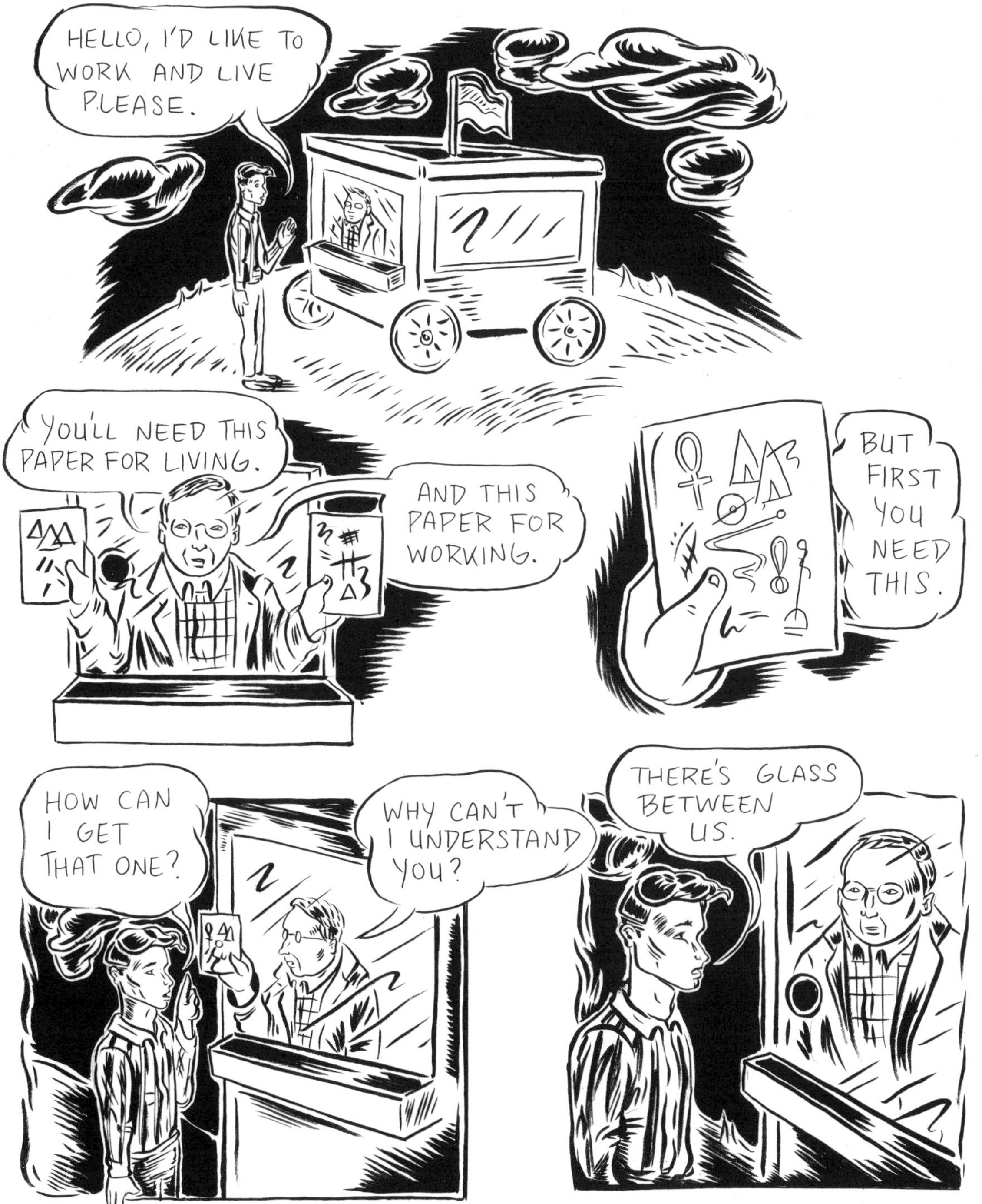
HELLO, I'D LIKE TO WORK AND LIVE PLEASE.
YOU'LL NEED THIS PAPER FOR LIVING.
AND THIS PAPER FOR WORKING.
BUT FIRST YOU NEED THIS.
HOW CAN I GET THAT ONE?
WHY CAN'T I UNDERSTAND YOU?
THERE'S GLASS BETWEEN US.

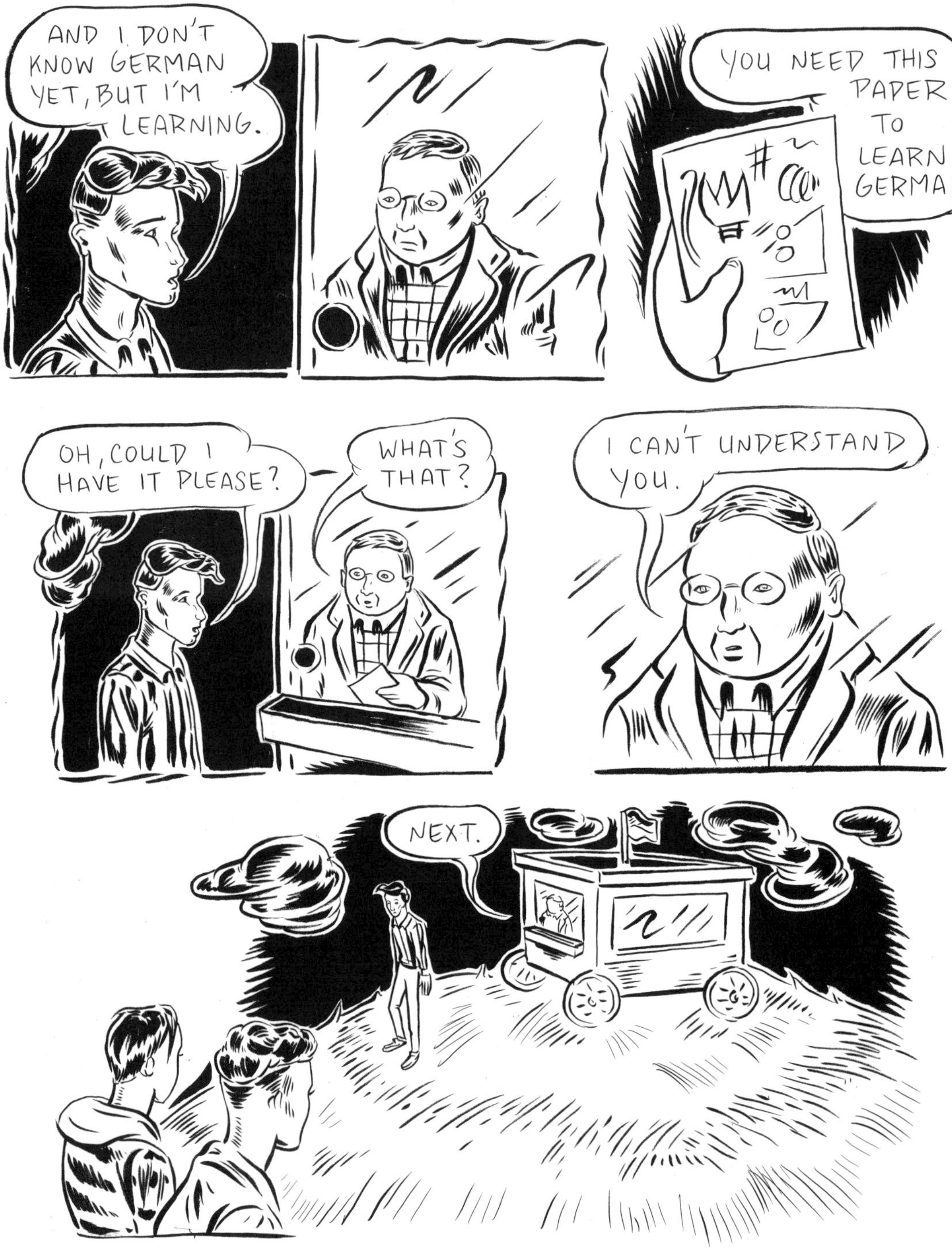
AND I DON'T KNOW GERMAN YET, BUT I'M LEARNING.
YOU NEED THIS PAPER TO LEARN GERMAN.
OH, COULD I HAVE IT PLEASE?
WHAT'S THAT?
I CAN'T UNDERSTAND YOU.
NEXT.

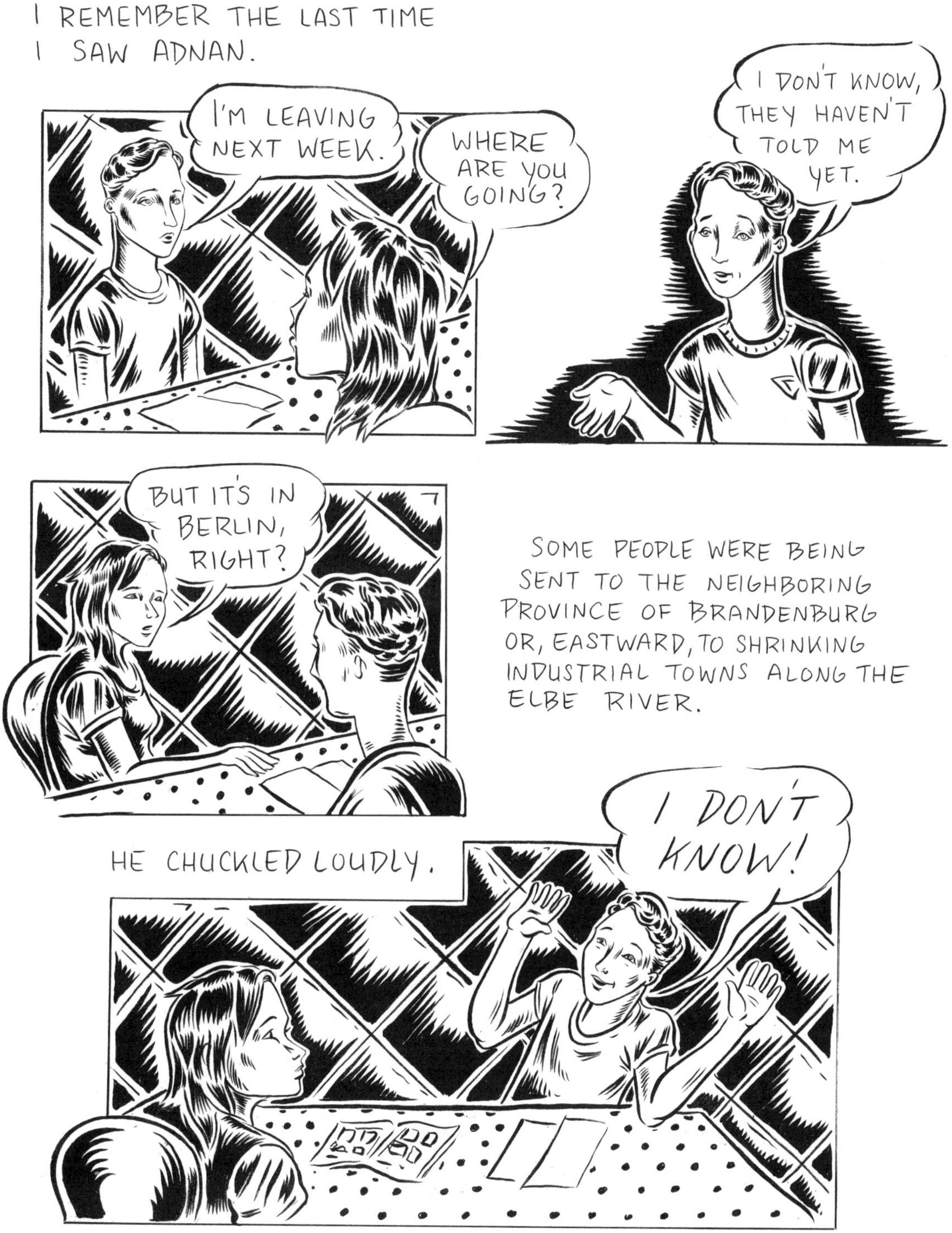
I REMEMBER THE LAST TIME
I SAW ADNAN.
I'M LEAVING NEXT WEEK.
WHERE ARE YOU GOING?
I DON'T KNOW, THEY HAVEN'T TOLD ME YET.
BUT IT'S IN BERLIN, RIGHT?
SOME PEOPLE WERE BEING SENT TO THE NEIGHBORING PROVINCE OF BRANDENBURG OR, EASTWARD, TO SHRINKING INDUSTRIAL TOWNS ALONG THE ELBE RIVER.
HE CHUCKLED LOUDLY.
I DON'T KNOW!

ROMANCE

IN THE FALL OF 2015, I WAS TEACHING AT THE SHELTER ONCE A WEEK. THE REST OF THE TIME, I DREW VICTORIAN PSYCHEDELIA AND TAUGHT ENGLISH TO GERMAN BUSINESSPEOPLE (MOSTLY MEN) FOR MONEY. I NODDED AS THEY SPOKE ABOUT FALCONRY, AVATAR AND UPCOMING TRIPS TO MALLORCA, OCCASIONALLY INTERJECTING: "*WE WOULD USE THE PRESENT PERFECT HERE,*" OR, "*REMEMBER ADVERBS!*"

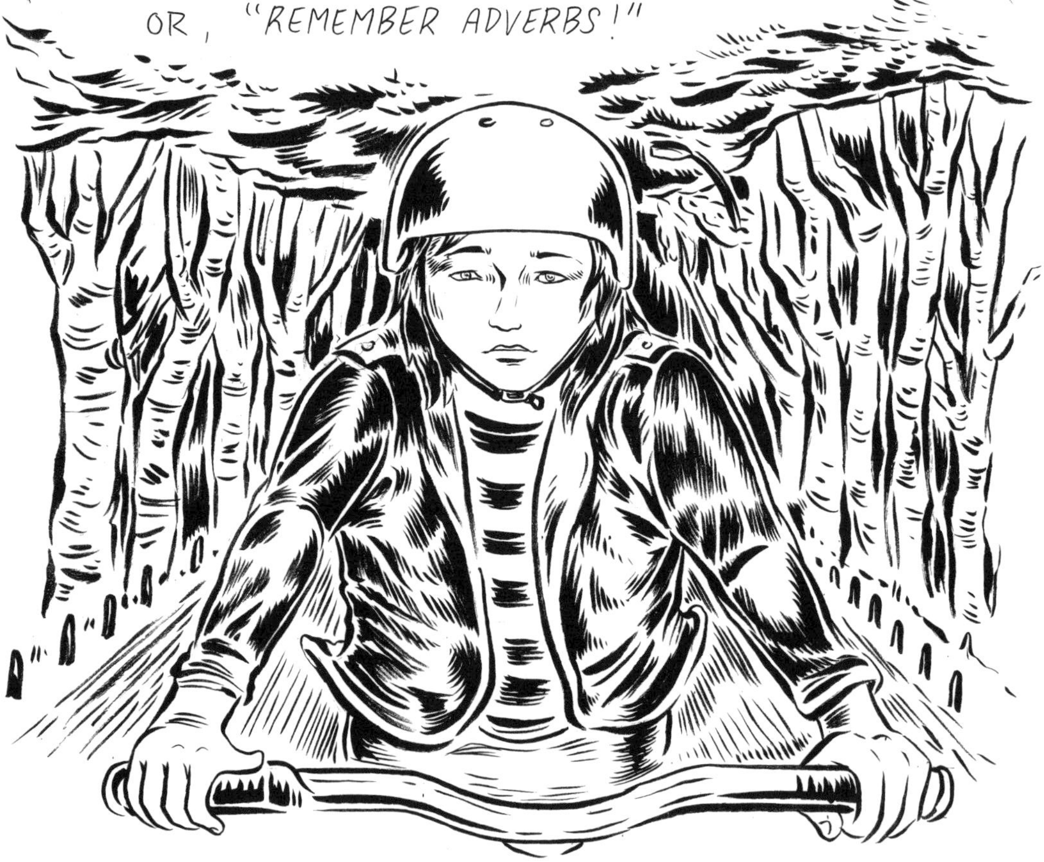

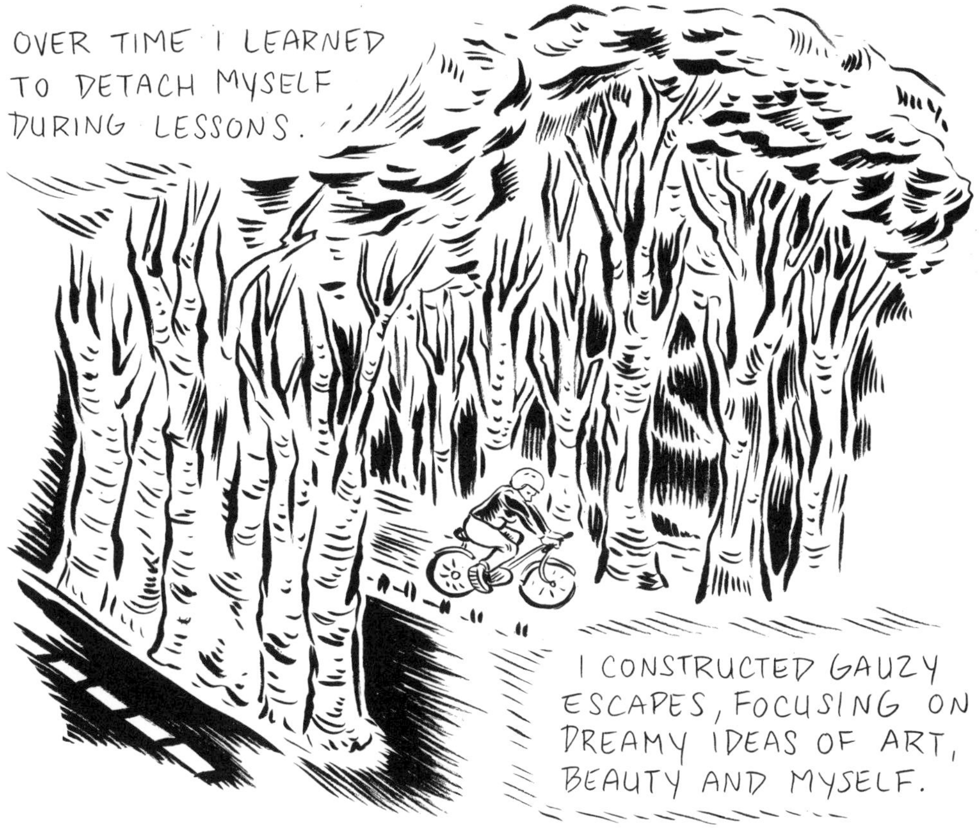
OVER TIME I LEARNED TO DETACH MYSELF DURING LESSONS.
I CONSTRUCTED GAUZY ESCAPES, FOCUSING ON DREAMY IDEAS OF ART, BEAUTY AND MYSELF.

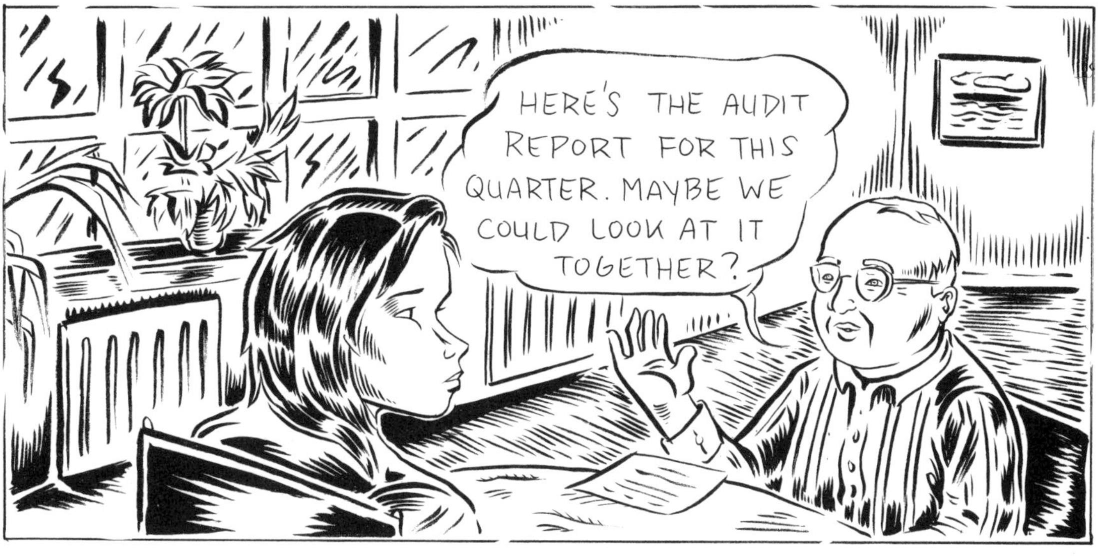
HERE'S THE AUDIT REPORT FOR THIS QUARTER. MAYBE WE COULD LOOK AT IT TOGETHER?

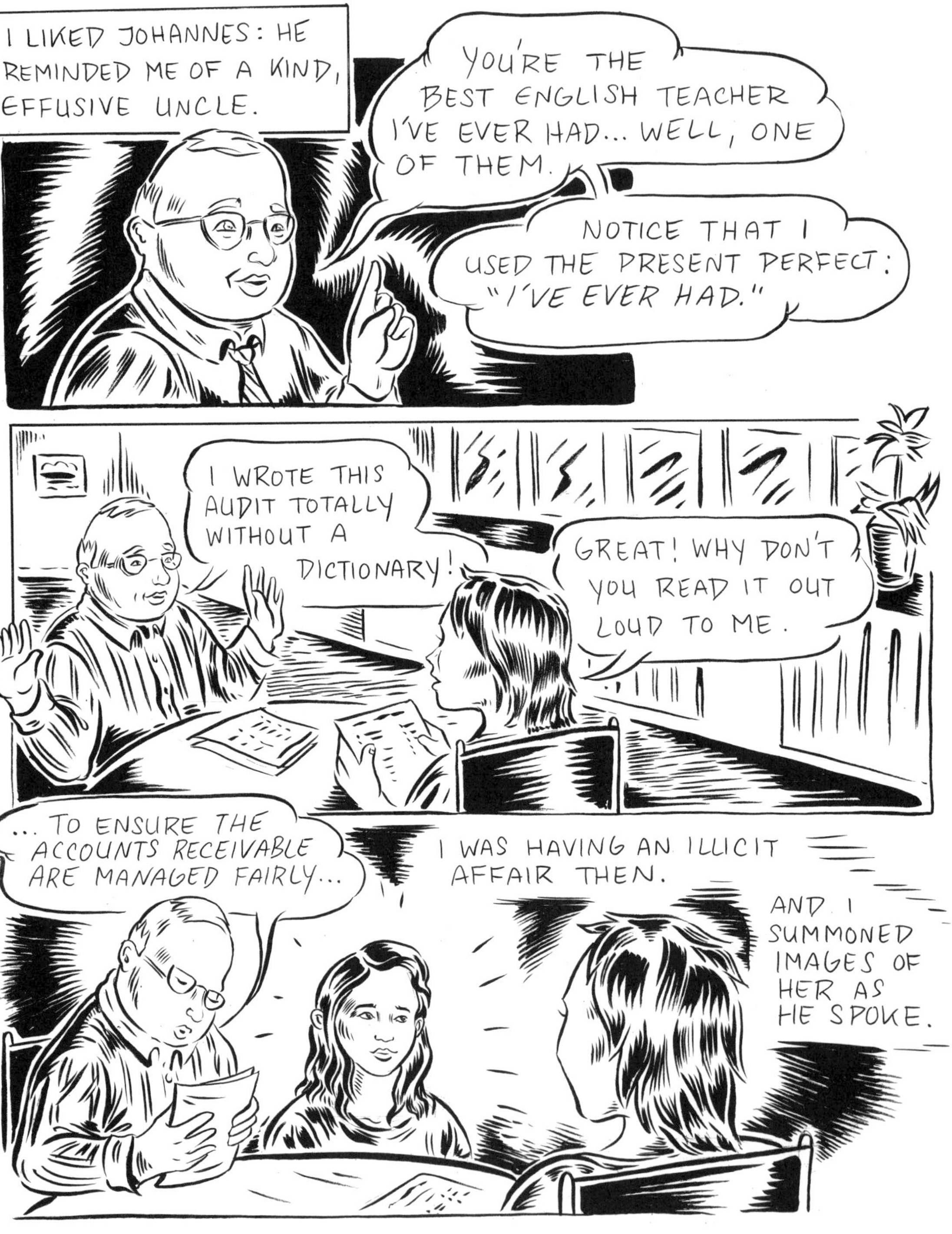
I LIKED JOHANNES: HE REMINDED ME OF A KIND, EFFUSIVE UNCLE.
YOU'RE THE BEST ENGLISH TEACHER I'VE EVER HAD... WELL, ONE OF THEM.
NOTICE THAT I USED THE PRESENT PERFECT: "I'VE EVER HAD."
I WROTE THIS AUDIT TOTALLY WITHOUT A DICTIONARY!
GREAT! WHY DON'T YOU READ IT OUT LOUD TO ME.
...TO ENSURE THE ACCOUNTS RECEIVABLE ARE MANAGED FAIRLY...
I WAS HAVING AN ILLICIT AFFAIR THEN.
AND I SUMMONED IMAGES OF HER AS HE SPOKE.

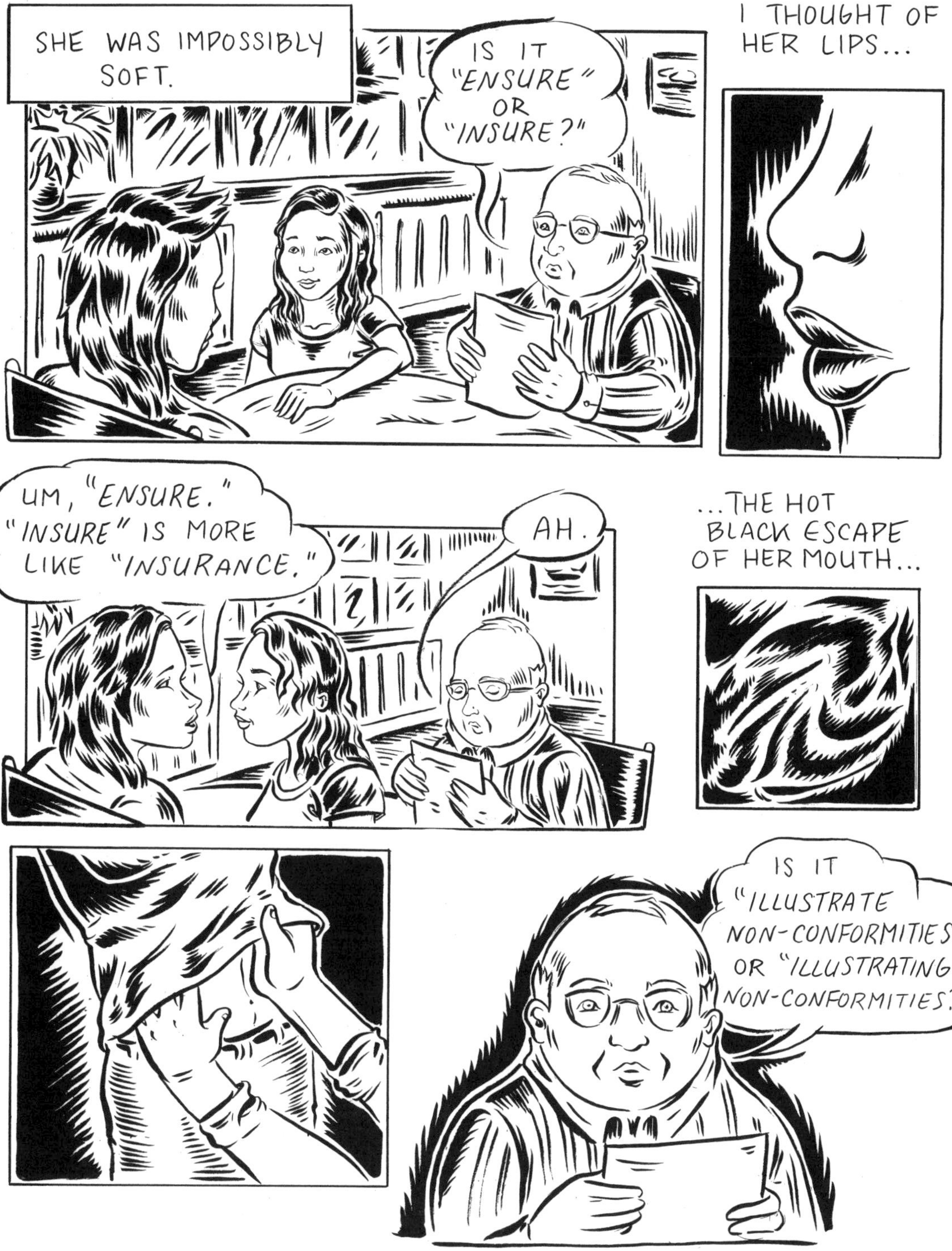
SHE WAS IMPOSSIBLY SOFT.
IS IT "ENSURE" OR "INSURE?"
I THOUGHT OF HER LIPS...
UM, "ENSURE." "INSURE" IS MORE LIKE "INSURANCE."
AH.
...THE HOT BLACK ESCAPE OF HER MOUTH...
IS IT "ILLUSTRATE NON-CONFORMITIES" OR "ILLUSTRATING NON-CONFORMITIES?"

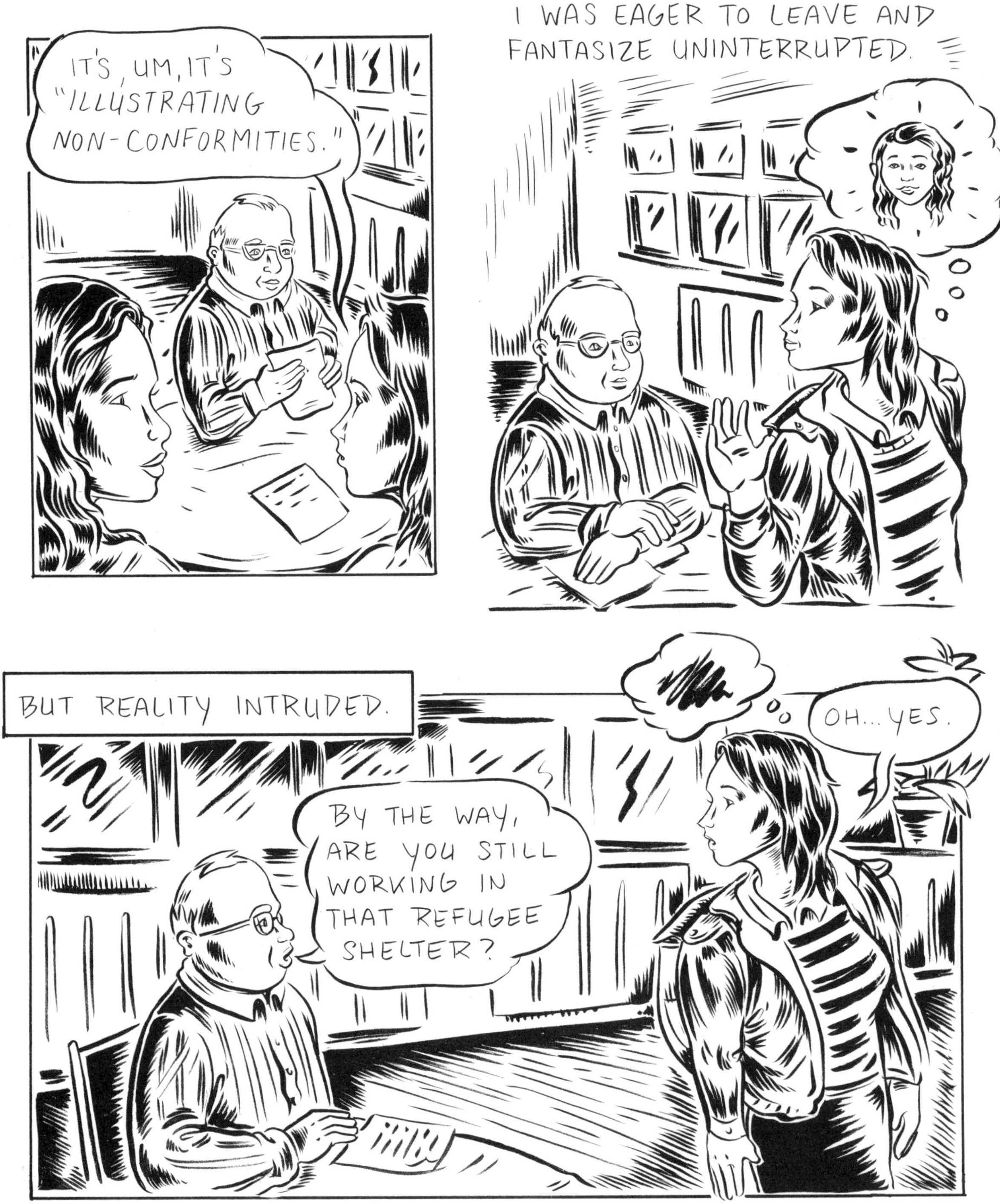
IT'S, UM, IT'S "ILLUSTRATING NON-CONFORMITIES."
I WAS EAGER TO LEAVE AND FANTASIZE UNINTERRUPTED.
BUT REALITY INTRUDED.
BY THE WAY, ARE YOU STILL WORKING IN THAT REFUGEE SHELTER?
OH... YES.

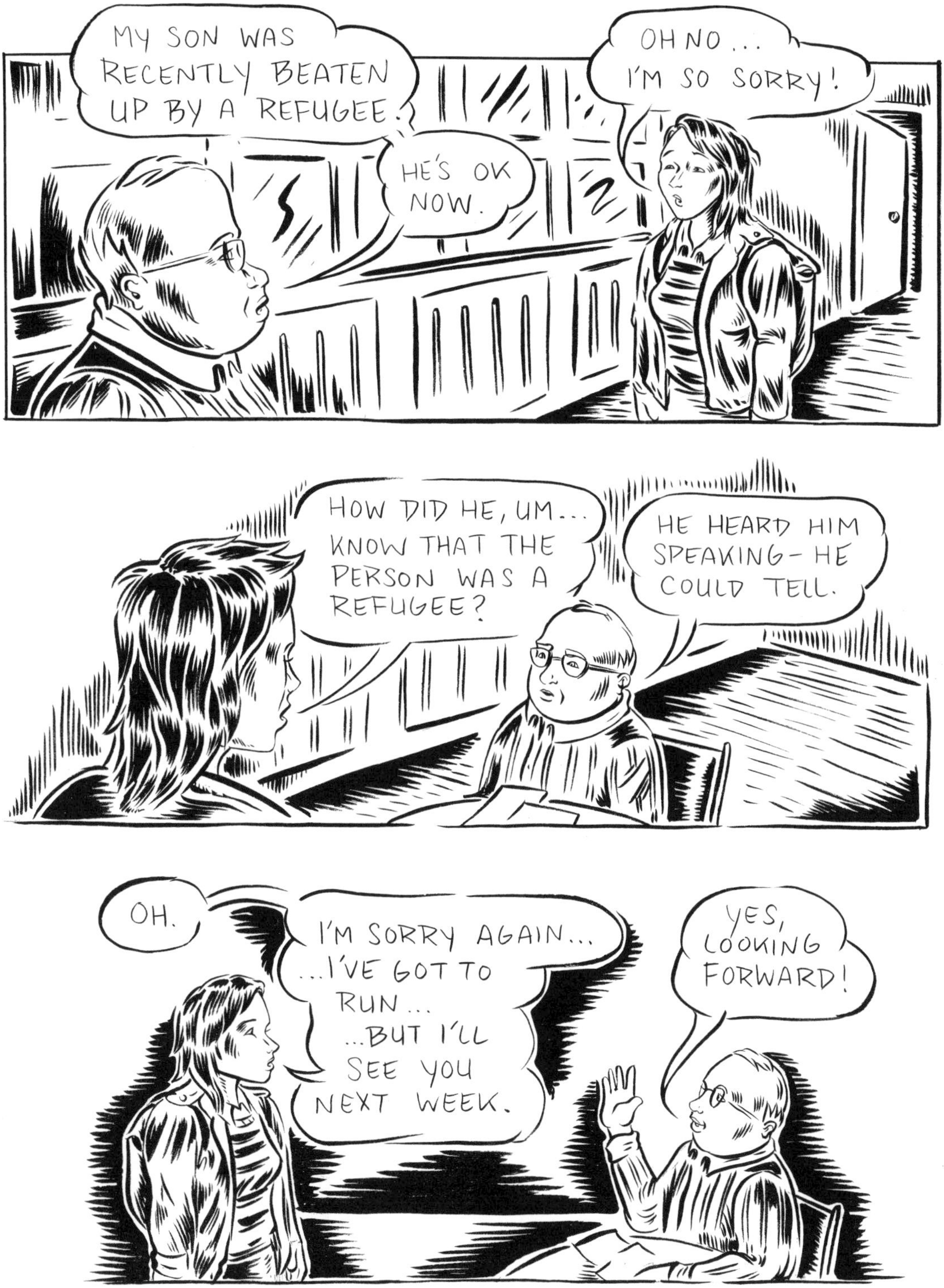
MY SON WAS RECENTLY BEATEN UP BY A REFUGEE.
HE'S OK NOW.
OH NO ... I'M SO SORRY!
HOW DID HE, UM... KNOW THAT THE PERSON WAS A REFUGEE?
HE HEARD HIM SPEAKING- HE COULD TELL.
OH.
I'M SORRY AGAIN... ...I'VE GOT TO RUN... ...BUT I'LL SEE YOU NEXT WEEK.
YES, LOOKING FORWARD!

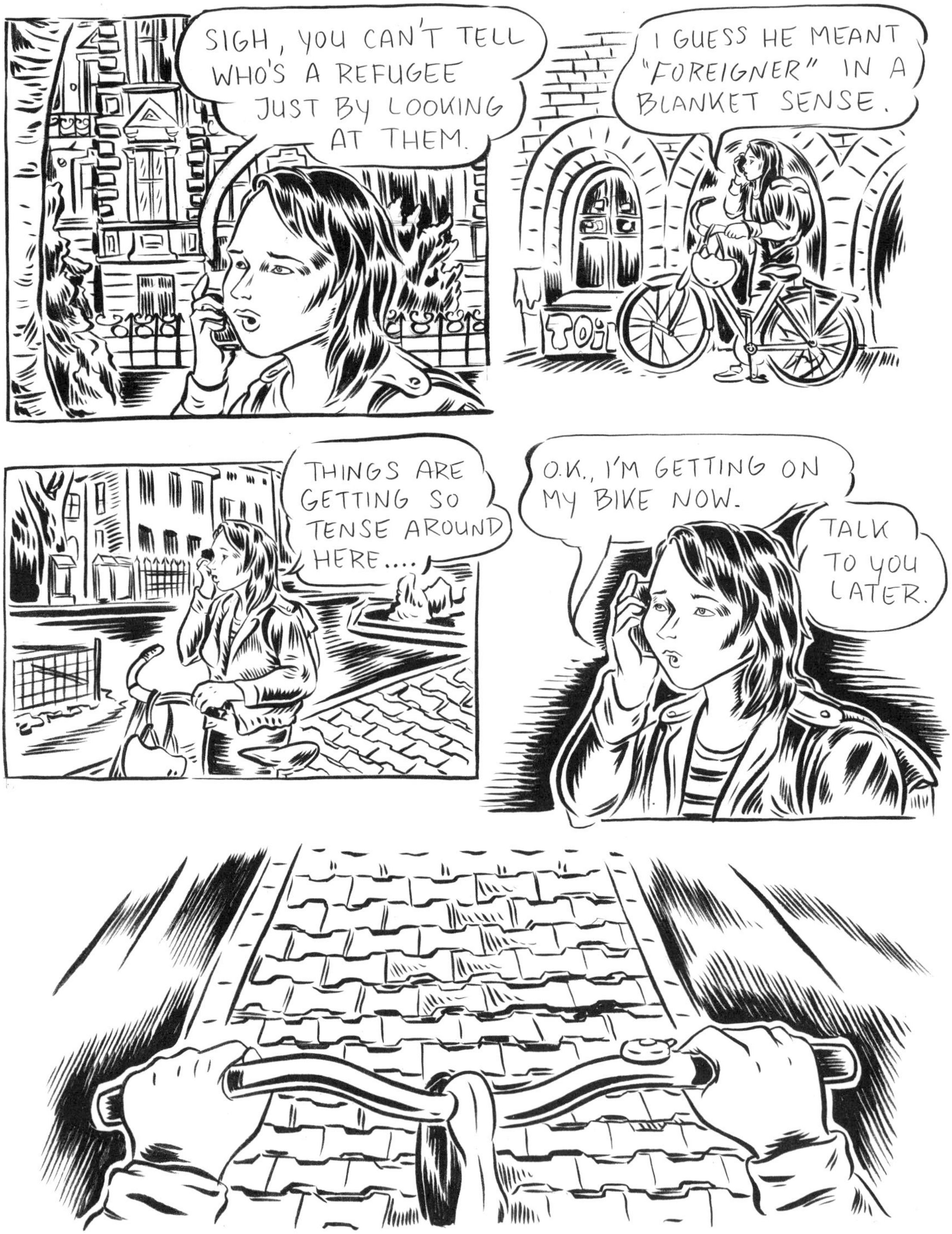
SIGH, YOU CAN'T TELL WHO'S A REFUGEE JUST BY LOOKING AT THEM.
I GUESS HE MEANT "FOREIGNER" IN A BLANKET SENSE.
THINGS ARE GETTING SO TENSE AROUND HERE....
O.K., I'M GETTING ON MY BIKE NOW.
TALK TO YOU LATER.

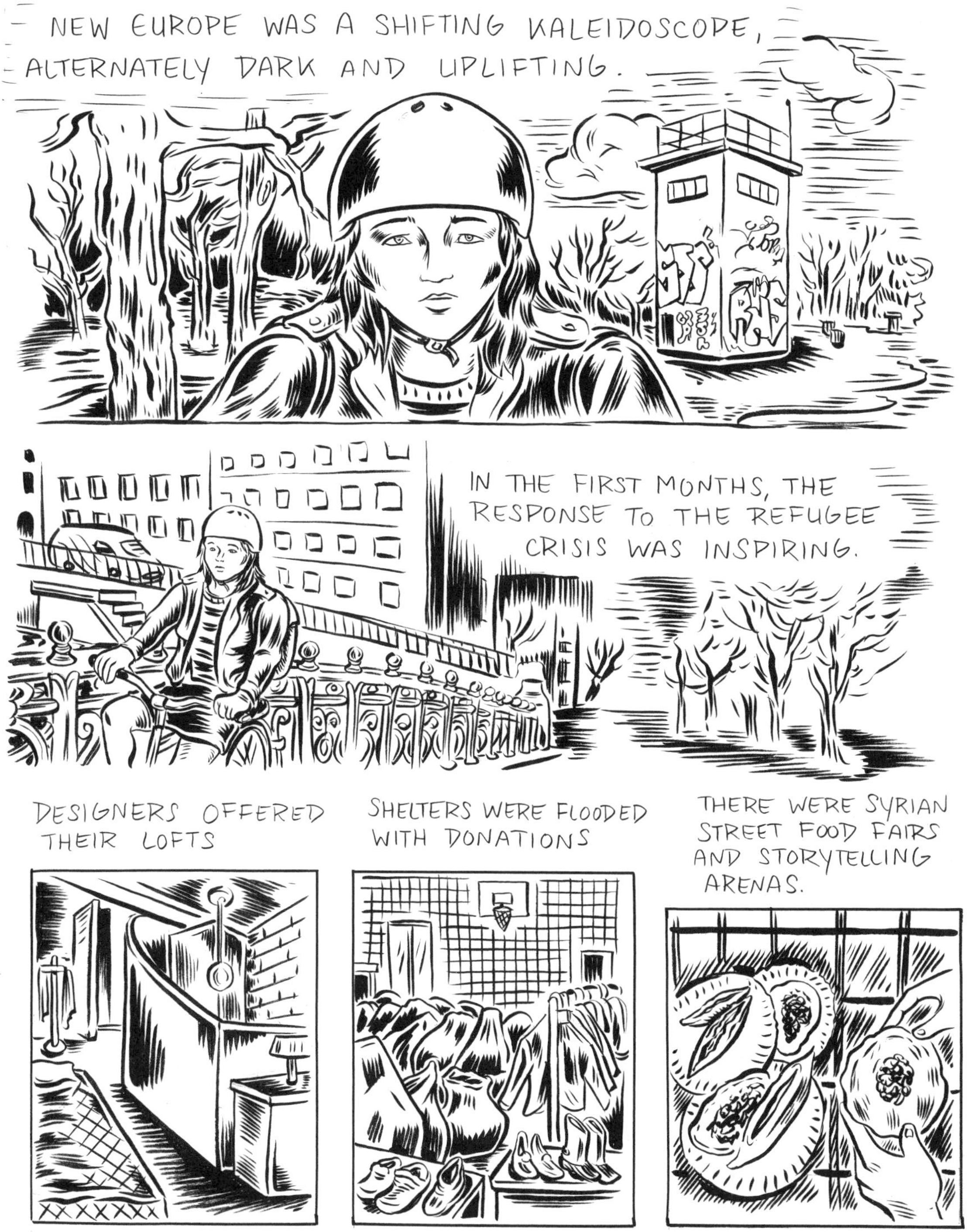
NEW EUROPE WAS A SHIFTING KALEIDOSCOPE, ALTERNATELY DARK AND UPLIFTING.
IN THE FIRST MONTHS, THE RESPONSE TO THE REFUGEE CRISIS WAS INSPIRING.
DESIGNERS OFFERED THEIR LOFTS
SHELTERS WERE FLOODED WITH DONATIONS
THERE WERE SYRIAN STREET FOOD FAIRS AND STORYTELLING ARENAS.

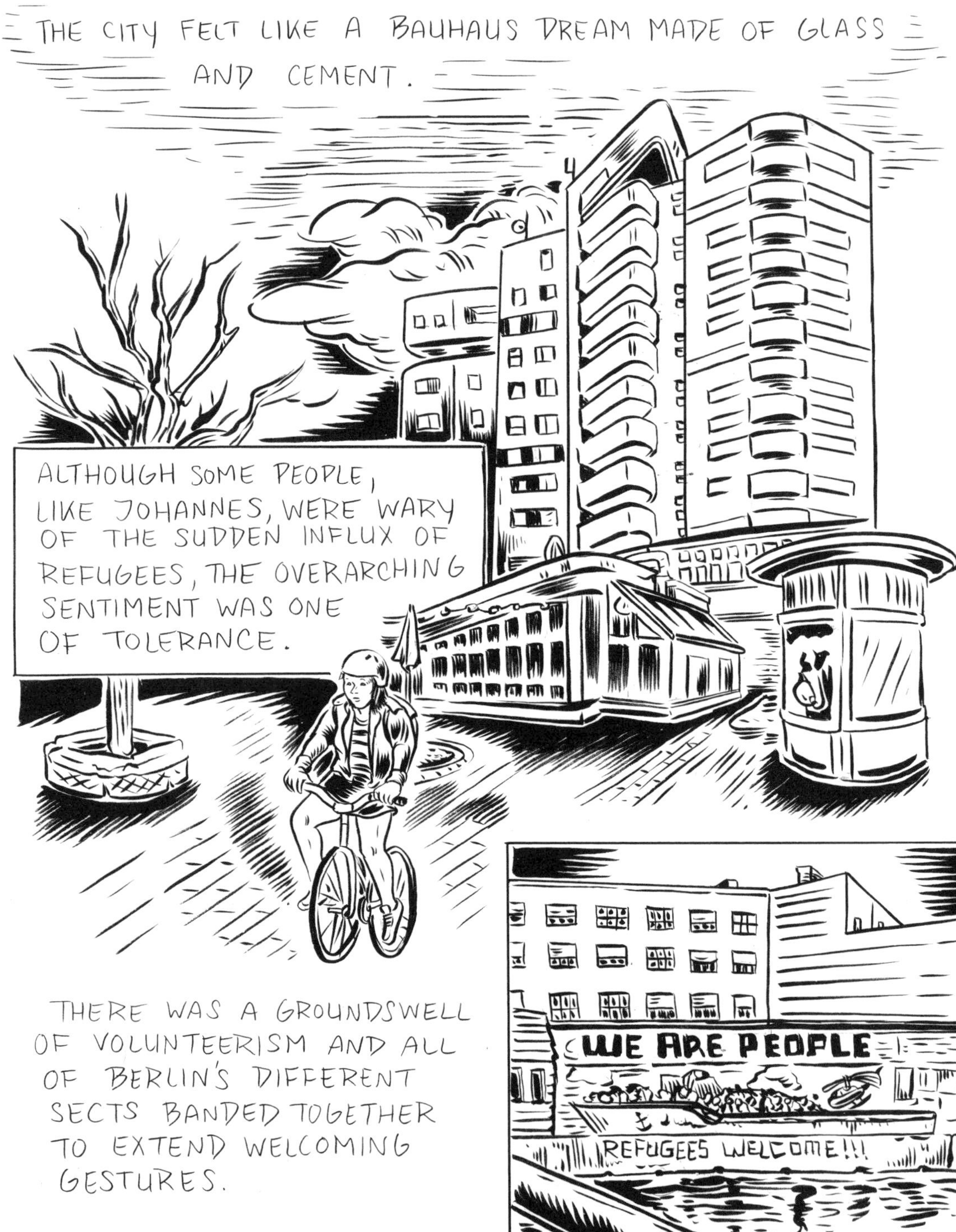
THE CITY FELT LIKE A BAUHAUS DREAM MADE OF GLASS AND CEMENT.
ALTHOUGH SOME PEOPLE, LIKE JOHANNES, WERE WARY OF THE SUDDEN INFLUX OF REFUGEES, THE OVERARCHING SENTIMENT WAS ONE OF TOLERANCE.
THERE WAS A GROUNDSWELL OF VOLUNTEERISM AND ALL OF BERLIN'S DIFFERENT SECTS BANDED TOGETHER TO EXTEND WELCOMING GESTURES.
WE ARE PEOPLE
REFUGEES WELCOME!!!

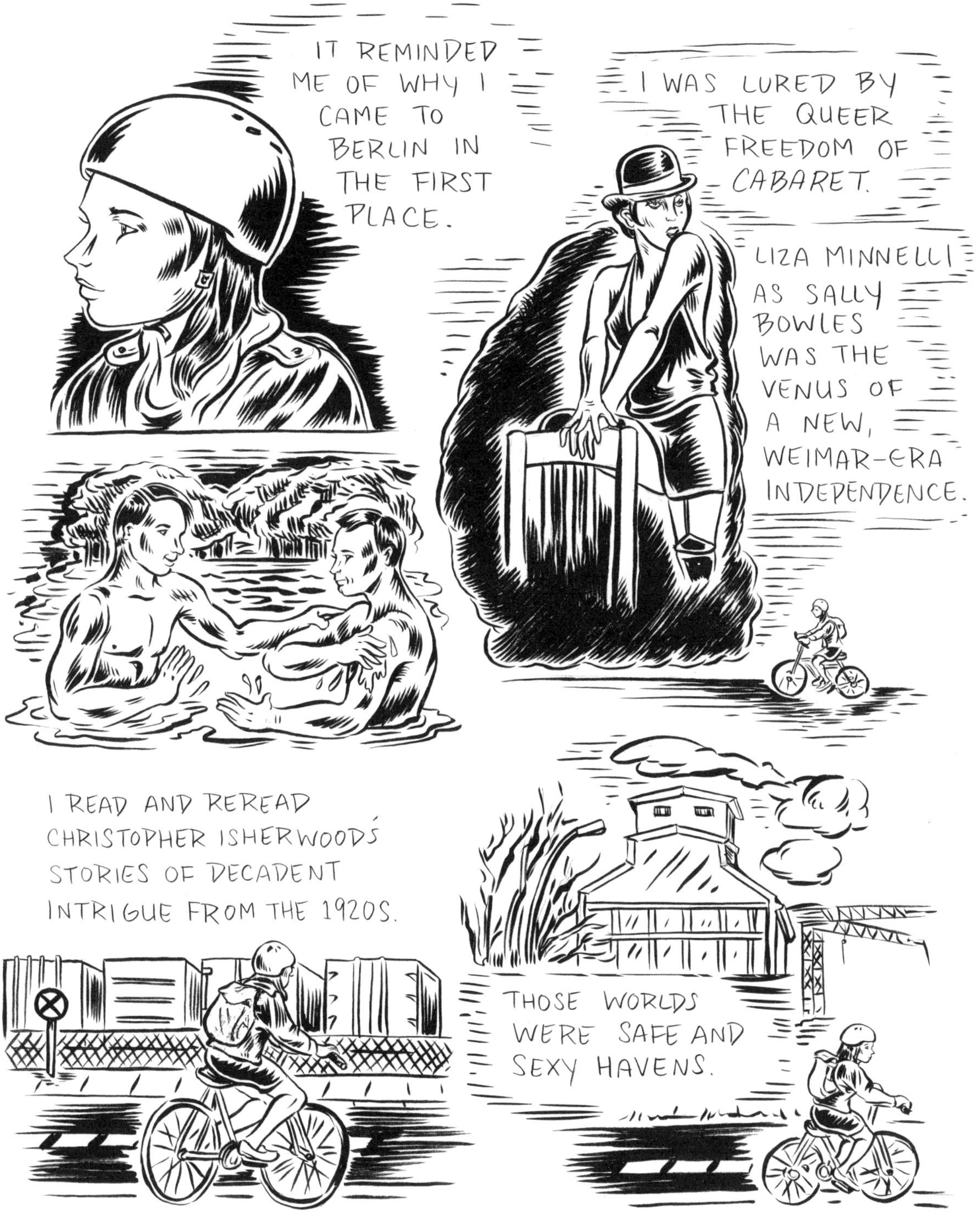
IT REMINDED ME OF WHY I CAME TO BERLIN IN THE FIRST PLACE.
I WAS LURED BY THE QUEER FREEDOM OF CABARET.
LIZA MINNELLI AS SALLY BOWLES WAS THE VENUS OF A NEW, WEIMAR-ERA INDEPENDENCE.
I READ AND REREAD CHRISTOPHER ISHERWOOD'S STORIES OF DECADENT INTRIGUE FROM THE 1920S.
THOSE WORLDS WERE SAFE AND SEXY HAVENS.

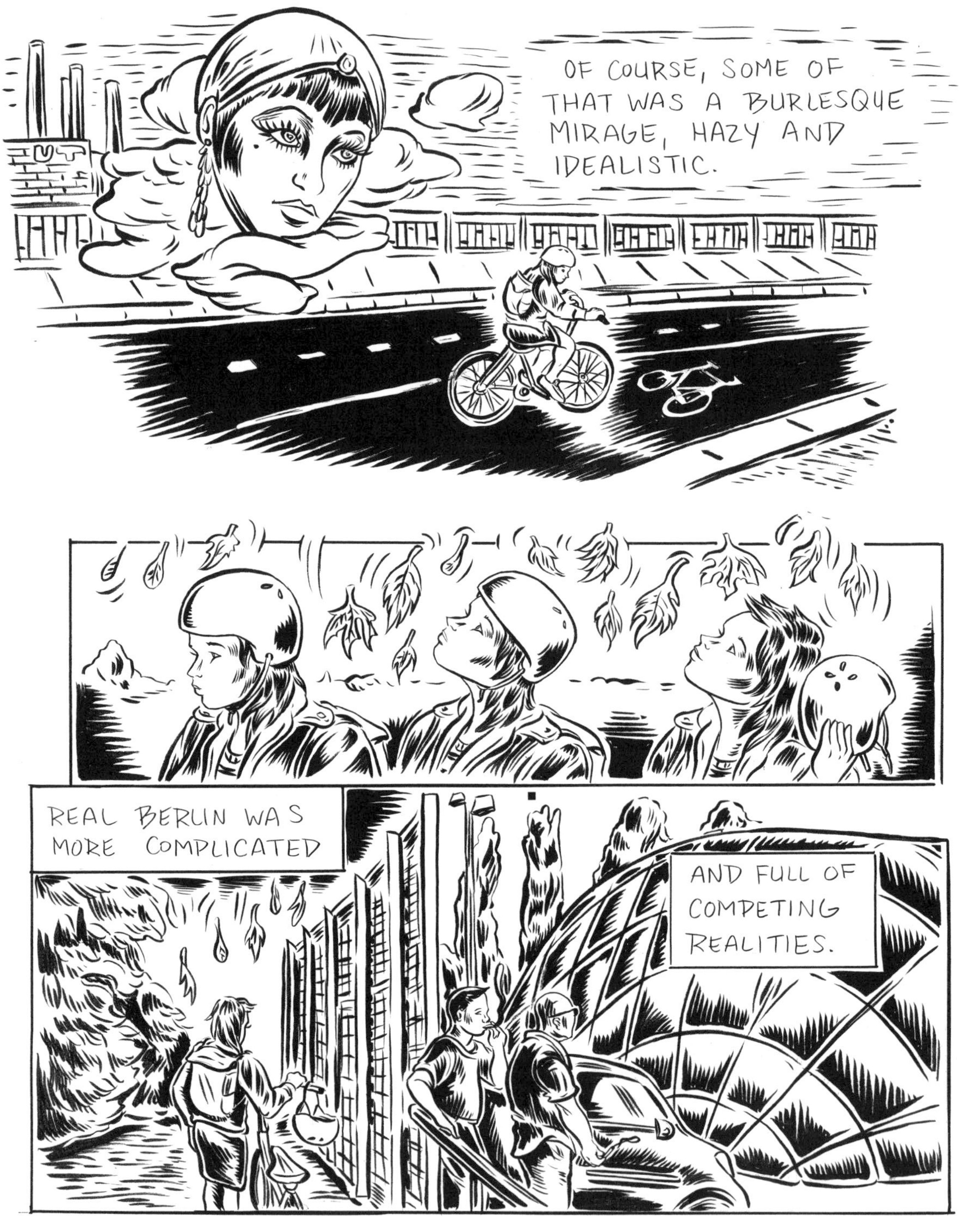
OF COURSE, SOME OF THAT WAS A BURLESQUE MIRAGE, HAZY AND IDEALISTIC.
REAL BERLIN WAS MORE COMPLICATED
AND FULL OF COMPETING REALITIES.

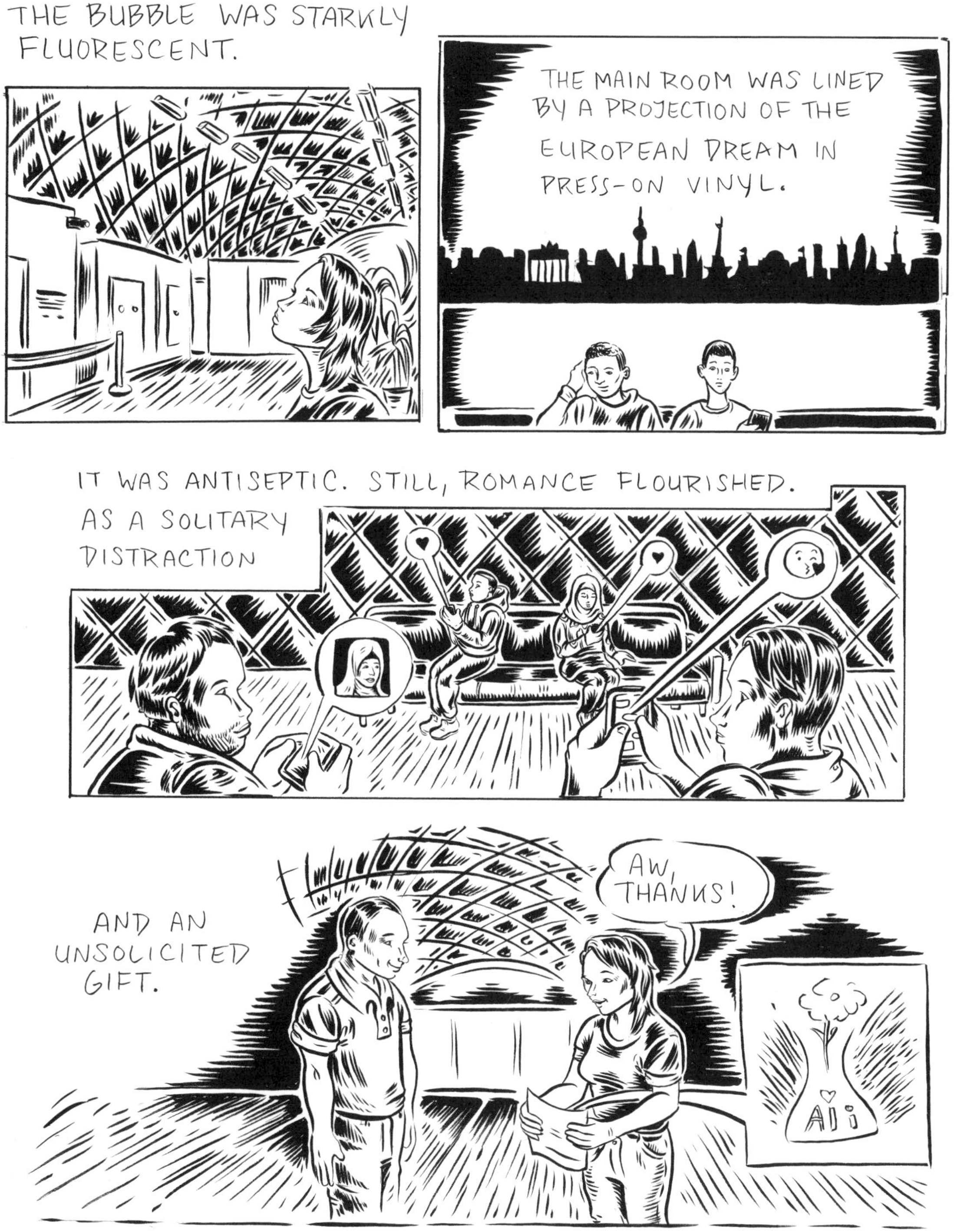
THE BUBBLE WAS STARKLY FLUORESCENT.
THE MAIN ROOM WAS LINED BY A PROJECTION OF THE EUROPEAN DREAM IN PRESS-ON VINYL.
IT WAS ANTISEPTIC. STILL, ROMANCE FLOURISHED.
AS A SOLITARY DISTRACTION
AND AN UNSOLICITED GIFT.
AW, THANKS!
Ali

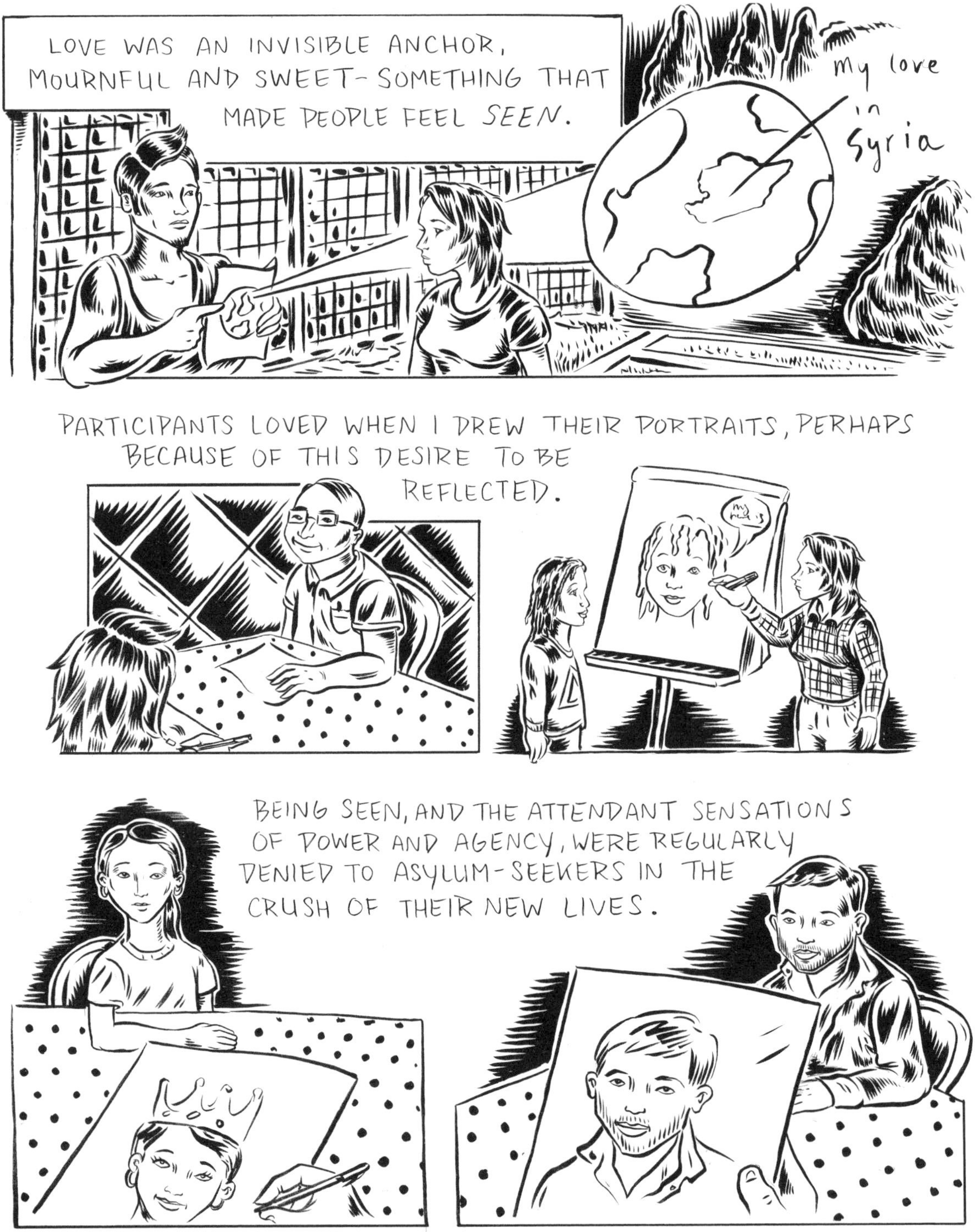
LOVE WAS AN INVISIBLE ANCHOR, MOURNFUL AND SWEET- SOMETHING THAT MADE PEOPLE FEEL *SEEN*.
my love in Syria
PARTICIPANTS LOVED WHEN I DREW THEIR PORTRAITS, PERHAPS BECAUSE OF THIS DESIRE TO BE REFLECTED.
BEING SEEN, AND THE ATTENDANT SENSATIONS OF POWER AND AGENCY, WERE REGULARLY DENIED TO ASYLUM-SEEKERS IN THE CRUSH OF THEIR NEW LIVES.

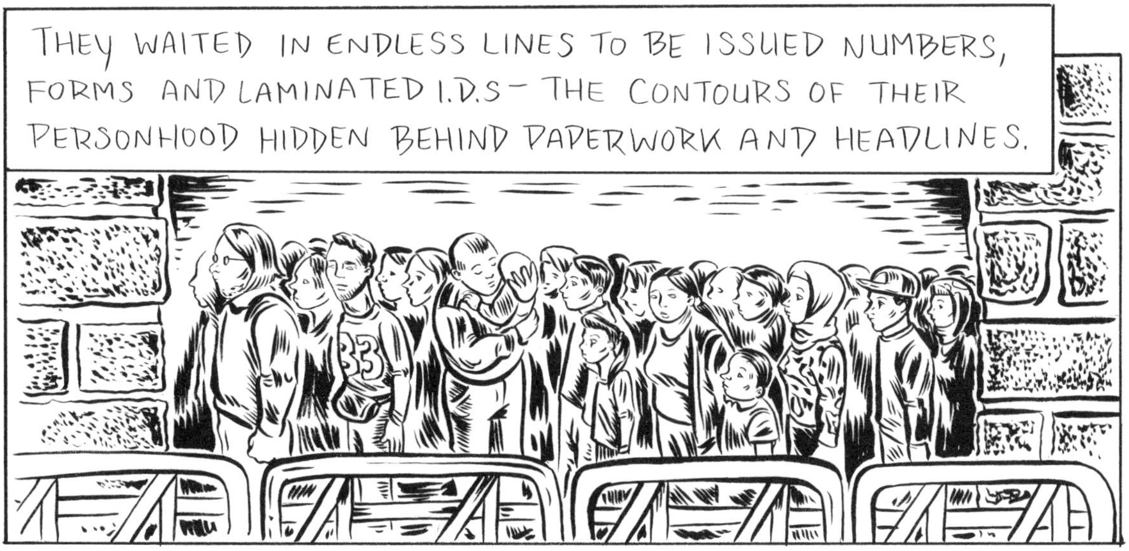
THEY WAITED IN ENDLESS LINES TO BE ISSUED NUMBERS, FORMS AND LAMINATED I.D.S – THE CONTOURS OF THEIR PERSONHOOD HIDDEN BEHIND PAPERWORK AND HEADLINES.
33

THEY USUALLY LEFT THEIR DRAWINGS, NO MATTER HOW I PROTESTED.

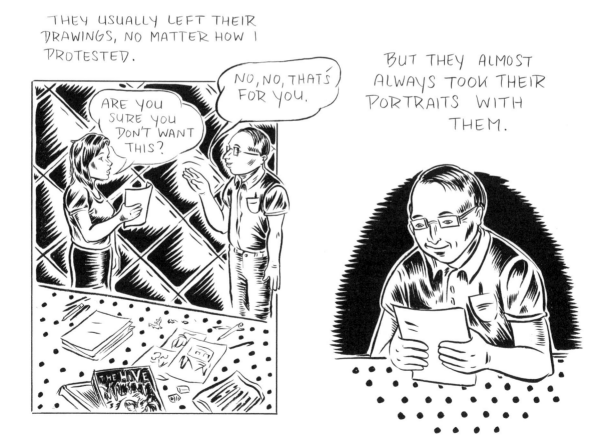

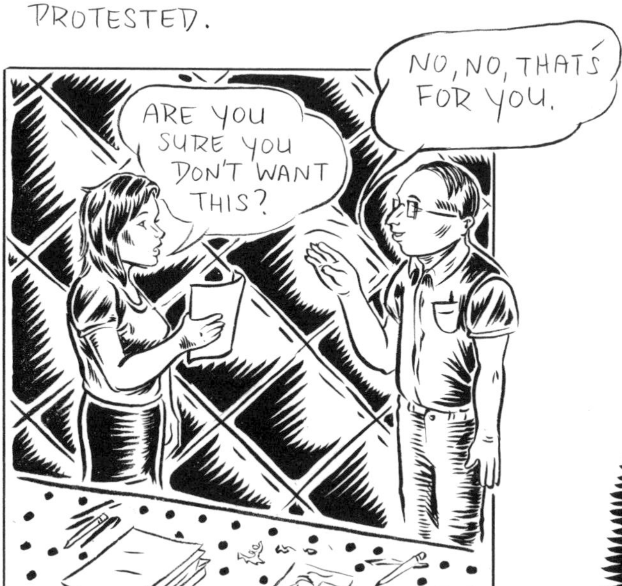
ARE YOU SURE YOU DON'T WANT THIS?
NO, NO, THAT'S FOR YOU.
THE LOVE

BUT THEY ALMOST ALWAYS TOOK THEIR PORTRAITS WITH THEM.

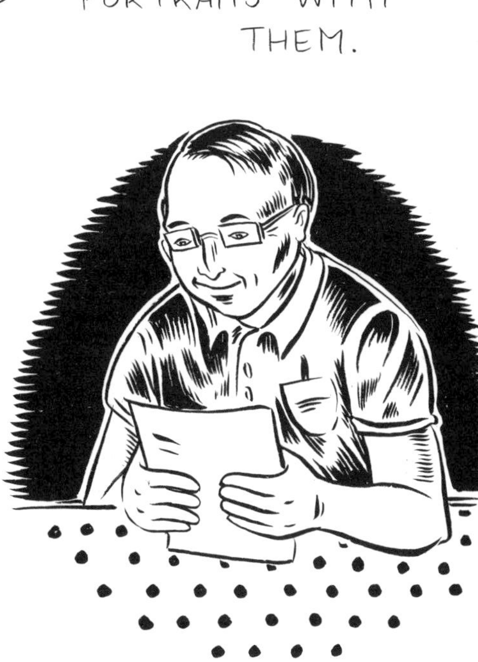

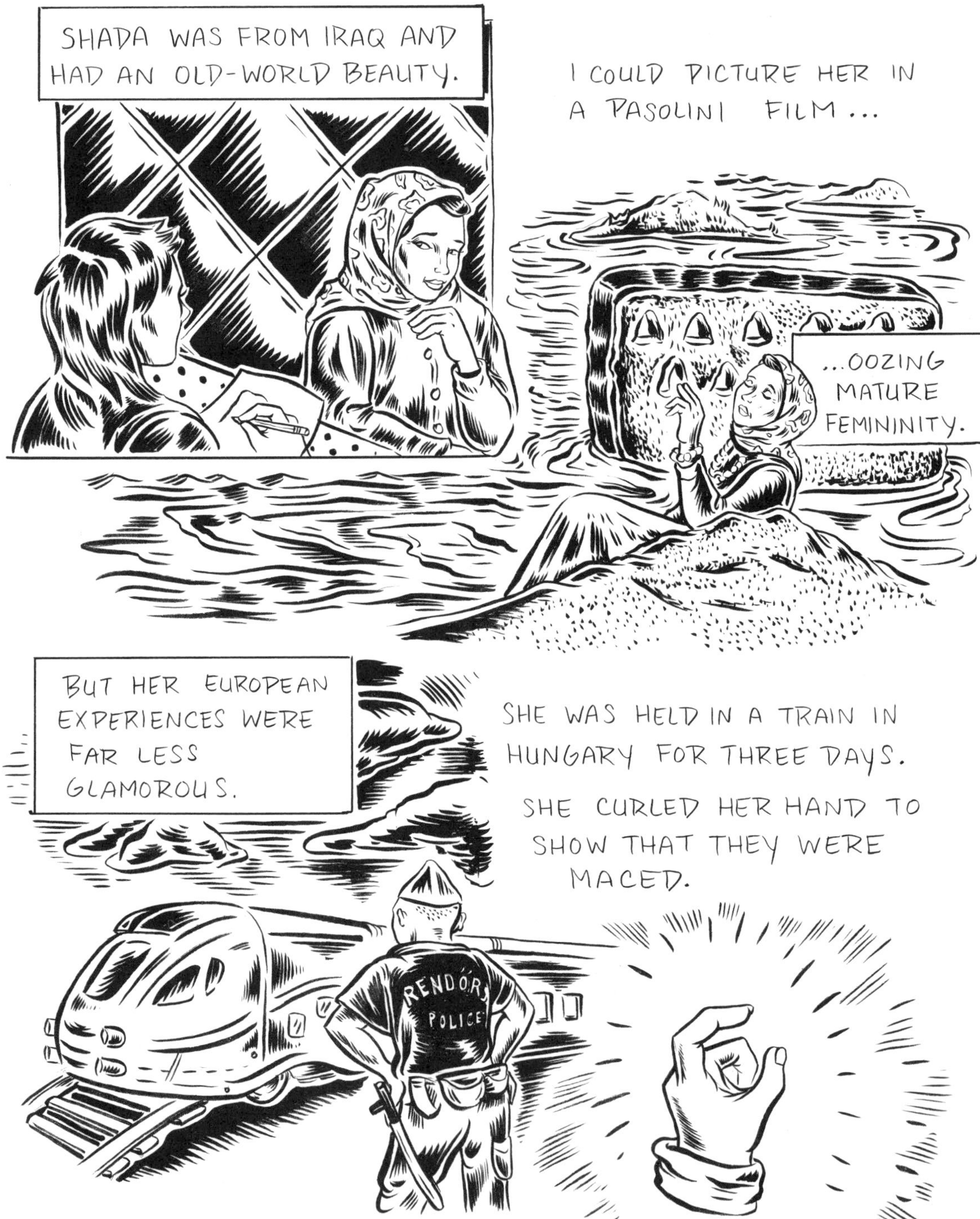
SHADA WAS FROM IRAQ AND HAD AN OLD-WORLD BEAUTY.
I COULD PICTURE HER IN A PASOLINI FILM...
...OOZING MATURE FEMININITY.
BUT HER EUROPEAN EXPERIENCES WERE FAR LESS GLAMOROUS.
SHE WAS HELD IN A TRAIN IN HUNGARY FOR THREE DAYS.
SHE CURLED HER HAND TO SHOW THAT THEY WERE MACED.
RENDŐRS
POLICE

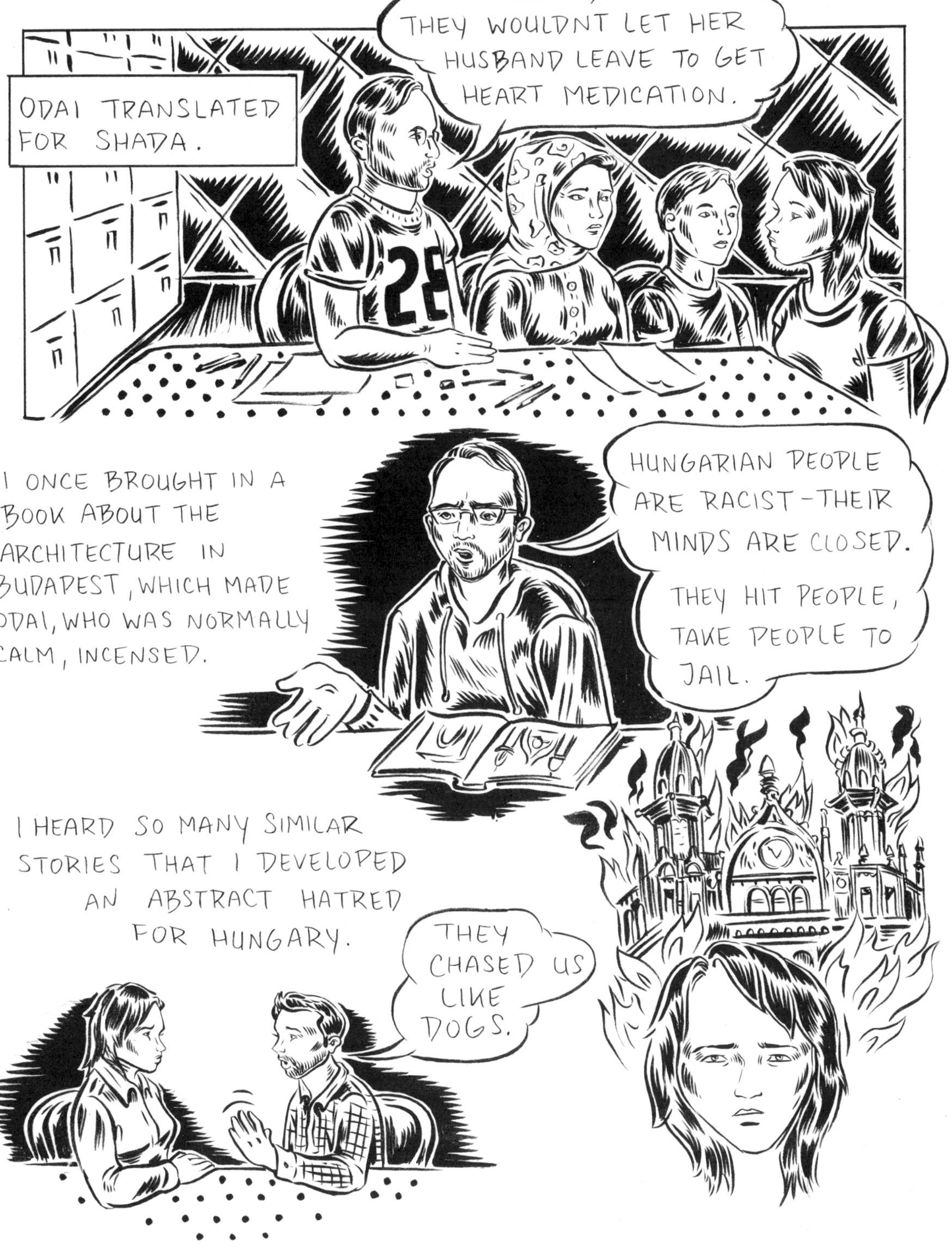

ODAI TRANSLATED FOR SHADA.
THEY WOULDN'T LET HER HUSBAND LEAVE TO GET HEART MEDICATION.
I ONCE BROUGHT IN A BOOK ABOUT THE ARCHITECTURE IN BUDAPEST, WHICH MADE ODAI, WHO WAS NORMALLY CALM, INCENSED.
HUNGARIAN PEOPLE ARE RACIST - THEIR MINDS ARE CLOSED.
THEY HIT PEOPLE, TAKE PEOPLE TO JAIL.
I HEARD SO MANY SIMILAR STORIES THAT I DEVELOPED AN ABSTRACT HATRED FOR HUNGARY.
THEY CHASED US LIKE DOGS.

SHADA SPENT MOST OF THE CLASS HELPING HER DISABLED SON DRAW SHINGLES AND CLOUDS.

SHE ALSO DREW A BIKE, BRIMMING WITH FLOWERS.

IT WAS LOVELY.

BEFORE LEAVING, SHE FOLDED MY PORTRAIT OF HER INTO SQUARES AND PUT IT INTO HER POCKET.

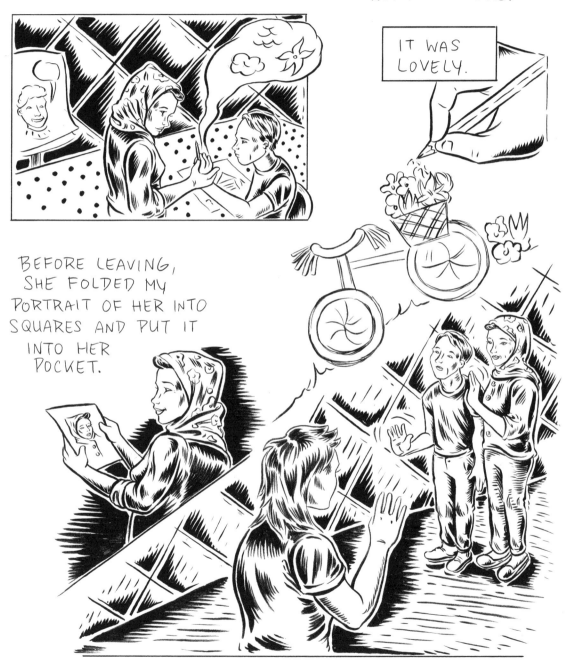

SAKER HAD A VERY DIFFERENT EXPERIENCE IN HUNGARY.

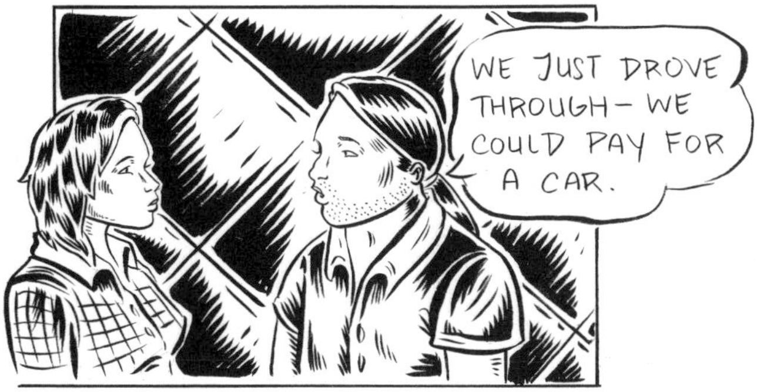
WE JUST DROVE THROUGH– WE COULD PAY FOR A CAR.

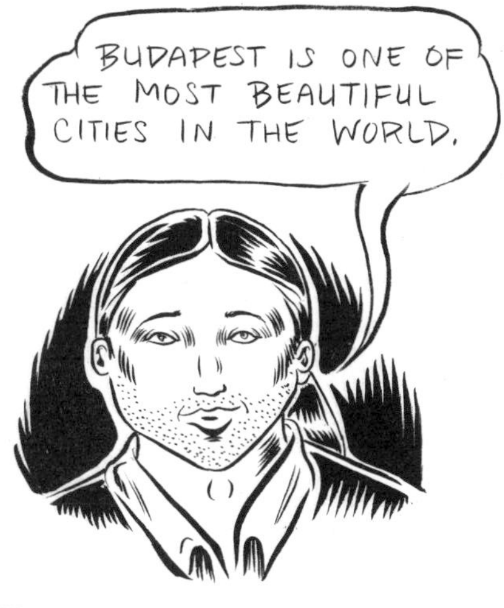
BUDAPEST IS ONE OF THE MOST BEAUTIFUL CITIES IN THE WORLD.

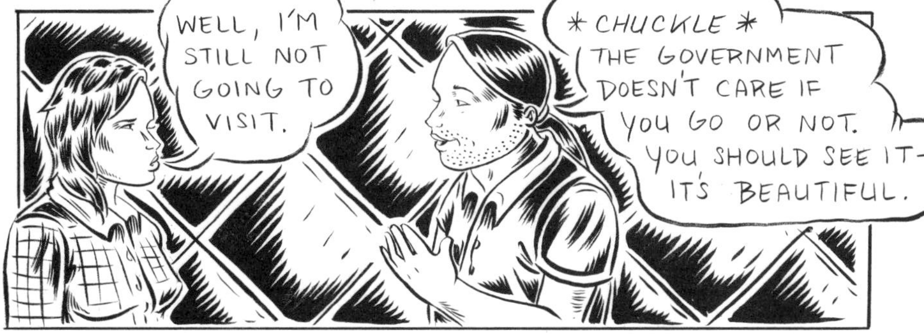
WELL, I'M STILL NOT GOING TO VISIT.
CHUCKLE THE GOVERNMENT DOESN'T CARE IF YOU GO OR NOT. YOU SHOULD SEE IT– IT'S BEAUTIFUL.

SAKER STUDIED BUSINESS ADMINISTRATION IN DAMASCUS AND LIKED TO ASK CURT, LOADED QUESTIONS.

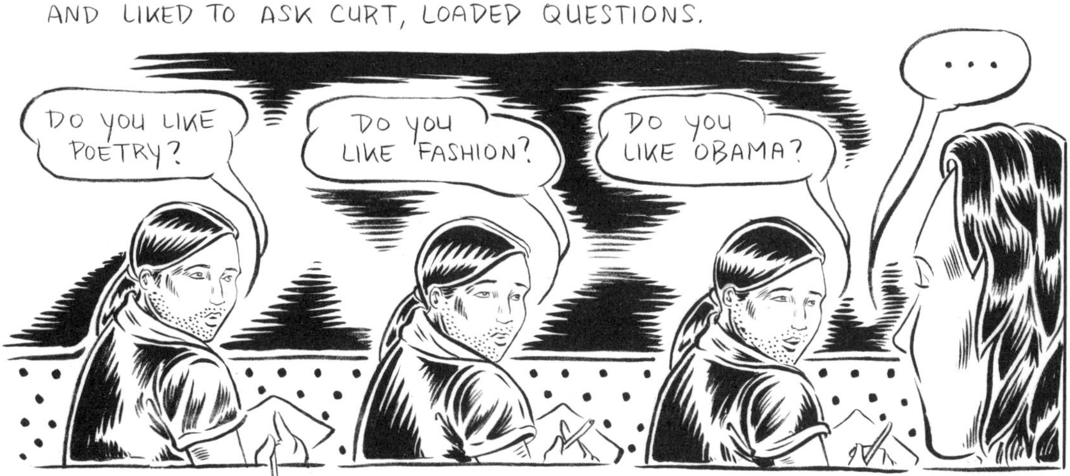
DO YOU LIKE POETRY?
DO YOU LIKE FASHION?
DO YOU LIKE OBAMA?
...

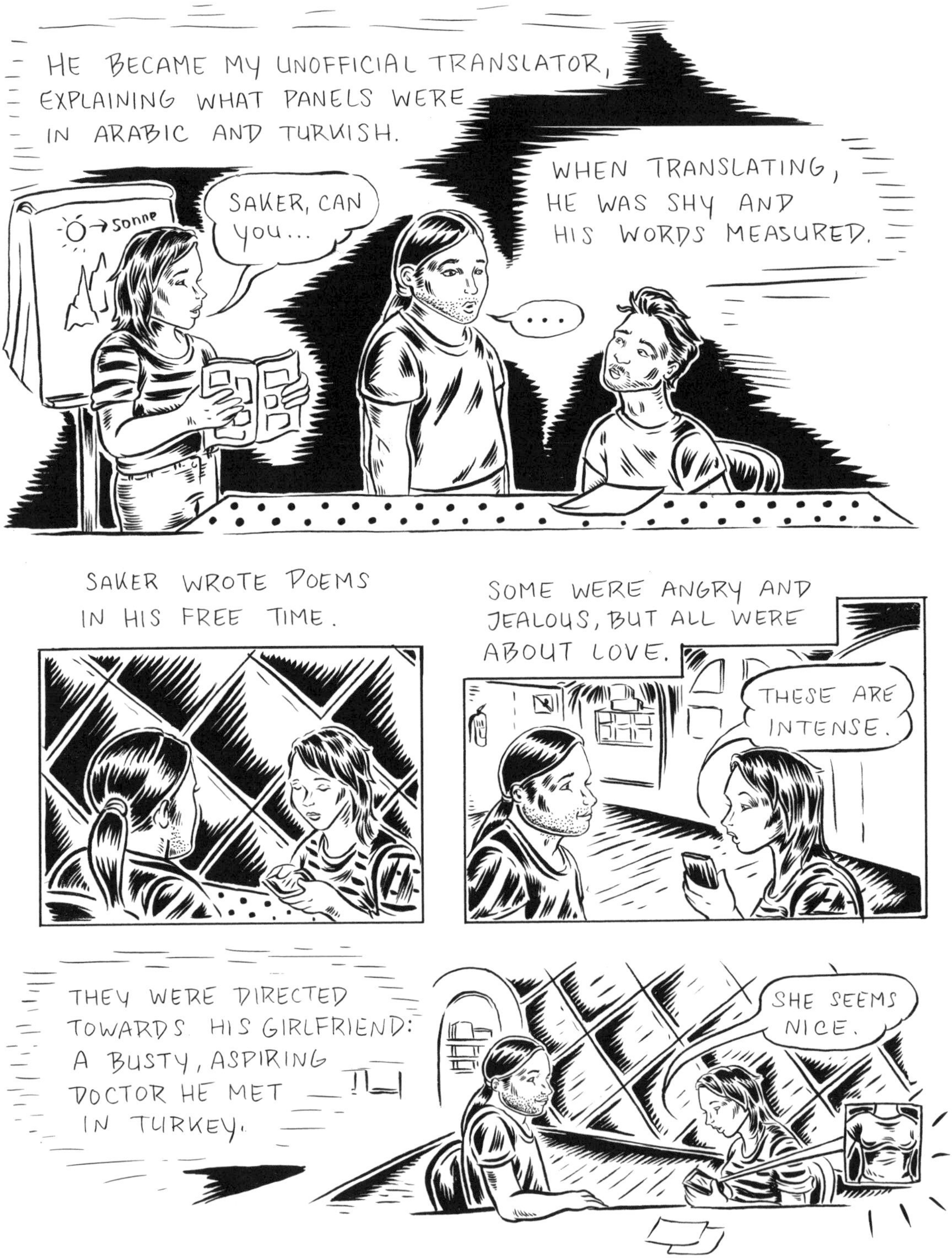
HE BECAME MY UNOFFICIAL TRANSLATOR, EXPLAINING WHAT PANELS WERE IN ARABIC AND TURKISH.
Sonne
SAKER, CAN YOU...
WHEN TRANSLATING, HE WAS SHY AND HIS WORDS MEASURED.
...
SAKER WROTE POEMS IN HIS FREE TIME.
SOME WERE ANGRY AND JEALOUS, BUT ALL WERE ABOUT LOVE.
THESE ARE INTENSE.
THEY WERE DIRECTED TOWARDS HIS GIRLFRIEND: A BUSTY, ASPIRING DOCTOR HE MET IN TURKEY.
SHE SEEMS NICE.

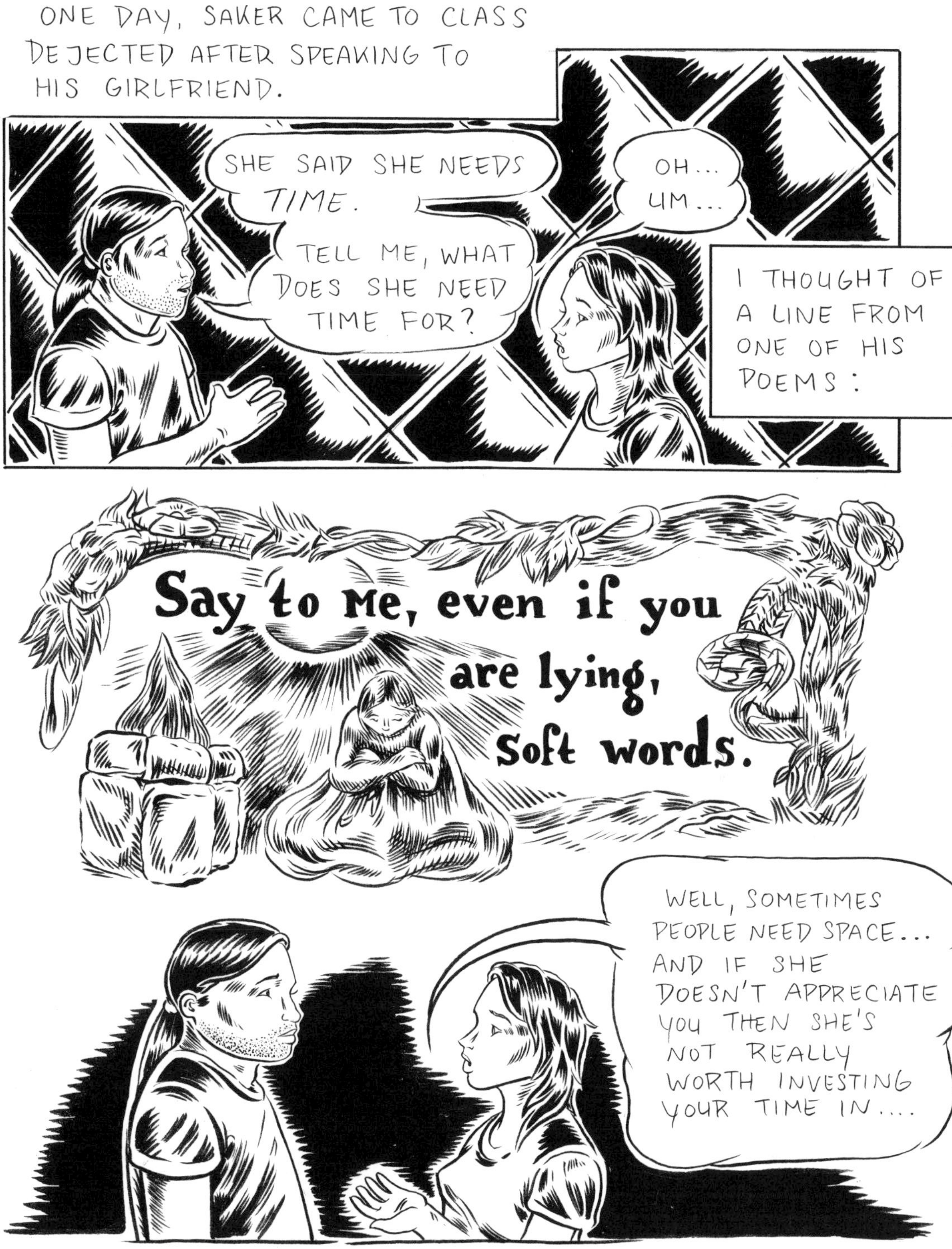
ONE DAY, SAKER CAME TO CLASS DEJECTED AFTER SPEAKING TO HIS GIRLFRIEND.
SHE SAID SHE NEEDS TIME.
TELL ME, WHAT DOES SHE NEED TIME FOR?
OH... UM...
I THOUGHT OF A LINE FROM ONE OF HIS POEMS:
Say to me, even if you are lying, soft words.
WELL, SOMETIMES PEOPLE NEED SPACE... AND IF SHE DOESN'T APPRECIATE YOU THEN SHE'S NOT REALLY WORTH INVESTING YOUR TIME IN....

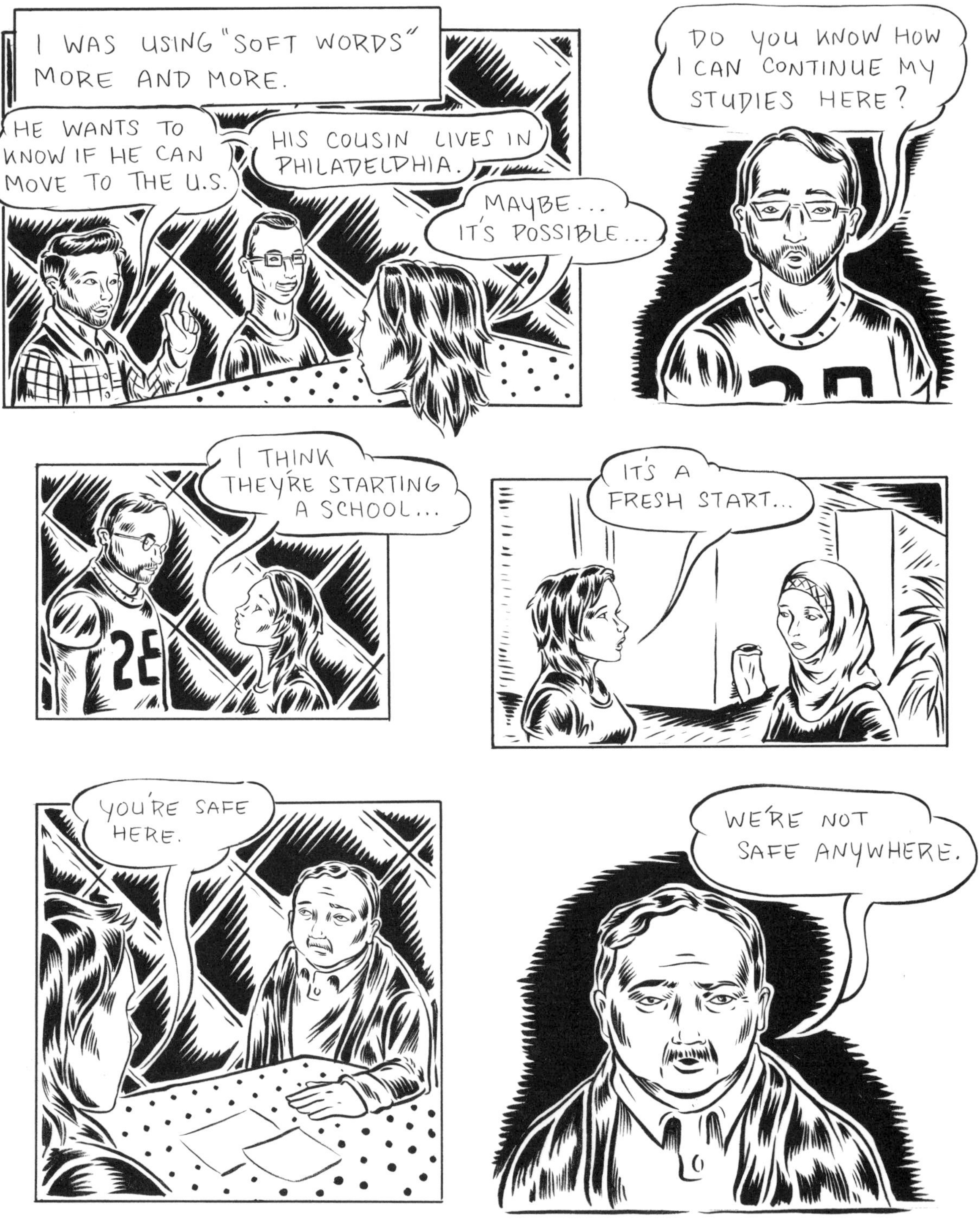
I WAS USING "SOFT WORDS" MORE AND MORE.
HE WANTS TO KNOW IF HE CAN MOVE TO THE U.S.
HIS COUSIN LIVES IN PHILADELPHIA.
MAYBE... IT'S POSSIBLE...
DO YOU KNOW HOW I CAN CONTINUE MY STUDIES HERE?
I THINK THEY'RE STARTING A SCHOOL...
IT'S A FRESH START...
YOU'RE SAFE HERE.
WE'RE NOT SAFE ANYWHERE.

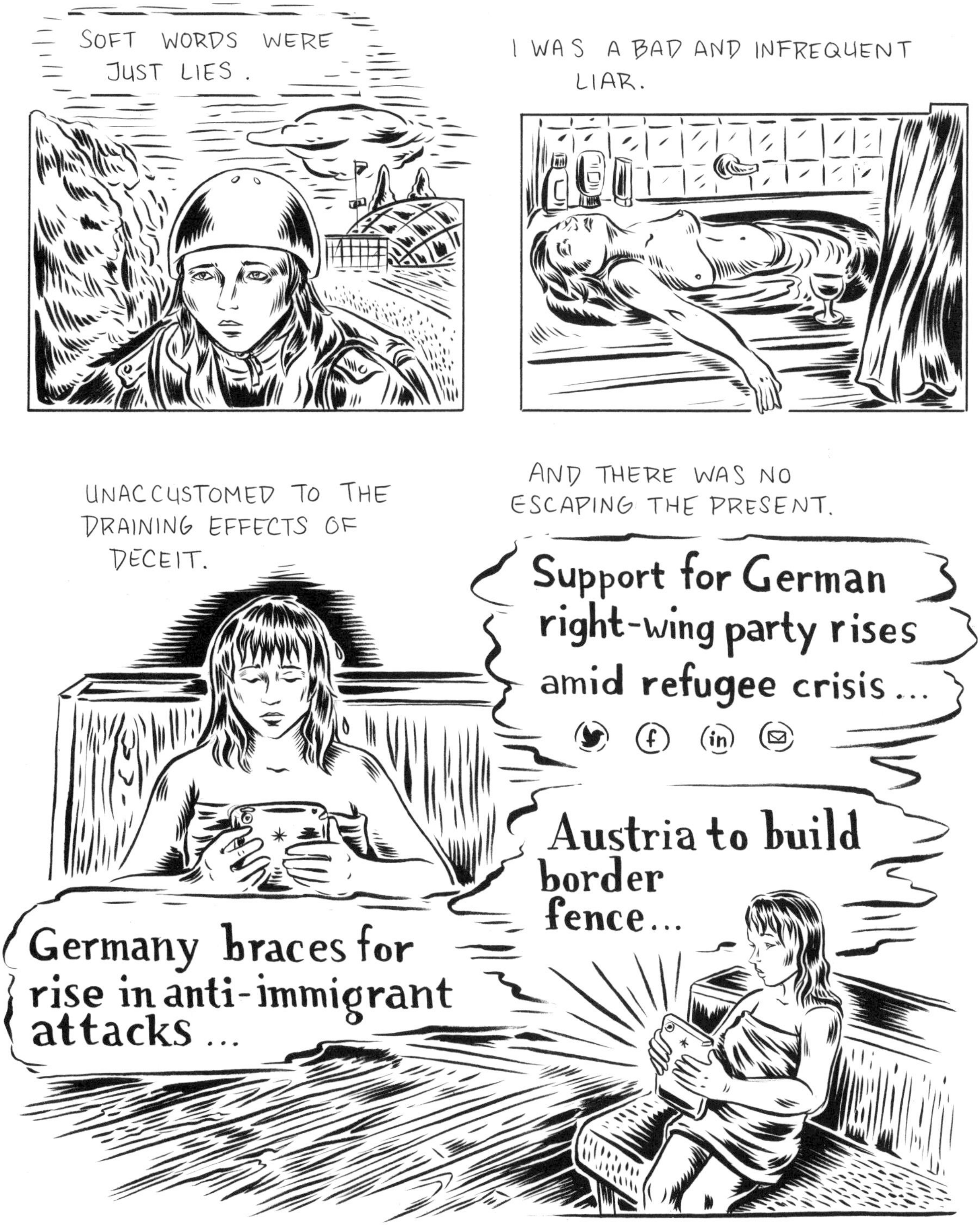
SOFT WORDS WERE JUST LIES.
I WAS A BAD AND INFREQUENT LIAR.
UNACCUSTOMED TO THE DRAINING EFFECTS OF DECEIT.
AND THERE WAS NO ESCAPING THE PRESENT.
Support for German right-wing party rises amid refugee crisis...
Austria to build border fence...
Germany braces for rise in anti-immigrant attacks...

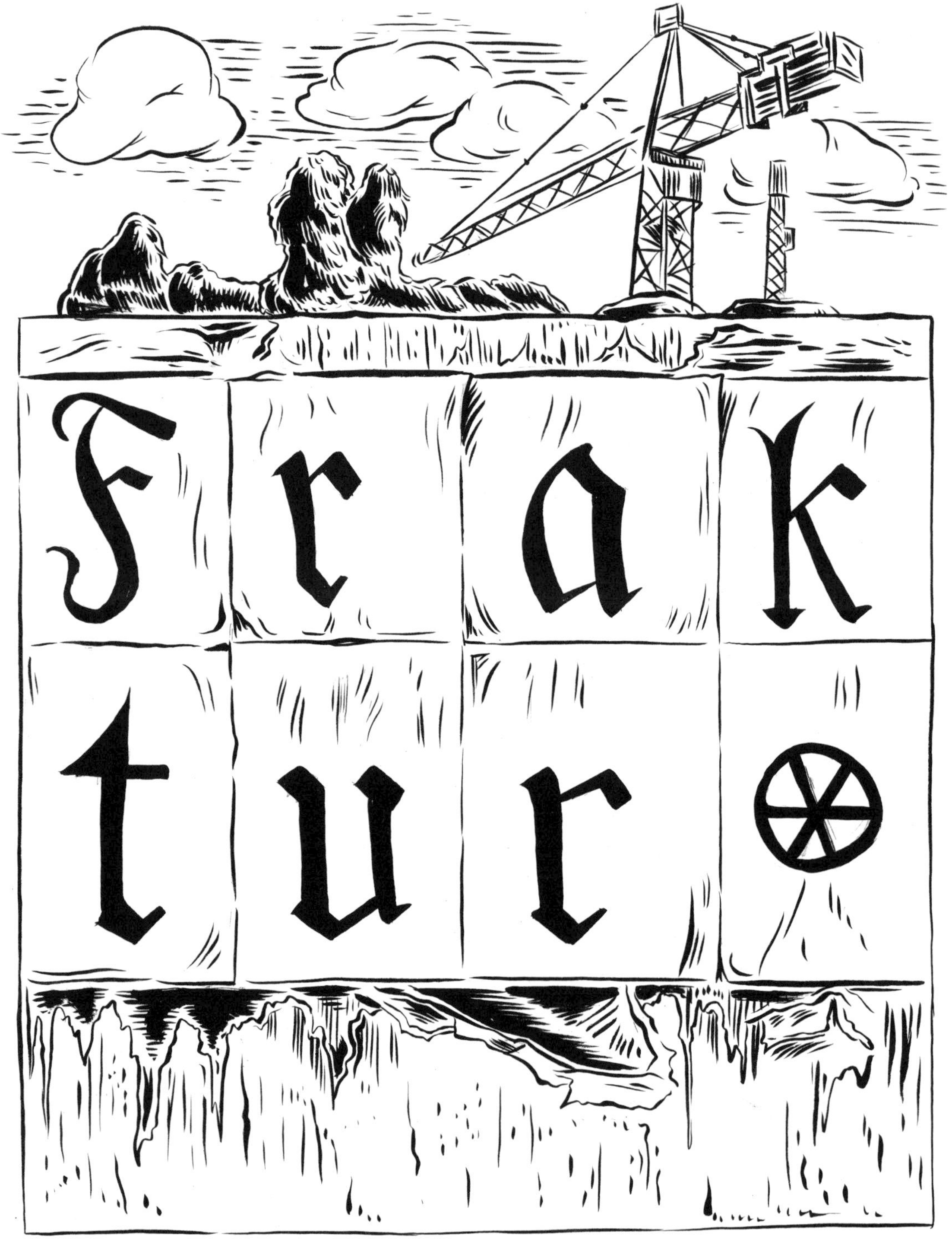
Frak
tur

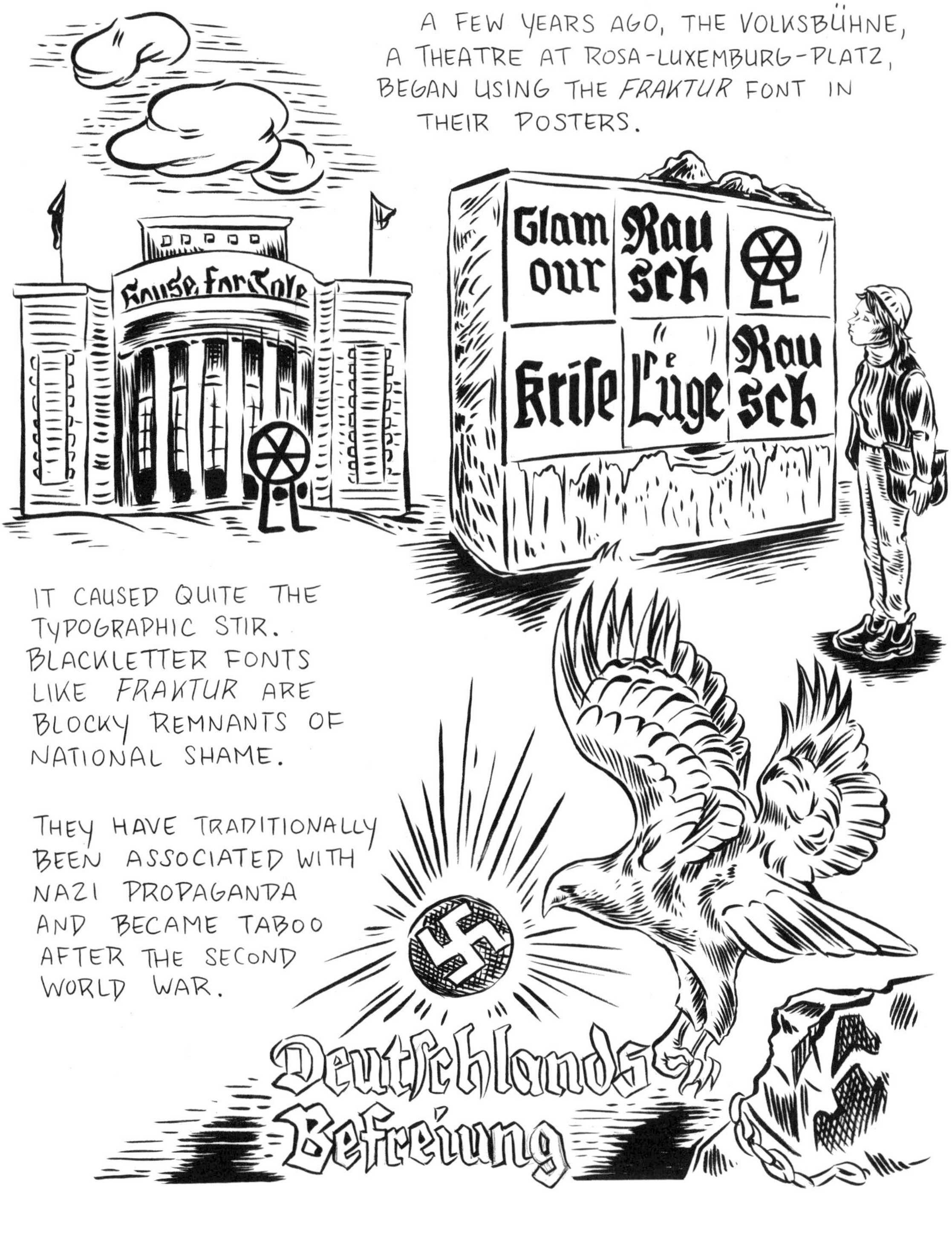
A FEW YEARS AGO, THE VOLKSBÜHNE, A THEATRE AT ROSA-LUXEMBURG-PLATZ, BEGAN USING THE *FRAKTUR* FONT IN THEIR POSTERS.
Glam our
Rau sch
Krise
Lüge
Rau sch
IT CAUSED QUITE THE TYPOGRAPHIC STIR. BLACKLETTER FONTS LIKE *FRAKTUR* ARE BLOCKY REMNANTS OF NATIONAL SHAME.
THEY HAVE TRADITIONALLY BEEN ASSOCIATED WITH NAZI PROPAGANDA AND BECAME TABOO AFTER THE SECOND WORLD WAR.
Deutschlands Befreiung

THE ULTRA-GERMANIC TYPEFACE FIRST APPEARED ALONGSIDE ALBRECHT DÜRER'S DRAWINGS IN THE 1500S.

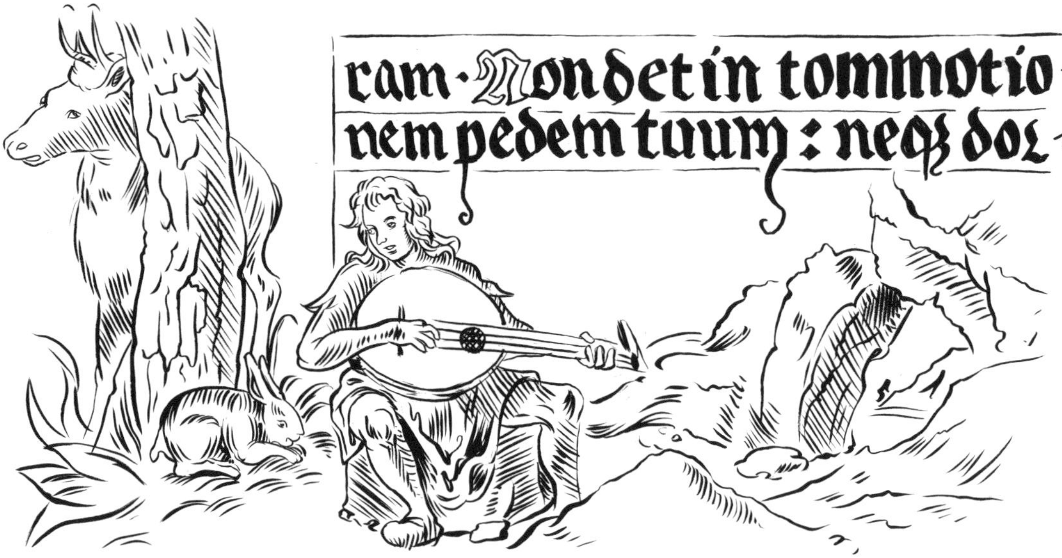
ram · Non det in tommotio
nem pedem tuum : neqz dol

FRAKTUR DECLINED IN THE EARLY 20TH CENTURY, THEN WAS RESURRECTED BY THE NATIONAL SOCIALISTS. ITS GOTHIC SOBRIETY WAS PERFECT TO ACCOMPANY HITLER'S ARYAN SUPERMEN.

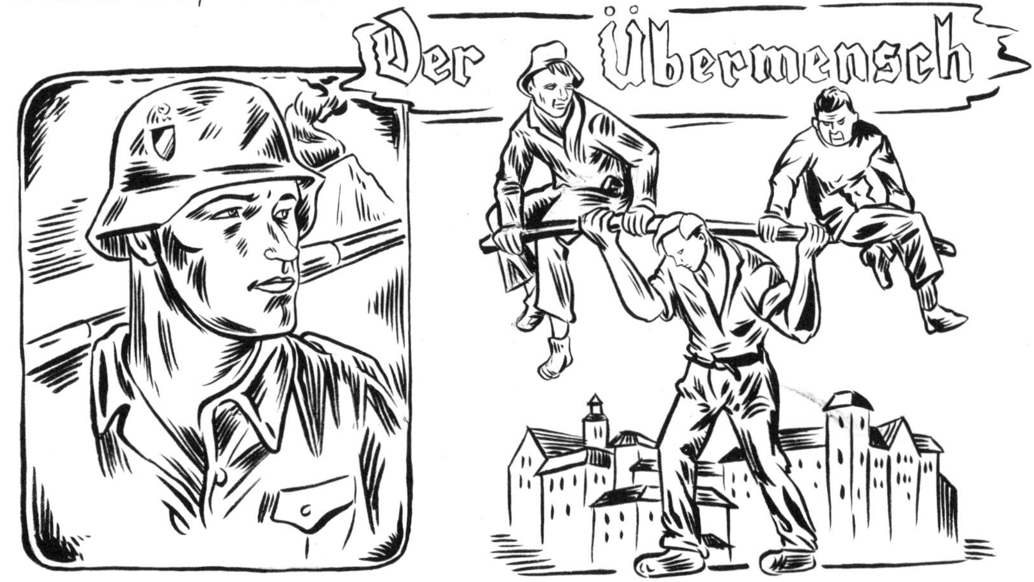
Der Übermensch

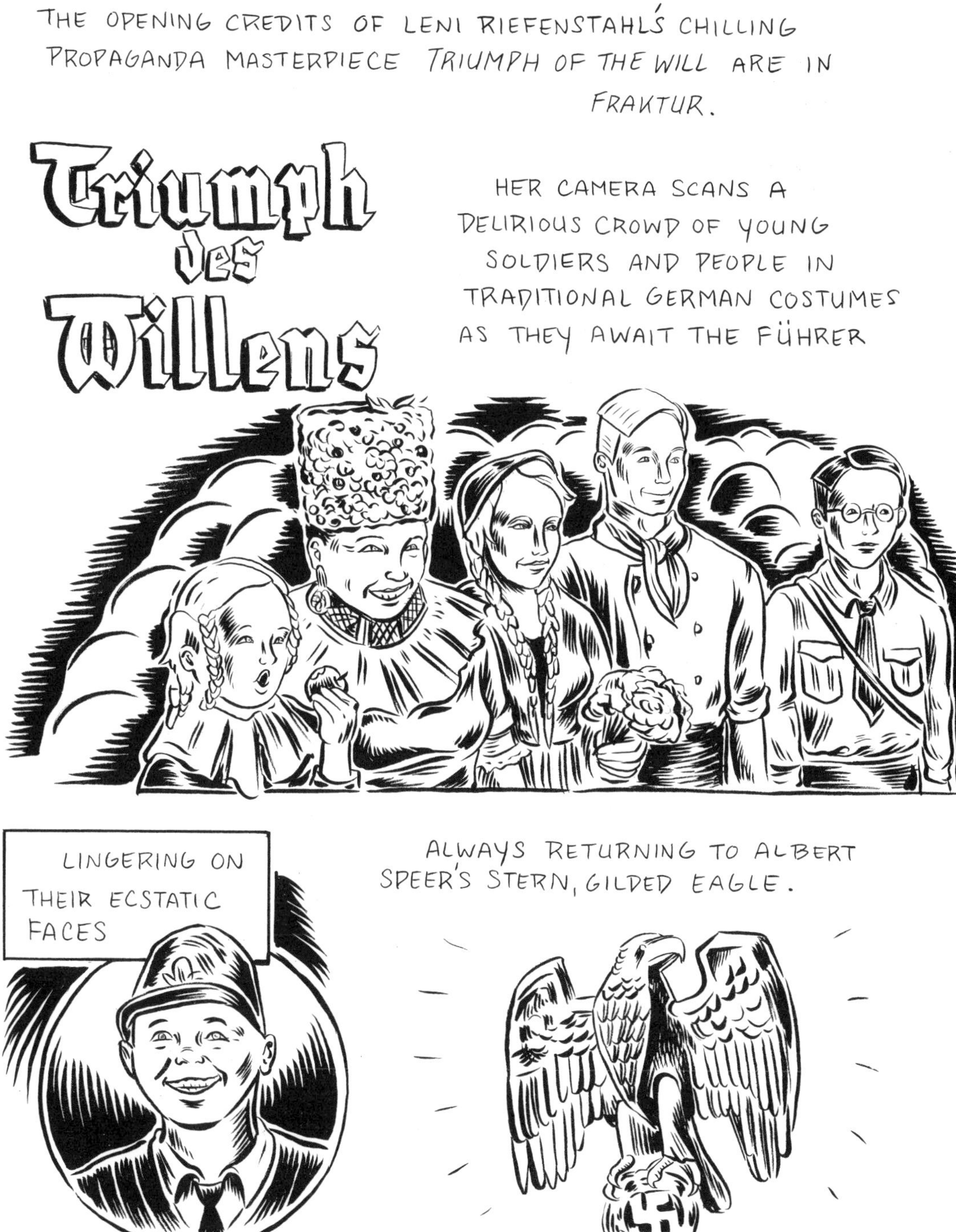
THE OPENING CREDITS OF LENI RIEFENSTAHL'S CHILLING PROPAGANDA MASTERPIECE *TRIUMPH OF THE WILL* ARE IN FRAKTUR.
Triumph des Willens
HER CAMERA SCANS A DELIRIOUS CROWD OF YOUNG SOLDIERS AND PEOPLE IN TRADITIONAL GERMAN COSTUMES AS THEY AWAIT THE FÜHRER
LINGERING ON THEIR ECSTATIC FACES
ALWAYS RETURNING TO ALBERT SPEER'S STERN, GILDED EAGLE.

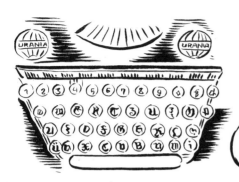

IN 1933, A NAZI MINISTER FORCIBLY INSTALLED *FRAKTUR*-READY TYPEWRITERS IN GOVERNMENT OFFICES.

HOWEVER, HITLER CHANGED COURSE IN 1940, DERIDING *FRAKTUR*'S "ROMANTICISM."

URANIA
URANIA

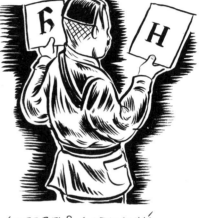

AT THAT TIME, GERMANY CONTROLLED MUCH OF EUROPE. HITLER CLAIMED THAT THE COMPARATIVE SIMPLICITY OF THE *ANTIQUA* FONT WOULD HELP GERMAN BECOME THE WORLD'S LANGUAGE.

SO IN 1941, *DAS REICH*, THE NAZI'S PROPAGANDA NEWSPAPER, BEGAN PRINTING IN *ANTIQUA*.

JOSEPH GOEBBELS, GERMANY'S PROPAGANDA MINISTER, LISTED THE ADVANTAGES OF *ANTIQUA* IN HIS DIARY:

DAS REICH

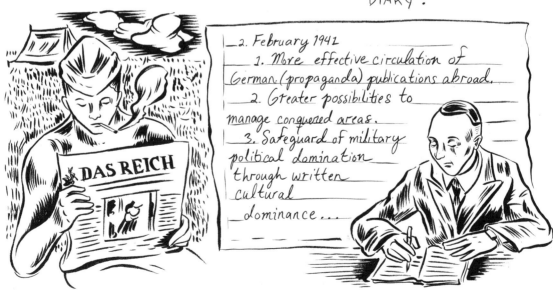

2. February 1941
1. More effective circulation of German (propaganda) publications abroad.
2. Greater possibilities to manage conquered areas.
3. Safeguard of military political domination through written cultural dominance...

AS VICTORY RECEDED, NAZI POSTERS SCREECHED DESPERATE WARNINGS IN BOLD AND SLANTED SAN SERIFS.

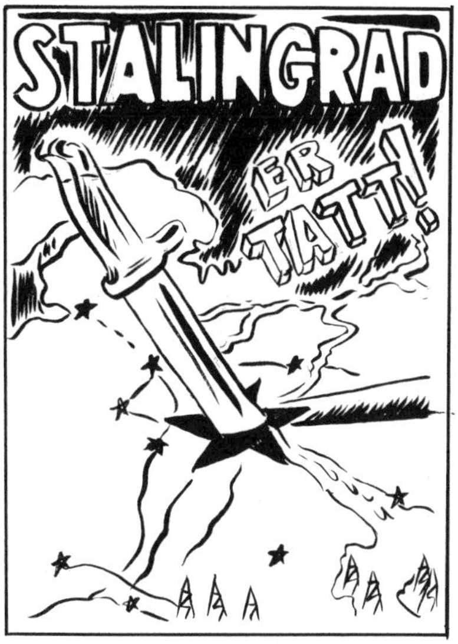
STALINGRAD
ER TATT!

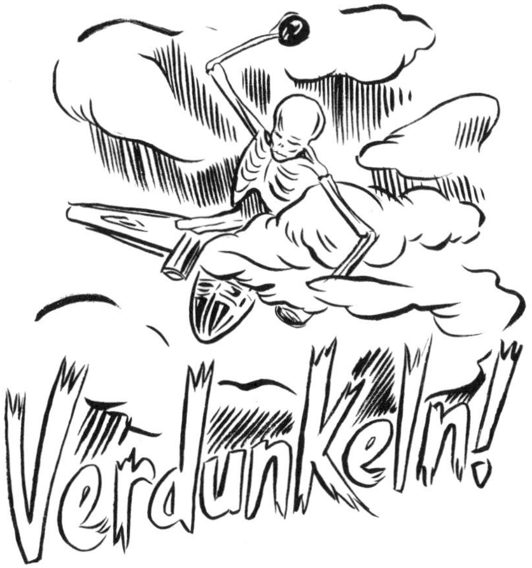
Verdunkeln!

AFTER THE WAR, BERLIN WAS SURROUNDED BY THE SPARE MODERNITY OF NEW, TALL TYPEFACES.

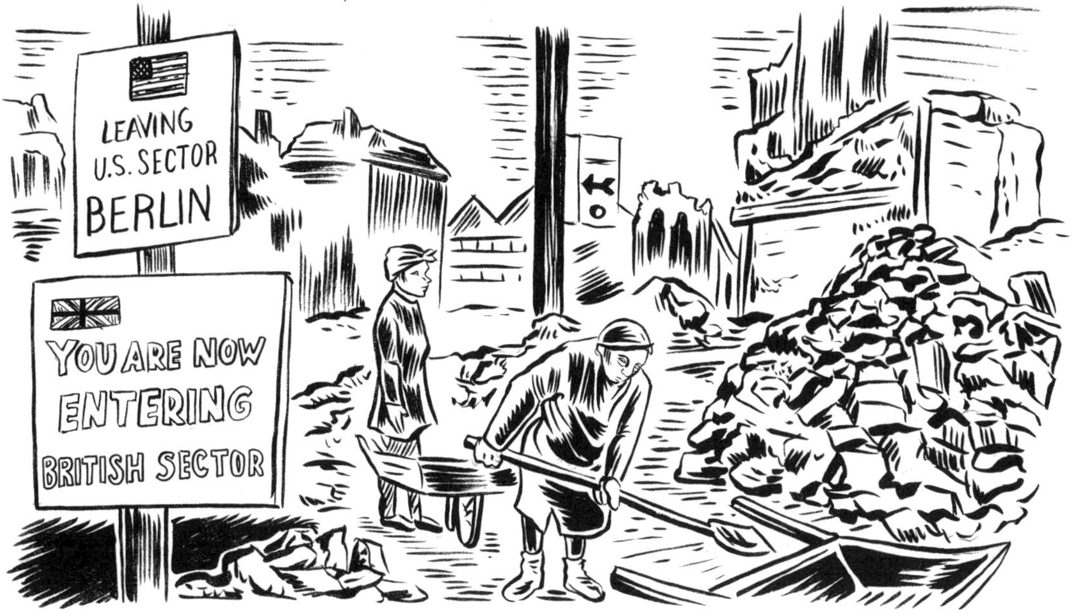
LEAVING
U.S. SECTOR
BERLIN
YOU ARE NOW
ENTERING
BRITISH SECTOR

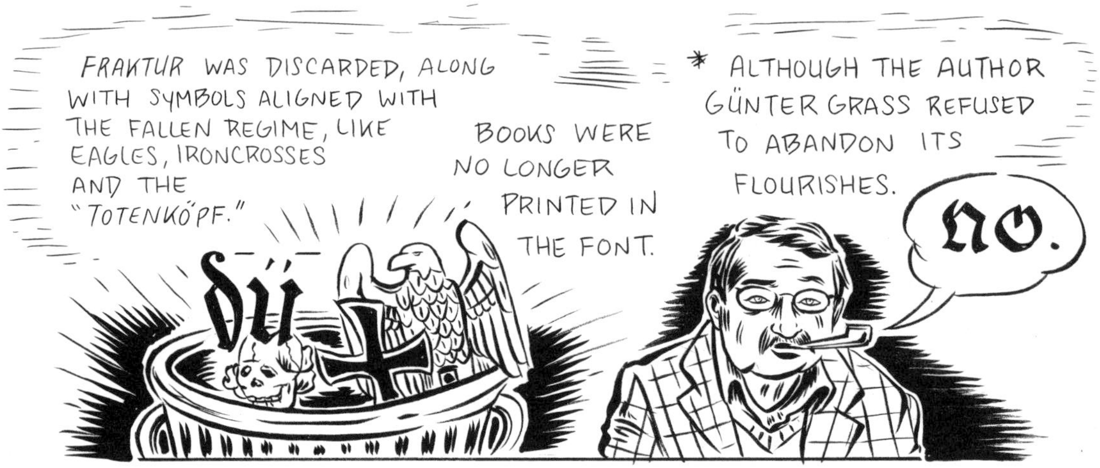
FRAKTUR WAS DISCARDED, ALONG WITH SYMBOLS ALIGNED WITH THE FALLEN REGIME, LIKE EAGLES, IRONCROSSES AND THE "TOTENKÖPF."
BOOKS WERE NO LONGER PRINTED IN THE FONT.
* ALTHOUGH THE AUTHOR GÜNTER GRASS REFUSED TO ABANDON ITS FLOURISHES.
NO.

FRAKTUR HAD ITS GOTHIC ROOTS IN GERMAN IDENTITY— AN IDENTITY MOST PEOPLE WANTED TO FORGET IN THE 20TH CENTURY.

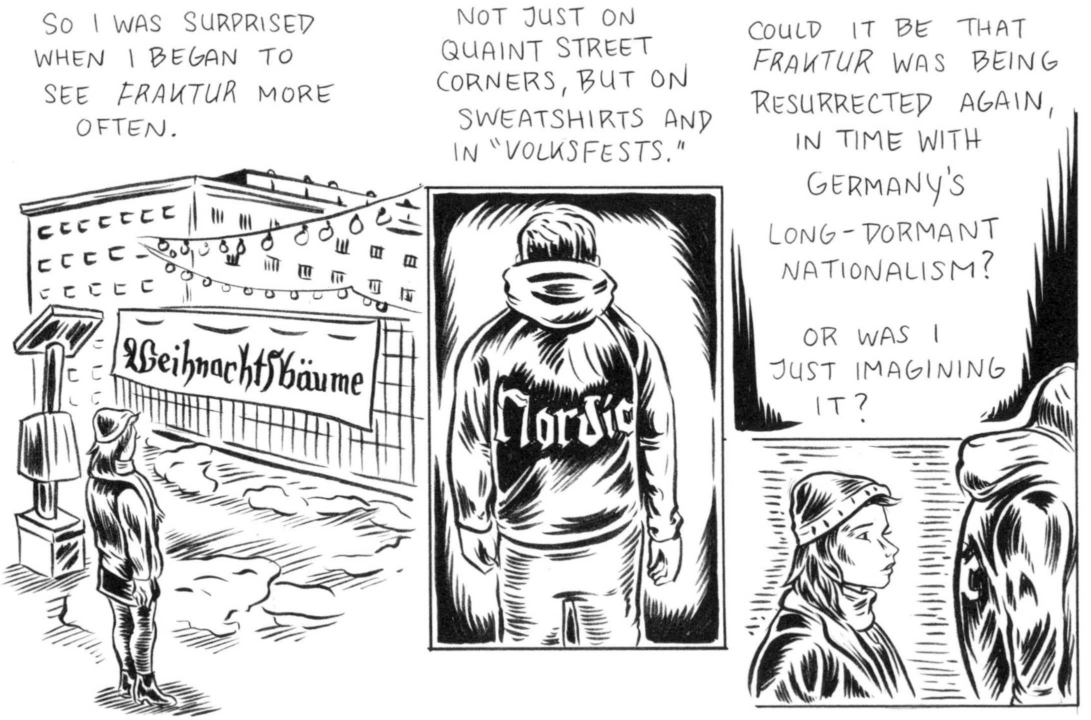
SO I WAS SURPRISED WHEN I BEGAN TO SEE FRAKTUR MORE OFTEN.
Weihnachtsbäume
NOT JUST ON QUAINT STREET CORNERS, BUT ON SWEATSHIRTS AND IN "VOLKSFESTS."
Nordic
COULD IT BE THAT FRAKTUR WAS BEING RESURRECTED AGAIN, IN TIME WITH GERMANY'S LONG-DORMANT NATIONALISM?
OR WAS I JUST IMAGINING IT?

GERMANY'S ASCENDANT RIGHT-WING PARTY, THE AFD, IS CAREFUL TO AVOID CHEEKY, AUSTERE NODS TO THE AESTHETICS OF FASCISM – THEY RARELY EMPLOY *FRAKTUR*.

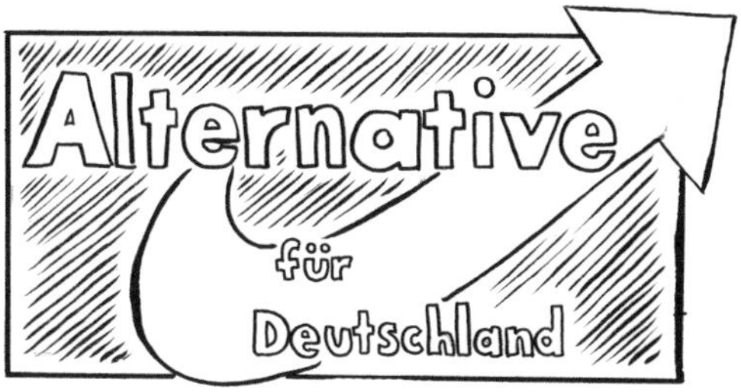
Alternative
für
Deutschland

THEIR LOGO RECALLS NOTHING OF THE PAST. INSTEAD, IT USES *BOLD FUTURA*.

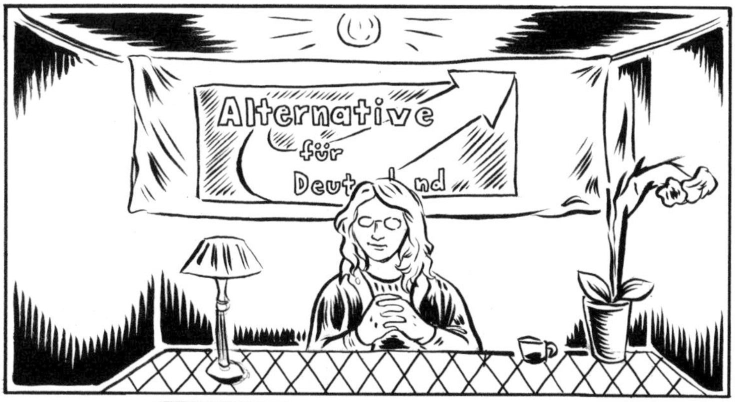
Alternative
für

IT READS AS UPLIFTING AND LIGHT – SOMETHING YOU MIGHT SEE IN THE OFFICE OF A CALIFORNIA LIFECOACH.

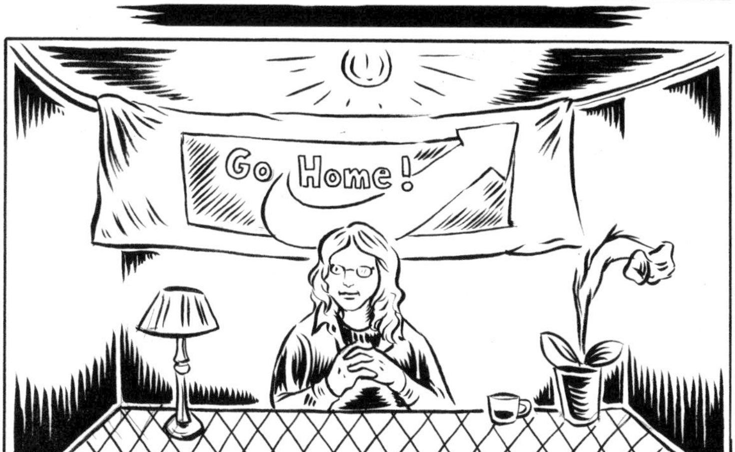
Go Home!

BUT ITS SKY BLUES OBSCURE A DARK, FRENZIED ANTI-IMMIGRANT STANCE.

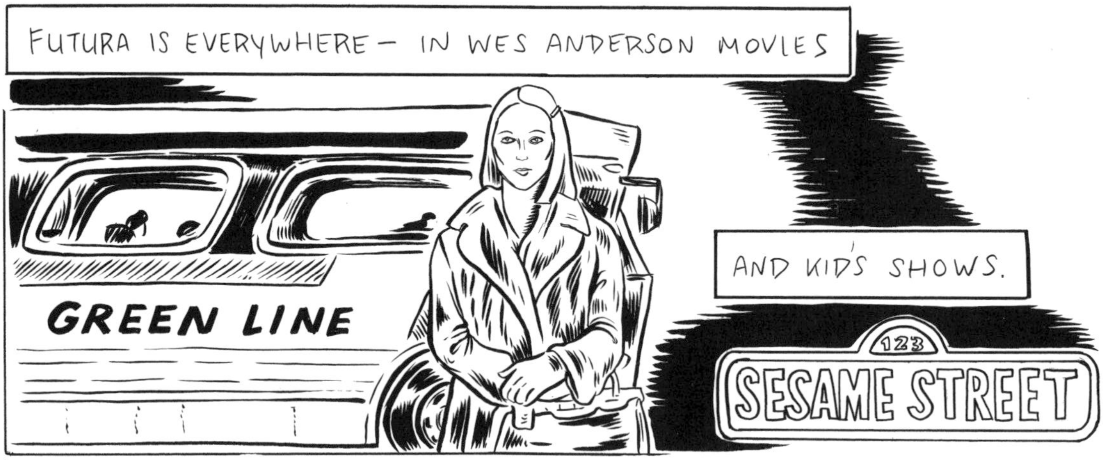
FUTURA IS EVERYWHERE – IN WES ANDERSON MOVIES
GREEN LINE
AND KID'S SHOWS.
123
SESAME STREET

IT WAS DESIGNED BY PAUL RENNER IN GERMANY IN 1927. IN KEEPING WITH BAUHAUS IDEALS, *FUTURA* WAS MEANT TO BE A FORWARD-LOOKING TYPEFACE – THE *ANTI-FRAKTUR* IF YOU WILL.

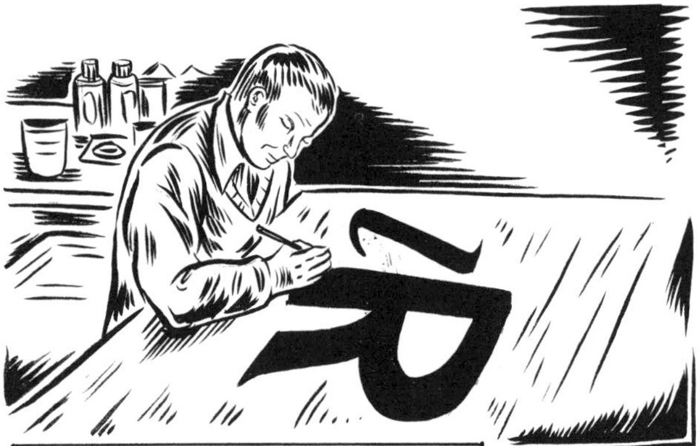

RENNER, A VOCAL CRITIC OF THE NAZIS, WAS ARRESTED AND REMOVED FROM HIS TEACHING POST IN MUNICH IN 1933.

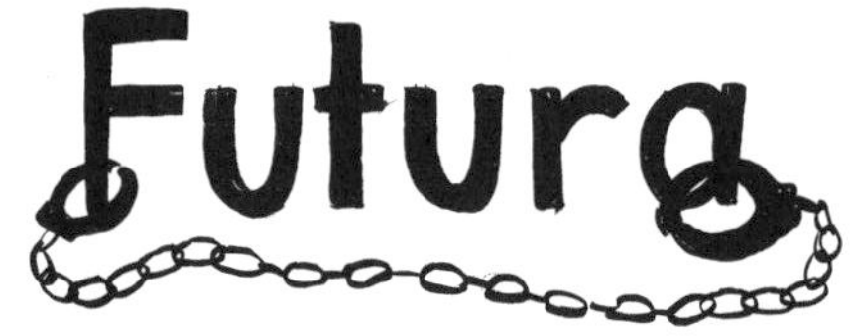
Futura

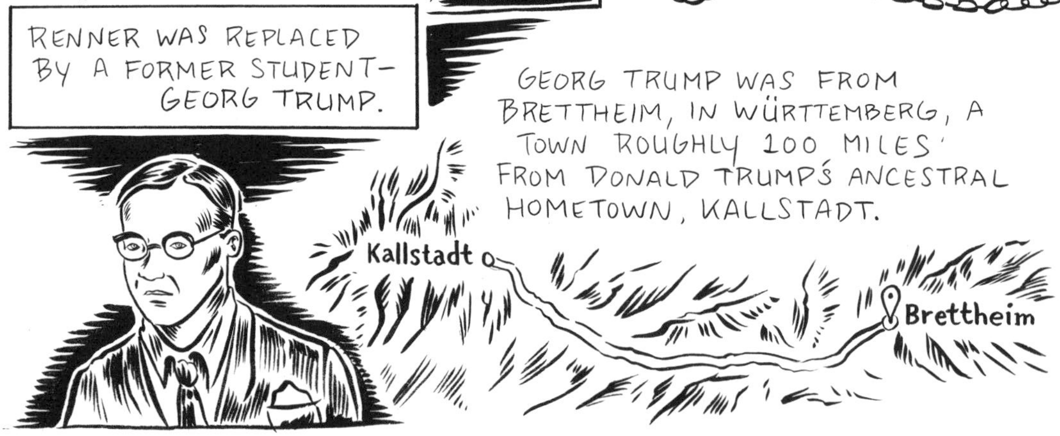
RENNER WAS REPLACED BY A FORMER STUDENT – GEORG TRUMP.
Kallstadt
Brettheim

GEORG TRUMP WAS FROM BRETTHEIM, IN WÜRTTEMBERG, A TOWN ROUGHLY 100 MILES FROM DONALD TRUMP'S ANCESTRAL HOMETOWN, KALLSTADT.

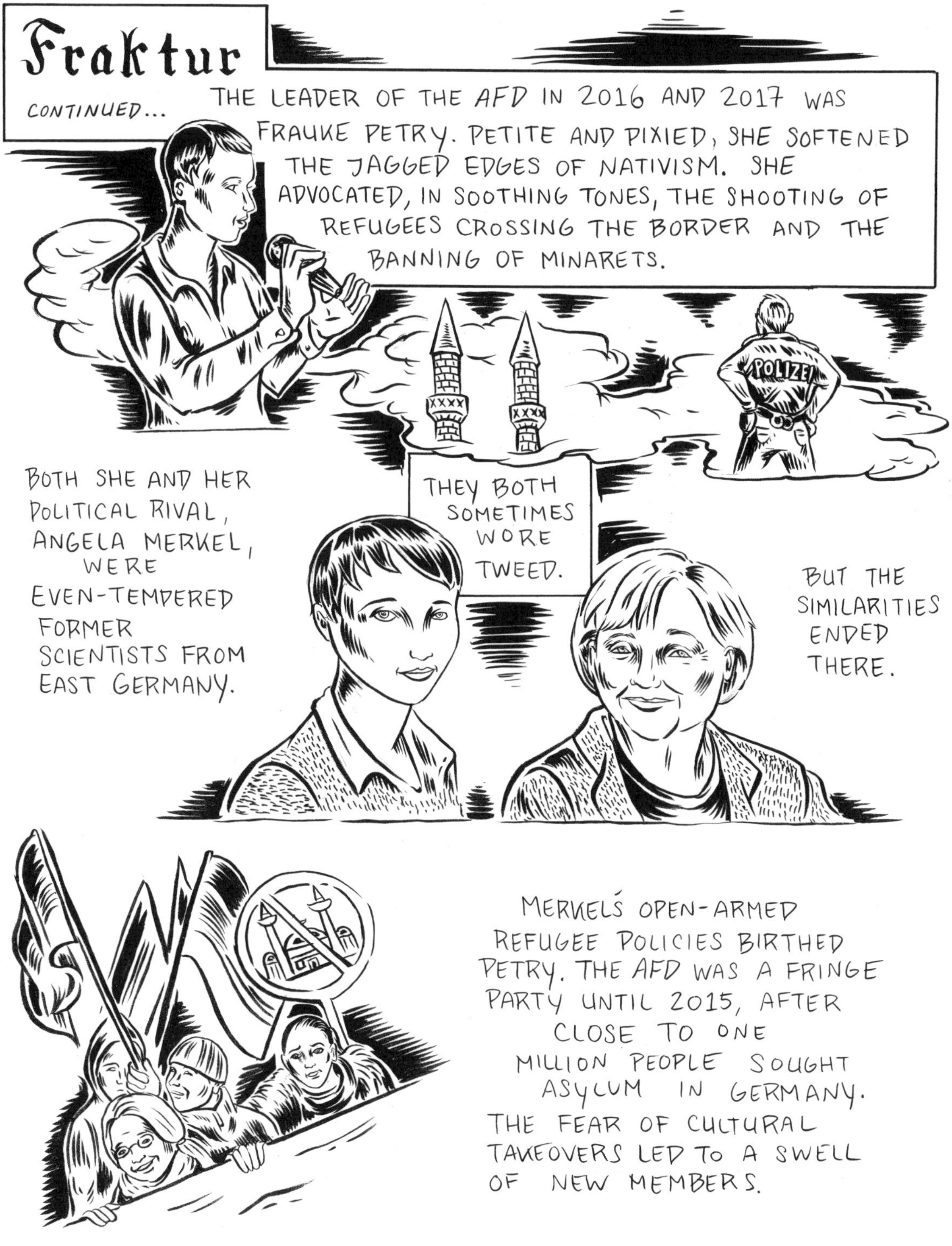
Fraktur
CONTINUED...
THE LEADER OF THE AFD IN 2016 AND 2017 WAS FRAUKE PETRY. PETITE AND PIXIED, SHE SOFTENED THE JAGGED EDGES OF NATIVISM. SHE ADVOCATED, IN SOOTHING TONES, THE SHOOTING OF REFUGEES CROSSING THE BORDER AND THE BANNING OF MINARETS.
POLIZEI
BOTH SHE AND HER POLITICAL RIVAL, ANGELA MERKEL, WERE EVEN-TEMPERED FORMER SCIENTISTS FROM EAST GERMANY.
THEY BOTH SOMETIMES WORE TWEED.
BUT THE SIMILARITIES ENDED THERE.
MERKEL'S OPEN-ARMED REFUGEE POLICIES BIRTHED PETRY. THE AFD WAS A FRINGE PARTY UNTIL 2015, AFTER CLOSE TO ONE MILLION PEOPLE SOUGHT ASYLUM IN GERMANY. THE FEAR OF CULTURAL TAKEOVERS LED TO A SWELL OF NEW MEMBERS.

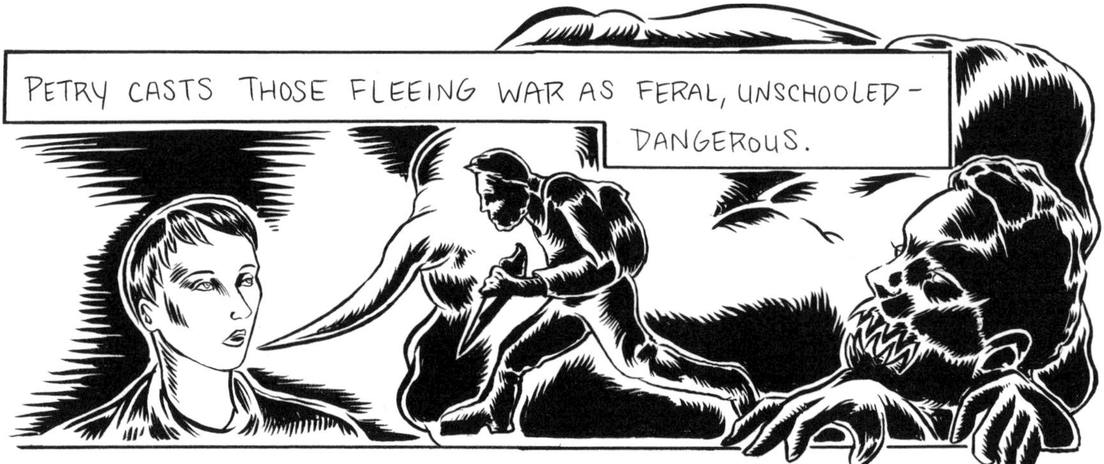
PETRY CASTS THOSE FLEEING WAR AS FERAL, UNSCHOOLED - DANGEROUS.

HER DEMONIC OUTLINES ARE JUST UNDEFINED ENOUGH FOR US TO CONNECT THE DOTS AND MAKE A MONSTER.

IN BADEN WÜRTTEMBERG, THE AFD PUBLISHED A PROPAGANDA NEWSPAPER. IN IT, SYRIAN MEN WERE CARICATURED.

CARICATURES CONTAIN TERRIFYING POTENCY.

IN THE SERVICE OF HATE, THEY STRIP AWAY HUMANITY, FLATTENING PEOPLE WITH SLIGHTLY ALTERED HATS AND NOSES.

THIS VENOM IS USED AGAIN AND AGAIN - BECAUSE IT WORKS.

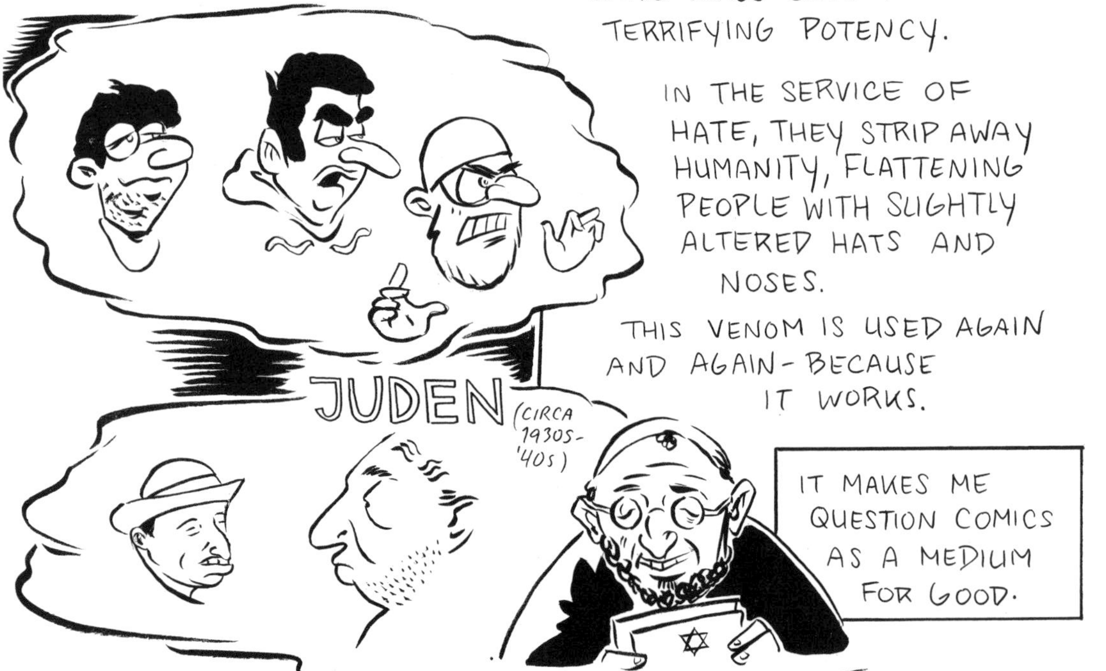
JUDEN
(CIRCA 1930S-'40S)
IT MAKES ME QUESTION COMICS AS A MEDIUM FOR GOOD.

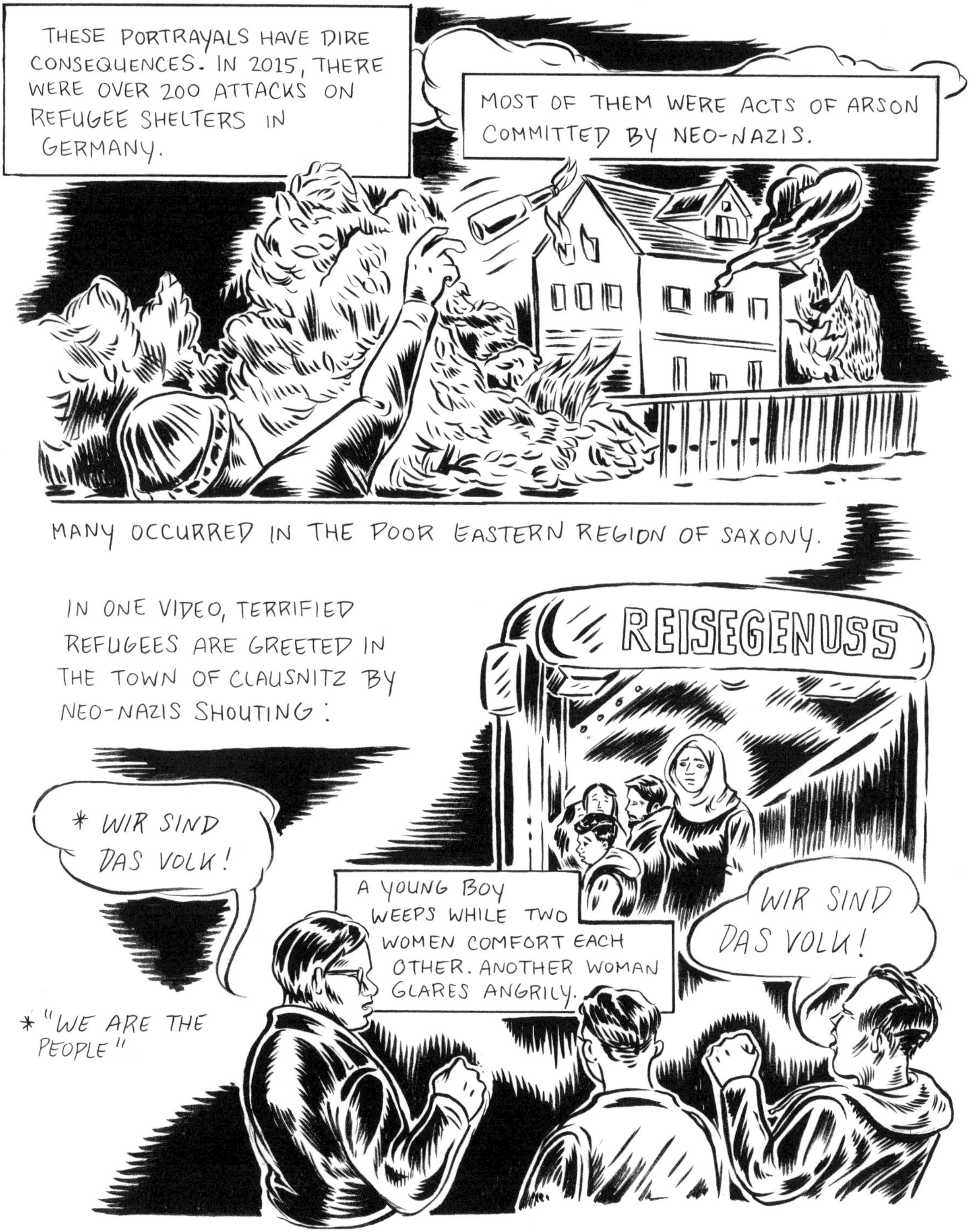
THESE PORTRAYALS HAVE DIRE CONSEQUENCES. IN 2015, THERE WERE OVER 200 ATTACKS ON REFUGEE SHELTERS IN GERMANY.
MOST OF THEM WERE ACTS OF ARSON COMMITTED BY NEO-NAZIS.
MANY OCCURRED IN THE POOR EASTERN REGION OF SAXONY.
IN ONE VIDEO, TERRIFIED REFUGEES ARE GREETED IN THE TOWN OF CLAUSNITZ BY NEO-NAZIS SHOUTING:
REISEGENUSS
* WIR SIND DAS VOLK!
A YOUNG BOY WEEPS WHILE TWO WOMEN COMFORT EACH OTHER. ANOTHER WOMAN GLARES ANGRILY.
WIR SIND DAS VOLK!
* "WE ARE THE PEOPLE"

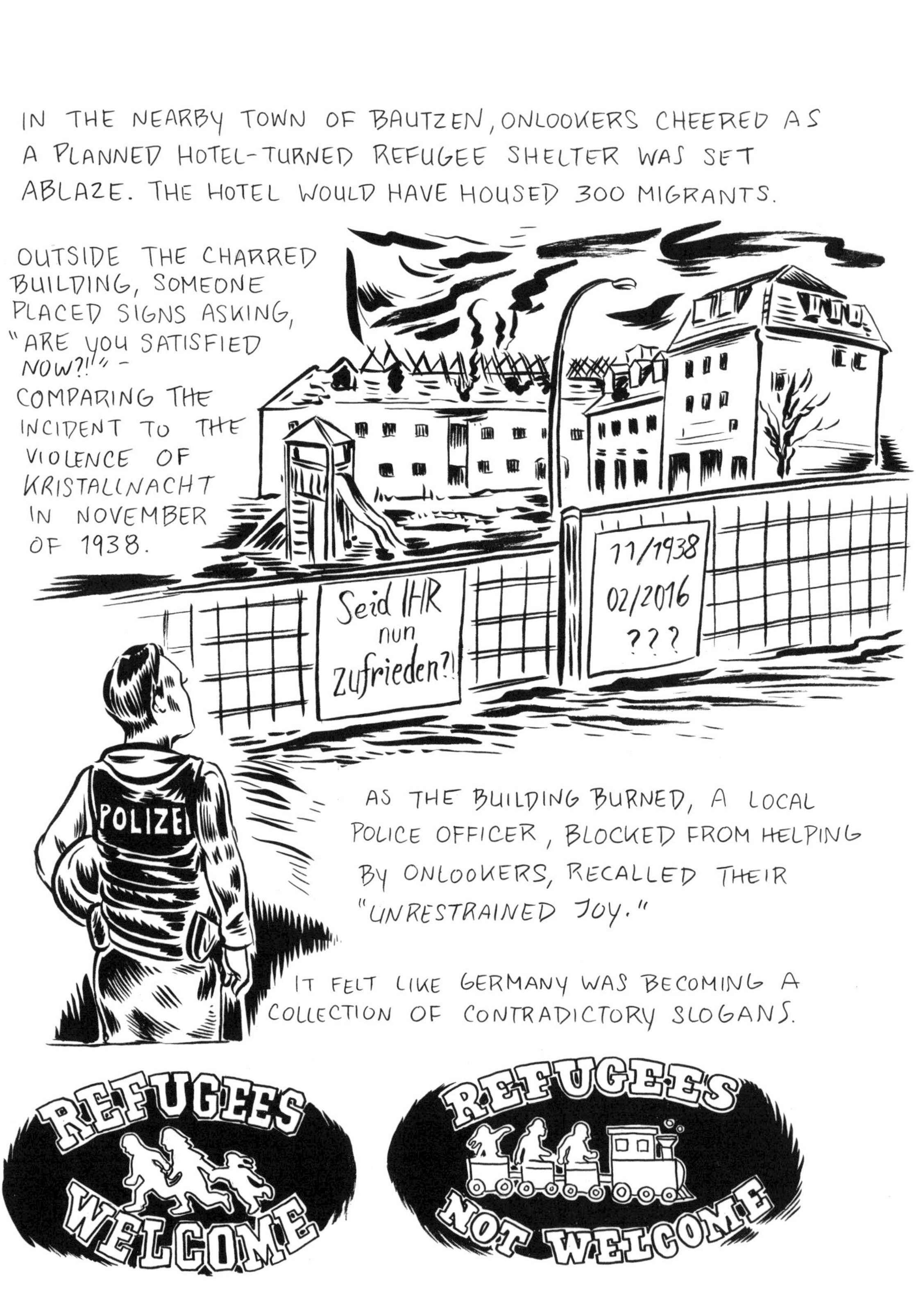
IN THE NEARBY TOWN OF BAUTZEN, ONLOOKERS CHEERED AS A PLANNED HOTEL-TURNED REFUGEE SHELTER WAS SET ABLAZE. THE HOTEL WOULD HAVE HOUSED 300 MIGRANTS.
OUTSIDE THE CHARRED BUILDING, SOMEONE PLACED SIGNS ASKING, "ARE YOU SATISFIED NOW?!" – COMPARING THE INCIDENT TO THE VIOLENCE OF KRISTALLNACHT IN NOVEMBER OF 1938.
Seid IHR nun zufrieden?!
11/1938 02/2016 ???
POLIZEI
AS THE BUILDING BURNED, A LOCAL POLICE OFFICER, BLOCKED FROM HELPING BY ONLOOKERS, RECALLED THEIR "UNRESTRAINED JOY."
IT FELT LIKE GERMANY WAS BECOMING A COLLECTION OF CONTRADICTORY SLOGANS.
REFUGEES WELCOME
REFUGEES NOT WELCOME

BERLIN WAS AGAIN A CENTER OF GLOBAL CONFLICT
BETWEEN EAST AND WEST

BETWEEN A
HARDENING TRIBALISM
AND A DELICATE
MULTI-ETHNIC DEMOCRACY.

THIS DIVISION WASN'T SO
APPARENT AT THE SHELTER—
PATRIOTISM FOR GERMANY WAS
EFFUSIVE AND UNMARRED BY
OUTSIDE POLITICS.

AT LEAST IN THE
BEGINNING.

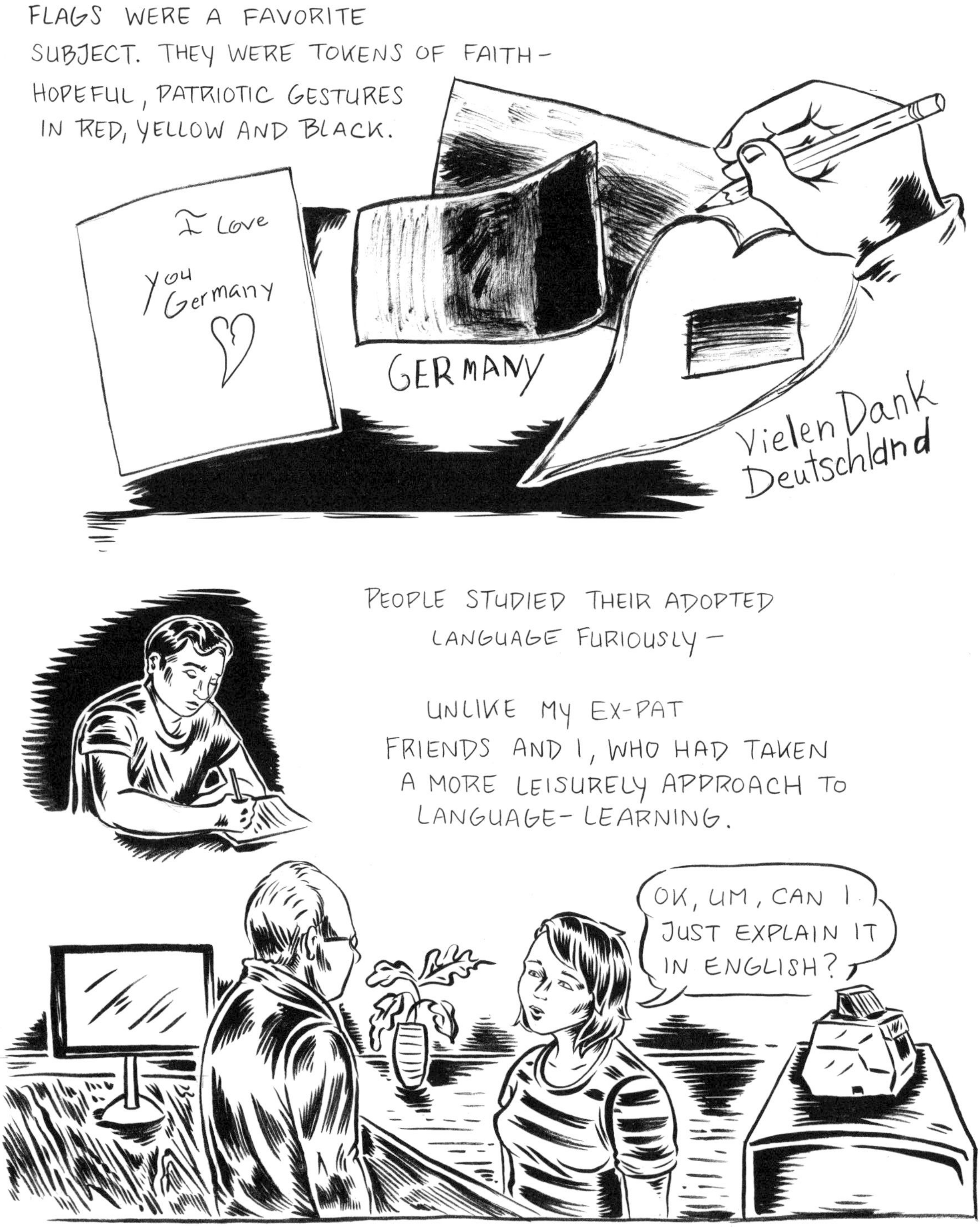
FLAGS WERE A FAVORITE SUBJECT. THEY WERE TOKENS OF FAITH - HOPEFUL, PATRIOTIC GESTURES IN RED, YELLOW AND BLACK.
I Love you Germany
GERMANY
Vielen Dank Deutschland
PEOPLE STUDIED THEIR ADOPTED LANGUAGE FURIOUSLY -
UNLIKE MY EX-PAT FRIENDS AND I, WHO HAD TAKEN A MORE LEISURELY APPROACH TO LANGUAGE-LEARNING.
OK, UM, CAN I JUST EXPLAIN IT IN ENGLISH?

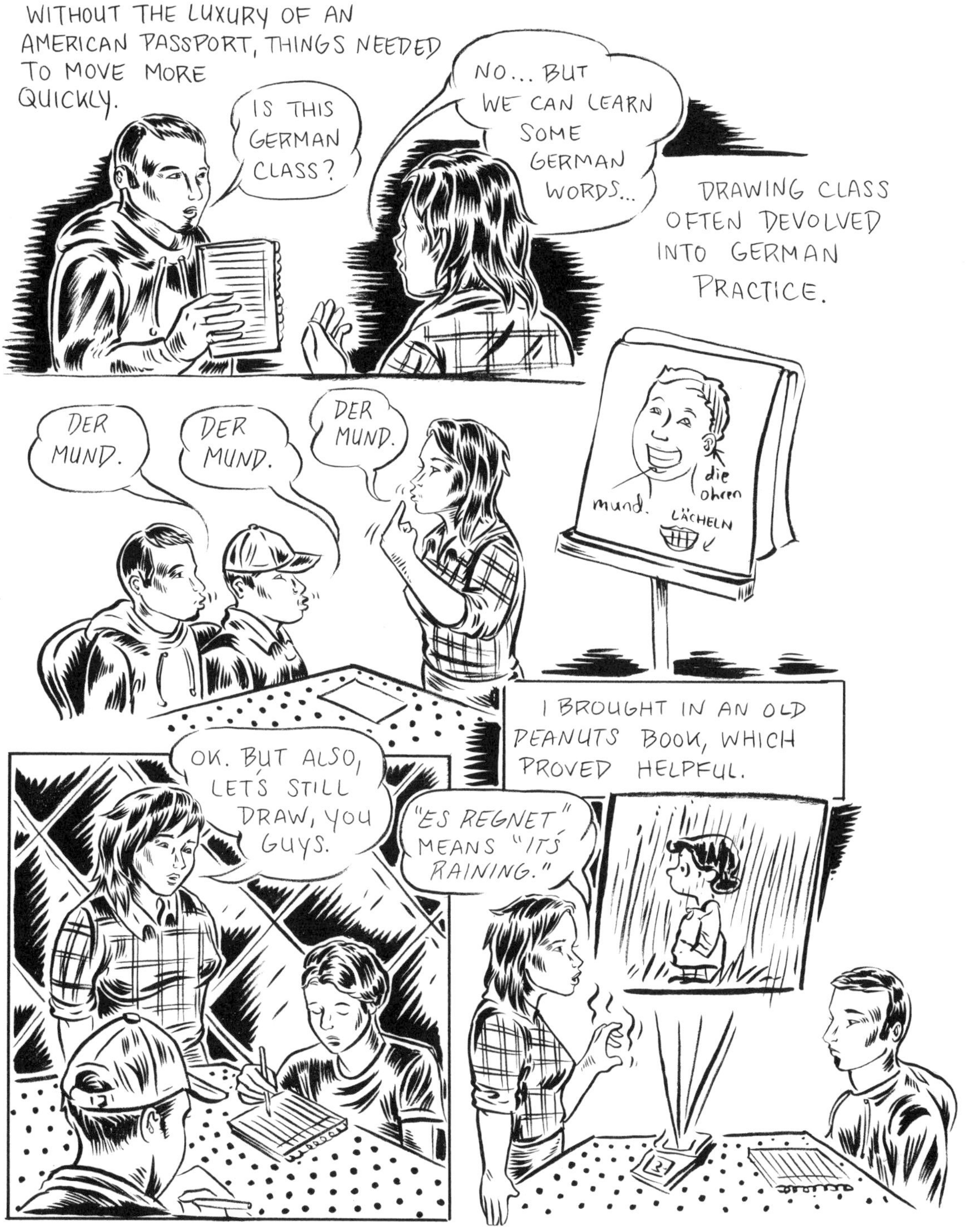
WITHOUT THE LUXURY OF AN AMERICAN PASSPORT, THINGS NEEDED TO MOVE MORE QUICKLY.
IS THIS GERMAN CLASS?
NO... BUT WE CAN LEARN SOME GERMAN WORDS...
DRAWING CLASS OFTEN DEVOLVED INTO GERMAN PRACTICE.
DER MUND.
DER MUND.
DER MUND.
die ohren
mund.
LÄCHELN
I BROUGHT IN AN OLD PEANUTS BOOK, WHICH PROVED HELPFUL.
OK. BUT ALSO, LET'S STILL DRAW, YOU GUYS.
"ES REGNET" MEANS "IT'S RAINING."

I'M SURE THE BUBBLE HAD AN EMERGENCY SPRINKLER SYSTEM, ALTHOUGH I DON'T REMEMBER SEEING IT.

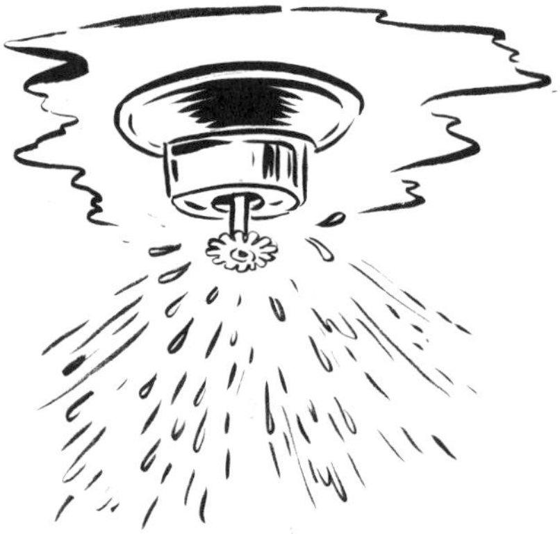

THERE WERE LOTS OF FIRE ESCAPE SIGNS—NORMALLY THE SIDE OPENINGS WERE LOCKED SO THE STRUCTURE WOULDN'T DEFLATE. THE THOUGHT OF A FIRE THERE WAS TERRIFYING.

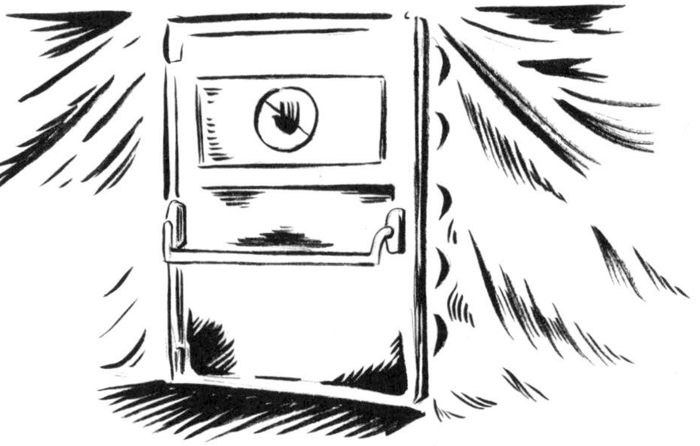

ONE DAY, THE DOOR BLEW OPEN VIOLENTLY. AN ALARM SOUNDED AND WE ALL STARED, TRANSFIXED, IN SILENCE.

WHO, OR WHAT, WAS COMING?

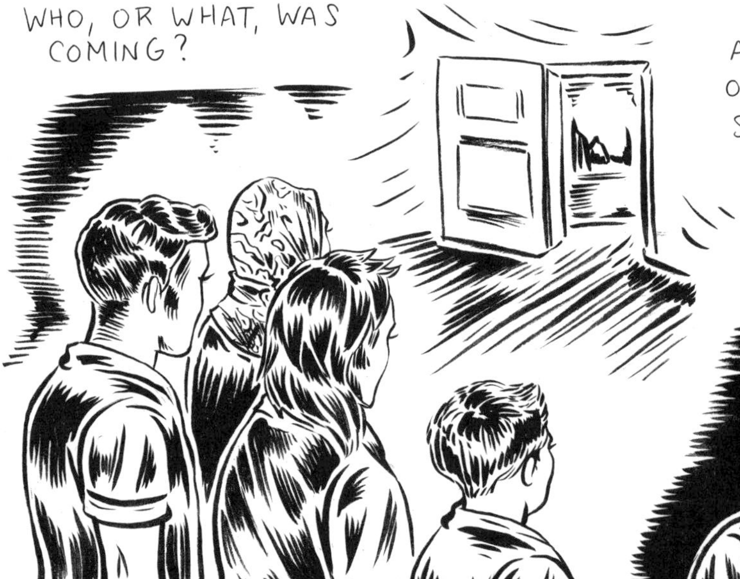

A GUARD RUSHED OVER AND CLOSED IT, SPEAKING QUICKLY,

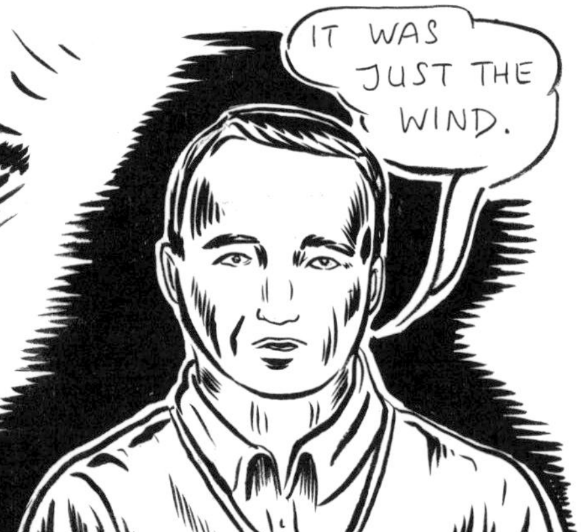
IT WAS JUST THE WIND.

MONSTERS

PART 1

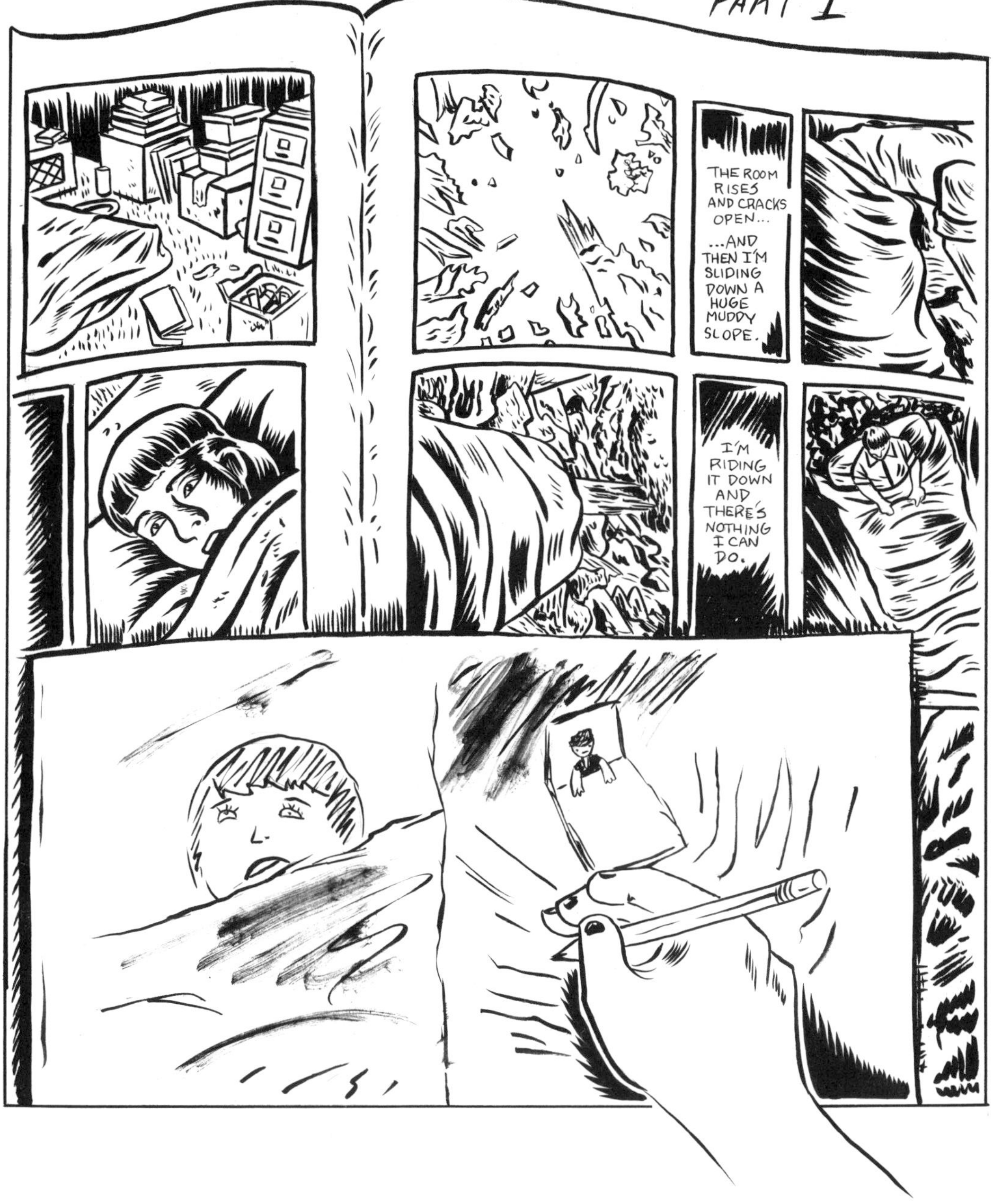
THE ROOM RISES AND CRACKS OPEN...
...AND THEN I'M SLIDING DOWN A HUGE MUDDY SLOPE.
I'M RIDING IT DOWN AND THERE'S NOTHING I CAN DO.

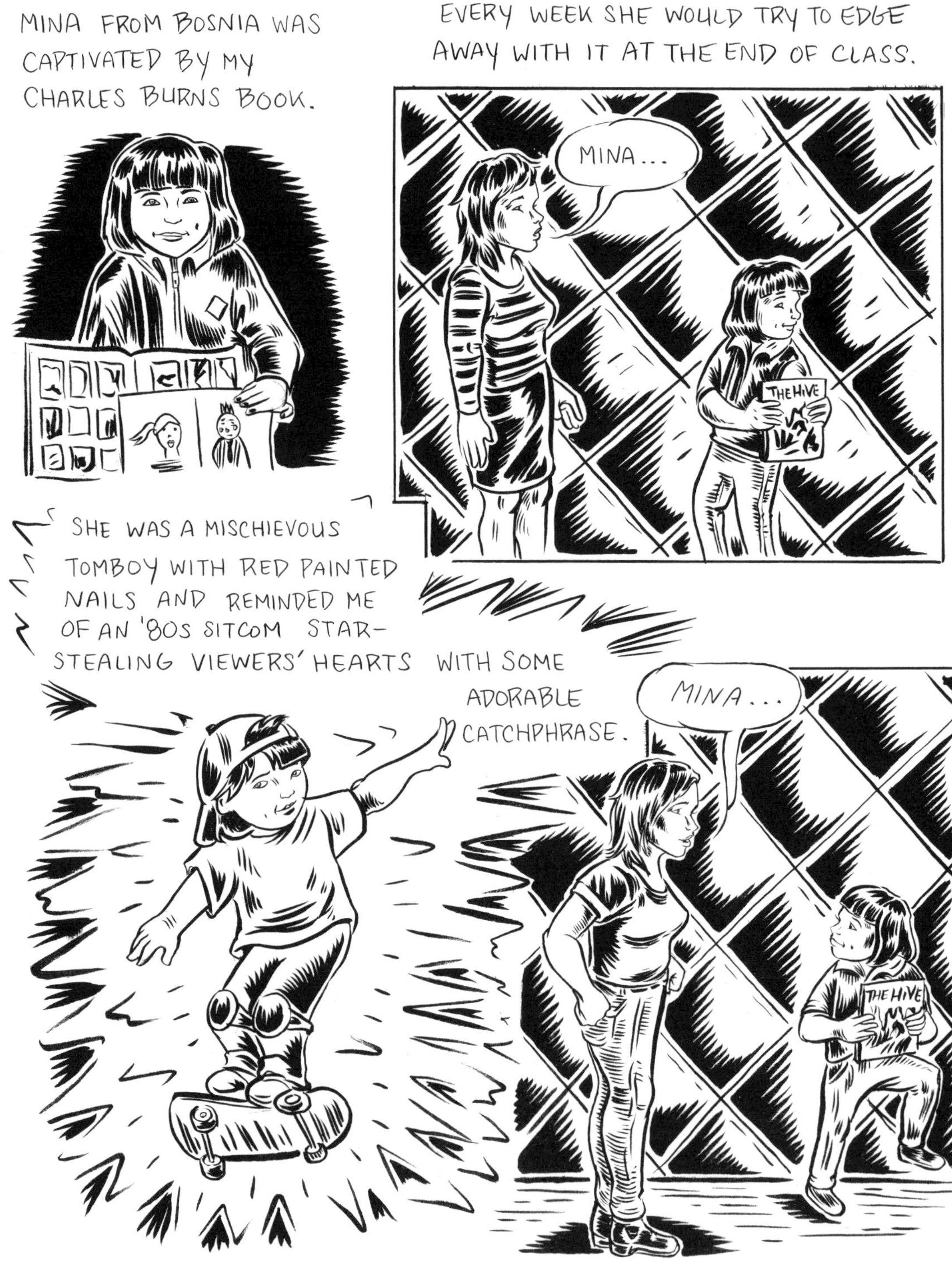
MINA FROM BOSNIA WAS CAPTIVATED BY MY CHARLES BURNS BOOK.
EVERY WEEK SHE WOULD TRY TO EDGE AWAY WITH IT AT THE END OF CLASS.
MINA...
THE HIVE
SHE WAS A MISCHIEVOUS TOMBOY WITH RED PAINTED NAILS AND REMINDED ME OF AN '80S SITCOM STAR-STEALING VIEWERS' HEARTS WITH SOME ADORABLE CATCHPHRASE.
MINA...
THE HIVE

LOOKING BACK, I WISH I HAD JUST GIVEN HER THE BOOK.

WHY DIDN'T I?
CHARLES BURNS
THE HIVE

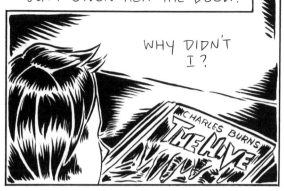

THERE ARE STILL GRAPHITE TRENCHES FROM HER TINY HANDIWORK.

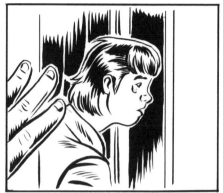

AND A NOTE IN THE MARGINS.

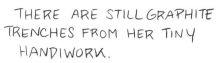

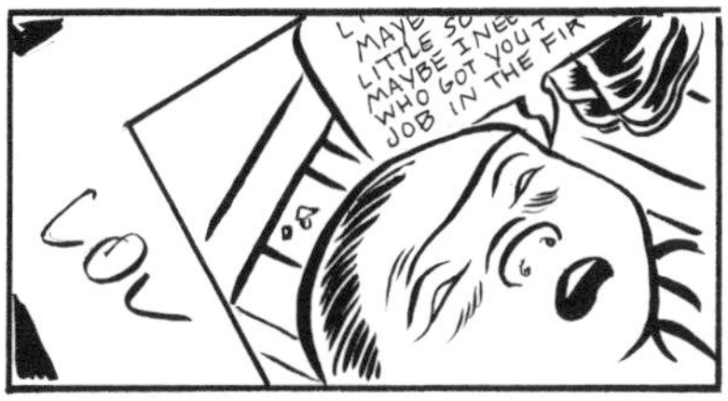

DID SHE WRITE IT?
WAS IT A MISSPELLING OF LOVE? VOV? LOL?
I HOPE THAT MINA WAS ABLE TO STAY IN BERLIN—BUT IT'S UNLIKELY.

AS THE CRISIS DEEPENED, MORE AND MORE ECONOMIC MIGRANTS WERE SENT BACK TO THE BALKANS.

I'M RIDING IT DOWN AND THERE'S NOTHING I CAN DO.

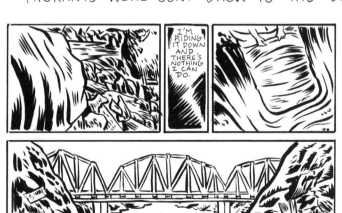

OVER 20,000 PEOPLE WERE DEPORTED IN 2015, MANY FROM IMPOVERISHED BUT NEWLY DECLARED "SAFE" STATES LIKE BOSNIA AND SERBIA.

IN 2014, ONLY ABOUT 0.3 PERCENT OF PEOPLE FROM THESE COUNTRIES WERE GRANTED ASYLUM. AND THINGS WEREN'T GETTING EASIER.

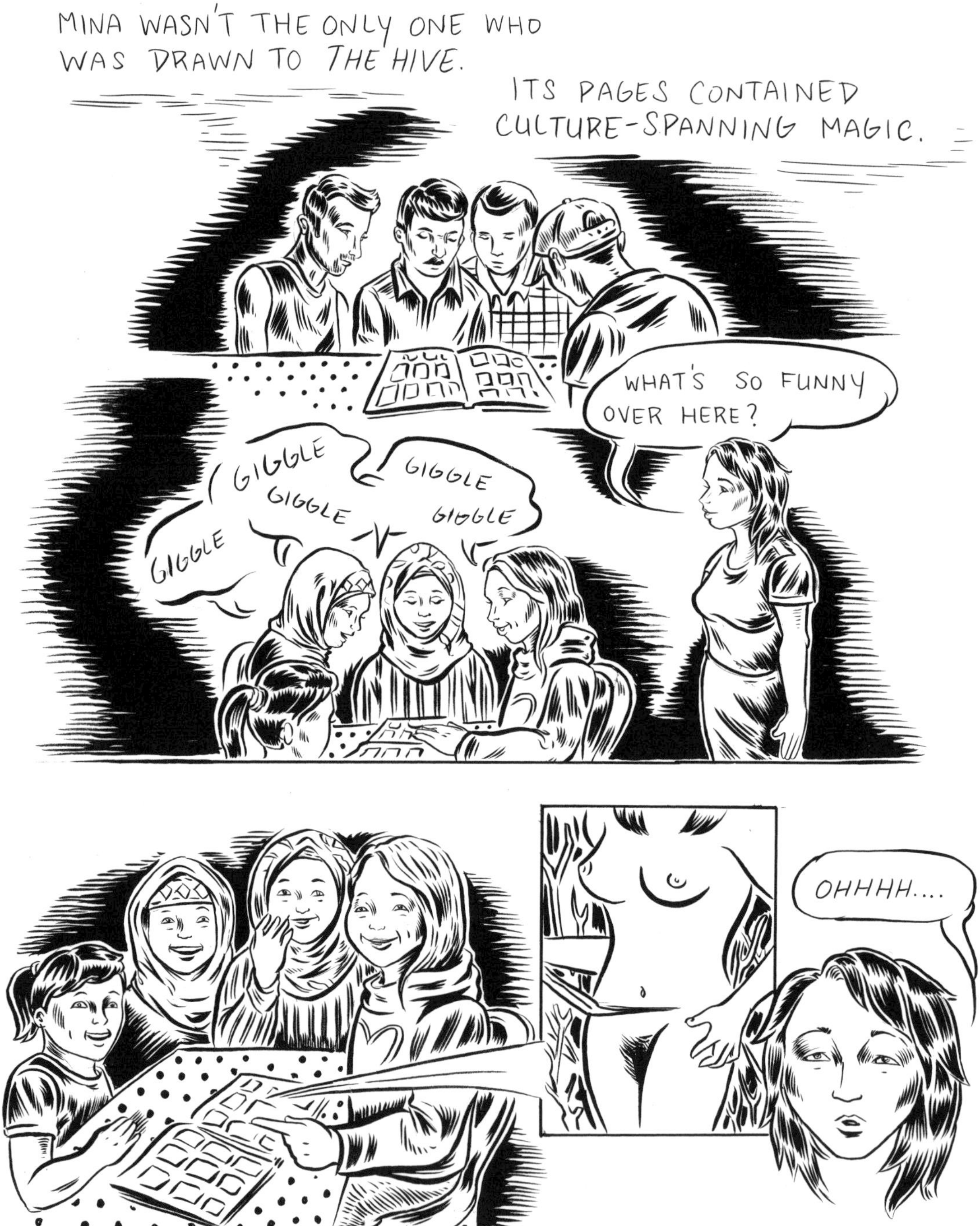
MINA WASN'T THE ONLY ONE WHO WAS DRAWN TO THE HIVE.
ITS PAGES CONTAINED CULTURE-SPANNING MAGIC.
WHAT'S SO FUNNY OVER HERE?
GIGGLE GIGGLE GIGGLE GIGGLE GIGGLE
OHHHH....

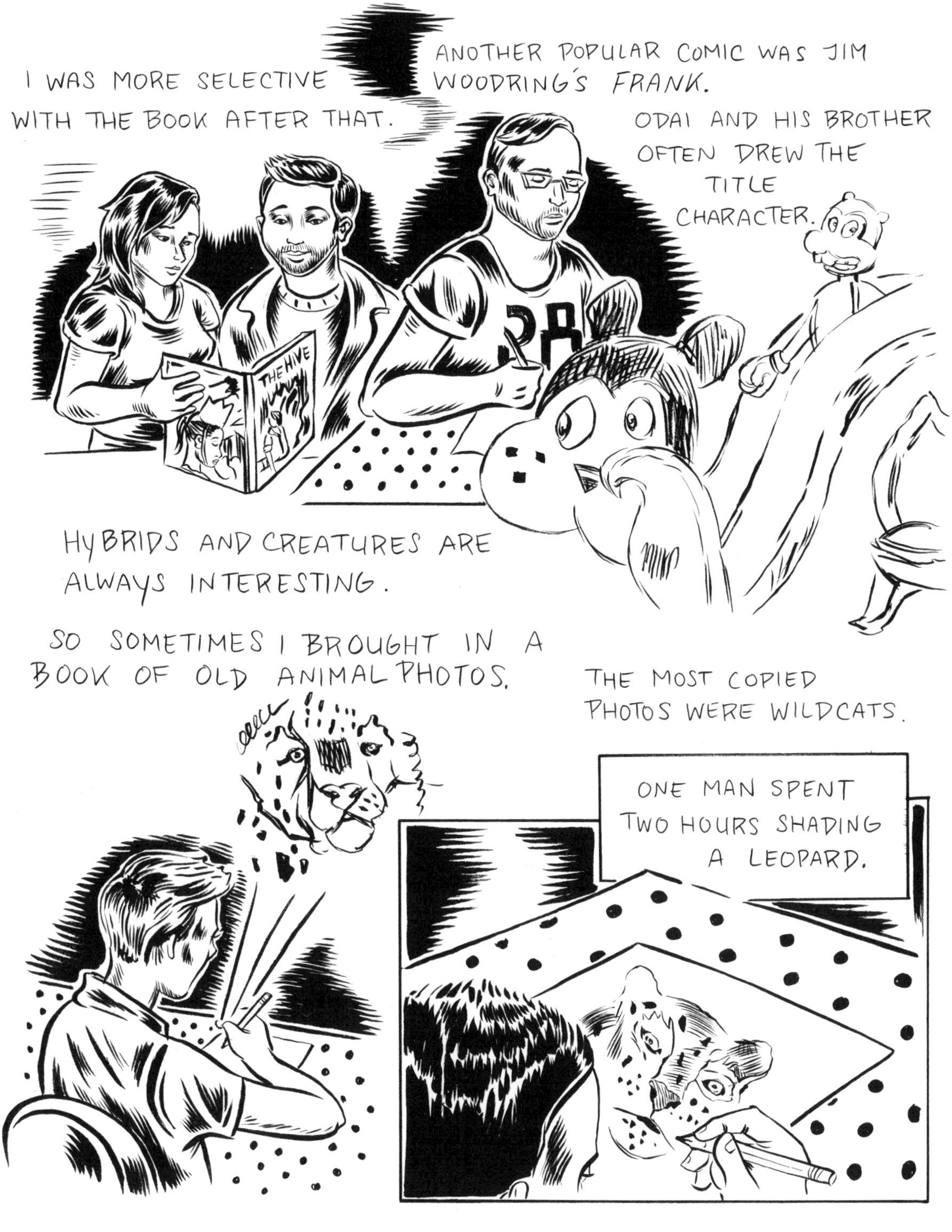
I WAS MORE SELECTIVE WITH THE BOOK AFTER THAT.
ANOTHER POPULAR COMIC WAS JIM WOODRING'S *FRANK*.
ODAI AND HIS BROTHER OFTEN DREW THE TITLE CHARACTER.
THE HIVE
HYBRIDS AND CREATURES ARE ALWAYS INTERESTING.
SO SOMETIMES I BROUGHT IN A BOOK OF OLD ANIMAL PHOTOS.
THE MOST COPIED PHOTOS WERE WILDCATS.
ONE MAN SPENT TWO HOURS SHADING A LEOPARD.

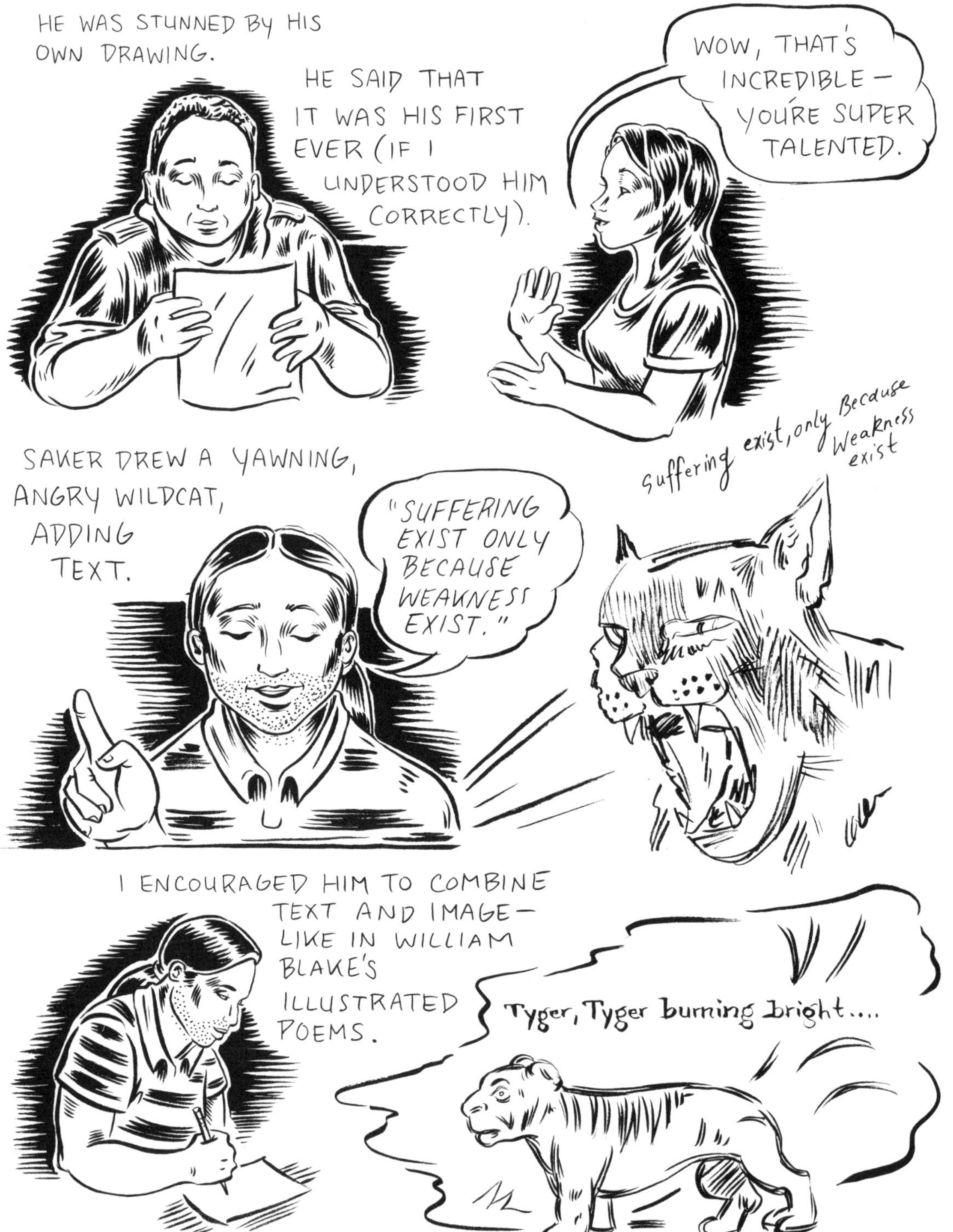
HE WAS STUNNED BY HIS OWN DRAWING.
HE SAID THAT IT WAS HIS FIRST EVER (IF I UNDERSTOOD HIM CORRECTLY).
WOW, THAT'S INCREDIBLE— YOU'RE SUPER TALENTED.
SAKER DREW A YAWNING, ANGRY WILDCAT, ADDING TEXT.
"SUFFERING EXIST ONLY BECAUSE WEAKNESS EXIST."
Suffering exist, only Because Weakness exist
I ENCOURAGED HIM TO COMBINE TEXT AND IMAGE— LIKE IN WILLIAM BLAKE'S ILLUSTRATED POEMS.
Tyger, Tyger burning bright....

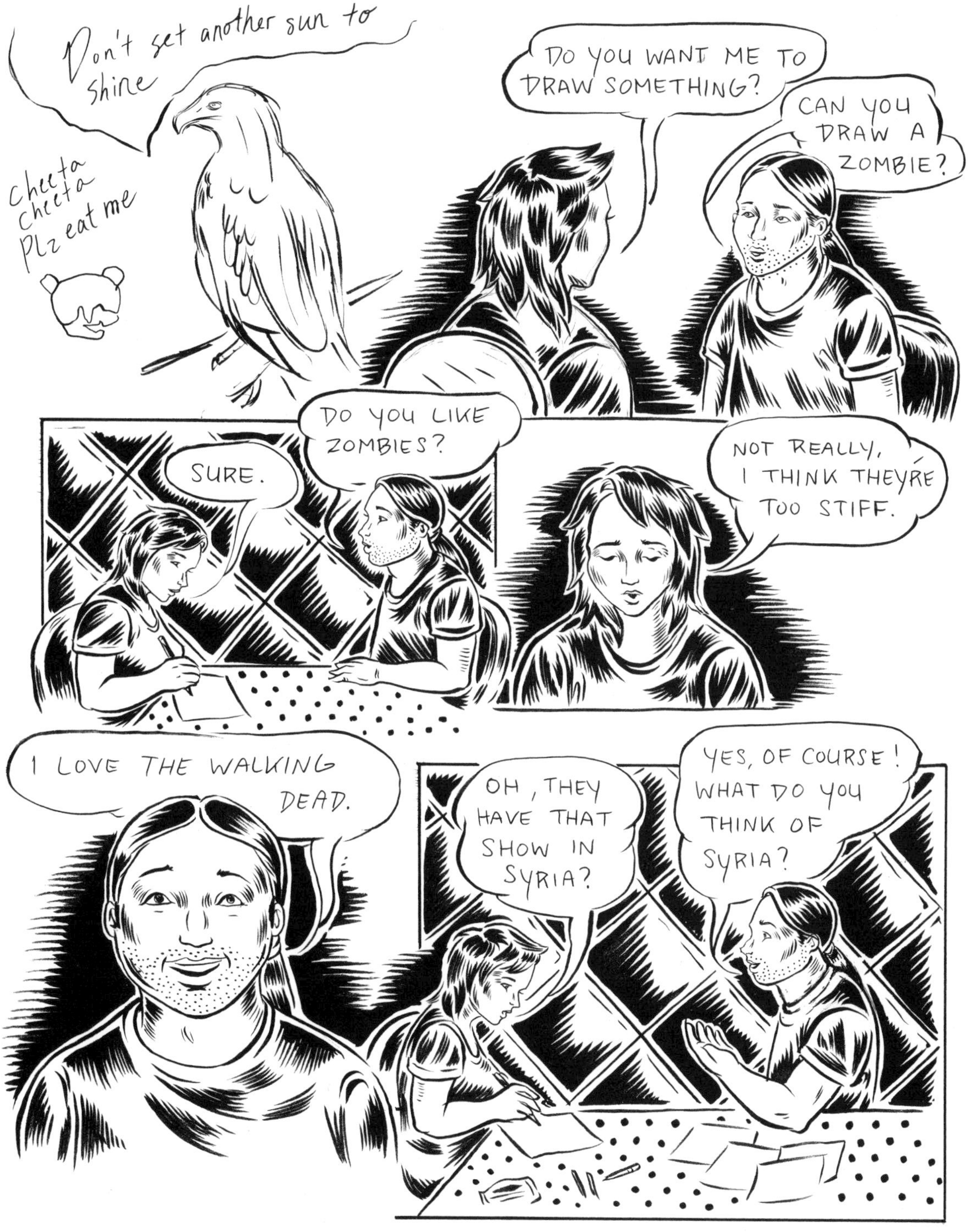
Don't set another sun to shine
cheeta cheeta plz eat me
DO YOU WANT ME TO DRAW SOMETHING?
CAN YOU DRAW A ZOMBIE?
DO YOU LIKE ZOMBIES?
SURE.
NOT REALLY, I THINK THEYRE TOO STIFF.
I LOVE THE WALKING DEAD.
OH, THEY HAVE THAT SHOW IN SYRIA?
YES, OF COURSE! WHAT DO YOU THINK OF SYRIA?

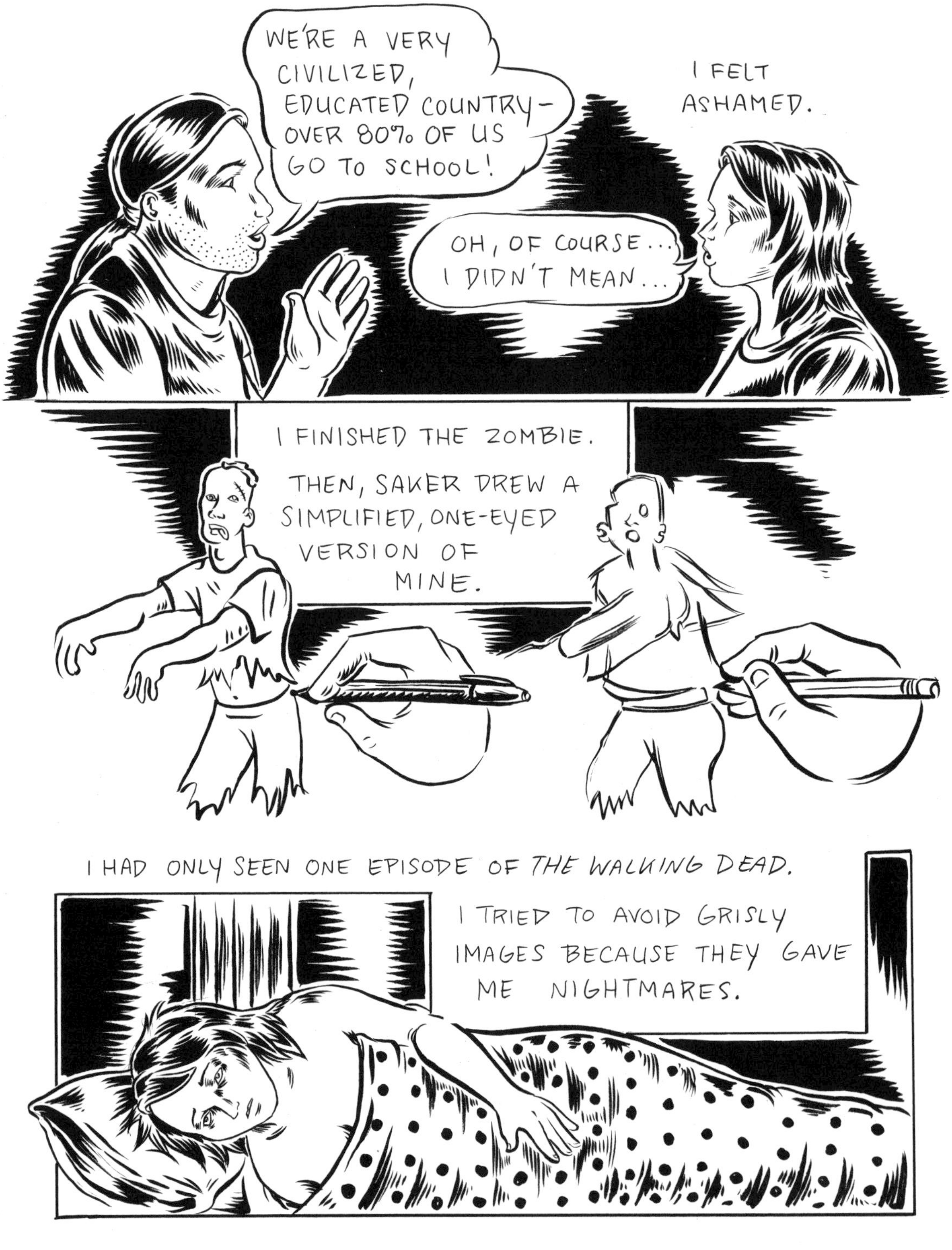
WE'RE A VERY CIVILIZED, EDUCATED COUNTRY- OVER 80% OF US GO TO SCHOOL!
I FELT ASHAMED.
OH, OF COURSE... I DIDN'T MEAN...
I FINISHED THE ZOMBIE.
THEN, SAKER DREW A SIMPLIFIED, ONE-EYED VERSION OF MINE.
I HAD ONLY SEEN ONE EPISODE OF *THE WALKING DEAD*.
I TRIED TO AVOID GRISLY IMAGES BECAUSE THEY GAVE ME NIGHTMARES.

WHEN I THOUGHT OF ZOMBIES, I THOUGHT OF PARTYMONSTERS AT THE *WARSCHAUERSTR.* TRAIN STATION.

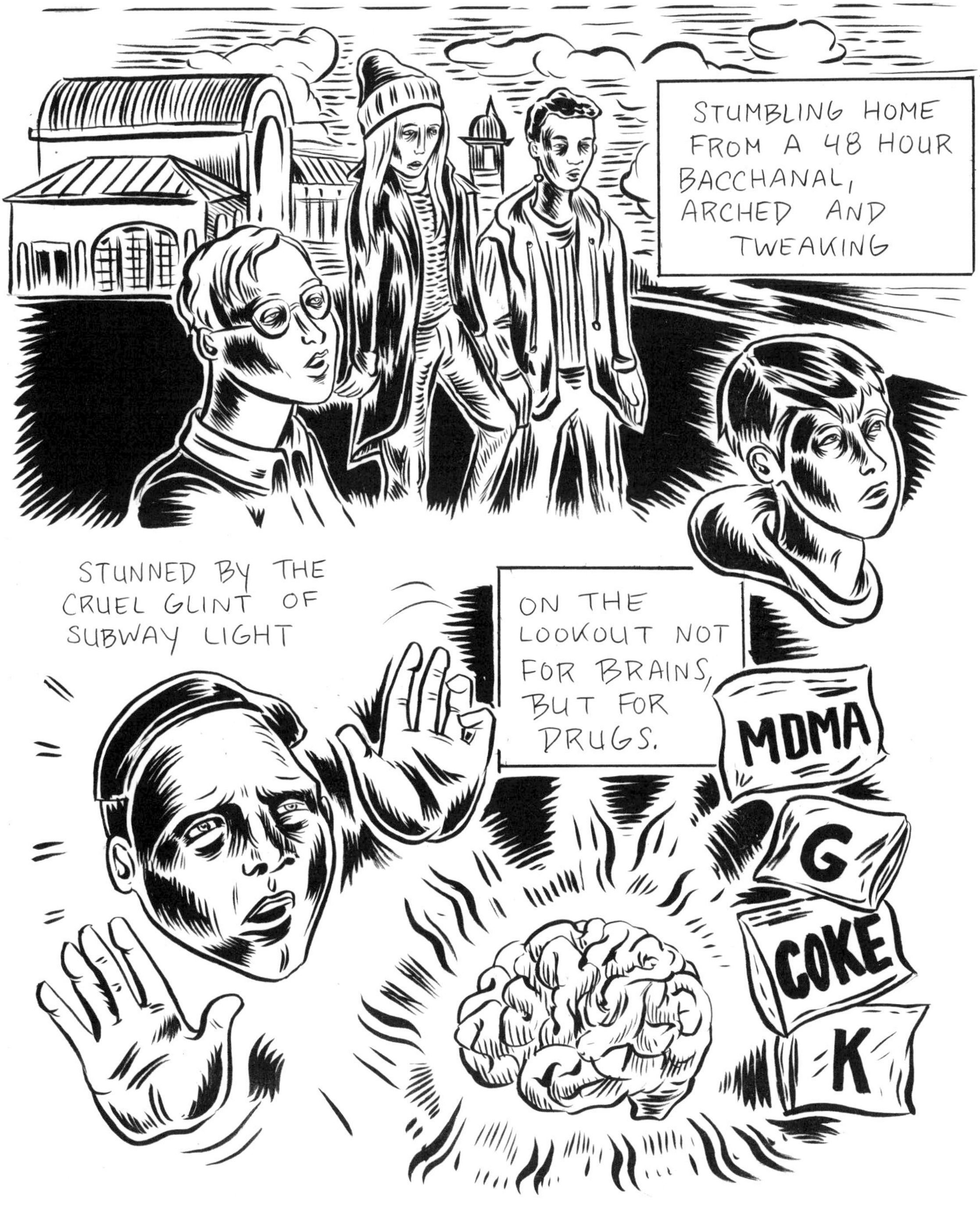
STUMBLING HOME FROM A 48 HOUR BACCHANAL, ARCHED AND TWEAKING
STUNNED BY THE CRUEL GLINT OF SUBWAY LIGHT
ON THE LOOKOUT NOT FOR BRAINS, BUT FOR DRUGS.
MDMA
G
COKE
K

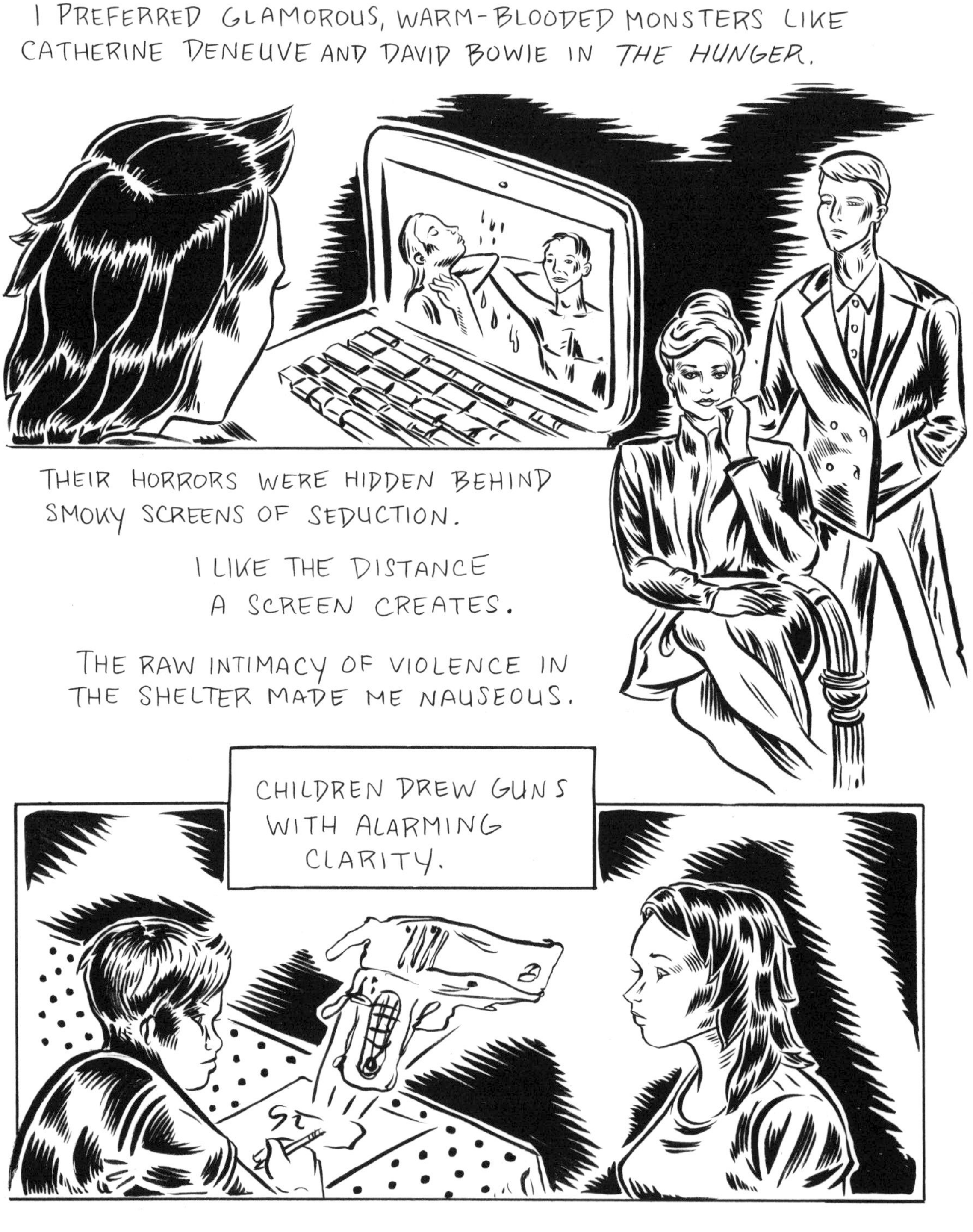
I PREFERRED GLAMOROUS, WARM-BLOODED MONSTERS LIKE CATHERINE DENEUVE AND DAVID BOWIE IN THE HUNGER.
THEIR HORRORS WERE HIDDEN BEHIND SMOKY SCREENS OF SEDUCTION.
I LIKE THE DISTANCE A SCREEN CREATES.
THE RAW INTIMACY OF VIOLENCE IN THE SHELTER MADE ME NAUSEOUS.
CHILDREN DREW GUNS WITH ALARMING CLARITY.

YOUNG MEN LIKE
SAYID MANUFACTURED LIMBS
AND MISSILES WITH DIZZYING
URGENCY.

THEIR EASE WITH WEAPONS
REMINDED ME OF MY OWN
TEENAGE FACILITY FOR
DRAWING BART SIMPSON.

WE ALL HAVE OUR
FAMILIAR SHAPES.

MY HAND WAS BRANDED BY YOUTH CORPORATIONS AND
1990s SUBURBAN AMERICA.

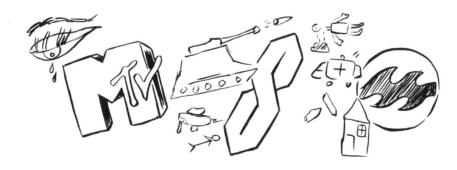

WHAT WAS THEIRS BRANDED BY?

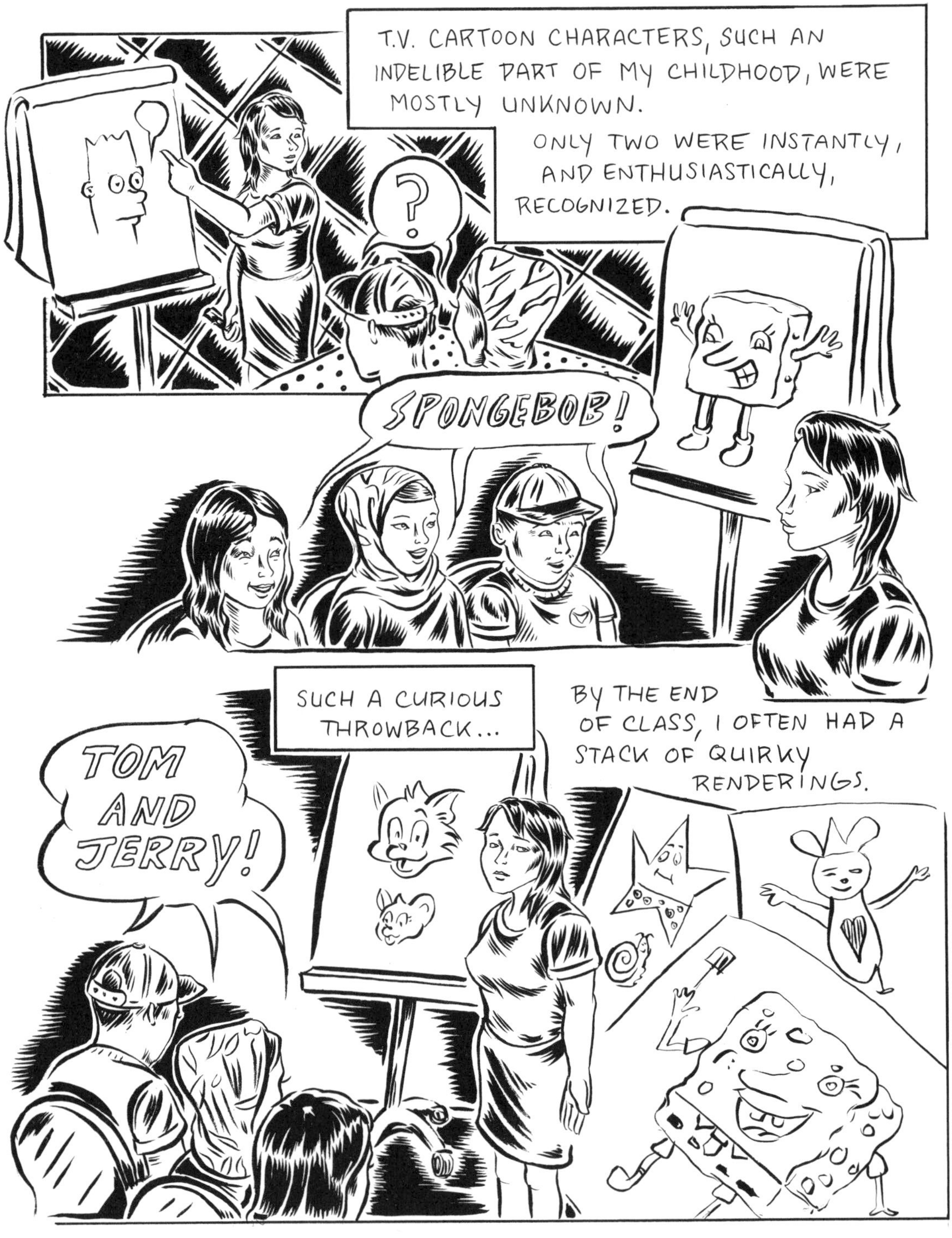
T.V. CARTOON CHARACTERS, SUCH AN INDELIBLE PART OF MY CHILDHOOD, WERE MOSTLY UNKNOWN.
ONLY TWO WERE INSTANTLY, AND ENTHUSIASTICALLY, RECOGNIZED.
?
SPONGEBOB!
SUCH A CURIOUS THROWBACK...
TOM AND JERRY!
BY THE END OF CLASS, I OFTEN HAD A STACK OF QUIRKY RENDERINGS.

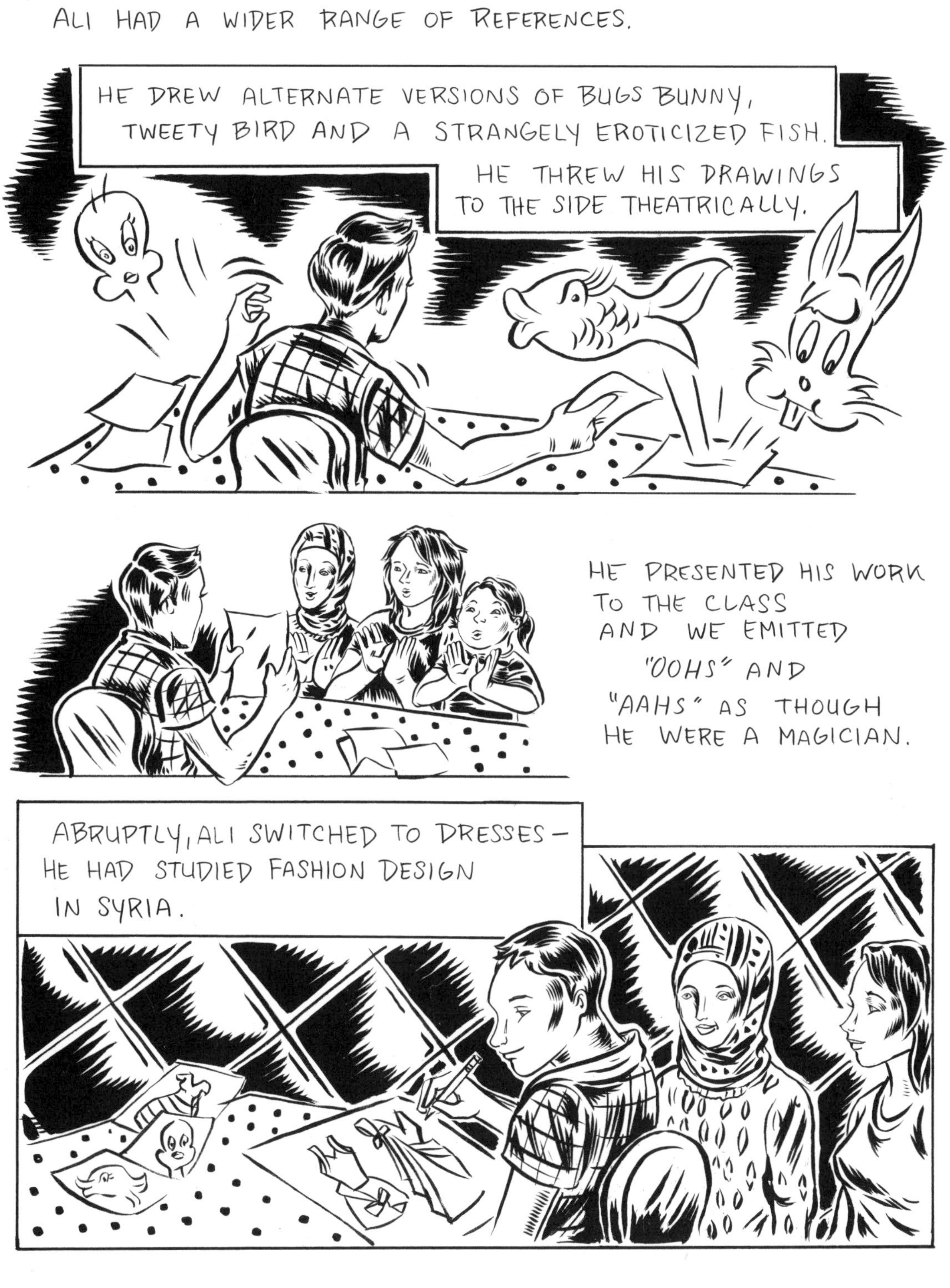
ALI HAD A WIDER RANGE OF REFERENCES.
HE DREW ALTERNATE VERSIONS OF BUGS BUNNY, TWEETY BIRD AND A STRANGELY EROTICIZED FISH.
HE THREW HIS DRAWINGS TO THE SIDE THEATRICALLY.
HE PRESENTED HIS WORK TO THE CLASS AND WE EMITTED "OOHS" AND "AAHS" AS THOUGH HE WERE A MAGICIAN.
ABRUPTLY, ALI SWITCHED TO DRESSES — HE HAD STUDIED FASHION DESIGN IN SYRIA.

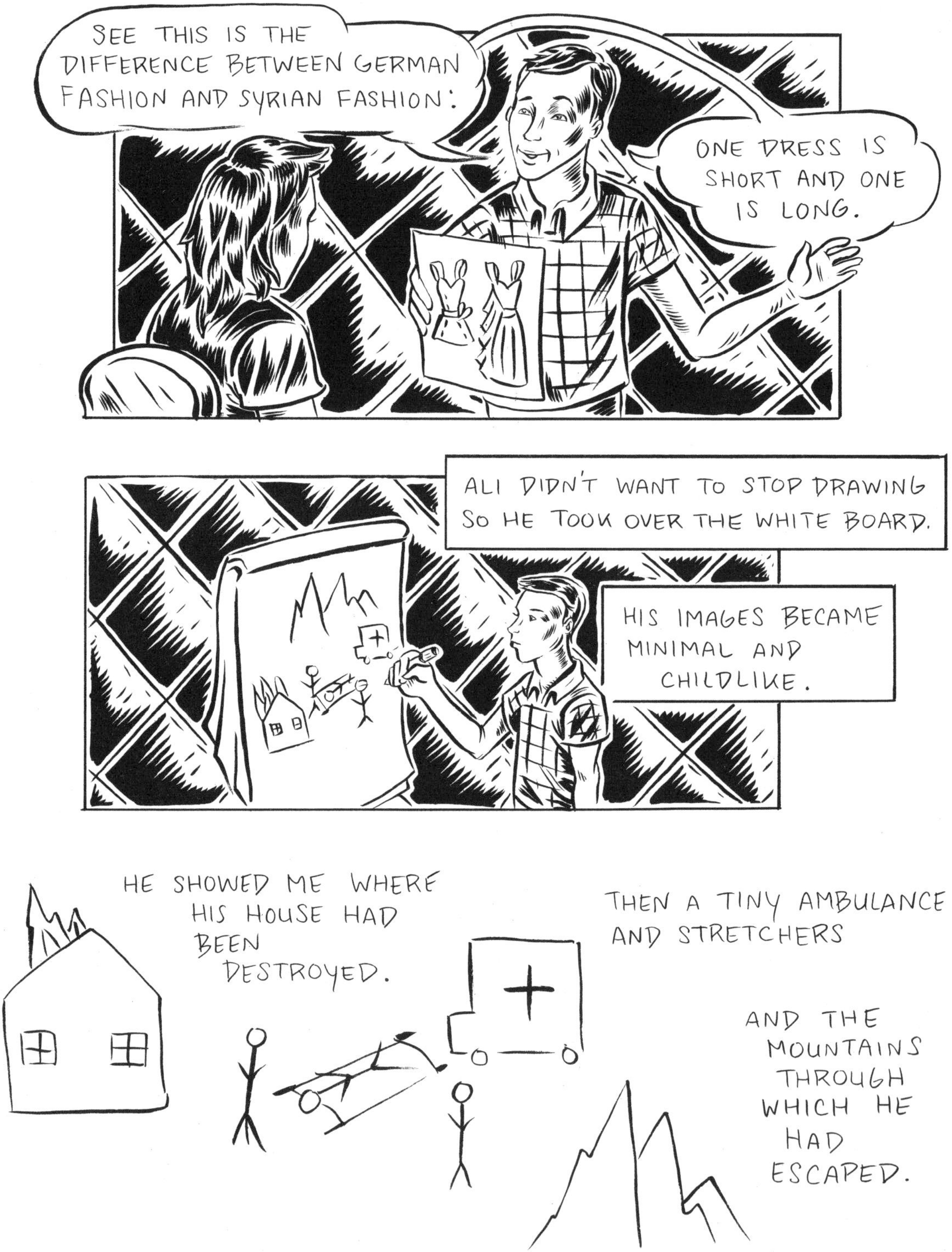
SEE THIS IS THE DIFFERENCE BETWEEN GERMAN FASHION AND SYRIAN FASHION:
ONE DRESS IS SHORT AND ONE IS LONG.
ALI DIDN'T WANT TO STOP DRAWING SO HE TOOK OVER THE WHITE BOARD.
HIS IMAGES BECAME MINIMAL AND CHILDLIKE.
HE SHOWED ME WHERE HIS HOUSE HAD BEEN DESTROYED.
THEN A TINY AMBULANCE AND STRETCHERS
AND THE MOUNTAINS THROUGH WHICH HE HAD ESCAPED.

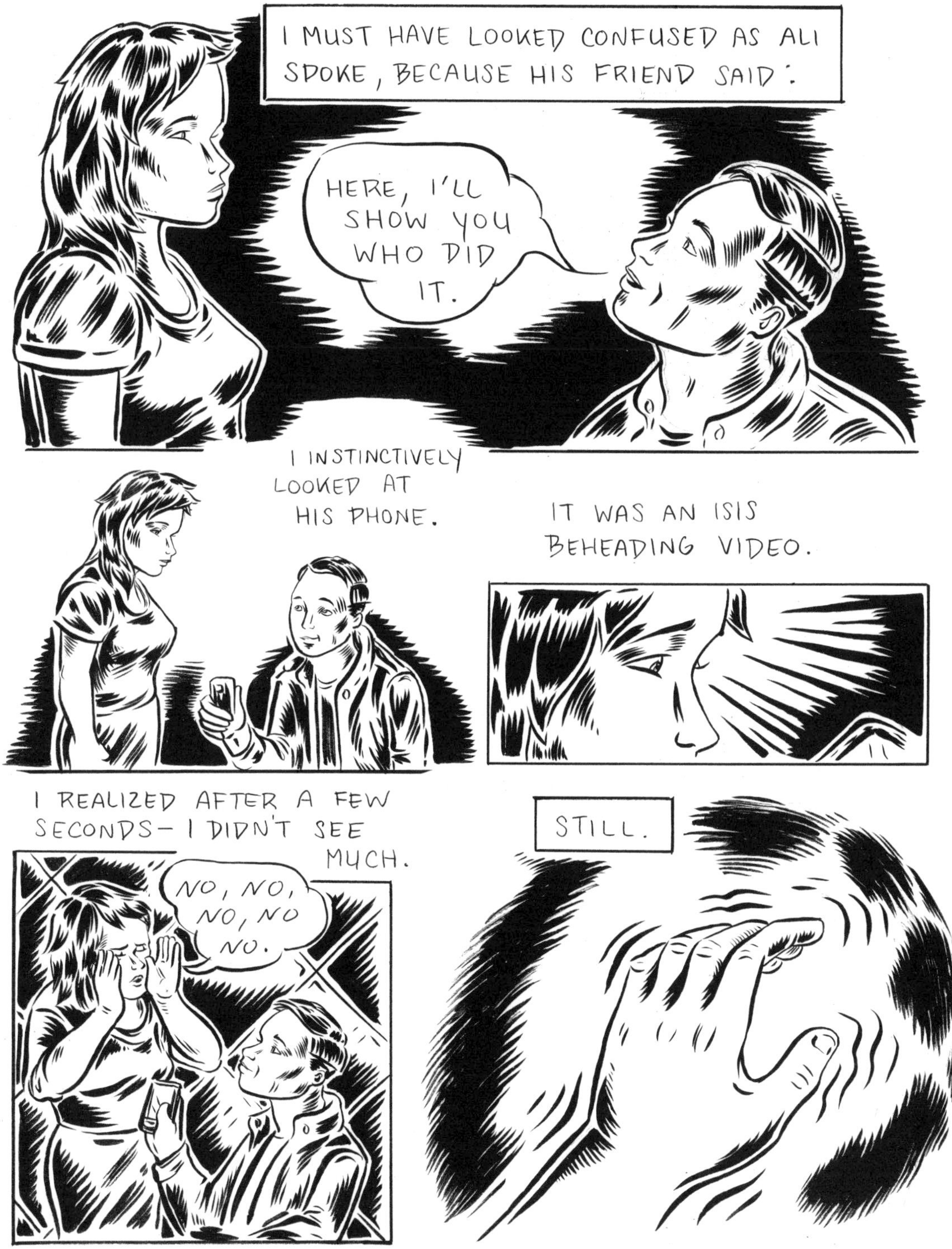
I MUST HAVE LOOKED CONFUSED AS ALI SPOKE, BECAUSE HIS FRIEND SAID:
HERE, I'LL SHOW YOU WHO DID IT.
I INSTINCTIVELY LOOKED AT HIS PHONE.
IT WAS AN ISIS BEHEADING VIDEO.
I REALIZED AFTER A FEW SECONDS- I DIDN'T SEE MUCH.
NO, NO, NO, NO NO.
STILL.

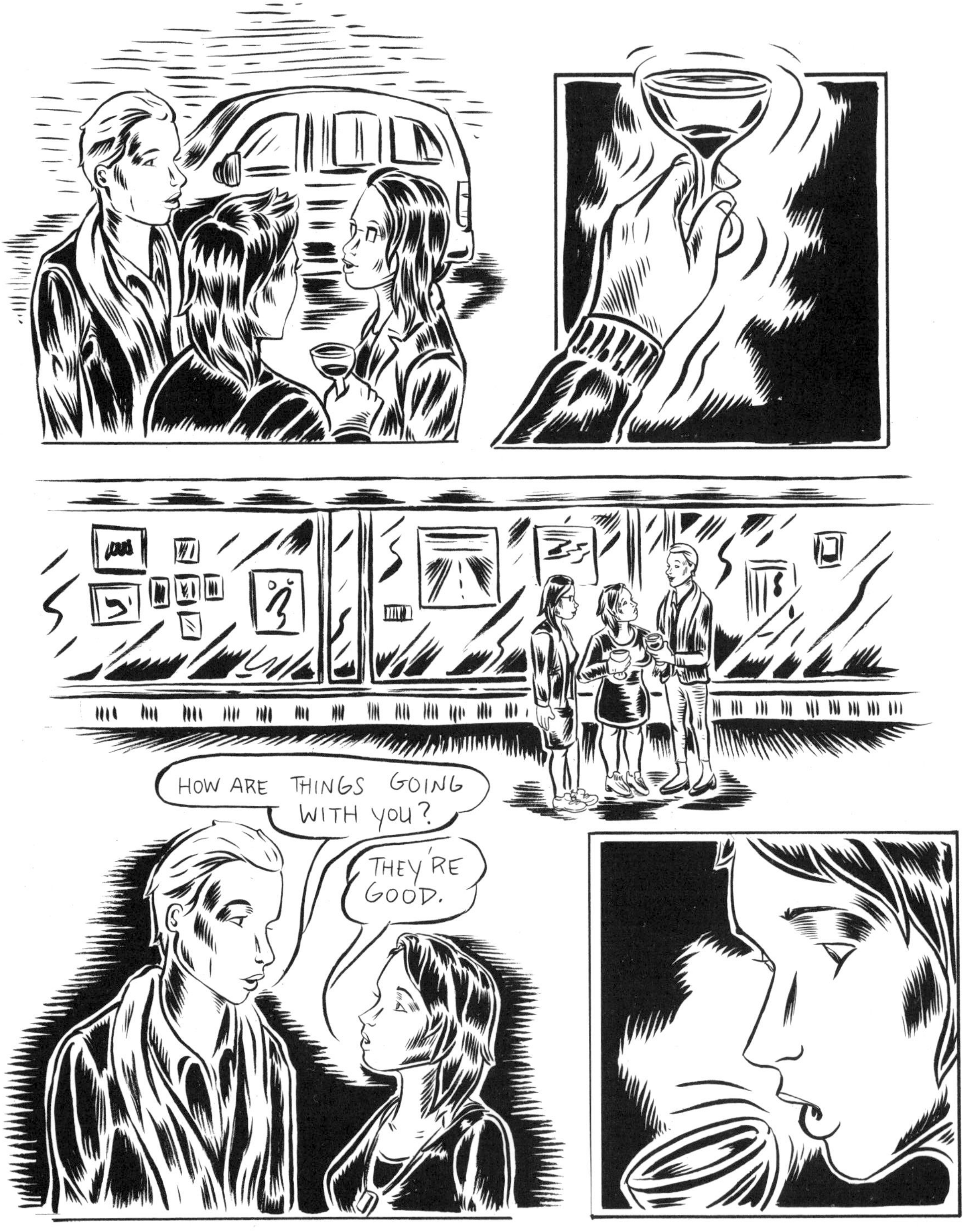
HOW ARE THINGS GOING WITH YOU?
THEY'RE GOOD.

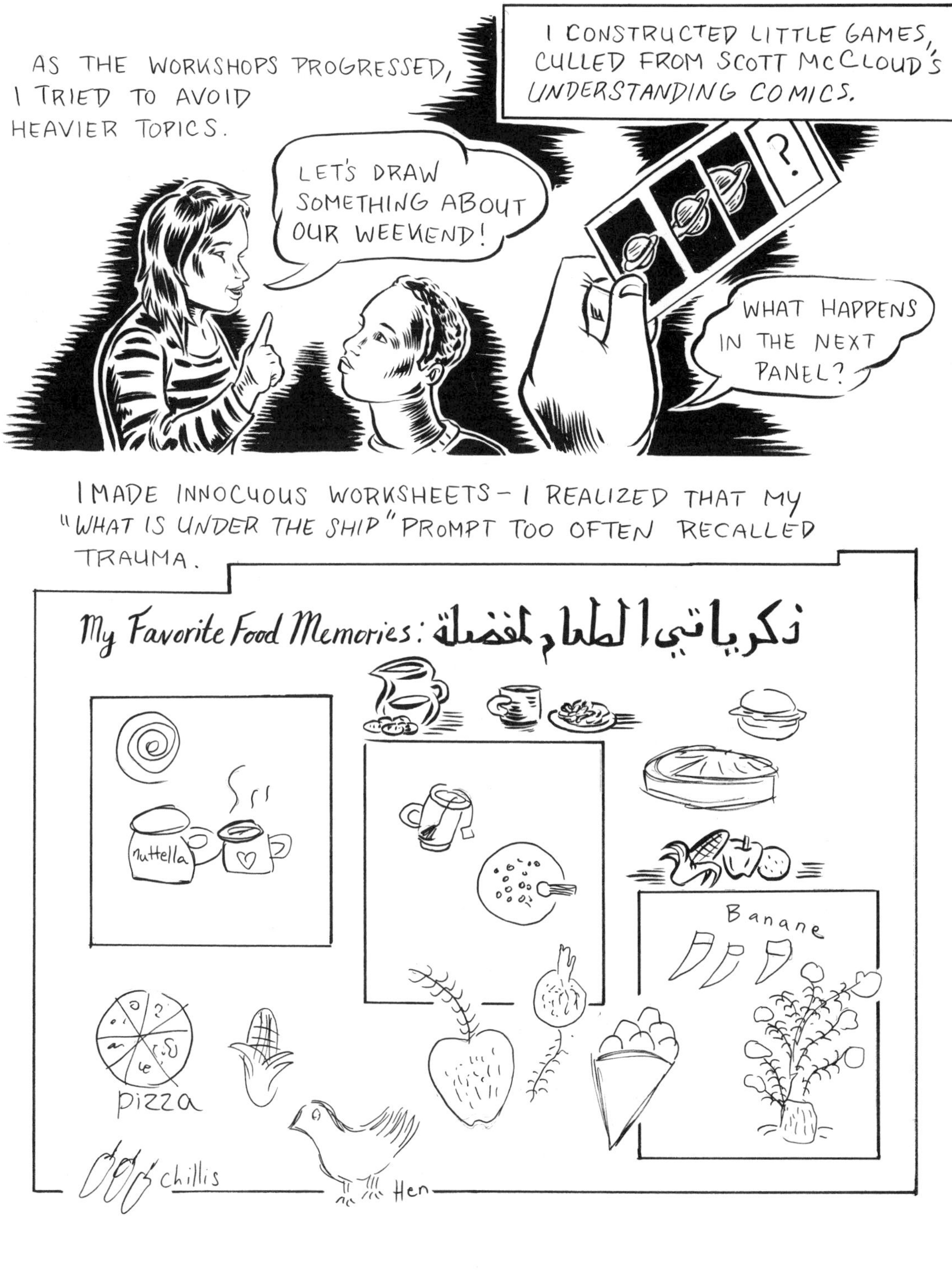
AS THE WORKSHOPS PROGRESSED, I TRIED TO AVOID HEAVIER TOPICS.
I CONSTRUCTED LITTLE GAMES, CULLED FROM SCOTT McCLOUD'S *UNDERSTANDING COMICS.*
LET'S DRAW SOMETHING ABOUT OUR WEEKEND!
?
WHAT HAPPENS IN THE NEXT PANEL?
I MADE INNOCUOUS WORKSHEETS — I REALIZED THAT MY "*WHAT IS UNDER THE SHIP*" PROMPT TOO OFTEN RECALLED TRAUMA.
My Favorite Food Memories: ذكرياتي الطعام لمفضلة
nutella
Banane
pizza
chillis
Hen

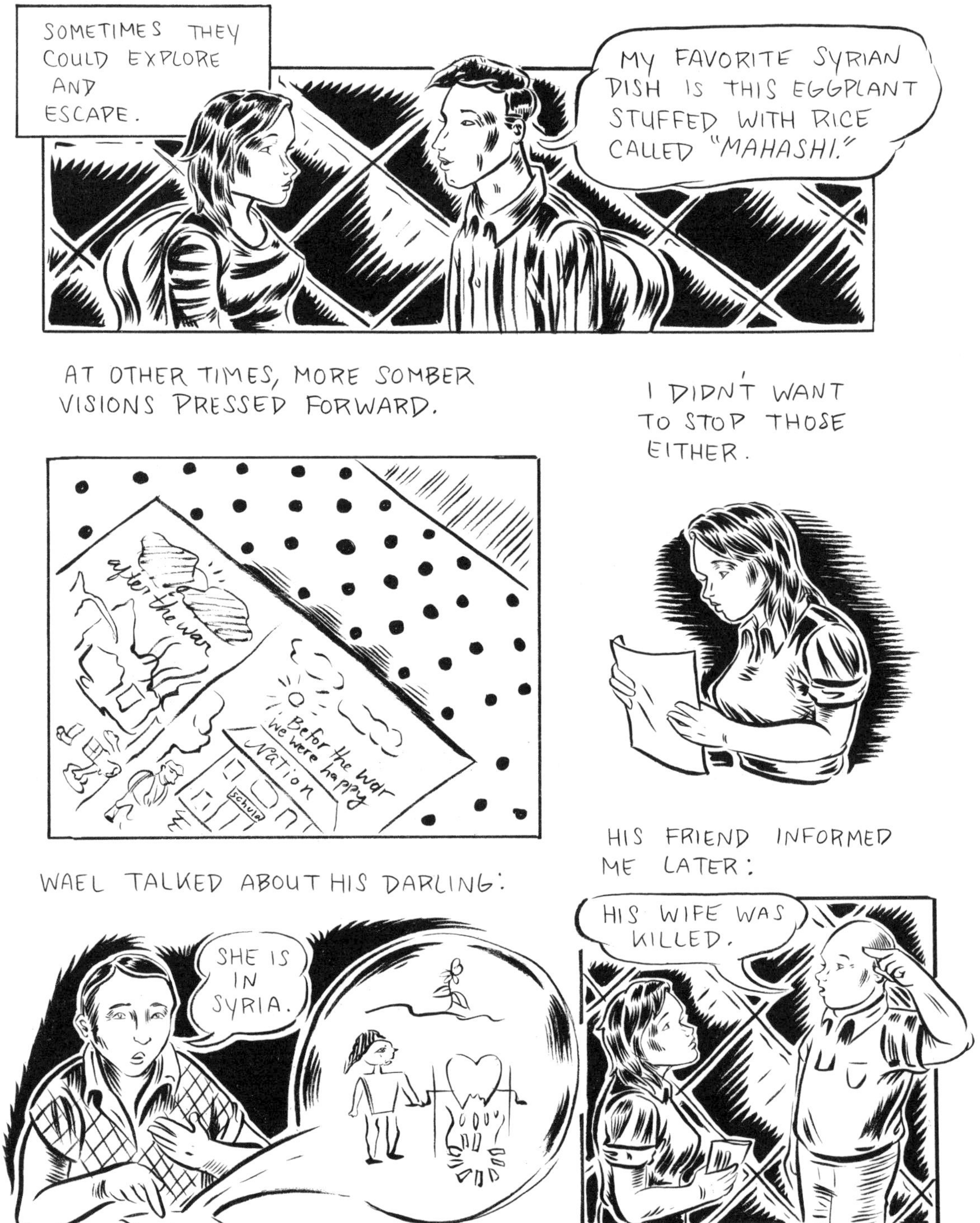
SOMETIMES THEY COULD EXPLORE AND ESCAPE.
MY FAVORITE SYRIAN DISH IS THIS EGGPLANT STUFFED WITH RICE CALLED "MAHASHI."
AT OTHER TIMES, MORE SOMBER VISIONS PRESSED FORWARD.
after the war
Befor the war we were happy
Nation
schula
I DIDN'T WANT TO STOP THOSE EITHER.
WAEL TALKED ABOUT HIS DARLING:
SHE IS IN SYRIA.
HIS FRIEND INFORMED ME LATER:
HIS WIFE WAS KILLED.

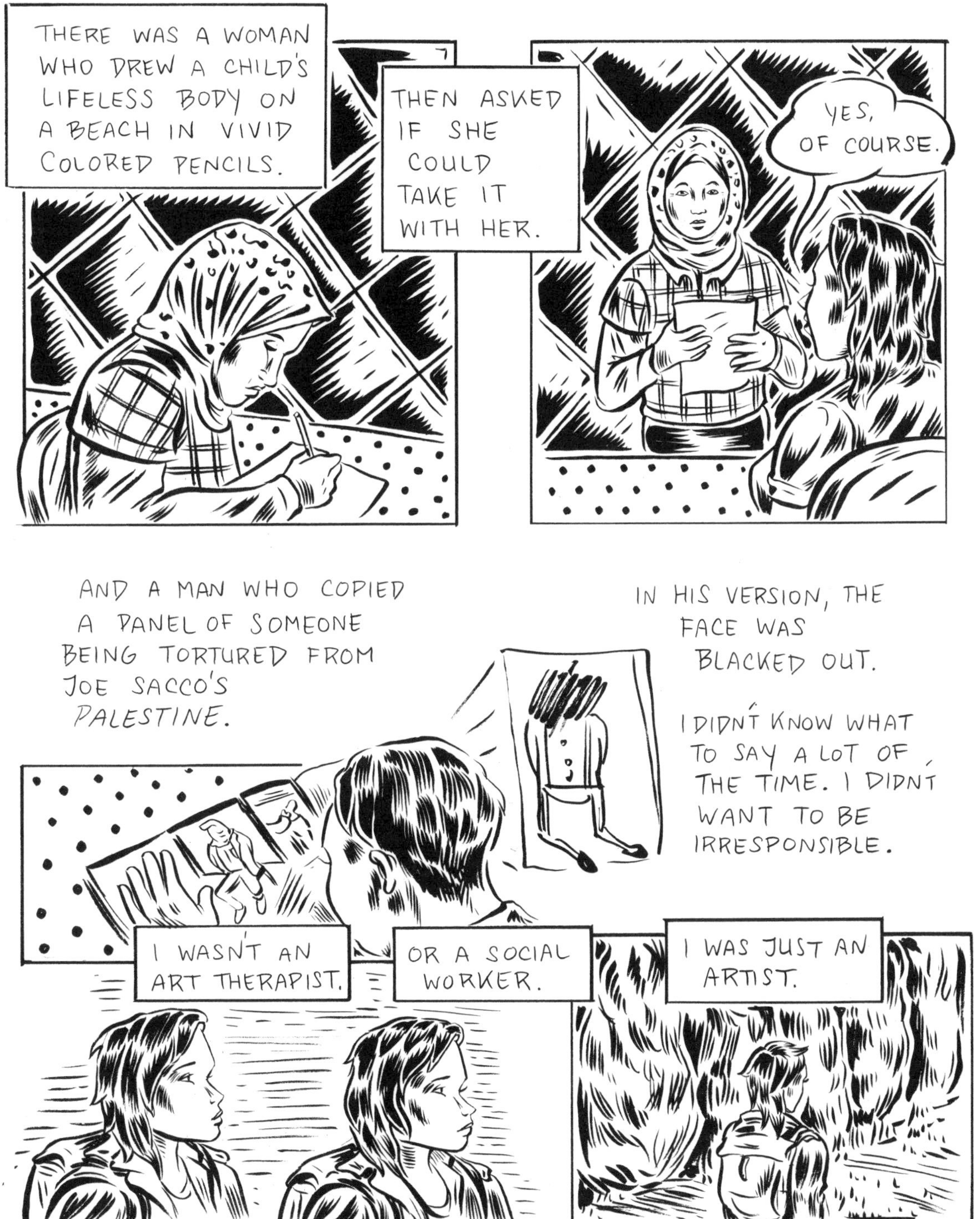
THERE WAS A WOMAN WHO DREW A CHILD'S LIFELESS BODY ON A BEACH IN VIVID COLORED PENCILS.
THEN ASKED IF SHE COULD TAKE IT WITH HER.
YES, OF COURSE.
AND A MAN WHO COPIED A PANEL OF SOMEONE BEING TORTURED FROM JOE SACCO'S *PALESTINE*.
IN HIS VERSION, THE FACE WAS BLACKED OUT.
I DIDN'T KNOW WHAT TO SAY A LOT OF THE TIME. I DIDN'T WANT TO BE IRRESPONSIBLE.
I WASN'T AN ART THERAPIST.
OR A SOCIAL WORKER.
I WAS JUST AN ARTIST.

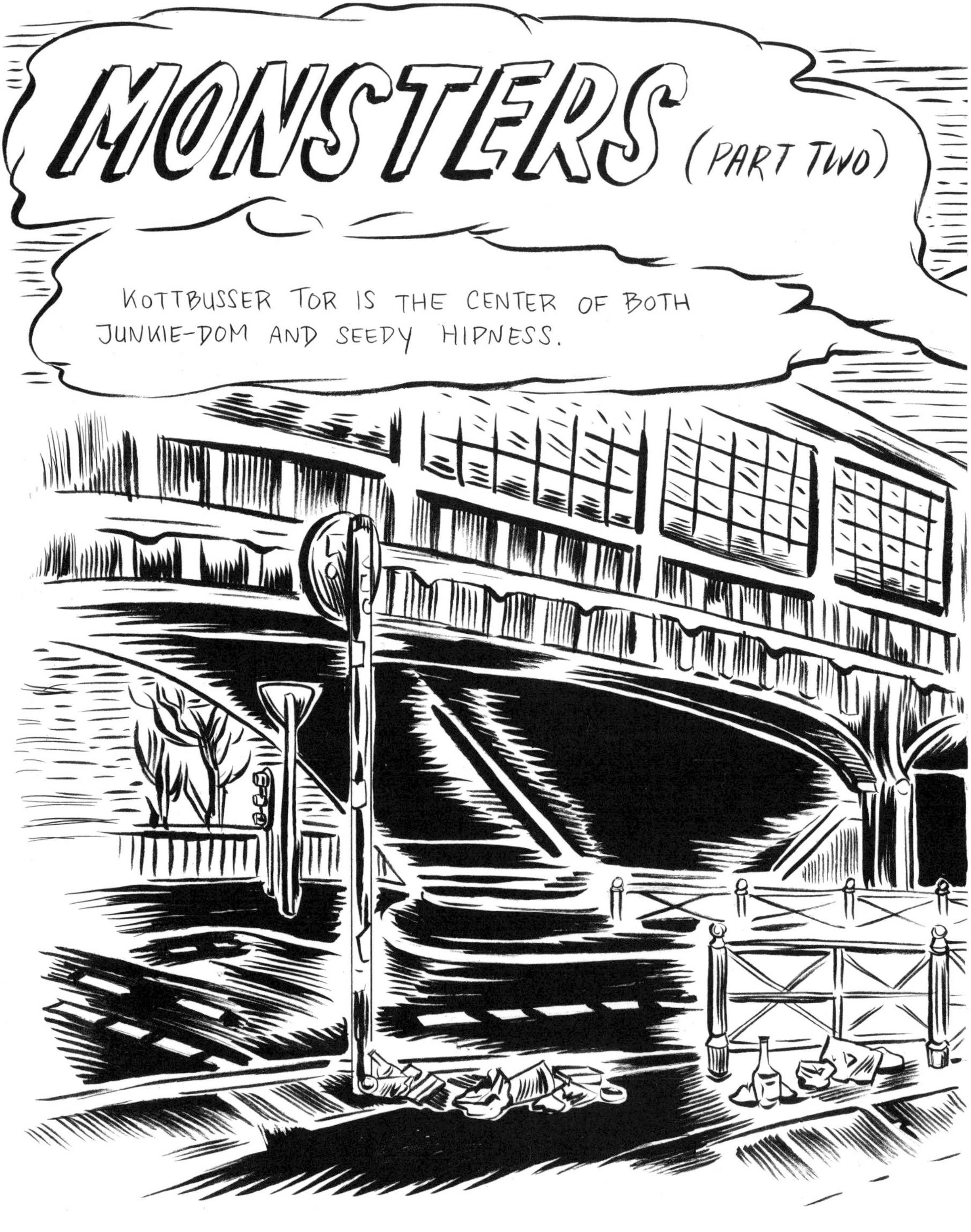
MONSTERS (PART TWO)
KOTTBUSSER TOR IS THE CENTER OF BOTH JUNKIE-DOM AND SEEDY HIPNESS.

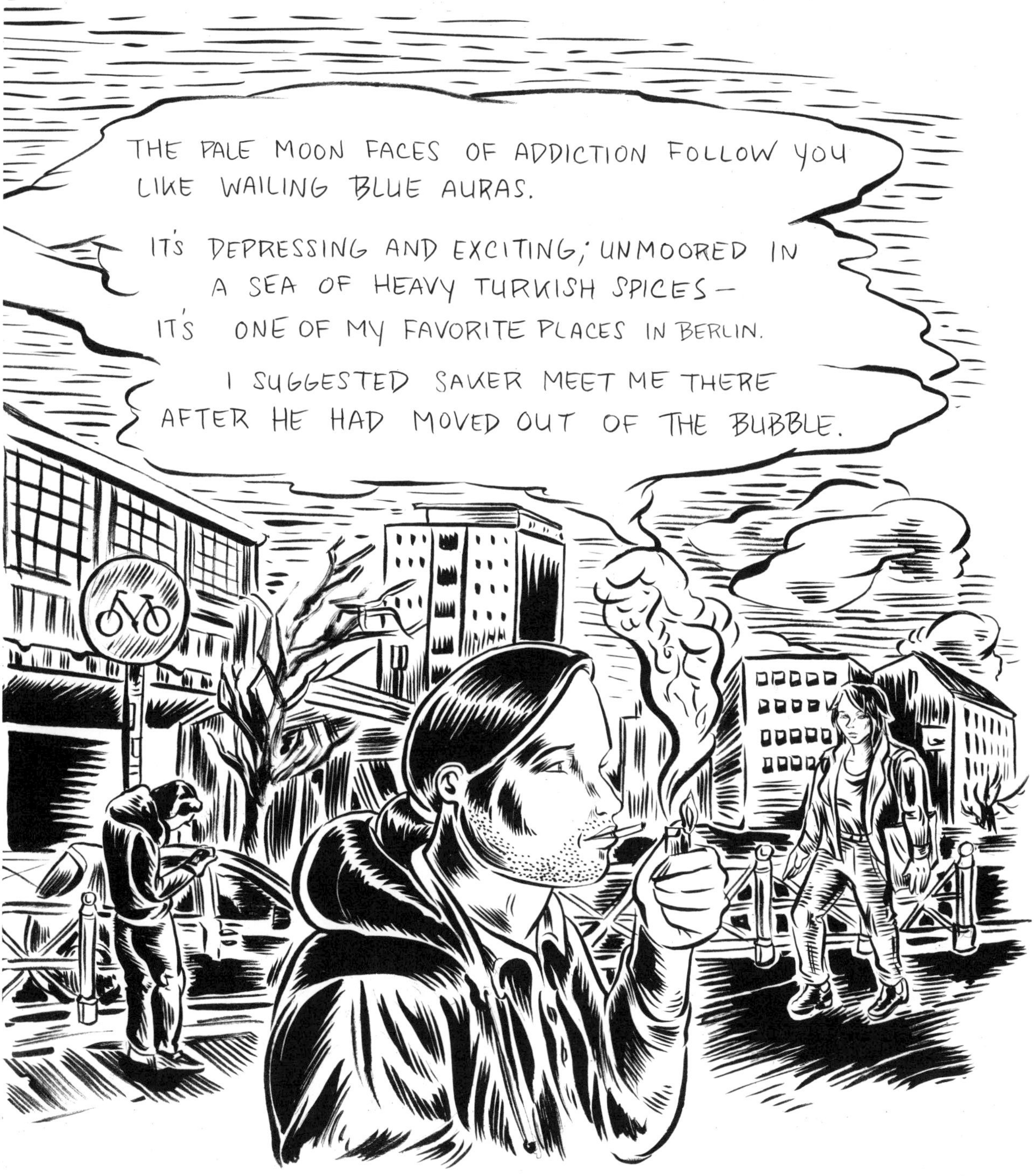
THE PALE MOON FACES OF ADDICTION FOLLOW YOU LIKE WAILING BLUE AURAS.
IT'S DEPRESSING AND EXCITING; UNMOORED IN A SEA OF HEAVY TURKISH SPICES—
IT'S ONE OF MY FAVORITE PLACES IN BERLIN.
I SUGGESTED SAKER MEET ME THERE AFTER HE HAD MOVED OUT OF THE BUBBLE.

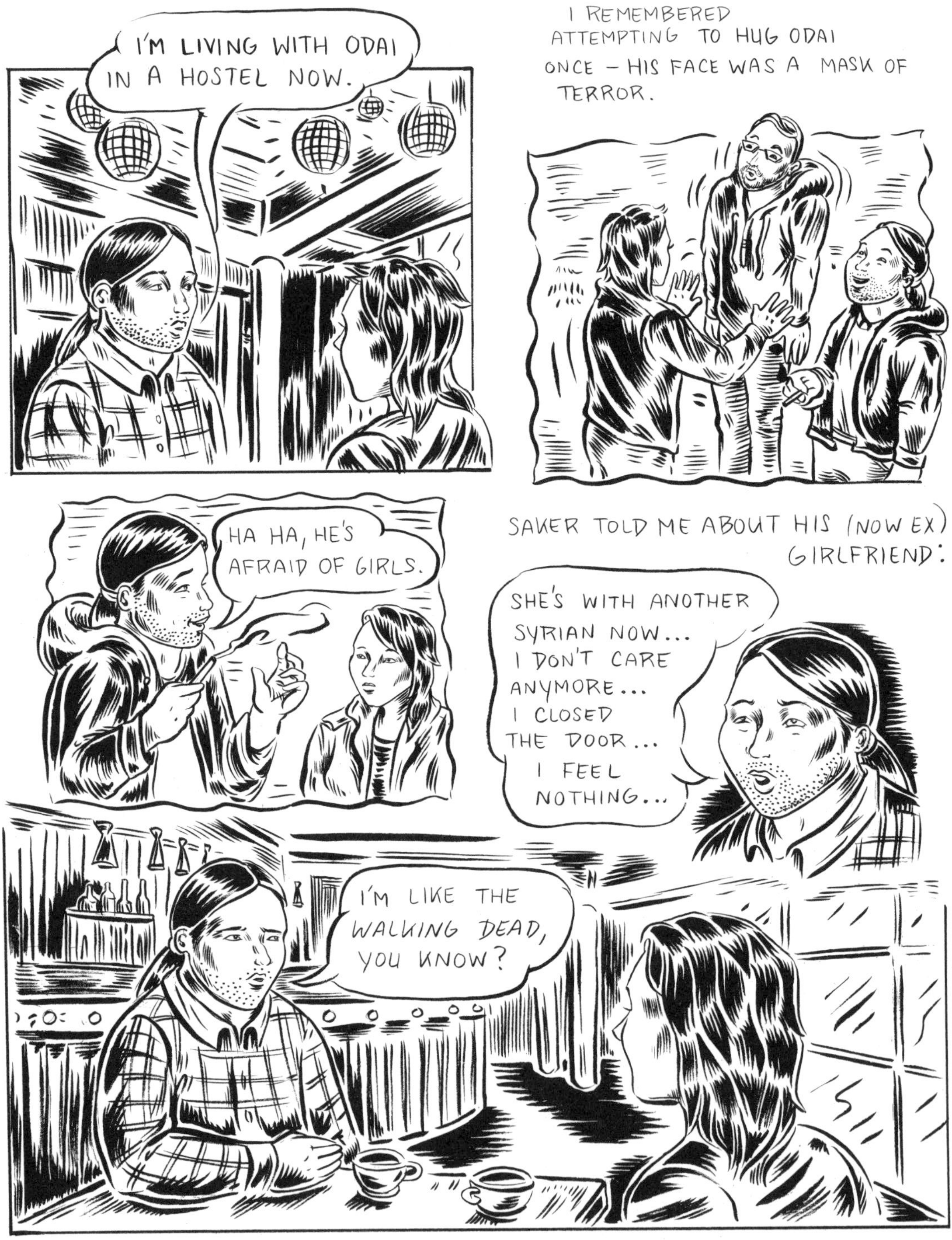
I'M LIVING WITH ODAI IN A HOSTEL NOW.
I REMEMBERED ATTEMPTING TO HUG ODAI ONCE – HIS FACE WAS A MASK OF TERROR.
HA HA, HE'S AFRAID OF GIRLS.
SAKER TOLD ME ABOUT HIS (NOW EX) GIRLFRIEND:
SHE'S WITH ANOTHER SYRIAN NOW... I DON'T CARE ANYMORE... I CLOSED THE DOOR... I FEEL NOTHING...
I'M LIKE THE WALKING DEAD, YOU KNOW?

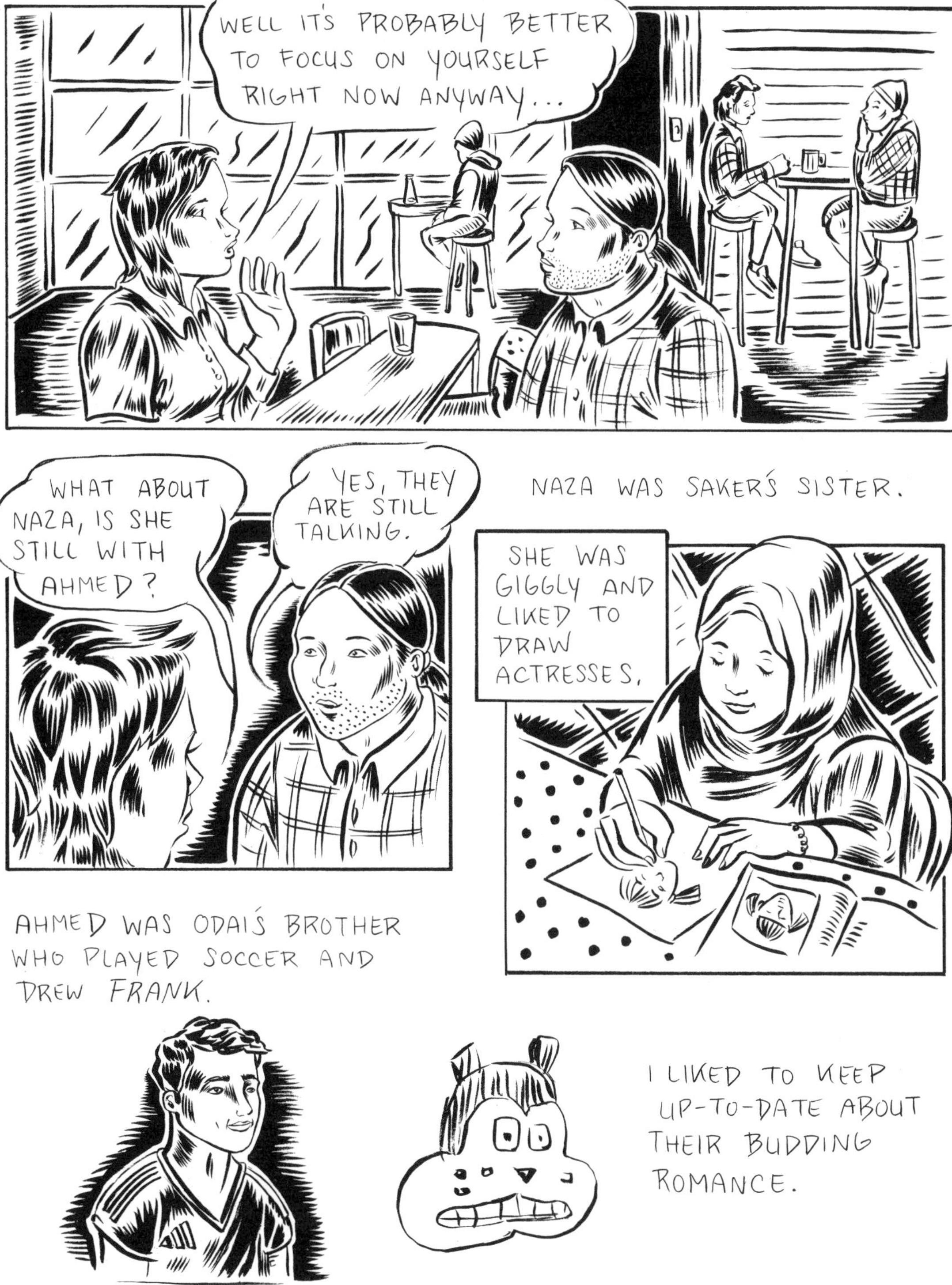
WELL IT'S PROBABLY BETTER TO FOCUS ON YOURSELF RIGHT NOW ANYWAY...
WHAT ABOUT NAZA, IS SHE STILL WITH AHMED?
YES, THEY ARE STILL TALKING.
NAZA WAS SAKER'S SISTER.
SHE WAS GIGGLY AND LIKED TO DRAW ACTRESSES.
AHMED WAS ODAI'S BROTHER WHO PLAYED SOCCER AND DREW FRANK.
I LIKED TO KEEP UP-TO-DATE ABOUT THEIR BUDDING ROMANCE.

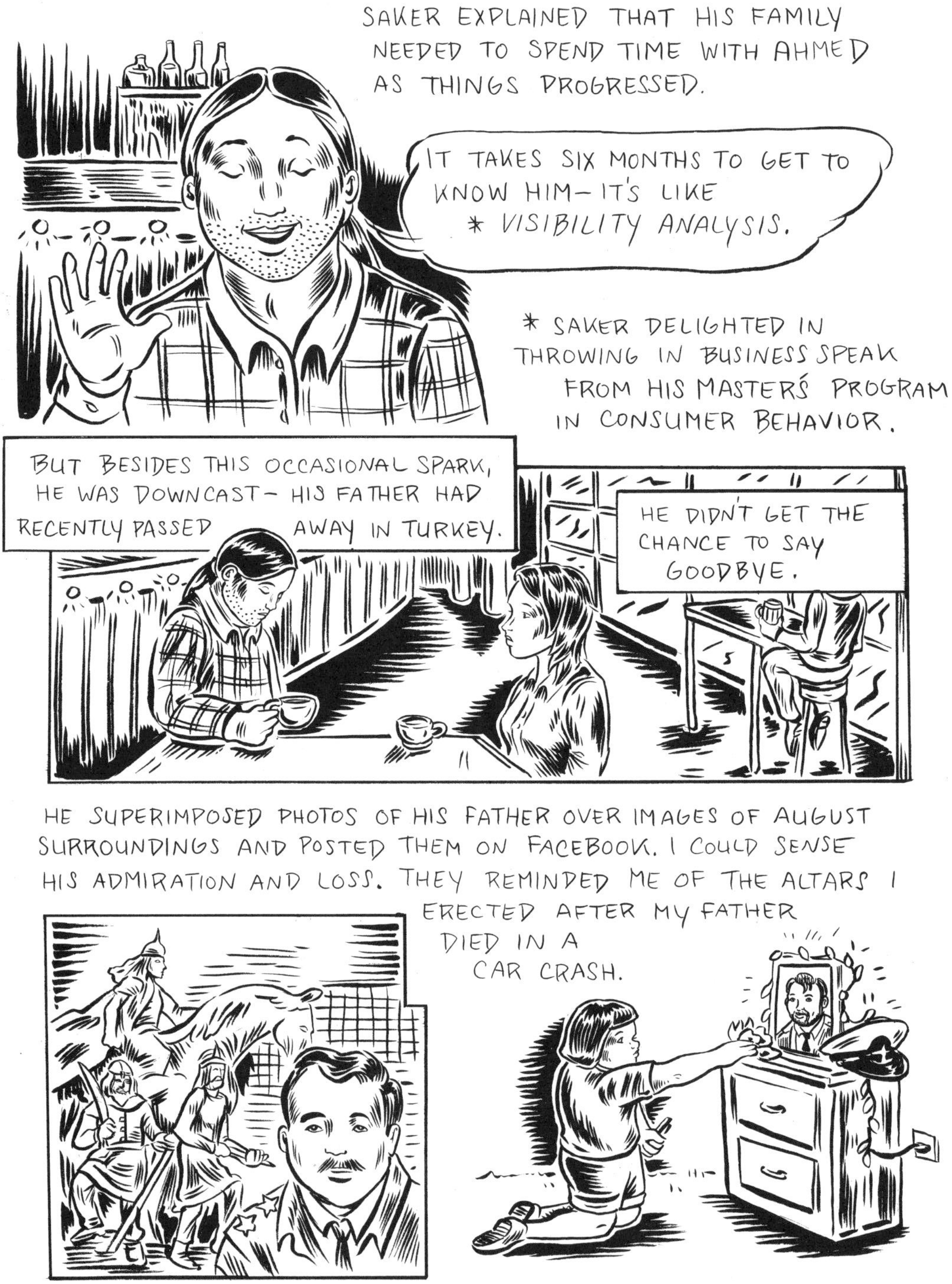
SAKER EXPLAINED THAT HIS FAMILY NEEDED TO SPEND TIME WITH AHMED AS THINGS PROGRESSED.
IT TAKES SIX MONTHS TO GET TO KNOW HIM– IT'S LIKE * VISIBILITY ANALYSIS.
* SAKER DELIGHTED IN THROWING IN BUSINESS SPEAK FROM HIS MASTER'S PROGRAM IN CONSUMER BEHAVIOR.
BUT BESIDES THIS OCCASIONAL SPARK, HE WAS DOWNCAST– HIS FATHER HAD RECENTLY PASSED AWAY IN TURKEY.
HE DIDN'T GET THE CHANCE TO SAY GOODBYE.
HE SUPERIMPOSED PHOTOS OF HIS FATHER OVER IMAGES OF AUGUST SURROUNDINGS AND POSTED THEM ON FACEBOOK. I COULD SENSE HIS ADMIRATION AND LOSS. THEY REMINDED ME OF THE ALTARS I ERECTED AFTER MY FATHER DIED IN A CAR CRASH.

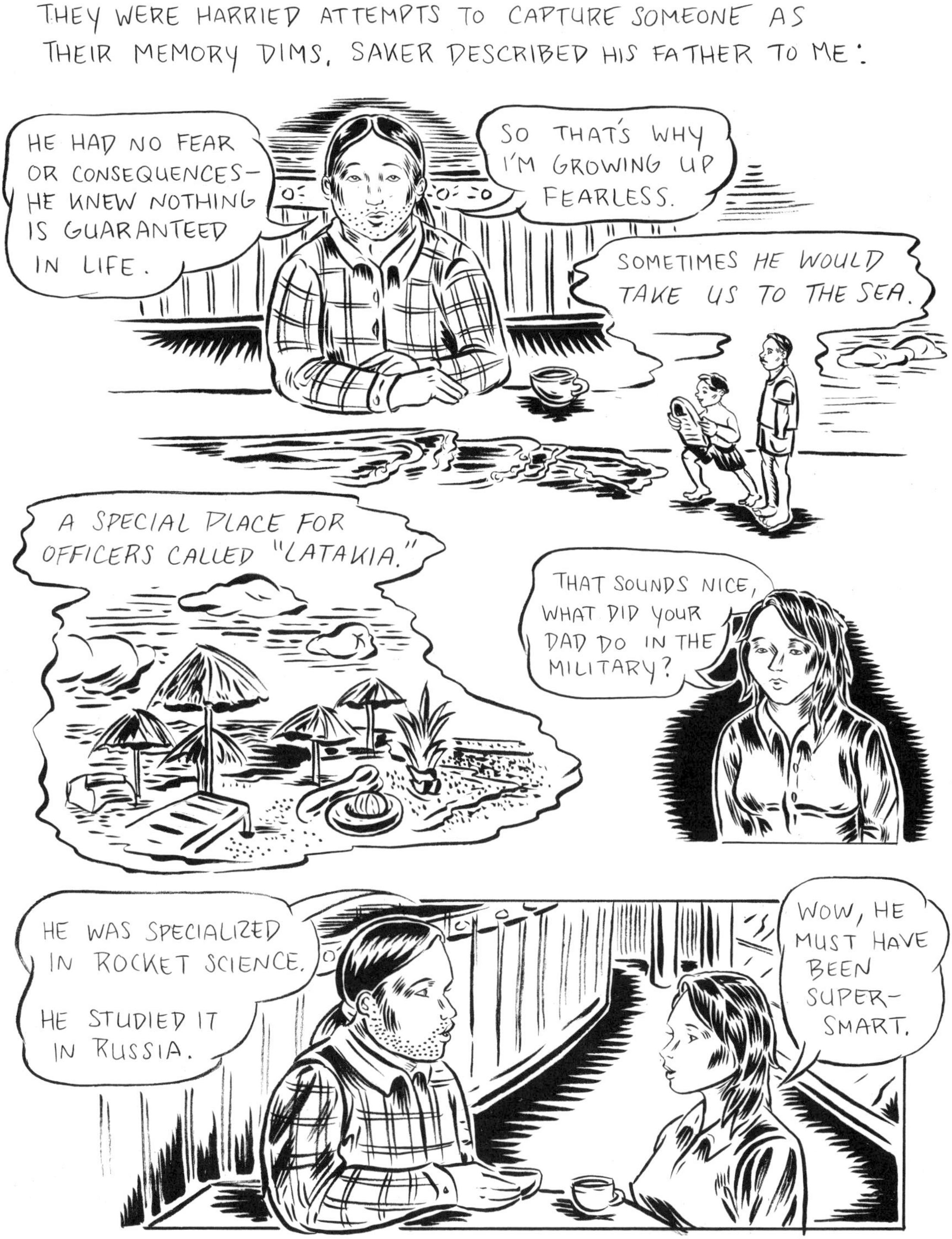
THEY WERE HARRIED ATTEMPTS TO CAPTURE SOMEONE AS THEIR MEMORY DIMS. SAKER DESCRIBED HIS FATHER TO ME:
HE HAD NO FEAR OR CONSEQUENCES— HE KNEW NOTHING IS GUARANTEED IN LIFE.
SO THAT'S WHY I'M GROWING UP FEARLESS.
SOMETIMES HE WOULD TAKE US TO THE SEA.
A SPECIAL PLACE FOR OFFICERS CALLED "LATAKIA."
THAT SOUNDS NICE, WHAT DID YOUR DAD DO IN THE MILITARY?
HE WAS SPECIALIZED IN ROCKET SCIENCE.
HE STUDIED IT IN RUSSIA.
WOW, HE MUST HAVE BEEN SUPER-SMART.

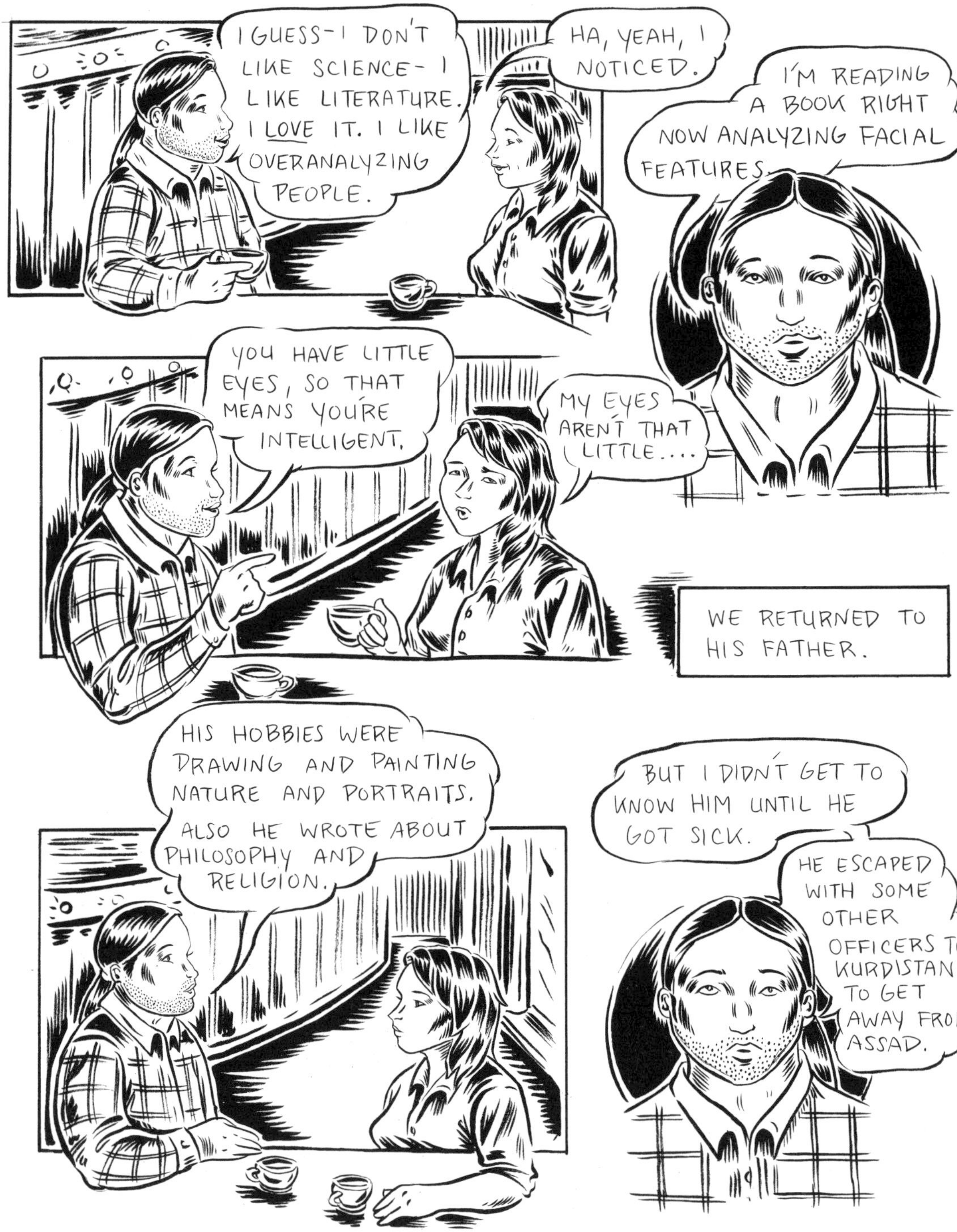
I GUESS- I DON'T LIKE SCIENCE- I LIKE LITERATURE. I LOVE IT. I LIKE OVERANALYZING PEOPLE.
HA, YEAH, I NOTICED.
I'M READING A BOOK RIGHT NOW ANALYZING FACIAL FEATURES.
YOU HAVE LITTLE EYES, SO THAT MEANS YOU'RE INTELLIGENT.
MY EYES AREN'T THAT LITTLE....
WE RETURNED TO HIS FATHER.
HIS HOBBIES WERE DRAWING AND PAINTING NATURE AND PORTRAITS.
ALSO HE WROTE ABOUT PHILOSOPHY AND RELIGION.
BUT I DIDN'T GET TO KNOW HIM UNTIL HE GOT SICK.
HE ESCAPED WITH SOME OTHER OFFICERS TO KURDISTAN - TO GET AWAY FROM ASSAD.

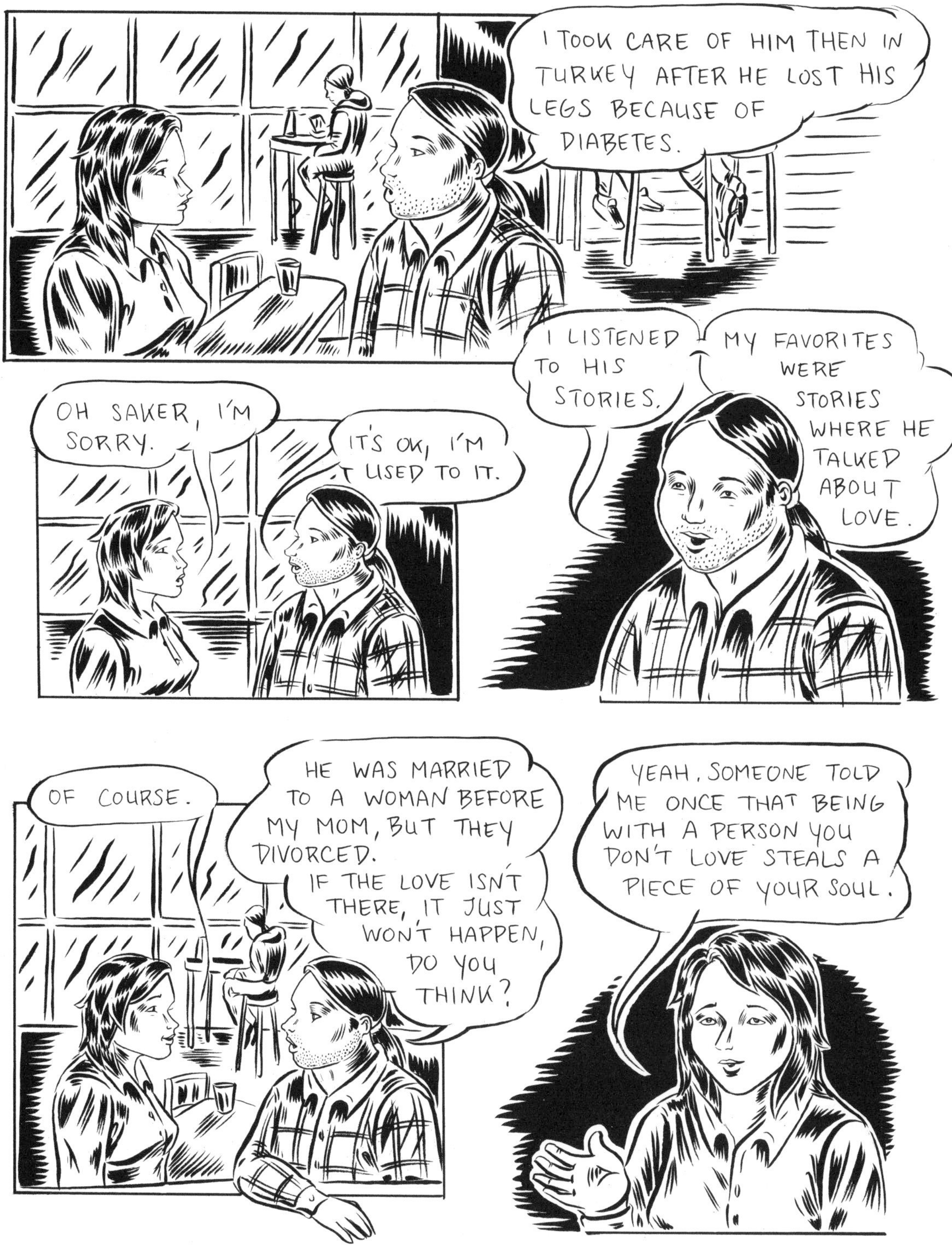
I TOOK CARE OF HIM THEN IN TURKEY AFTER HE LOST HIS LEGS BECAUSE OF DIABETES.
OH SAKER, I'M SORRY.
IT'S OK, I'M USED TO IT.
I LISTENED TO HIS STORIES.
MY FAVORITES WERE STORIES WHERE HE TALKED ABOUT LOVE.
OF COURSE.
HE WAS MARRIED TO A WOMAN BEFORE MY MOM, BUT THEY DIVORCED.
IF THE LOVE ISN'T THERE, IT JUST WON'T HAPPEN, DO YOU THINK?
YEAH, SOMEONE TOLD ME ONCE THAT BEING WITH A PERSON YOU DON'T LOVE STEALS A PIECE OF YOUR SOUL.

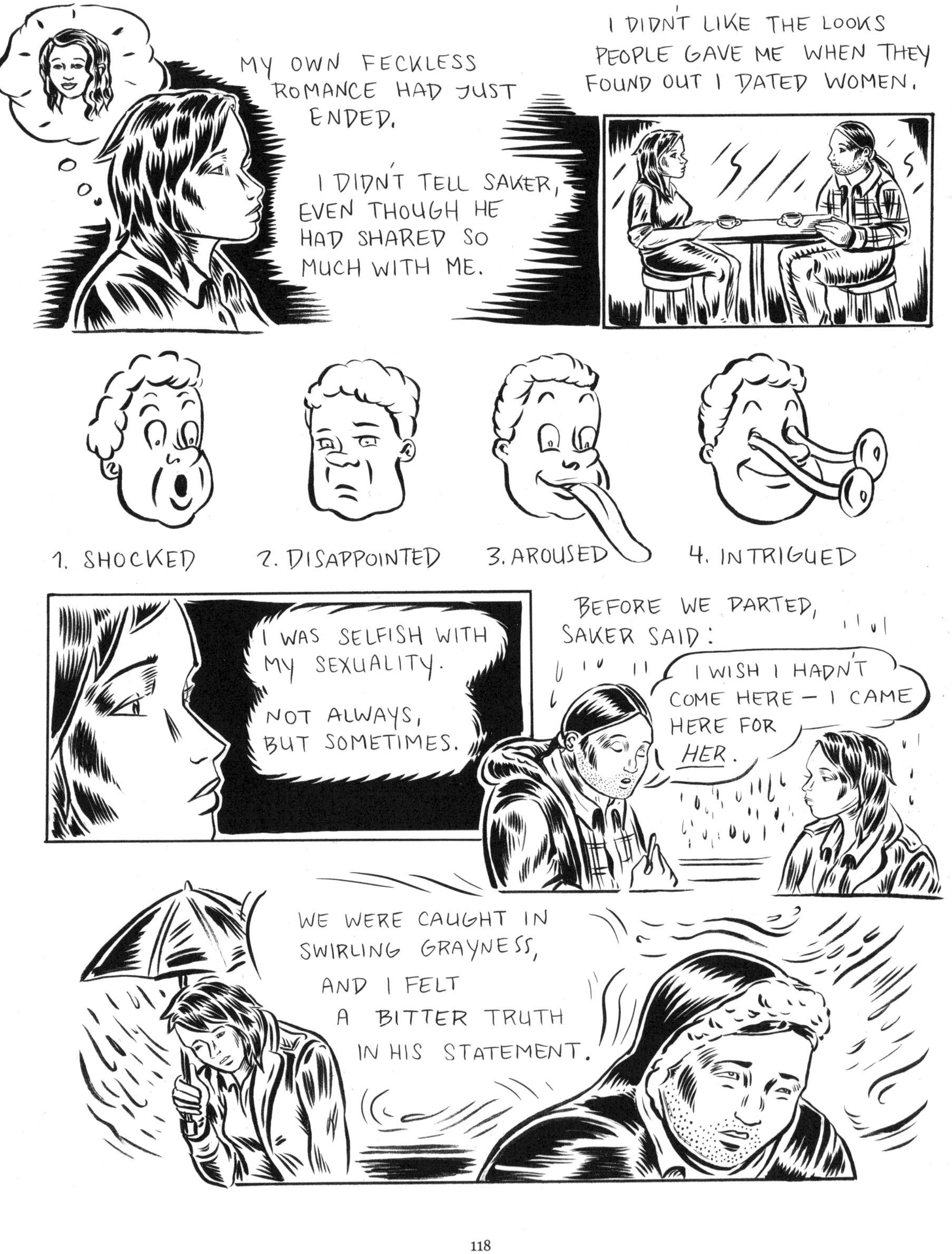
MY OWN FECKLESS ROMANCE HAD JUST ENDED.
I DIDN'T TELL SAKER, EVEN THOUGH HE HAD SHARED SO MUCH WITH ME.
I DIDN'T LIKE THE LOOKS PEOPLE GAVE ME WHEN THEY FOUND OUT I DATED WOMEN.
1. SHOCKED
2. DISAPPOINTED
3. AROUSED
4. INTRIGUED
I WAS SELFISH WITH MY SEXUALITY.
NOT ALWAYS, BUT SOMETIMES.
BEFORE WE PARTED, SAKER SAID:
I WISH I HADN'T COME HERE - I CAME HERE FOR HER.
WE WERE CAUGHT IN SWIRLING GRAYNESS,
AND I FELT A BITTER TRUTH IN HIS STATEMENT.

MICHAEL AND THE CHRISTMAS MARKET

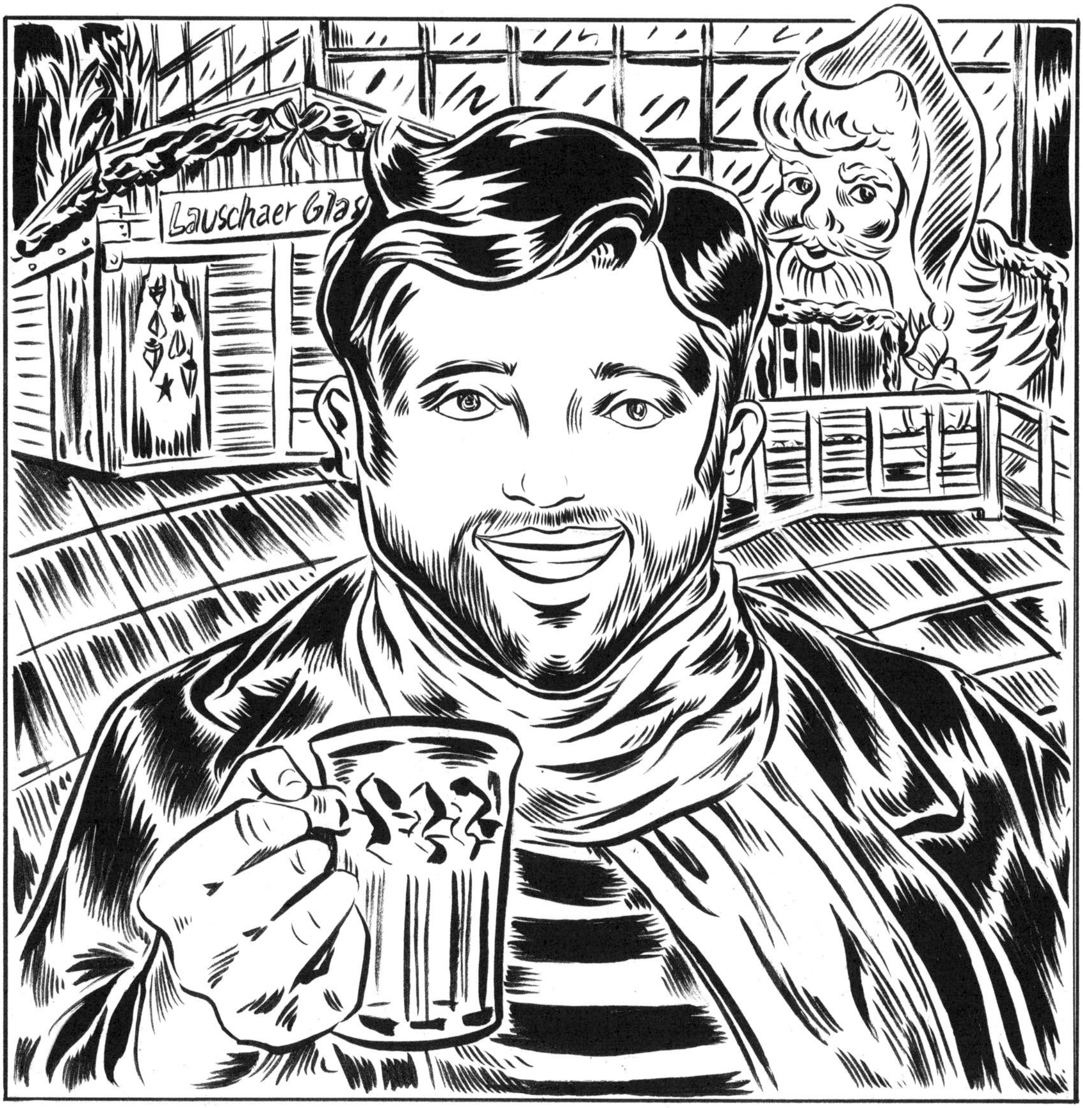
Lauschaer Glas

LIKE SAKER, MICHAEL WAS MY OCCASIONAL TRANSLATOR. I WAS THE FIRST AMERICAN HE HAD MET.

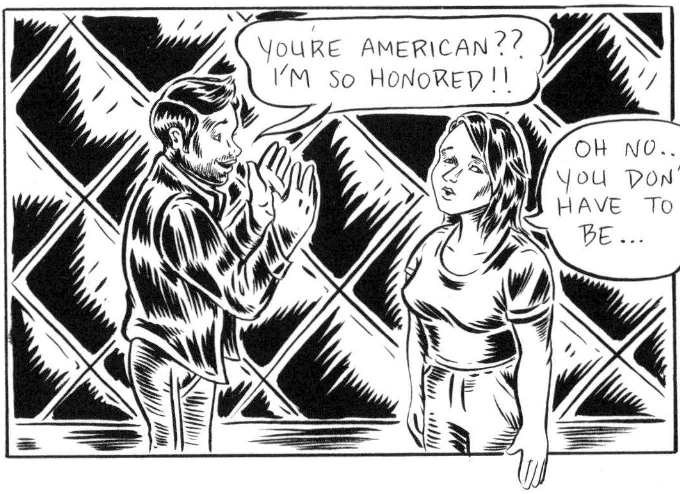
YOU'RE AMERICAN?? I'M SO HONORED!!
OH NO... YOU DON'T HAVE TO BE...

MICHAEL'S ENGLISH HAD BEEN HONED ENTIRELY FROM POP MUSIC AND T.V. SO HE HAD A CUTE TWANG.

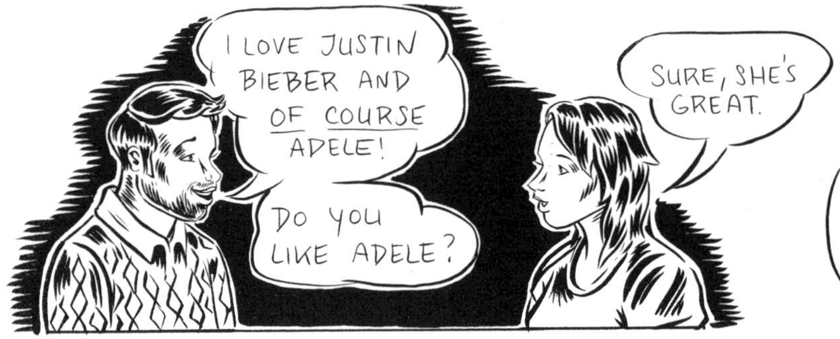
I LOVE JUSTIN BIEBER AND OF COURSE ADELE!
DO YOU LIKE ADELE?
SURE, SHE'S GREAT.

HIS FAVORITE T.V. SHOW WAS *NARUTO*.

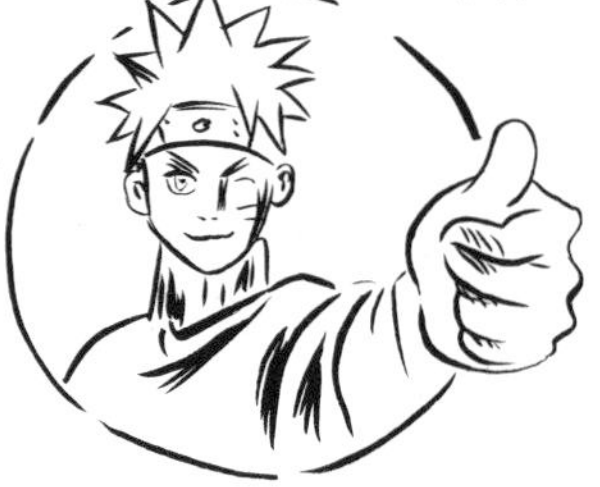

AS MUCH AS HE HELPED ME, MICHAEL RARELY PARTICIPATED HIMSELF.

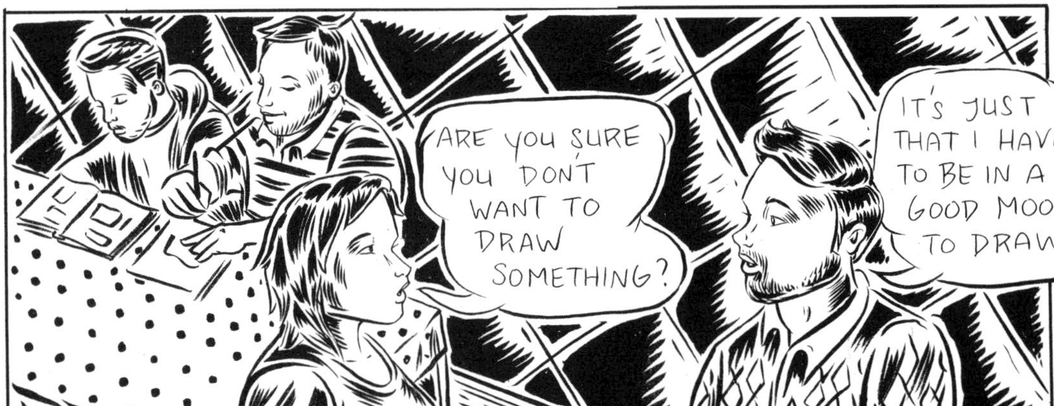
ARE YOU SURE YOU DON'T WANT TO DRAW SOMETHING?
IT'S JUST THAT I HAVE TO BE IN A GOOD MOOD TO DRAW...

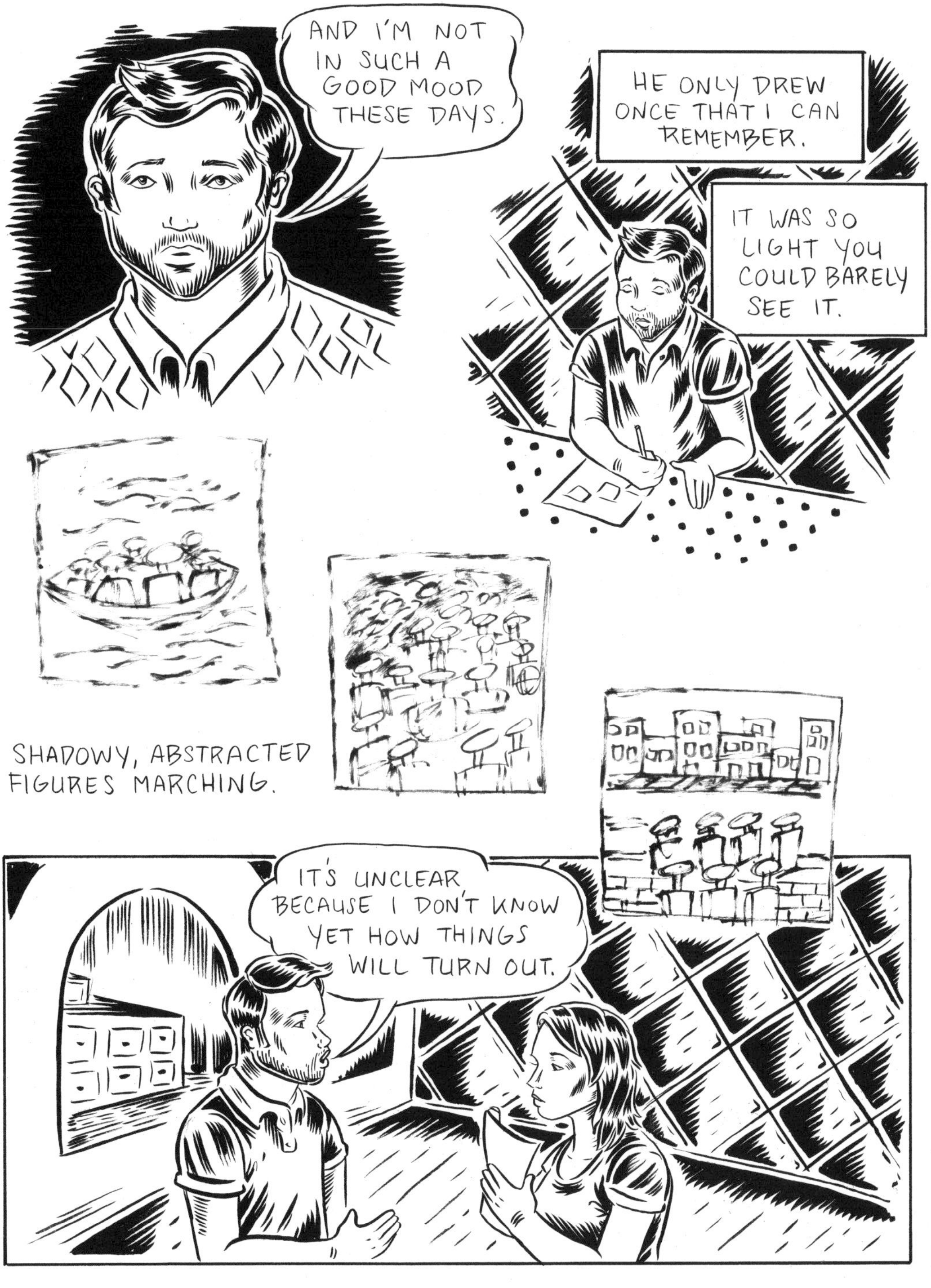
AND I'M NOT IN SUCH A GOOD MOOD THESE DAYS.
HE ONLY DREW ONCE THAT I CAN REMEMBER.
IT WAS SO LIGHT YOU COULD BARELY SEE IT.
SHADOWY, ABSTRACTED FIGURES MARCHING.
IT'S UNCLEAR BECAUSE I DON'T KNOW YET HOW THINGS WILL TURN OUT.

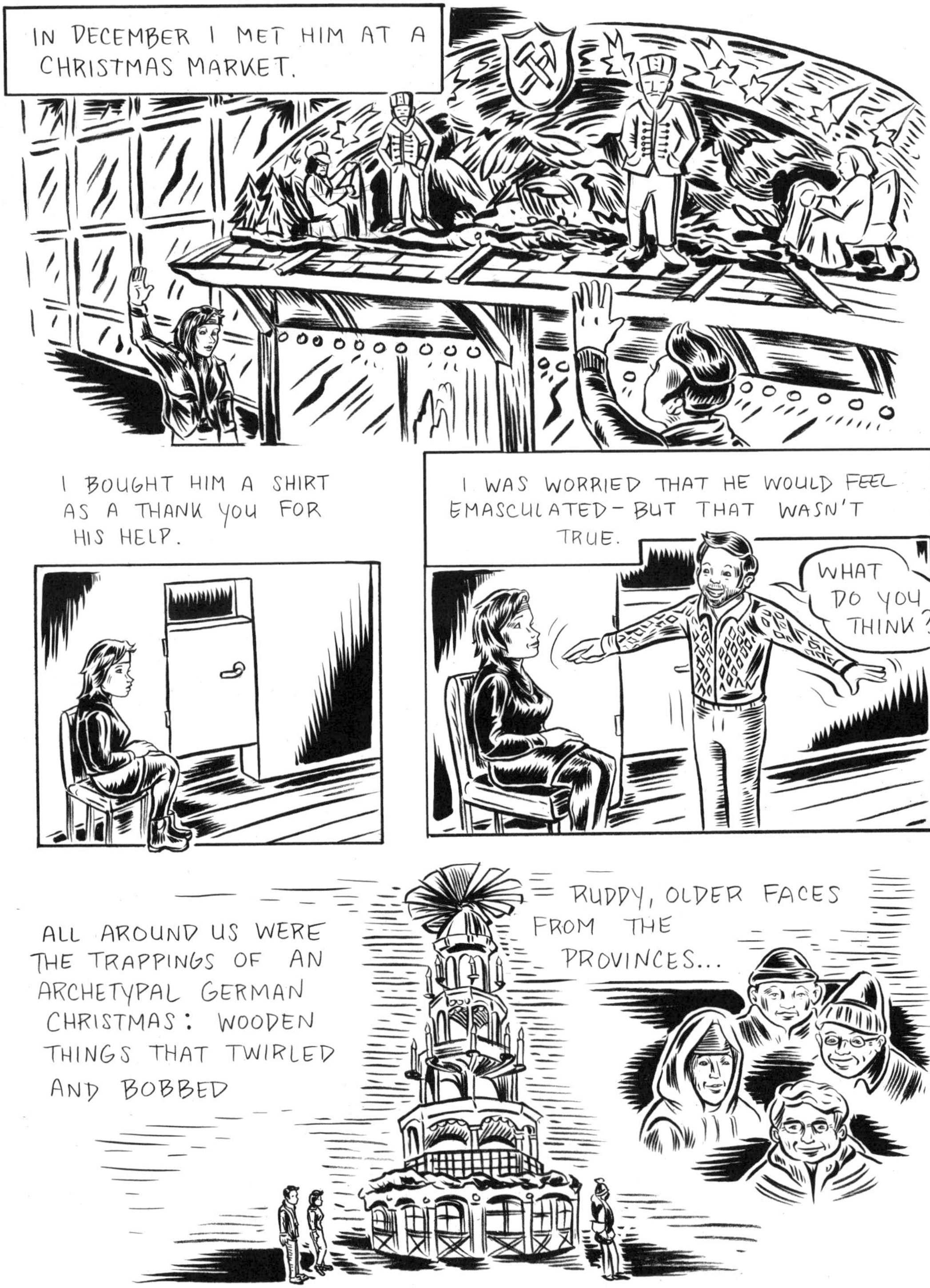
IN DECEMBER I MET HIM AT A CHRISTMAS MARKET.
I BOUGHT HIM A SHIRT AS A THANK YOU FOR HIS HELP.
I WAS WORRIED THAT HE WOULD FEEL EMASCULATED - BUT THAT WASN'T TRUE.
WHAT DO YOU THINK?
ALL AROUND US WERE THE TRAPPINGS OF AN ARCHETYPAL GERMAN CHRISTMAS: WOODEN THINGS THAT TWIRLED AND BOBBED
RUDDY, OLDER FACES FROM THE PROVINCES...

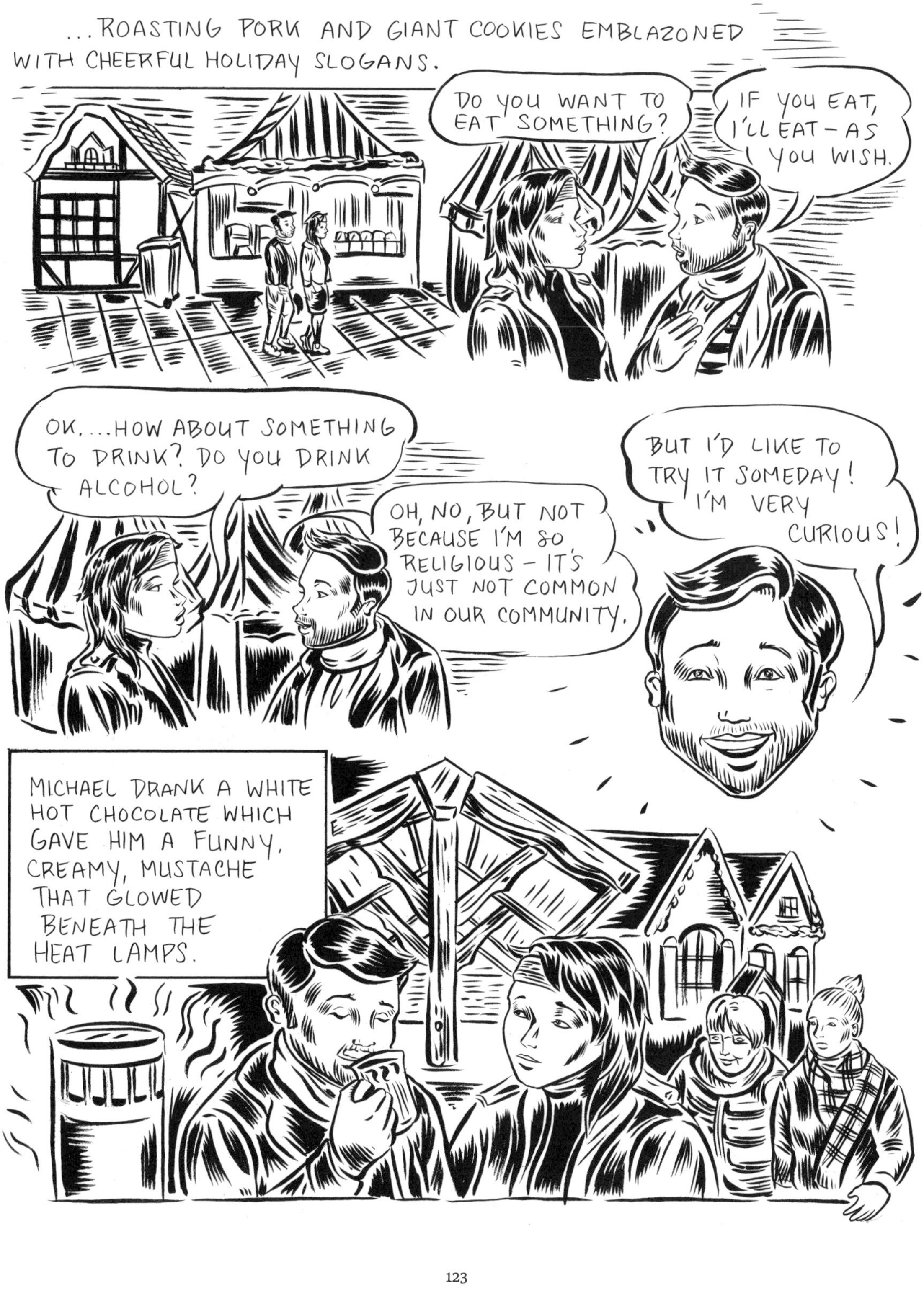
...ROASTING PORK AND GIANT COOKIES EMBLAZONED WITH CHEERFUL HOLIDAY SLOGANS.
DO YOU WANT TO EAT SOMETHING?
IF YOU EAT, I'LL EAT - AS YOU WISH.
OK, ...HOW ABOUT SOMETHING TO DRINK? DO YOU DRINK ALCOHOL?
OH, NO, BUT NOT BECAUSE I'M SO RELIGIOUS - IT'S JUST NOT COMMON IN OUR COMMUNITY.
BUT I'D LIKE TO TRY IT SOMEDAY! I'M VERY CURIOUS!
MICHAEL DRANK A WHITE HOT CHOCOLATE WHICH GAVE HIM A FUNNY, CREAMY, MUSTACHE THAT GLOWED BENEATH THE HEAT LAMPS.

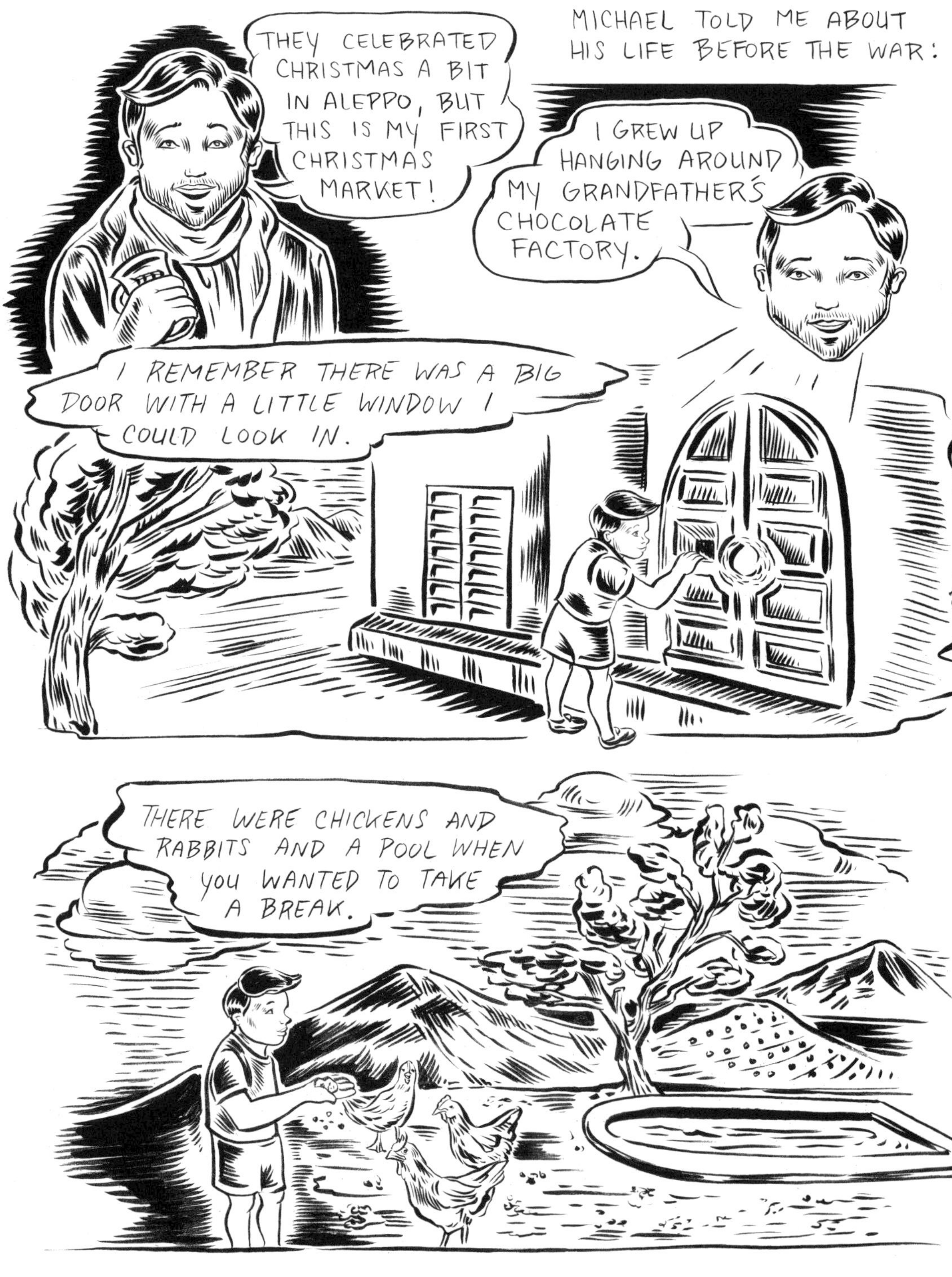
THEY CELEBRATED CHRISTMAS A BIT IN ALEPPO, BUT THIS IS MY FIRST CHRISTMAS MARKET!
MICHAEL TOLD ME ABOUT HIS LIFE BEFORE THE WAR:
I GREW UP HANGING AROUND MY GRANDFATHER'S CHOCOLATE FACTORY.
I REMEMBER THERE WAS A BIG DOOR WITH A LITTLE WINDOW I COULD LOOK IN.
THERE WERE CHICKENS AND RABBITS AND A POOL WHEN YOU WANTED TO TAKE A BREAK.

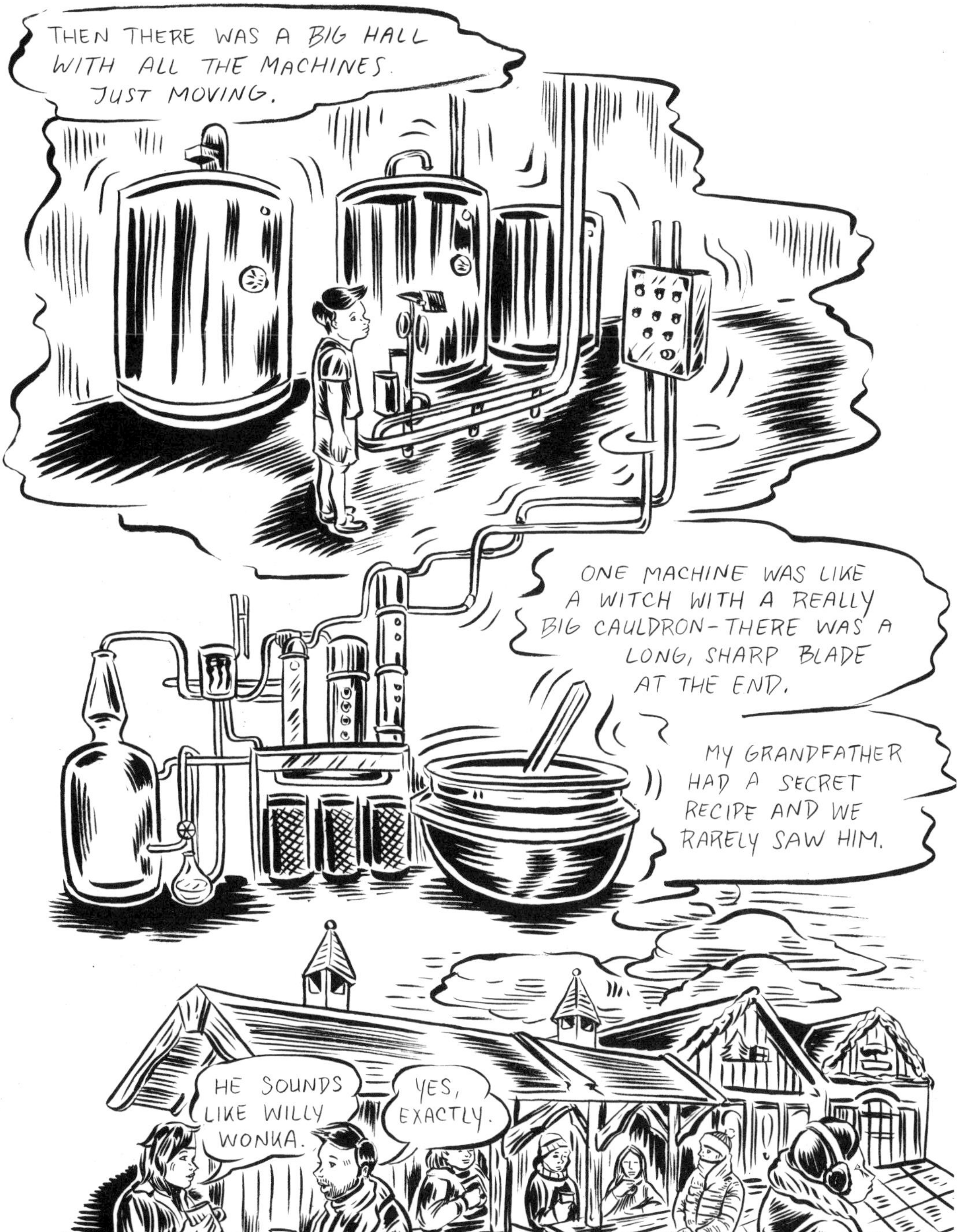
THEN THERE WAS A BIG HALL WITH ALL THE MACHINES JUST MOVING.
ONE MACHINE WAS LIKE A WITCH WITH A REALLY BIG CAULDRON- THERE WAS A LONG, SHARP BLADE AT THE END.
MY GRANDFATHER HAD A SECRET RECIPE AND WE RARELY SAW HIM.
HE SOUNDS LIKE WILLY WONKA.
YES, EXACTLY.

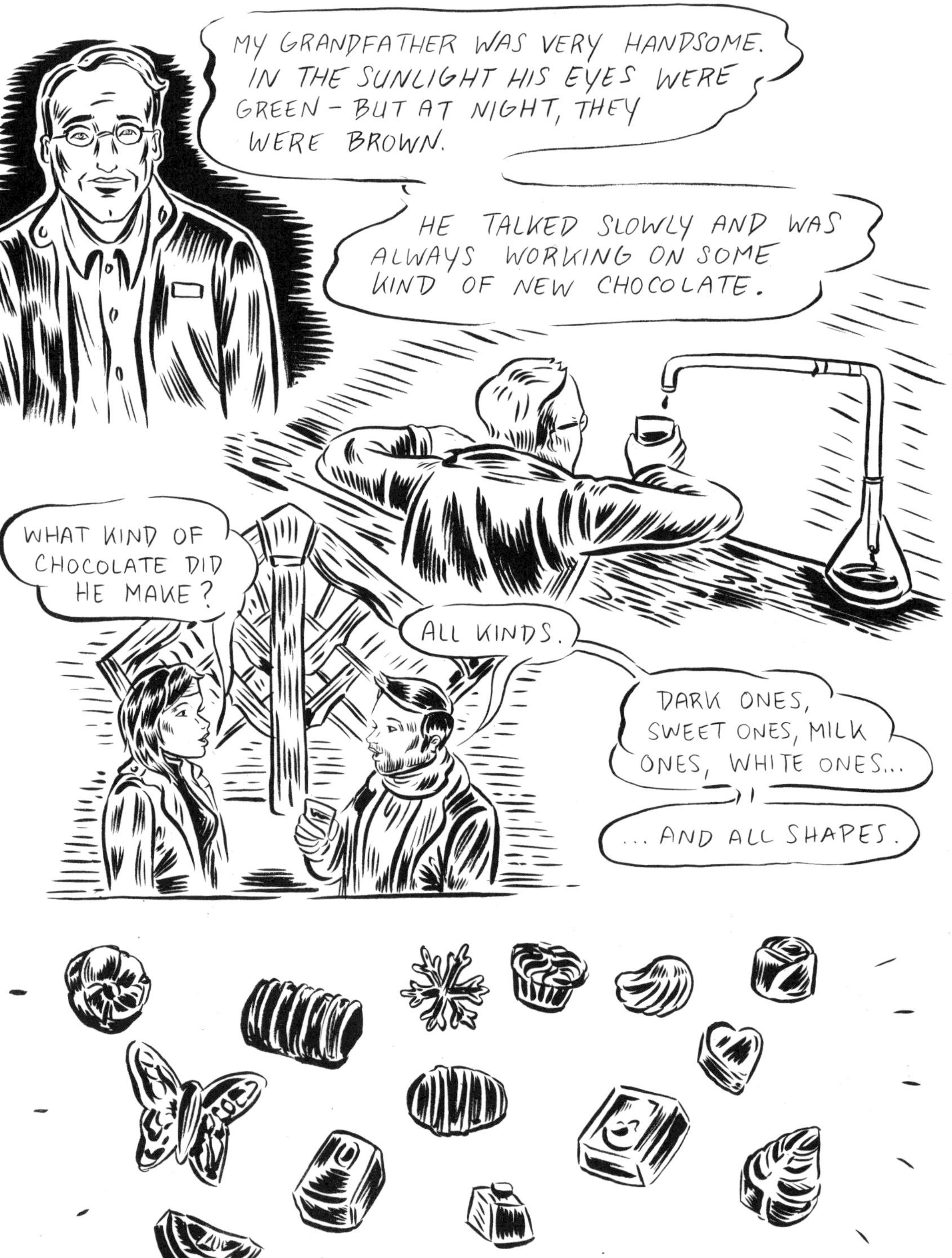
MY GRANDFATHER WAS VERY HANDSOME. IN THE SUNLIGHT HIS EYES WERE GREEN - BUT AT NIGHT, THEY WERE BROWN.
HE TALKED SLOWLY AND WAS ALWAYS WORKING ON SOME KIND OF NEW CHOCOLATE.
WHAT KIND OF CHOCOLATE DID HE MAKE?
ALL KINDS.
DARK ONES, SWEET ONES, MILK ONES, WHITE ONES...
... AND ALL SHAPES.

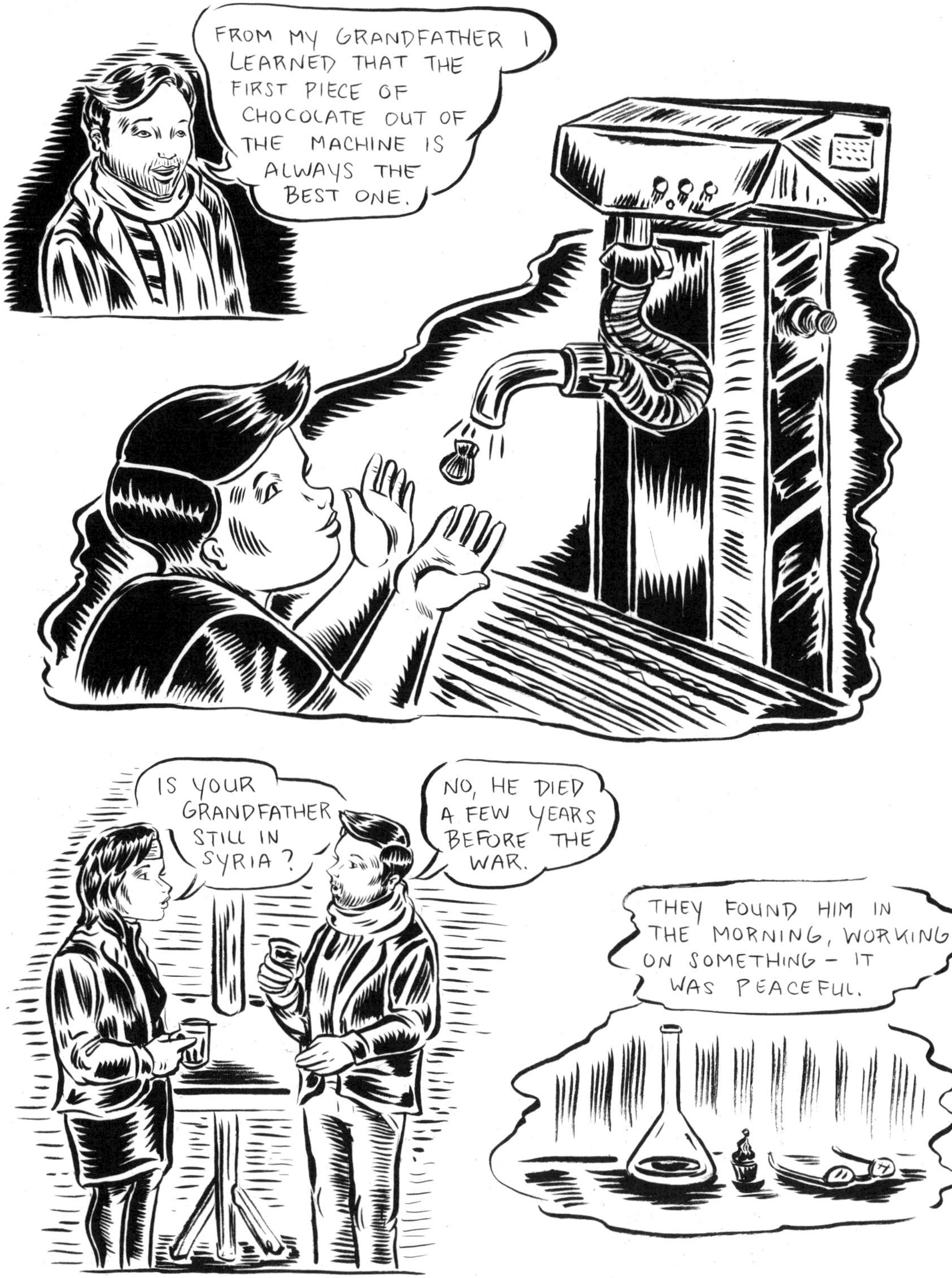
FROM MY GRANDFATHER I LEARNED THAT THE FIRST PIECE OF CHOCOLATE OUT OF THE MACHINE IS ALWAYS THE BEST ONE.
IS YOUR GRANDFATHER STILL IN SYRIA?
NO, HE DIED A FEW YEARS BEFORE THE WAR.
THEY FOUND HIM IN THE MORNING, WORKING ON SOMETHING - IT WAS PEACEFUL.

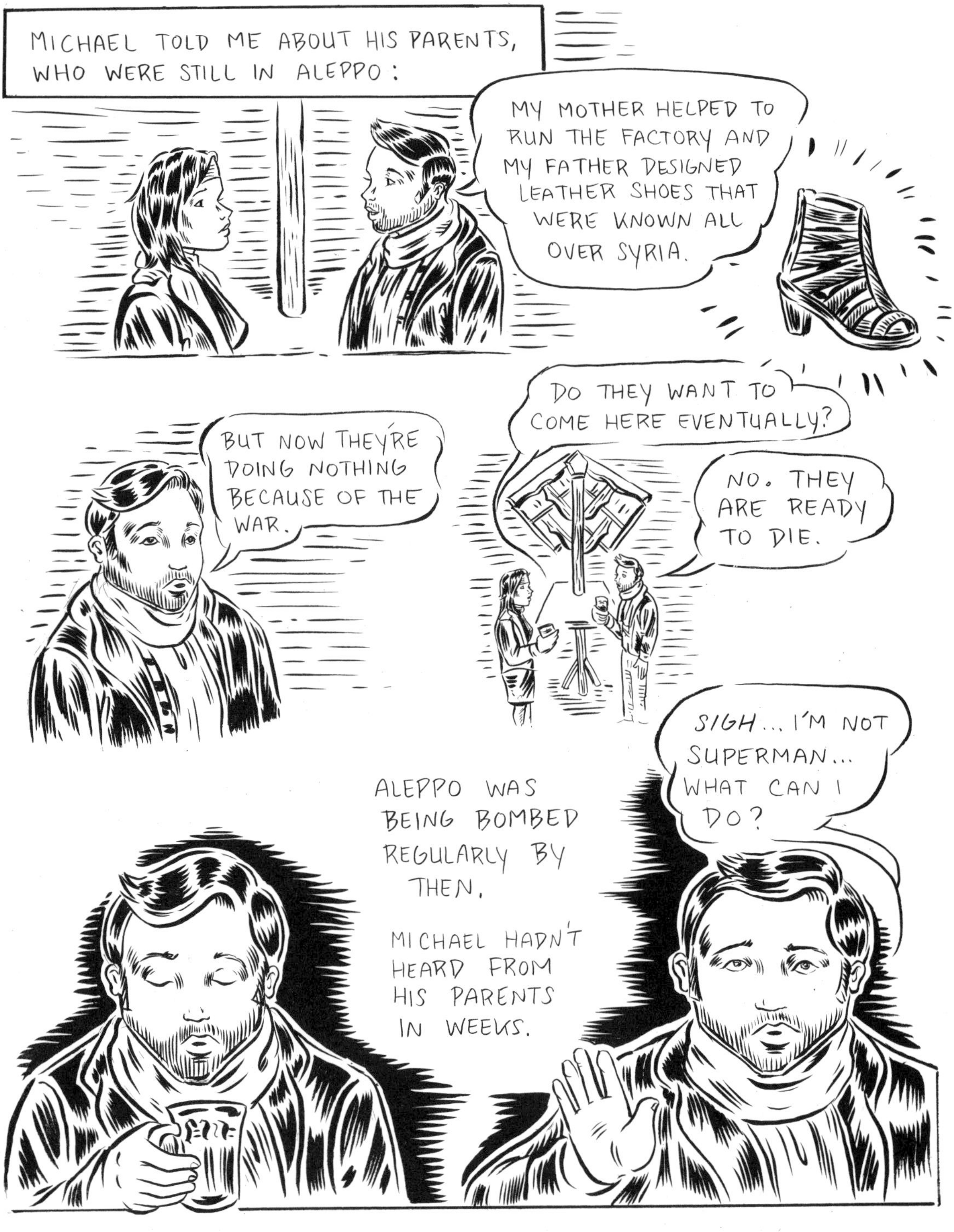
MICHAEL TOLD ME ABOUT HIS PARENTS, WHO WERE STILL IN ALEPPO:
MY MOTHER HELPED TO RUN THE FACTORY AND MY FATHER DESIGNED LEATHER SHOES THAT WERE KNOWN ALL OVER SYRIA.
BUT NOW THEY'RE DOING NOTHING BECAUSE OF THE WAR.
DO THEY WANT TO COME HERE EVENTUALLY?
NO. THEY ARE READY TO DIE.
ALEPPO WAS BEING BOMBED REGULARLY BY THEN.
MICHAEL HADN'T HEARD FROM HIS PARENTS IN WEEKS.
SIGH... I'M NOT SUPERMAN... WHAT CAN I DO?

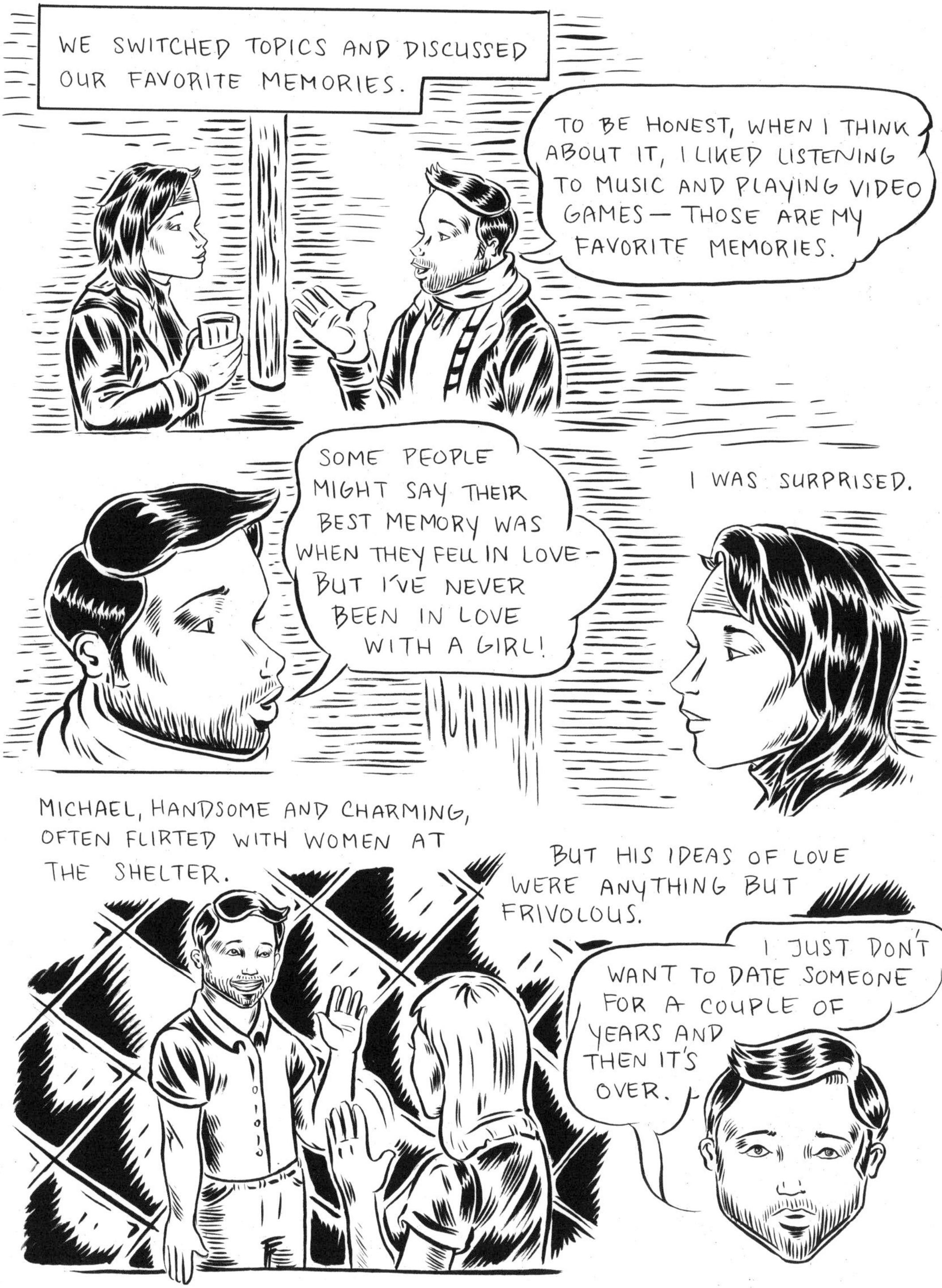
WE SWITCHED TOPICS AND DISCUSSED OUR FAVORITE MEMORIES.
TO BE HONEST, WHEN I THINK ABOUT IT, I LIKED LISTENING TO MUSIC AND PLAYING VIDEO GAMES— THOSE ARE MY FAVORITE MEMORIES.
SOME PEOPLE MIGHT SAY THEIR BEST MEMORY WAS WHEN THEY FELL IN LOVE— BUT I'VE NEVER BEEN IN LOVE WITH A GIRL!
I WAS SURPRISED.
MICHAEL, HANDSOME AND CHARMING, OFTEN FLIRTED WITH WOMEN AT THE SHELTER.
BUT HIS IDEAS OF LOVE WERE ANYTHING BUT FRIVOLOUS.
I JUST DON'T WANT TO DATE SOMEONE FOR A COUPLE OF YEARS AND THEN IT'S OVER.

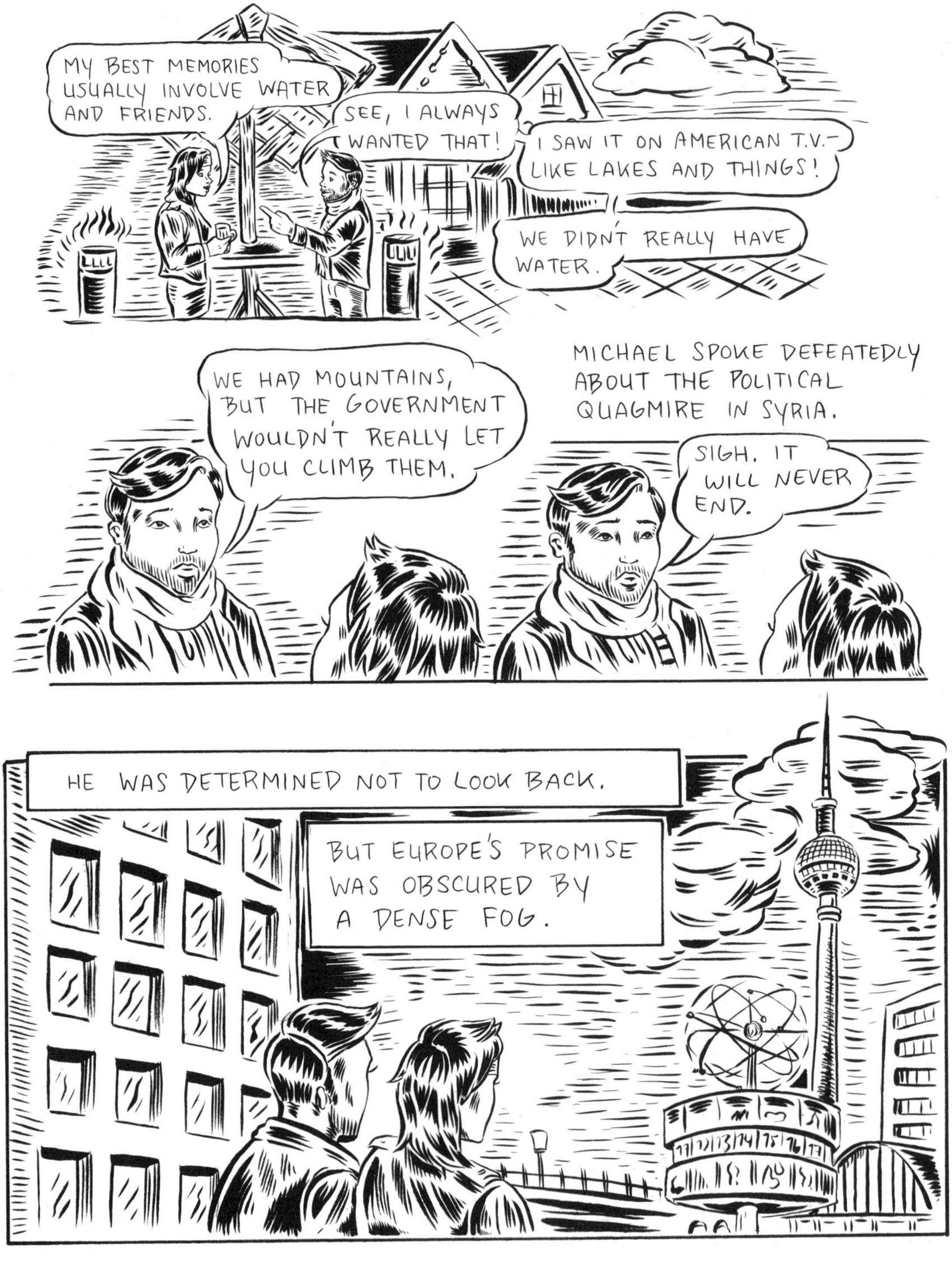
MY BEST MEMORIES USUALLY INVOLVE WATER AND FRIENDS.
SEE, I ALWAYS WANTED THAT!
I SAW IT ON AMERICAN T.V.– LIKE LAKES AND THINGS!
WE DIDN'T REALLY HAVE WATER.
WE HAD MOUNTAINS, BUT THE GOVERNMENT WOULDN'T REALLY LET YOU CLIMB THEM.
MICHAEL SPOKE DEFEATEDLY ABOUT THE POLITICAL QUAGMIRE IN SYRIA.
SIGH. IT WILL NEVER END.
HE WAS DETERMINED NOT TO LOOK BACK.
BUT EUROPE'S PROMISE WAS OBSCURED BY A DENSE FOG.

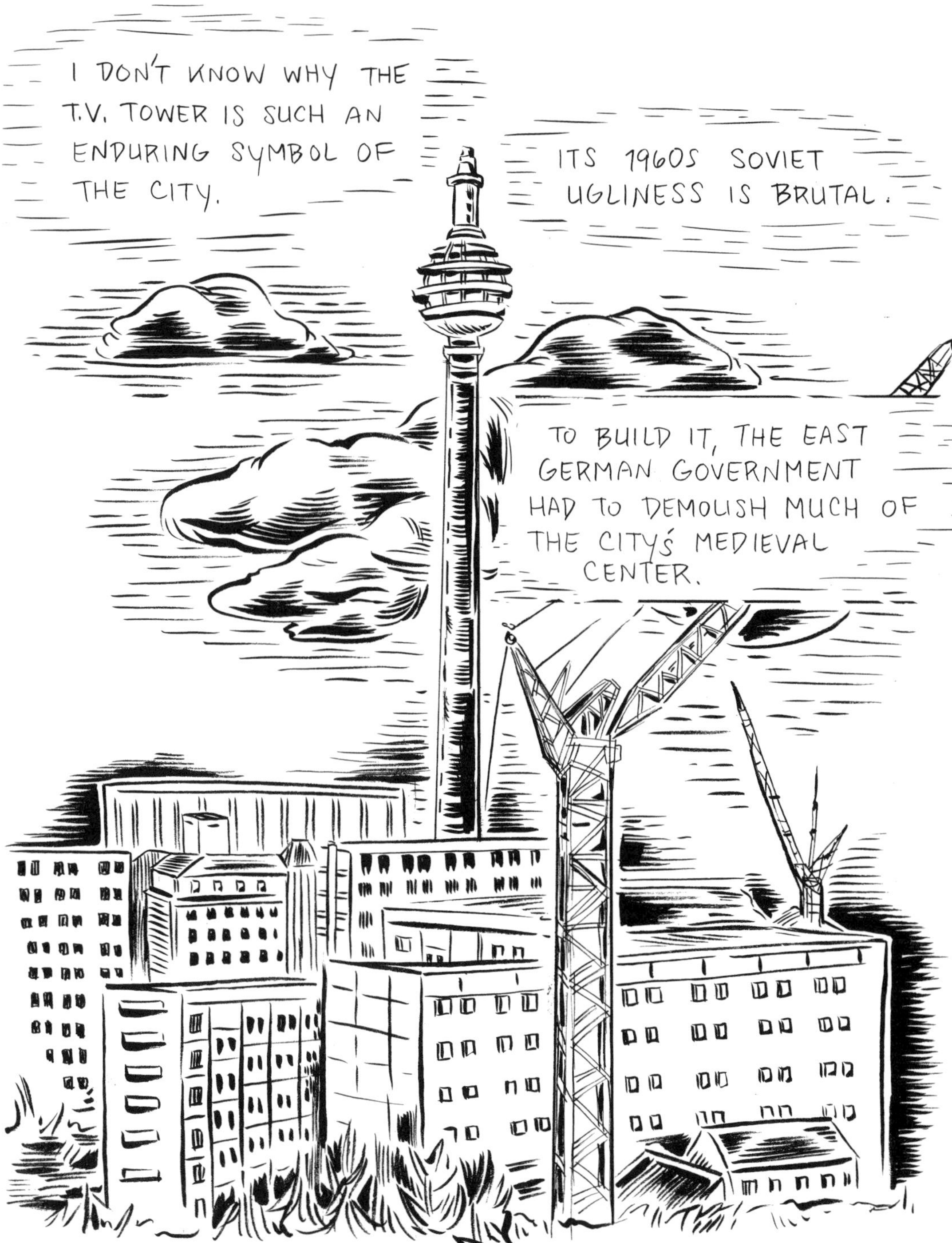
I DON'T KNOW WHY THE T.V. TOWER IS SUCH AN ENDURING SYMBOL OF THE CITY.
ITS 1960S SOVIET UGLINESS IS BRUTAL.
TO BUILD IT, THE EAST GERMAN GOVERNMENT HAD TO DEMOLISH MUCH OF THE CITY'S MEDIEVAL CENTER.

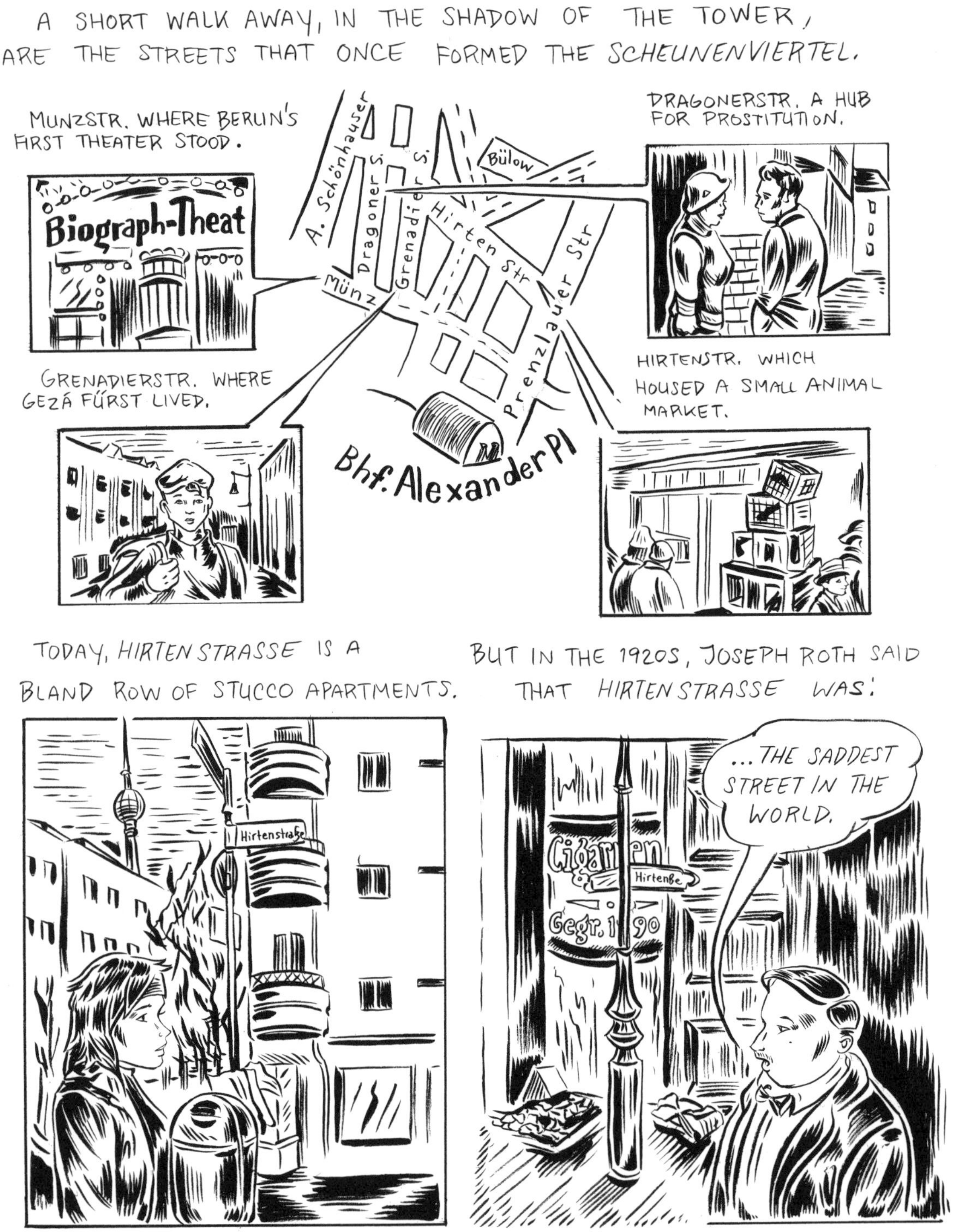
A SHORT WALK AWAY, IN THE SHADOW OF THE TOWER, ARE THE STREETS THAT ONCE FORMED THE SCHEUNENVIERTEL.
MUNZSTR. WHERE BERLIN'S FIRST THEATER STOOD.
Biograph-Theat
A. Schönhauser
Dragoner S.
Grenadier S.
Bülow
Hirten Str
Prenzlauer Str
Münz
Bhf. Alexander Pl
DRAGONERSTR. A HUB FOR PROSTITUTION.
GRENADIERSTR. WHERE GEZÁ FŰRST LIVED.
HIRTENSTR. WHICH HOUSED A SMALL ANIMAL MARKET.
TODAY, HIRTENSTRASSE IS A BLAND ROW OF STUCCO APARTMENTS.
Hirtenstraße
BUT IN THE 1920S, JOSEPH ROTH SAID THAT HIRTENSTRASSE WAS:
...THE SADDEST STREET IN THE WORLD.

PERIL OF THE EAST (PART 2)

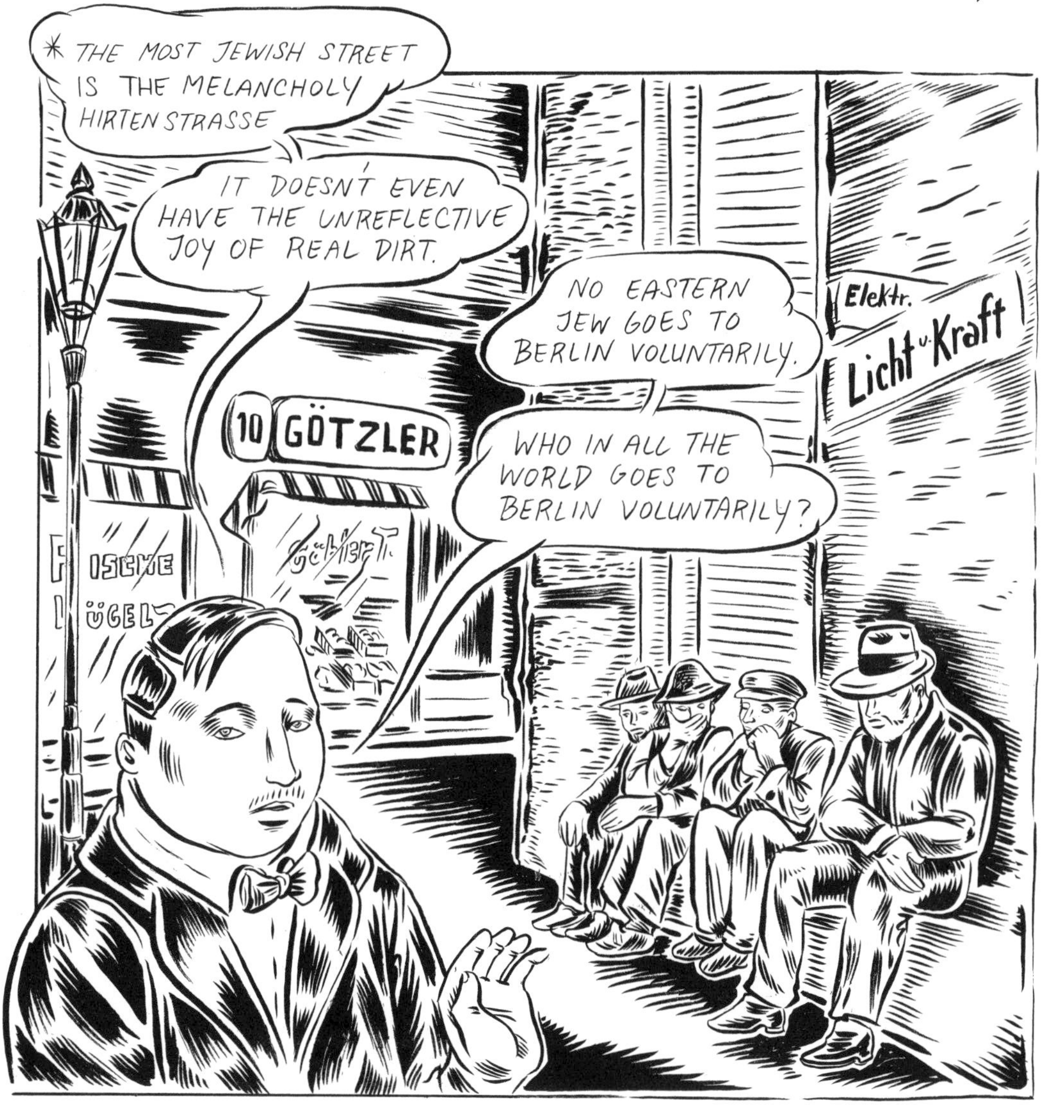
* THE MOST JEWISH STREET IS THE MELANCHOLY HIRTENSTRASSE
IT DOESN'T EVEN HAVE THE UNREFLECTIVE JOY OF REAL DIRT.
NO EASTERN JEW GOES TO BERLIN VOLUNTARILY.
WHO IN ALL THE WORLD GOES TO BERLIN VOLUNTARILY?
Elektr. Licht u. Kraft
10 GÖTZLER

* FROM THE WANDERING JEWS

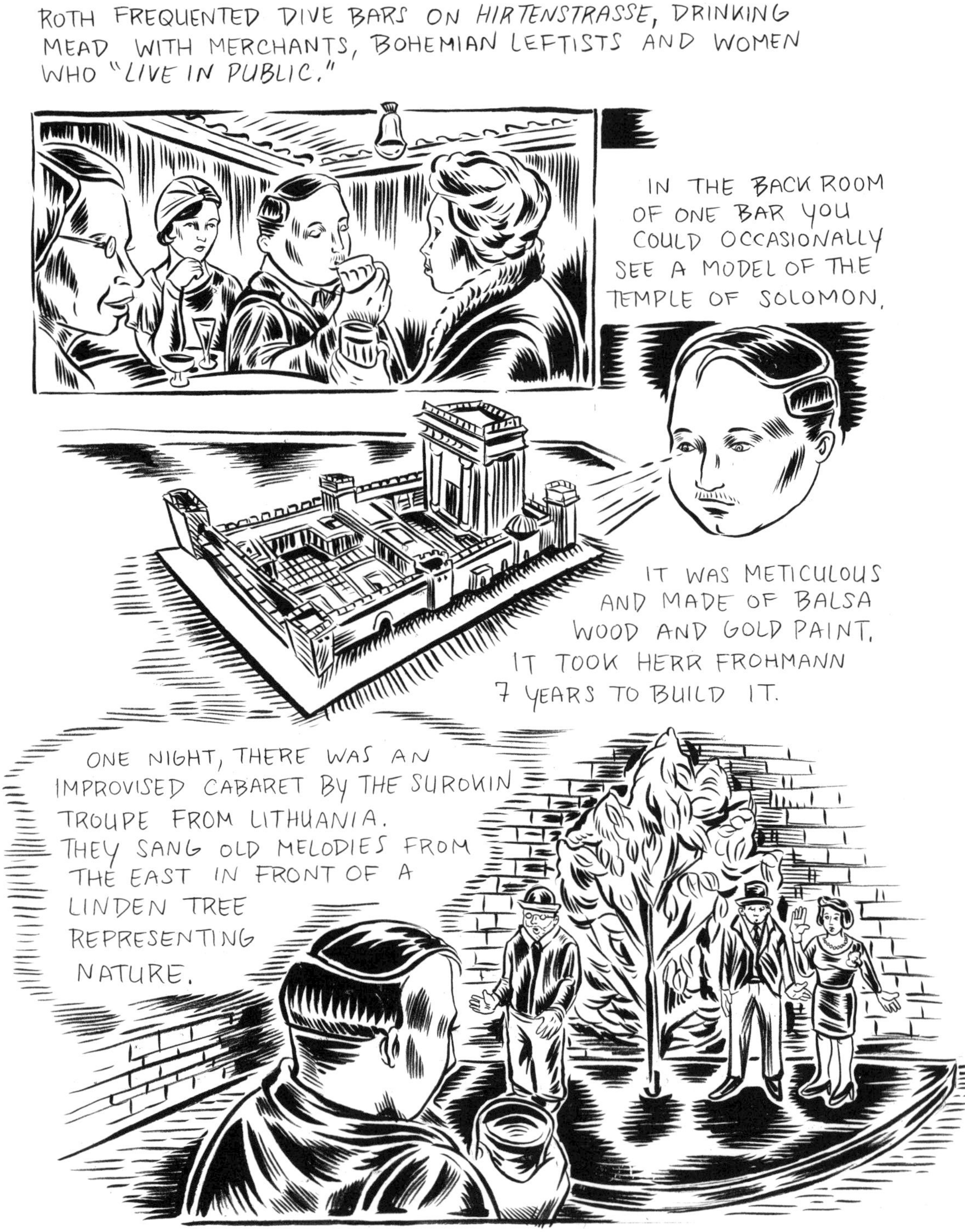
ROTH FREQUENTED DIVE BARS ON *HIRTENSTRASSE*, DRINKING MEAD WITH MERCHANTS, BOHEMIAN LEFTISTS AND WOMEN WHO "*LIVE IN PUBLIC.*"
IN THE BACK ROOM OF ONE BAR YOU COULD OCCASIONALLY SEE A MODEL OF THE TEMPLE OF SOLOMON.
IT WAS METICULOUS AND MADE OF BALSA WOOD AND GOLD PAINT.
IT TOOK HERR FROHMANN 7 YEARS TO BUILD IT.
ONE NIGHT, THERE WAS AN IMPROVISED CABARET BY THE SUROKIN TROUPE FROM LITHUANIA.
THEY SANG OLD MELODIES FROM THE EAST IN FRONT OF A LINDEN TREE REPRESENTING NATURE.

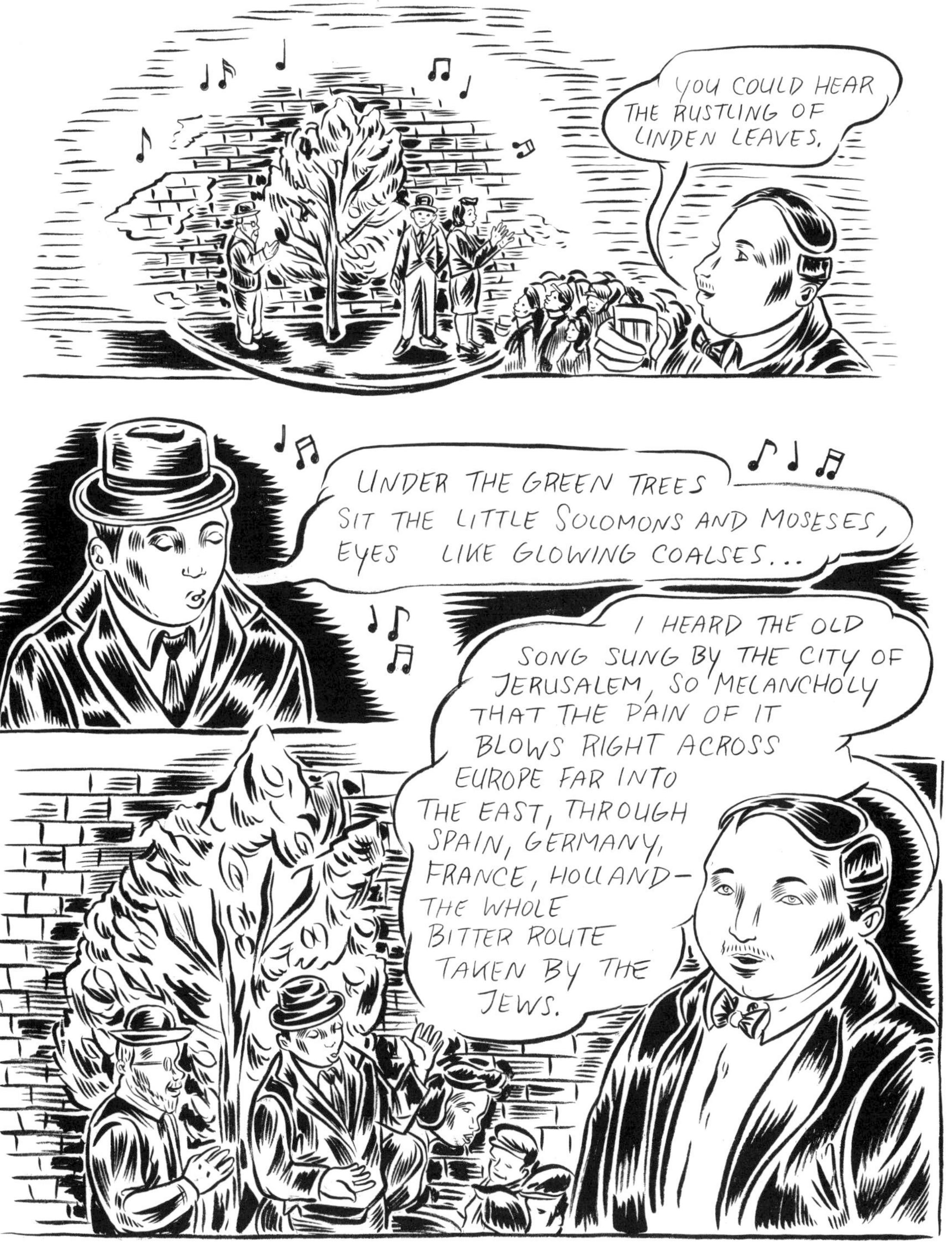
YOU COULD HEAR THE RUSTLING OF LINDEN LEAVES.
UNDER THE GREEN TREES SIT THE LITTLE SOLOMONS AND MOSESES, EYES LIKE GLOWING COALSES...
I HEARD THE OLD SONG SUNG BY THE CITY OF JERUSALEM, SO MELANCHOLY THAT THE PAIN OF IT BLOWS RIGHT ACROSS EUROPE FAR INTO THE EAST, THROUGH SPAIN, GERMANY, FRANCE, HOLLAND— THE WHOLE BITTER ROUTE TAKEN BY THE JEWS.

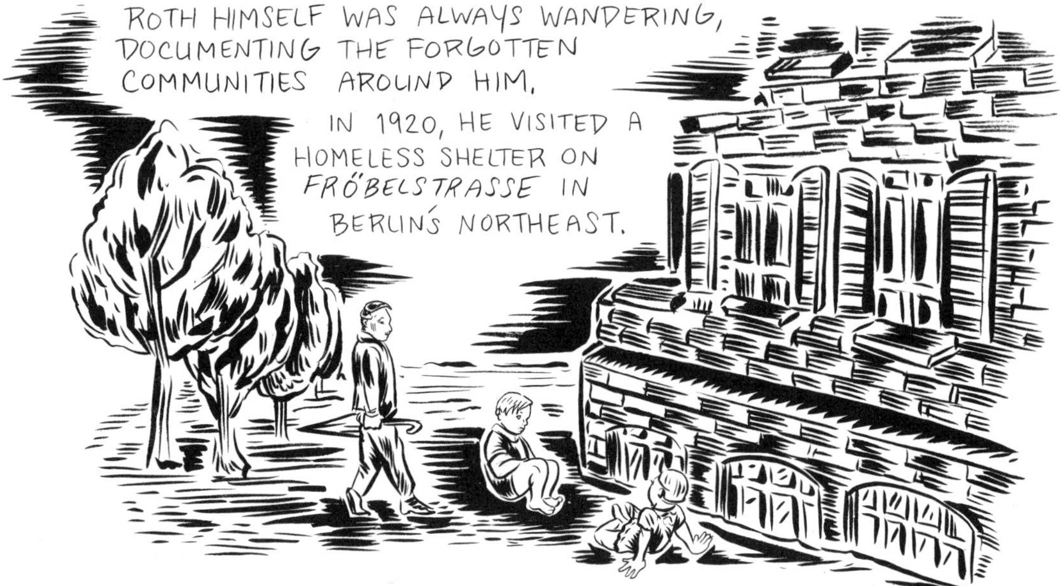
ROTH HIMSELF WAS ALWAYS WANDERING, DOCUMENTING THE FORGOTTEN COMMUNITIES AROUND HIM.
IN 1920, HE VISITED A HOMELESS SHELTER ON *FRÖBELSTRASSE* IN BERLIN'S NORTHEAST.

THE PEOPLE THERE WERE REFUGEES FROM PRUSSIA, THE RHINELAND AND HOLSTEIN. HE DESCRIBED THE CHILDREN:

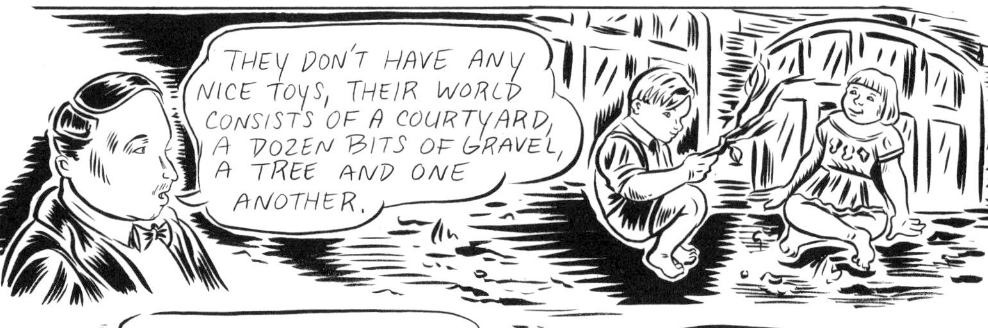
THEY DON'T HAVE ANY NICE TOYS, THEIR WORLD CONSISTS OF A COURTYARD, A DOZEN BITS OF GRAVEL, A TREE AND ONE ANOTHER.

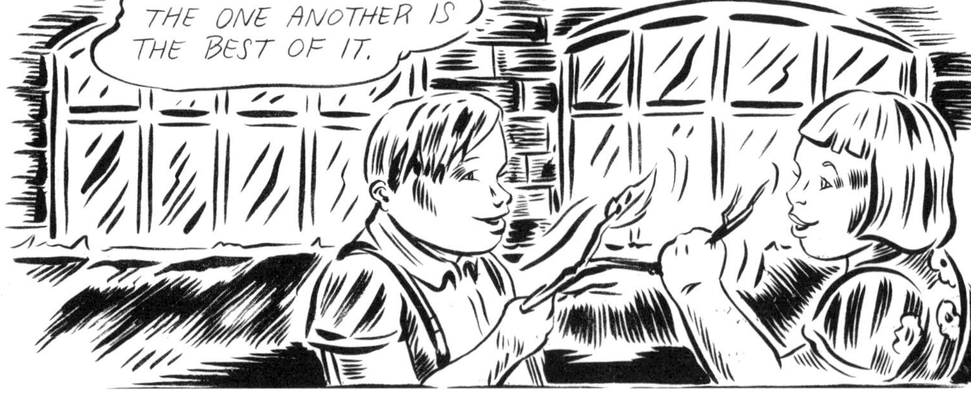
THE ONE ANOTHER IS THE BEST OF IT.

THE SHELTER WAS CALLED "THE PALMS" BECAUSE OF A PALM TREE NEAR ITS ENTRANCE.

ROTH DESCRIBED A POPULATION IN FLUX:

"SOME OF THESE PEOPLE HAVE WALKED ALL THEIR LIVES."

THE ARTIST KÄTHE KOLLWITZ MADE A LITHOGRAPH DEPICTING A WEARY FAMILY AT THE PALMS IN 1926.

ANOTHER ARTIST, WILLIBALD KRAIN, DREW MEN WAITING IN A SNAKING LINE FOR ROOMS IN 1925.

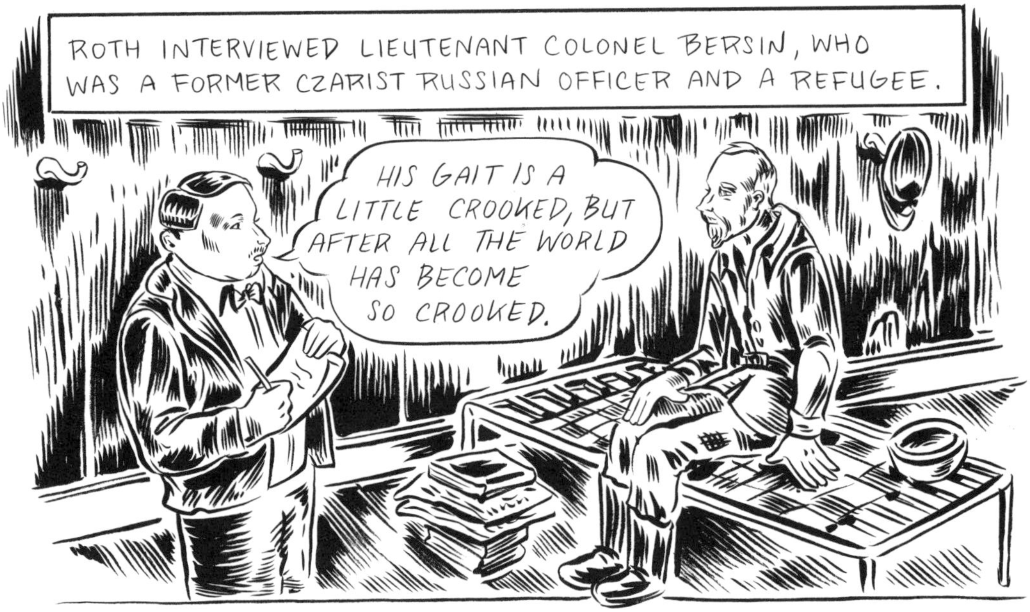
ROTH INTERVIEWED LIEUTENANT COLONEL BERSIN, WHO WAS A FORMER CZARIST RUSSIAN OFFICER AND A REFUGEE.
HIS GAIT IS A LITTLE CROOKED, BUT AFTER ALL THE WORLD HAS BECOME SO CROOKED.

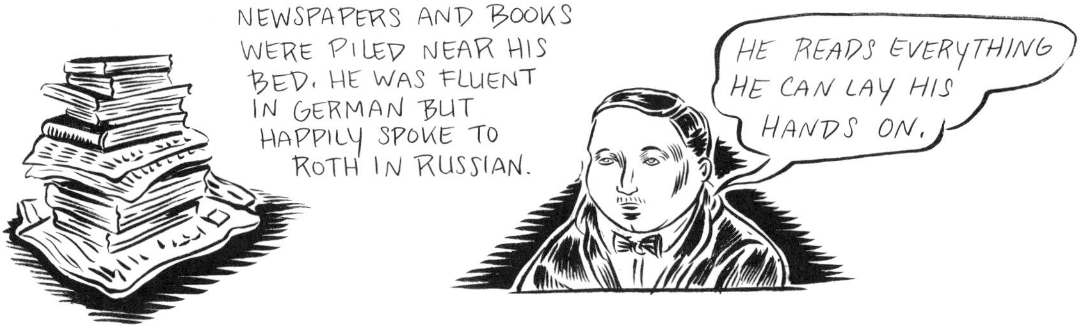
NEWSPAPERS AND BOOKS WERE PILED NEAR HIS BED. HE WAS FLUENT IN GERMAN BUT HAPPILY SPOKE TO ROTH IN RUSSIAN.
HE READS EVERYTHING HE CAN LAY HIS HANDS ON.

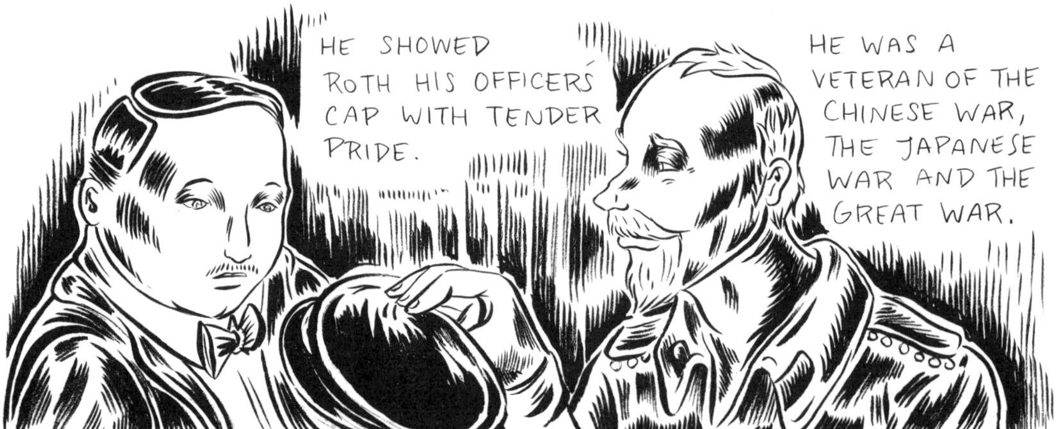
HE SHOWED ROTH HIS OFFICERS' CAP WITH TENDER PRIDE.
HE WAS A VETERAN OF THE CHINESE WAR, THE JAPANESE WAR AND THE GREAT WAR.

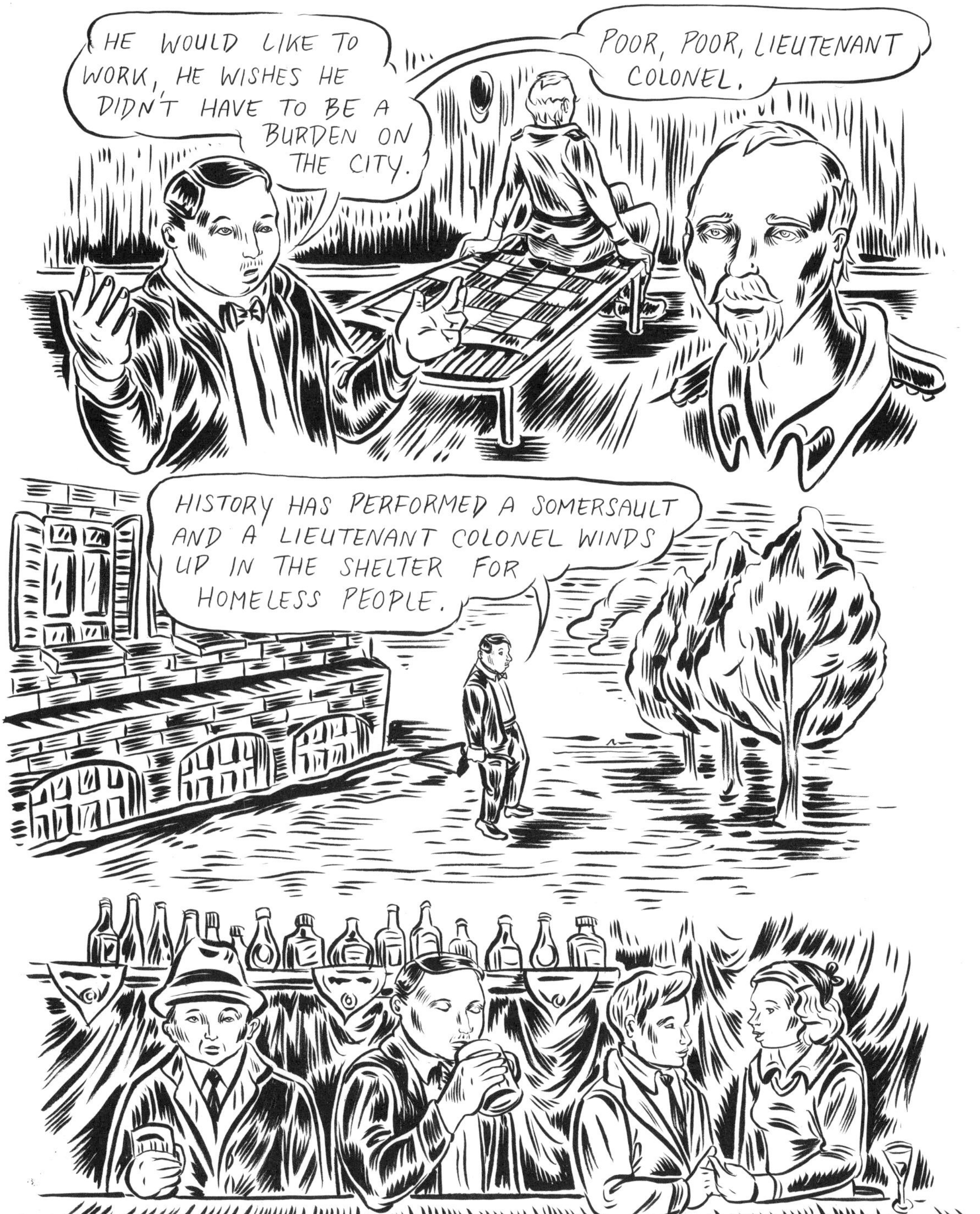
HE WOULD LIKE TO WORK, HE WISHES HE DIDN'T HAVE TO BE A BURDEN ON THE CITY.
POOR, POOR, LIEUTENANT COLONEL.
HISTORY HAS PERFORMED A SOMERSAULT AND A LIEUTENANT COLONEL WINDS UP IN THE SHELTER FOR HOMELESS PEOPLE.

Winter

WINTER IN BERLIN ARRIVES WITH CRUSHING EFFICIENCY.

THE CHRISTMAS MARKETS CLOSE, AND SUDDENLY THERE ARE NO MORE DOTTED LIGHTS AND MULLED WINE TO LENGTHEN THE DAYS.

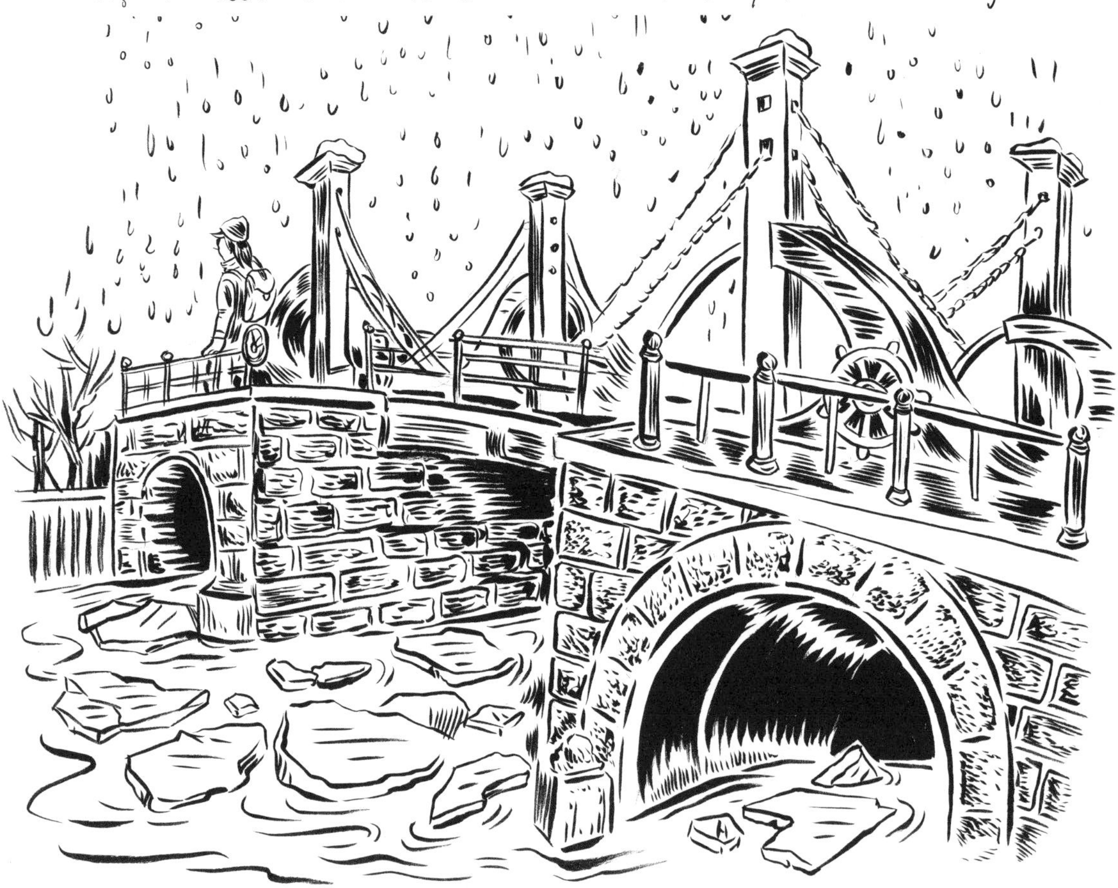

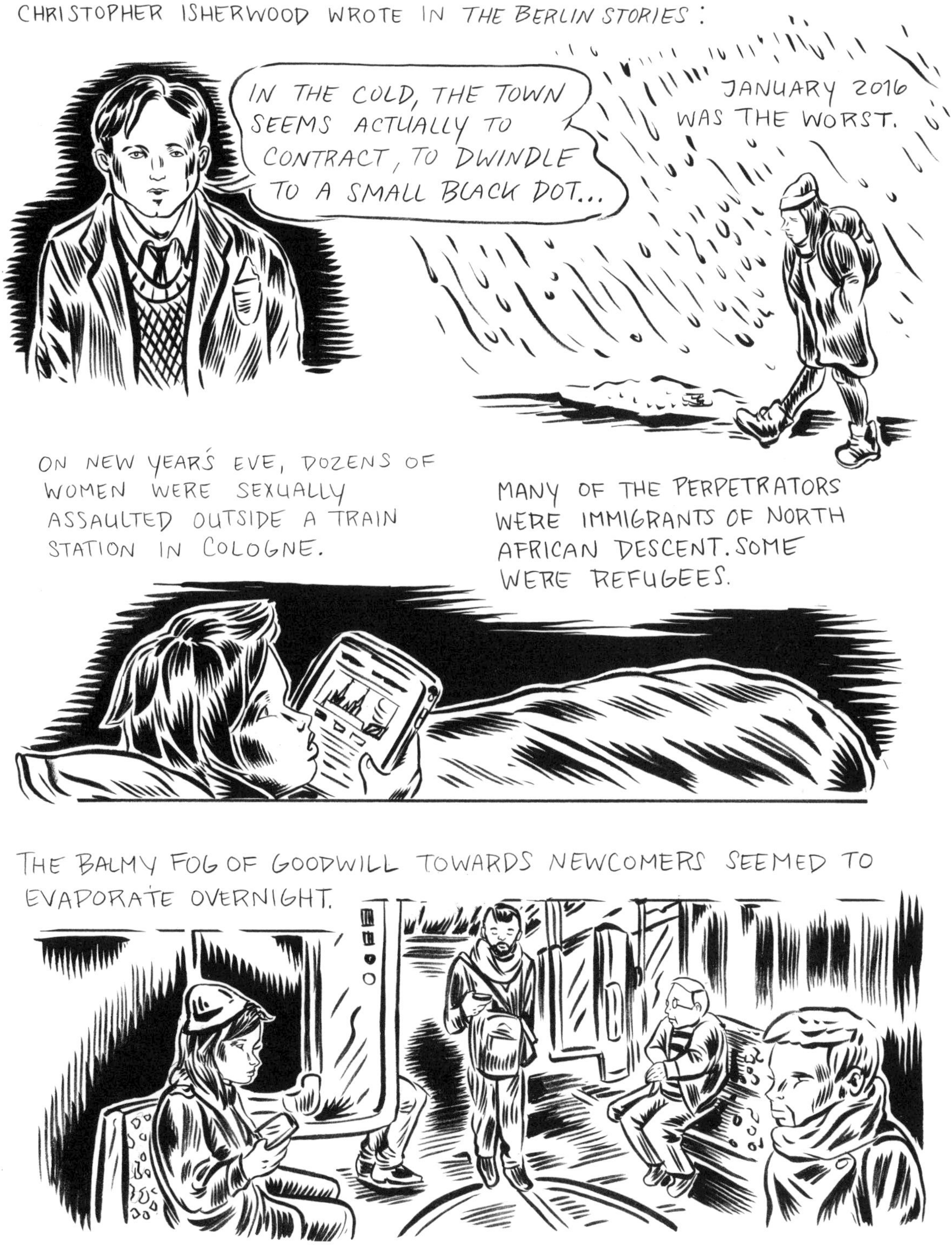
CHRISTOPHER ISHERWOOD WROTE IN THE BERLIN STORIES:
IN THE COLD, THE TOWN SEEMS ACTUALLY TO CONTRACT, TO DWINDLE TO A SMALL BLACK DOT...
JANUARY 2016 WAS THE WORST.
ON NEW YEAR'S EVE, DOZENS OF WOMEN WERE SEXUALLY ASSAULTED OUTSIDE A TRAIN STATION IN COLOGNE.
MANY OF THE PERPETRATORS WERE IMMIGRANTS OF NORTH AFRICAN DESCENT. SOME WERE REFUGEES.
THE BALMY FOG OF GOODWILL TOWARDS NEWCOMERS SEEMED TO EVAPORATE OVERNIGHT.

SUSPICION AND FEAR WERE PALPABLE— I WONDERED IF IT FELT THE SAME DURING THE ERA OF STASI SURVEILLANCE AND INFORMANTS.

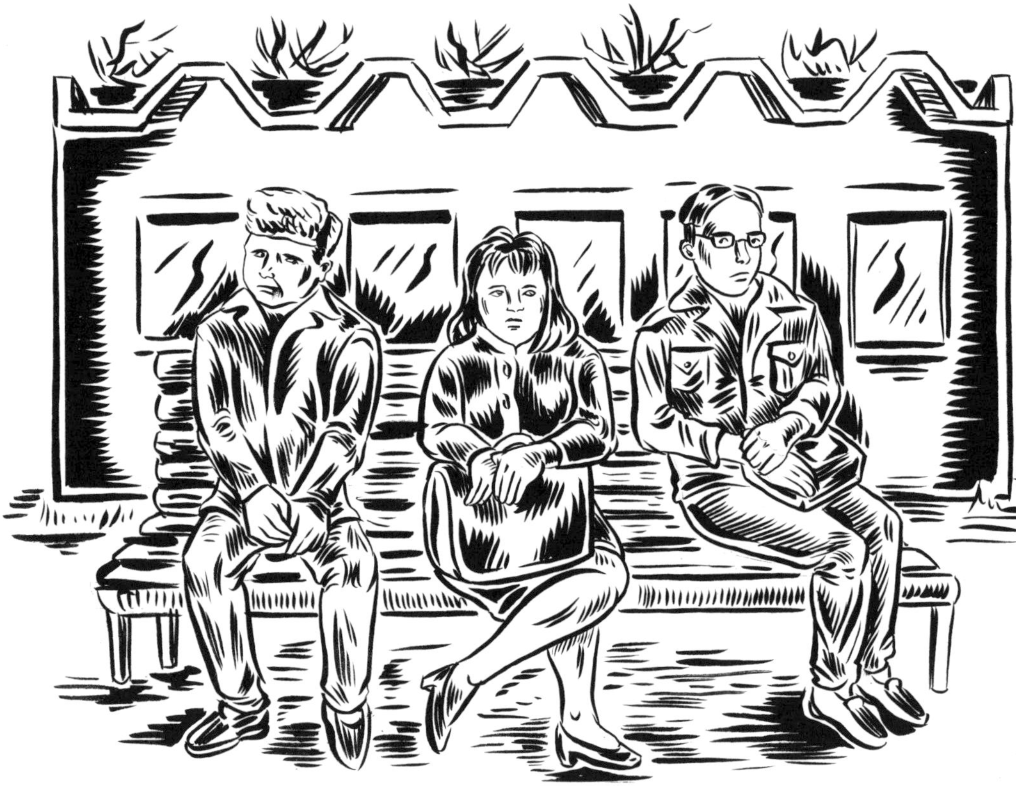

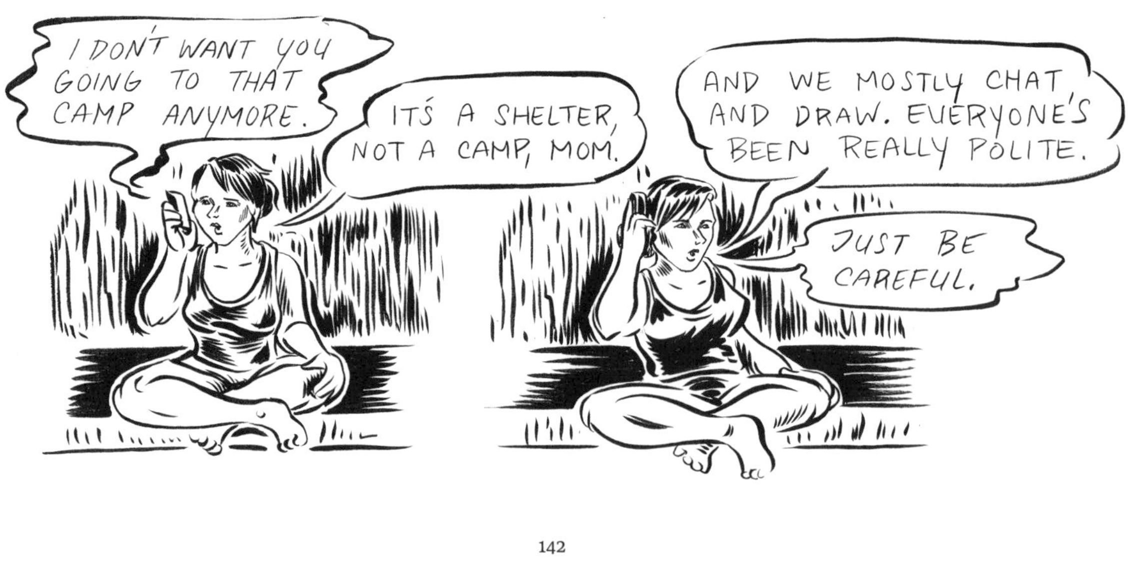
I DON'T WANT YOU GOING TO THAT CAMP ANYMORE.
IT'S A SHELTER, NOT A CAMP, MOM.
AND WE MOSTLY CHAT AND DRAW. EVERYONE'S BEEN REALLY POLITE.
JUST BE CAREFUL.

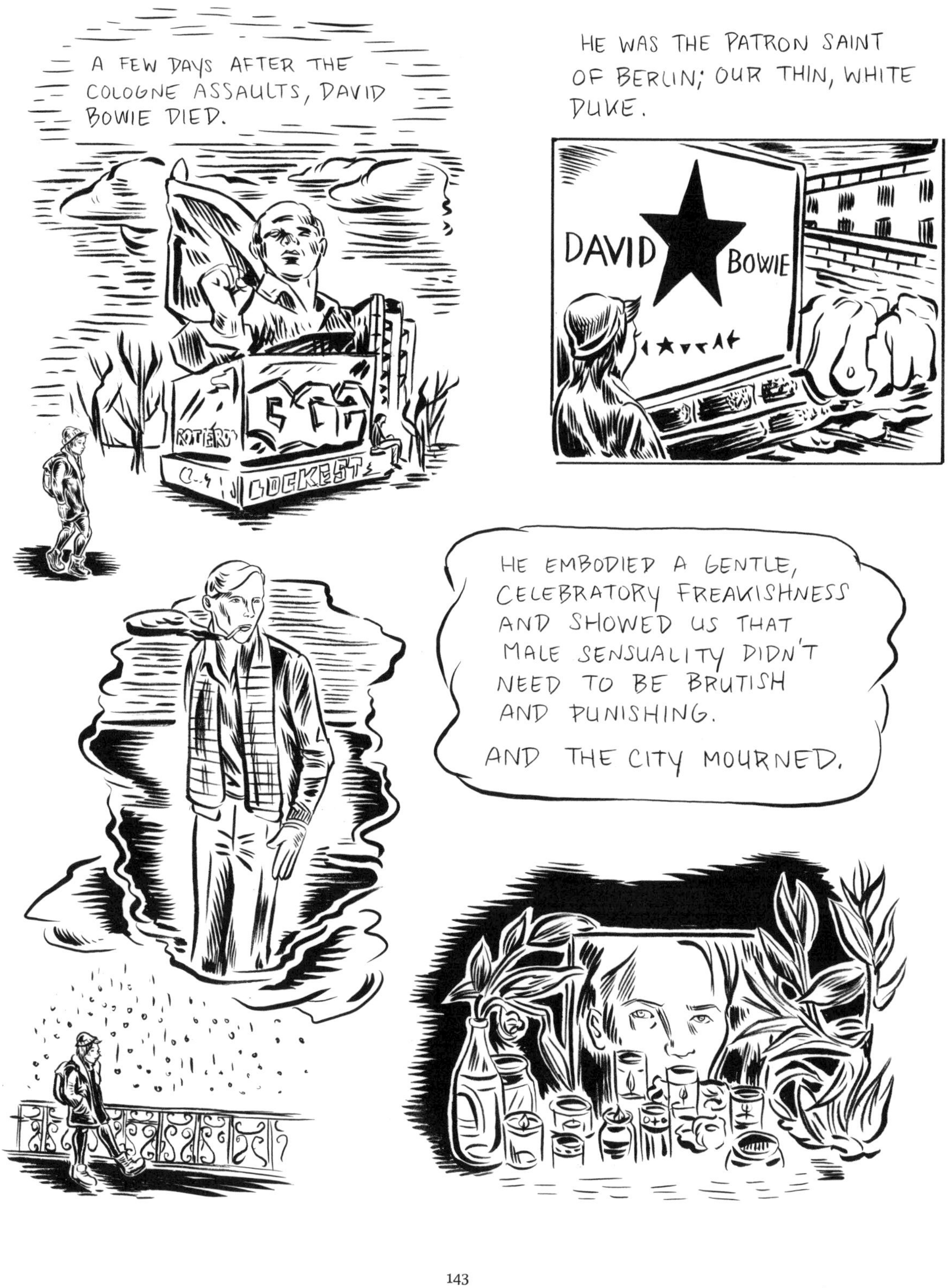
A FEW DAYS AFTER THE COLOGNE ASSAULTS, DAVID BOWIE DIED.
HE WAS THE PATRON SAINT OF BERLIN; OUR THIN, WHITE DUKE.
DAVID BOWIE
HE EMBODIED A GENTLE, CELEBRATORY FREAKISHNESS AND SHOWED US THAT MALE SENSUALITY DIDN'T NEED TO BE BRUTISH AND PUNISHING.
AND THE CITY MOURNED.

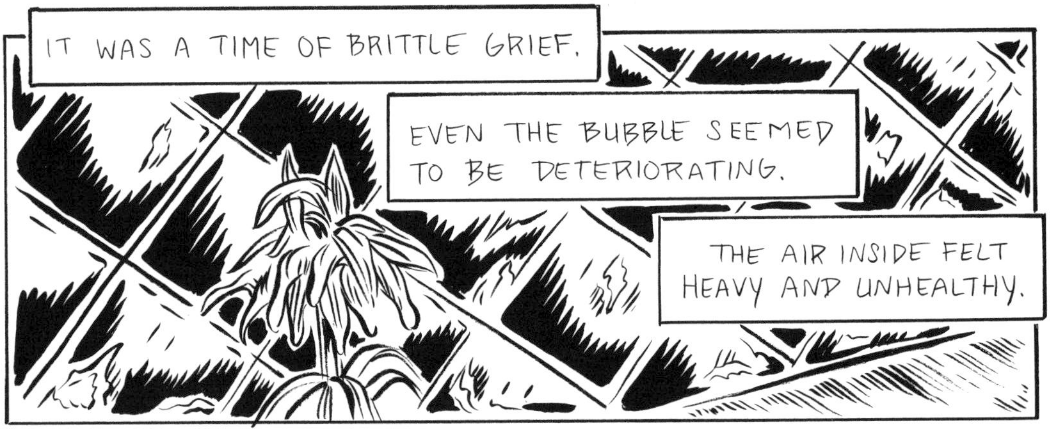
IT WAS A TIME OF BRITTLE GRIEF.
EVEN THE BUBBLE SEEMED TO BE DETERIORATING.
THE AIR INSIDE FELT HEAVY AND UNHEALTHY.

PEOPLE'S APPLICATIONS WERE DELAYED AGAIN AND AGAIN.

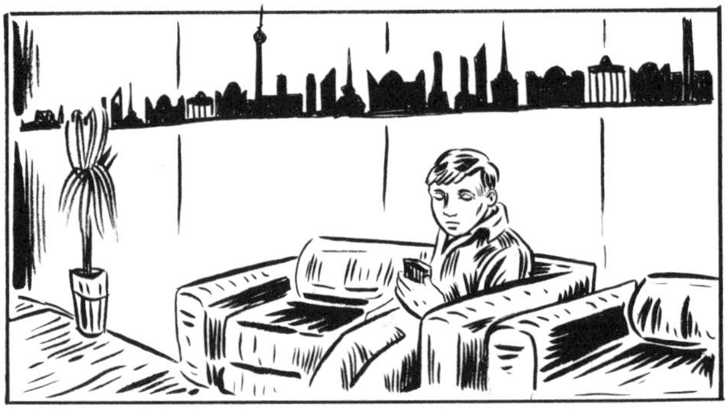

THE EMERGENCY SHELTER WAS MEANT TO HOUSE RESIDENTS FOR WEEKS, NOT MONTHS. BUT THE DEPTH OF THE CRISIS WAS TESTING THE LIMITS OF GERMAN BUREAUCRACY.

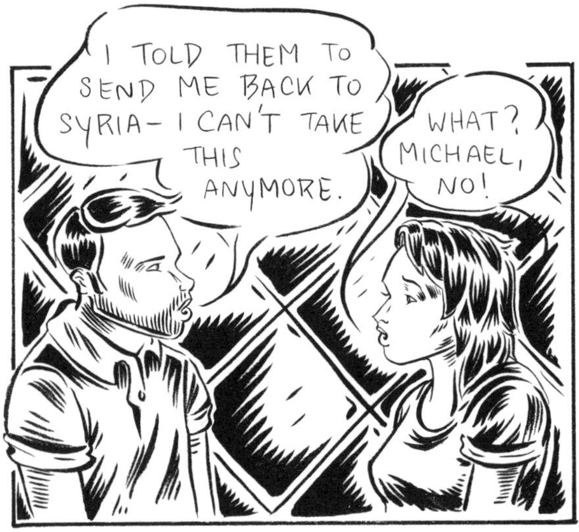
I TOLD THEM TO SEND ME BACK TO SYRIA– I CAN'T TAKE THIS ANYMORE.
WHAT? MICHAEL, NO!

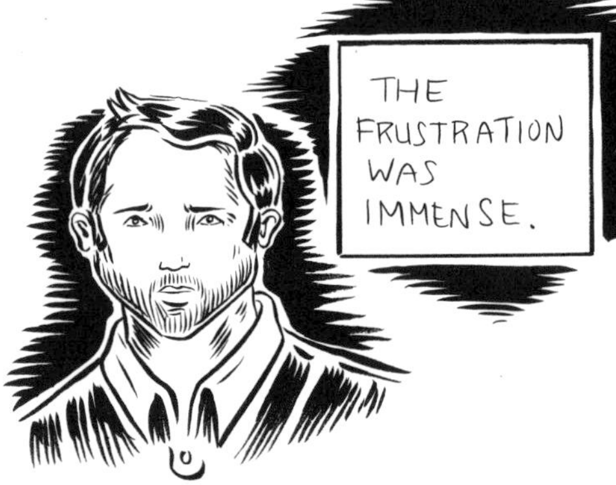
THE FRUSTRATION WAS IMMENSE.

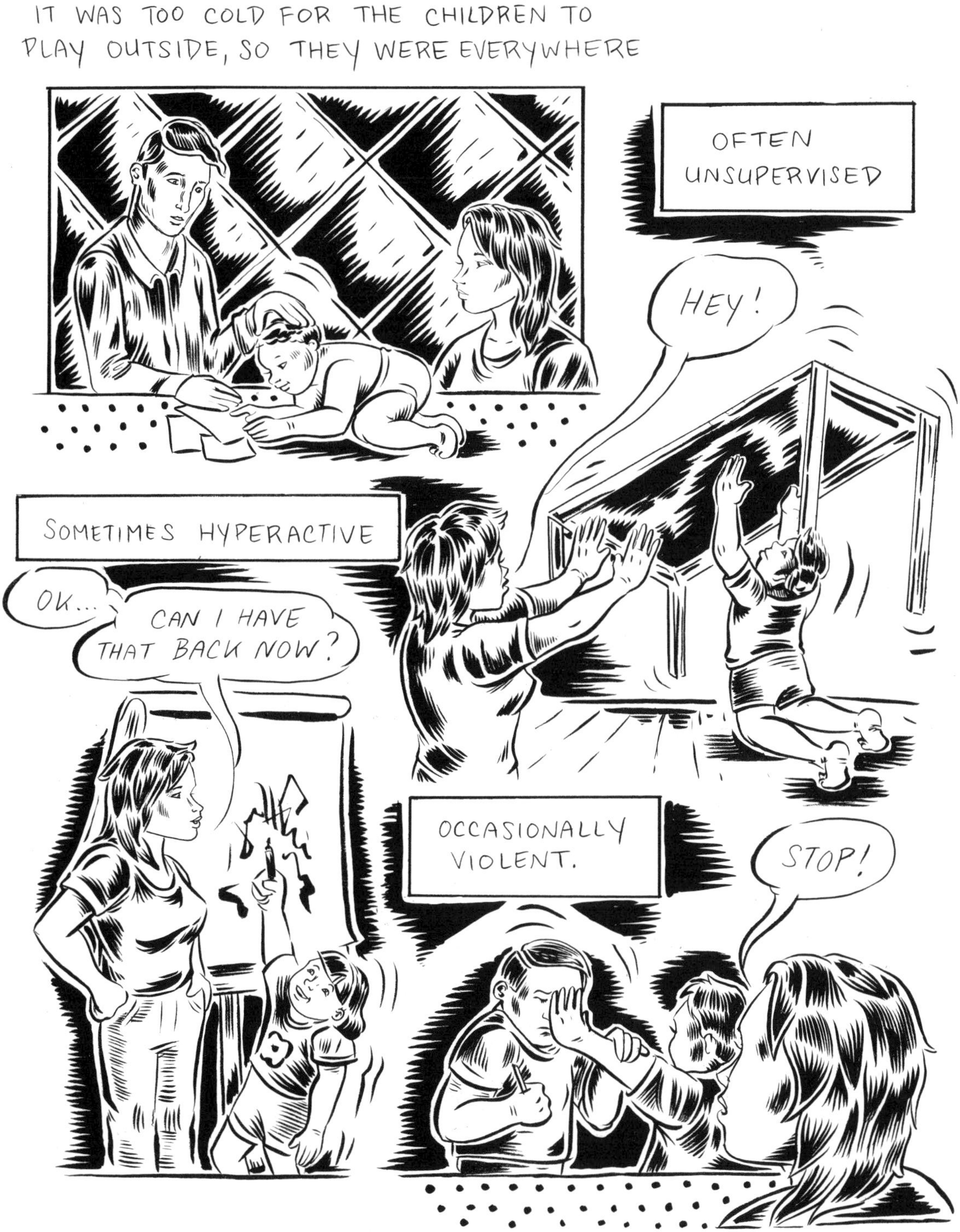
IT WAS TOO COLD FOR THE CHILDREN TO PLAY OUTSIDE, SO THEY WERE EVERYWHERE
OFTEN UNSUPERVISED
HEY!
SOMETIMES HYPERACTIVE
OK...
CAN I HAVE THAT BACK NOW?
OCCASIONALLY VIOLENT.
STOP!

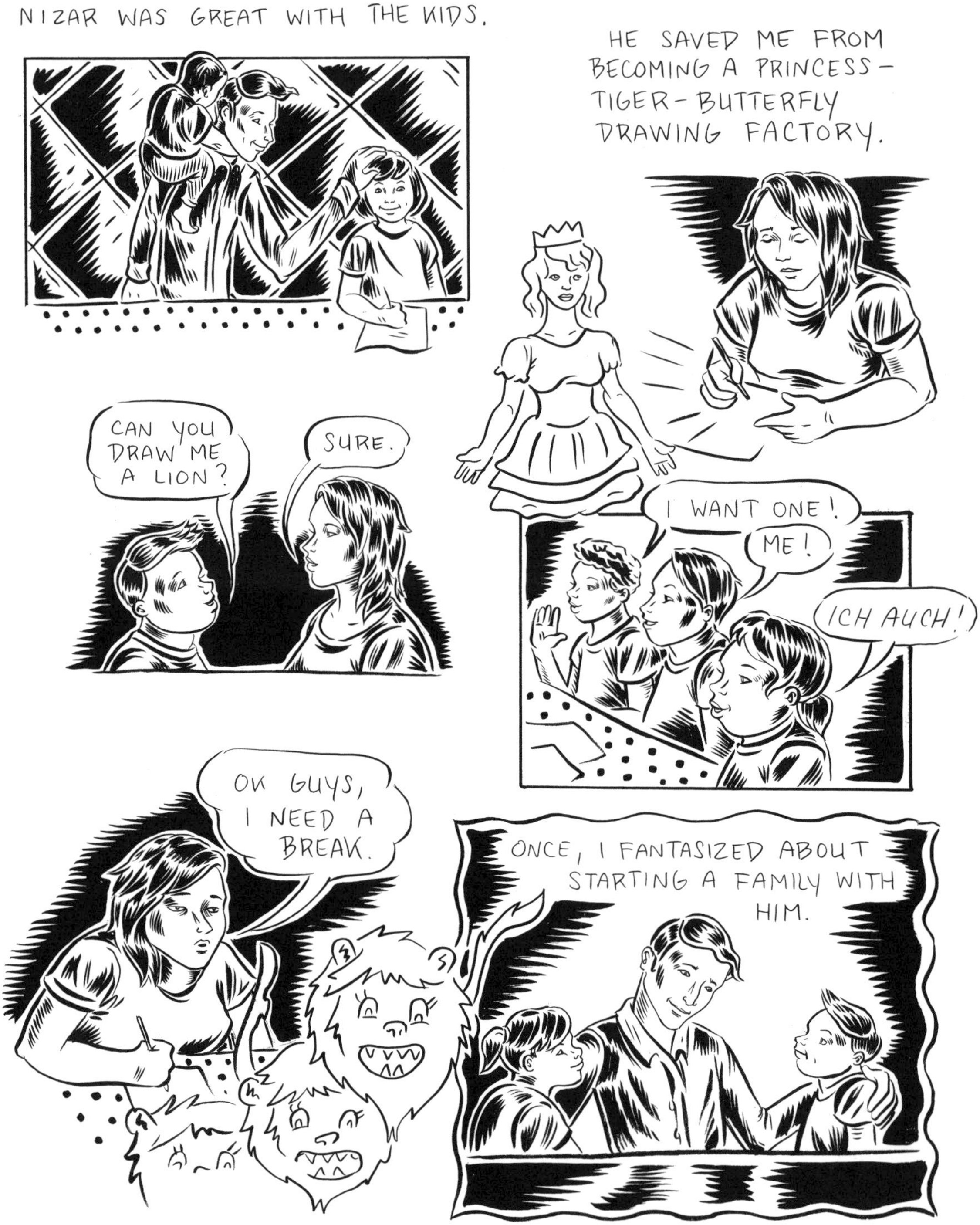
NIZAR WAS GREAT WITH THE KIDS.
HE SAVED ME FROM BECOMING A PRINCESS-TIGER-BUTTERFLY DRAWING FACTORY.
CAN YOU DRAW ME A LION?
SURE.
I WANT ONE!
ME!
ICH AUCH!
OK GUYS, I NEED A BREAK.
ONCE, I FANTASIZED ABOUT STARTING A FAMILY WITH HIM.

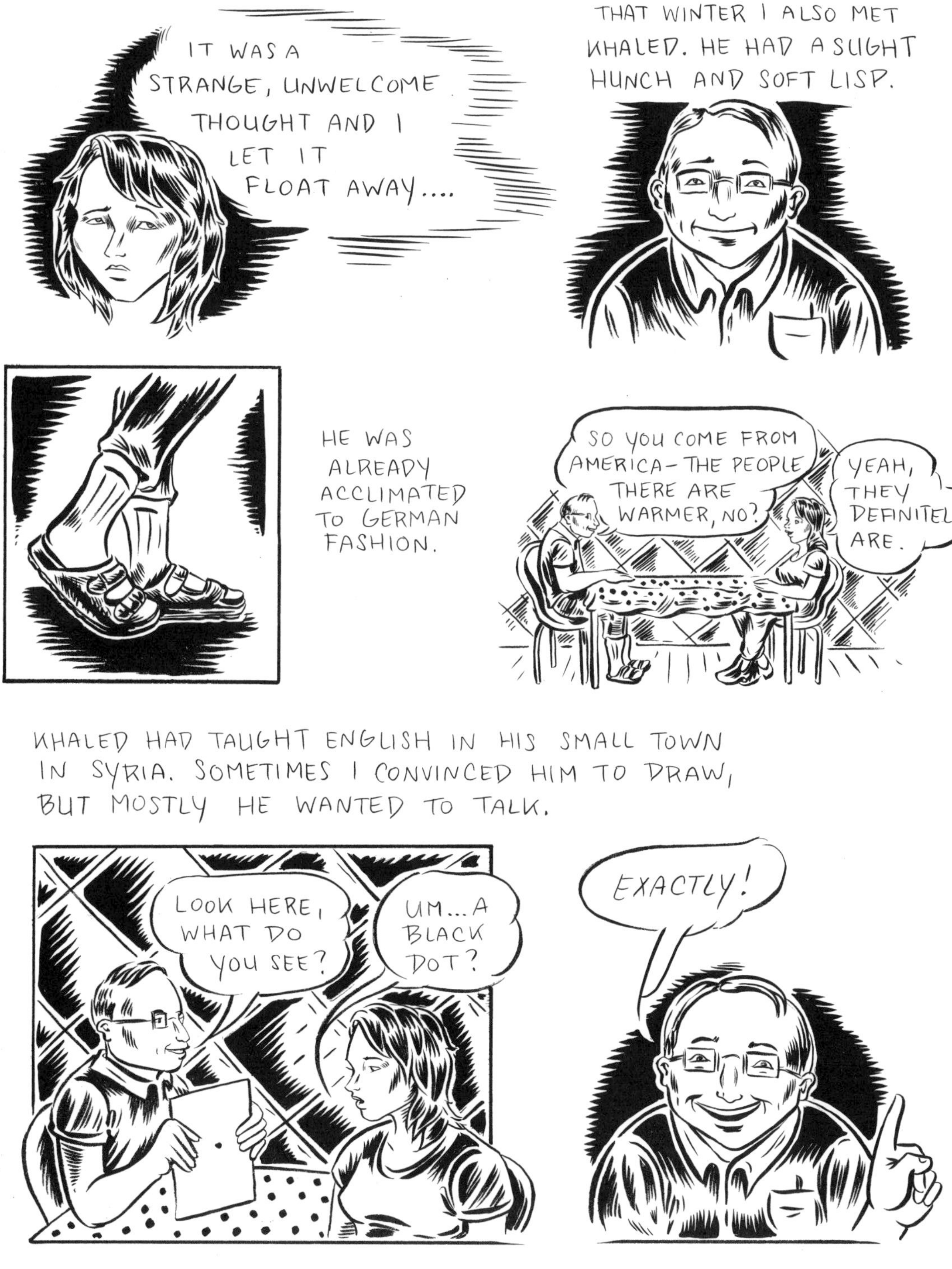
IT WAS A STRANGE, UNWELCOME THOUGHT AND I LET IT FLOAT AWAY....
THAT WINTER I ALSO MET KHALED. HE HAD A SLIGHT HUNCH AND SOFT LISP.
HE WAS ALREADY ACCLIMATED TO GERMAN FASHION.
SO YOU COME FROM AMERICA- THE PEOPLE THERE ARE WARMER, NO?
YEAH, THEY DEFINITELY ARE.
KHALED HAD TAUGHT ENGLISH IN HIS SMALL TOWN IN SYRIA. SOMETIMES I CONVINCED HIM TO DRAW, BUT MOSTLY HE WANTED TO TALK.
LOOK HERE, WHAT DO YOU SEE?
UM... A BLACK DOT?
EXACTLY!

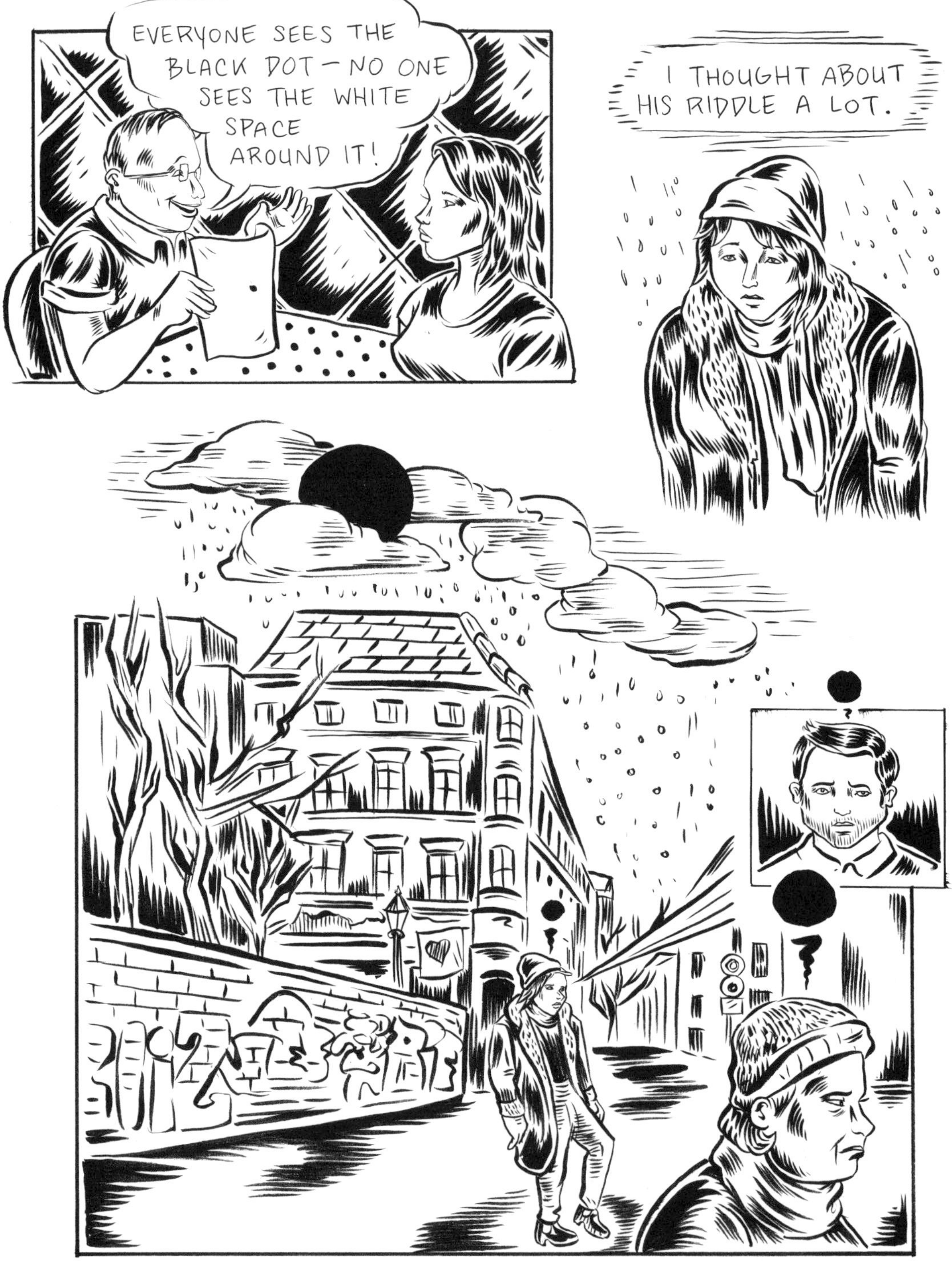
EVERYONE SEES THE BLACK DOT—NO ONE SEES THE WHITE SPACE AROUND IT!
I THOUGHT ABOUT HIS RIDDLE A LOT.

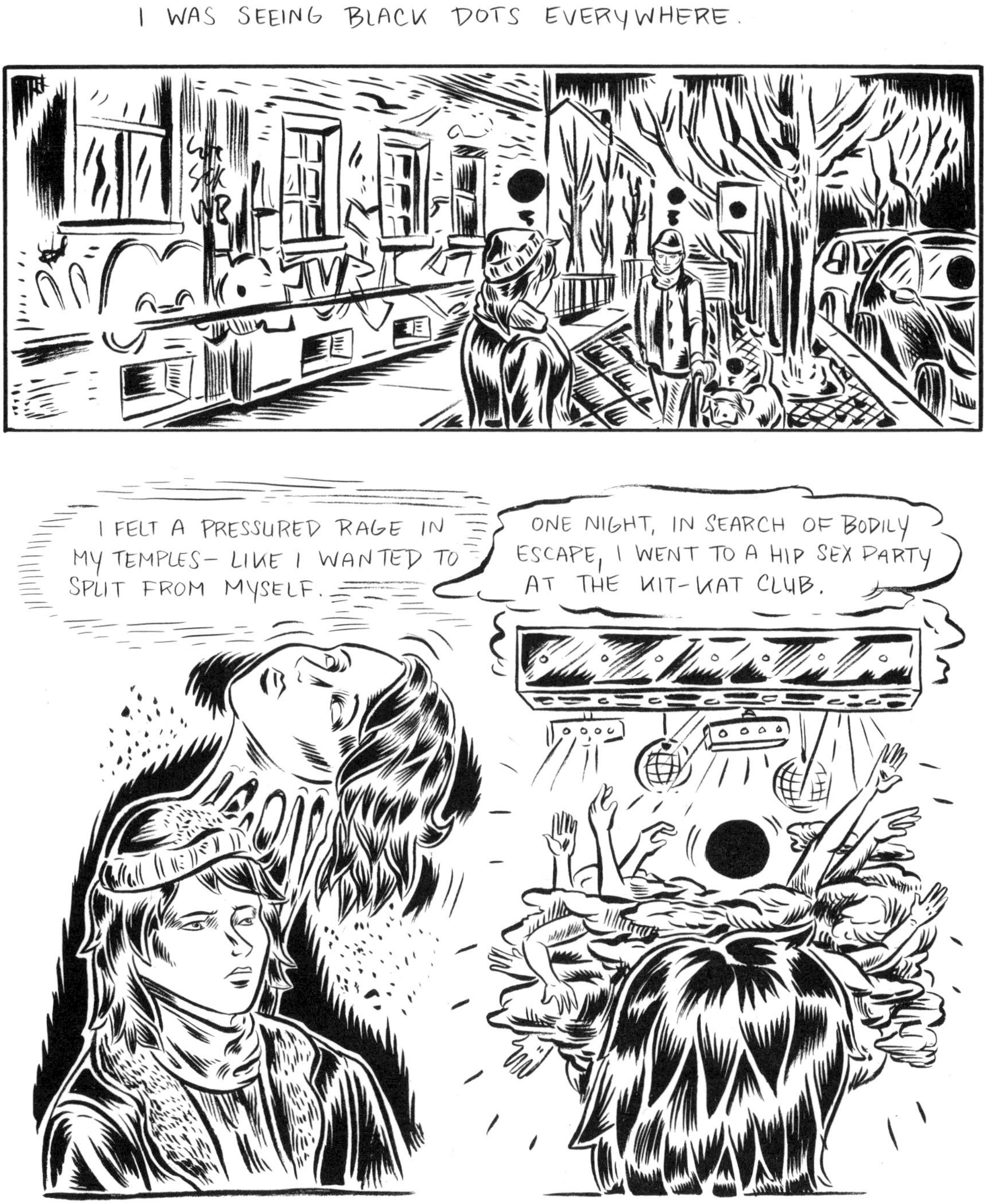
I WAS SEEING BLACK DOTS EVERYWHERE.
I FELT A PRESSURED RAGE IN MY TEMPLES— LIKE I WANTED TO SPLIT FROM MYSELF.
ONE NIGHT, IN SEARCH OF BODILY ESCAPE, I WENT TO A HIP SEX PARTY AT THE KIT-KAT CLUB.

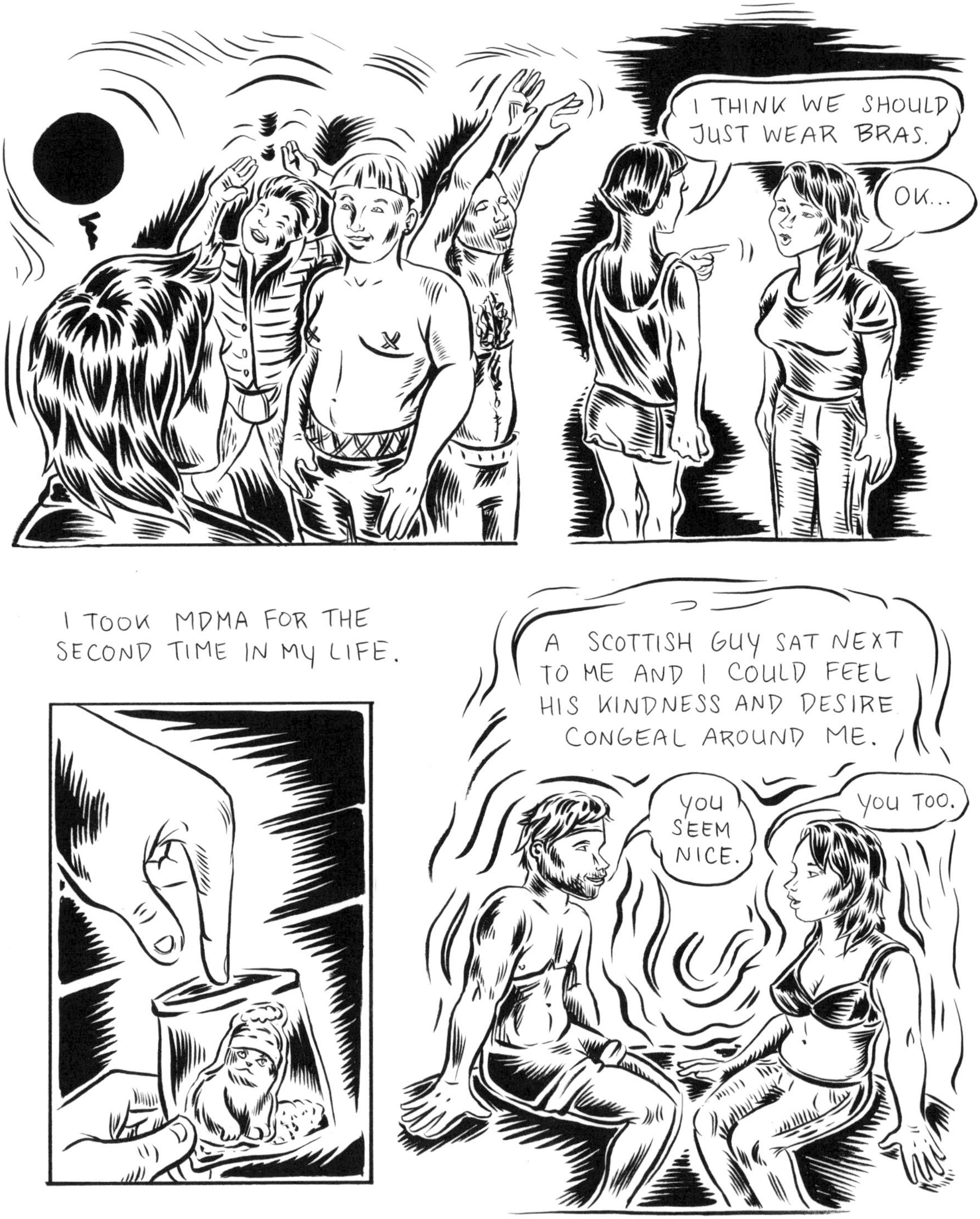
I THINK WE SHOULD JUST WEAR BRAS.
OK...
I TOOK MDMA FOR THE SECOND TIME IN MY LIFE.
A SCOTTISH GUY SAT NEXT TO ME AND I COULD FEEL HIS KINDNESS AND DESIRE CONGEAL AROUND ME.
YOU SEEM NICE.
YOU TOO.

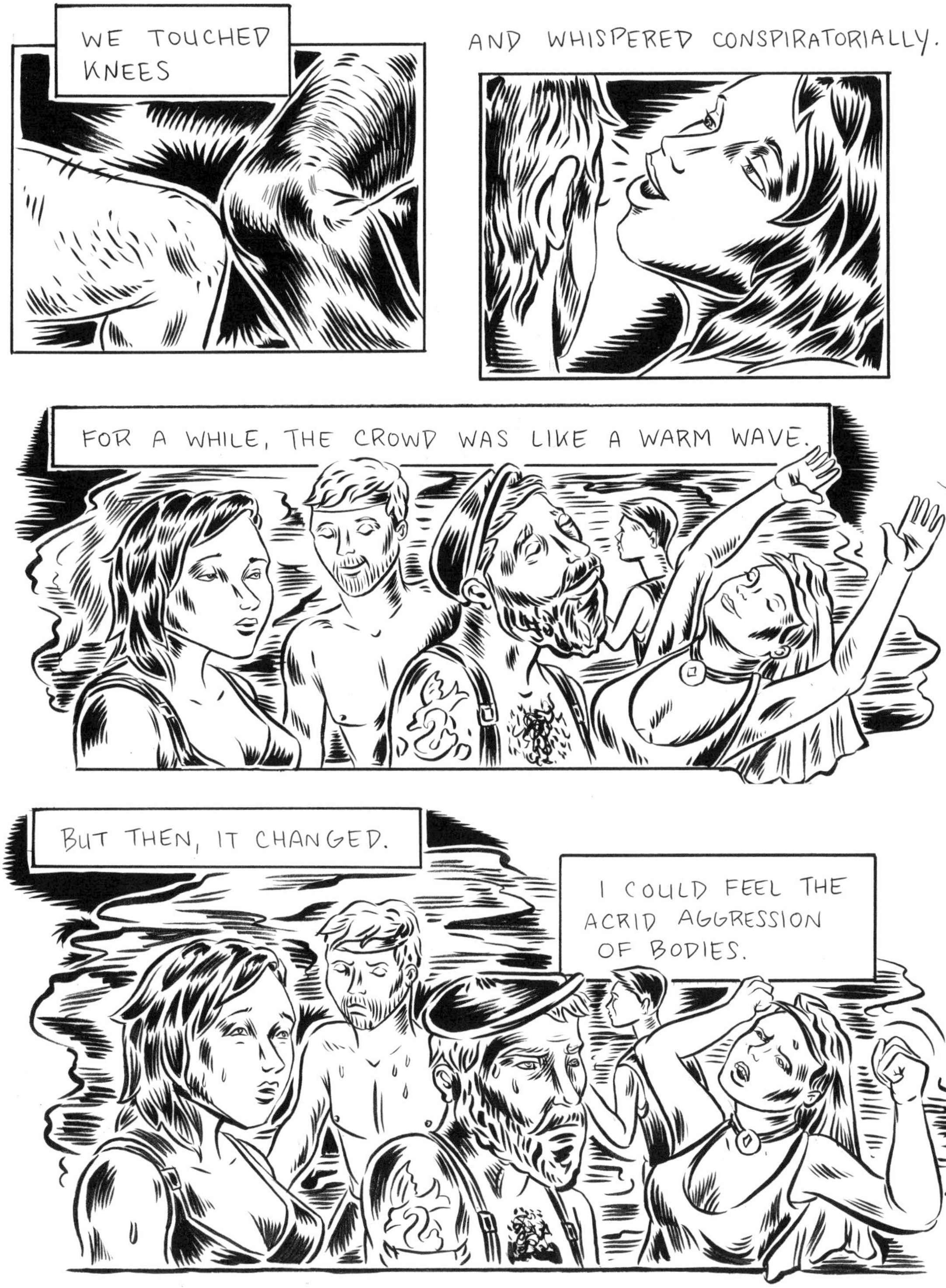
WE TOUCHED KNEES
AND WHISPERED CONSPIRATORIALLY.
FOR A WHILE, THE CROWD WAS LIKE A WARM WAVE.
BUT THEN, IT CHANGED.
I COULD FEEL THE ACRID AGGRESSION OF BODIES.

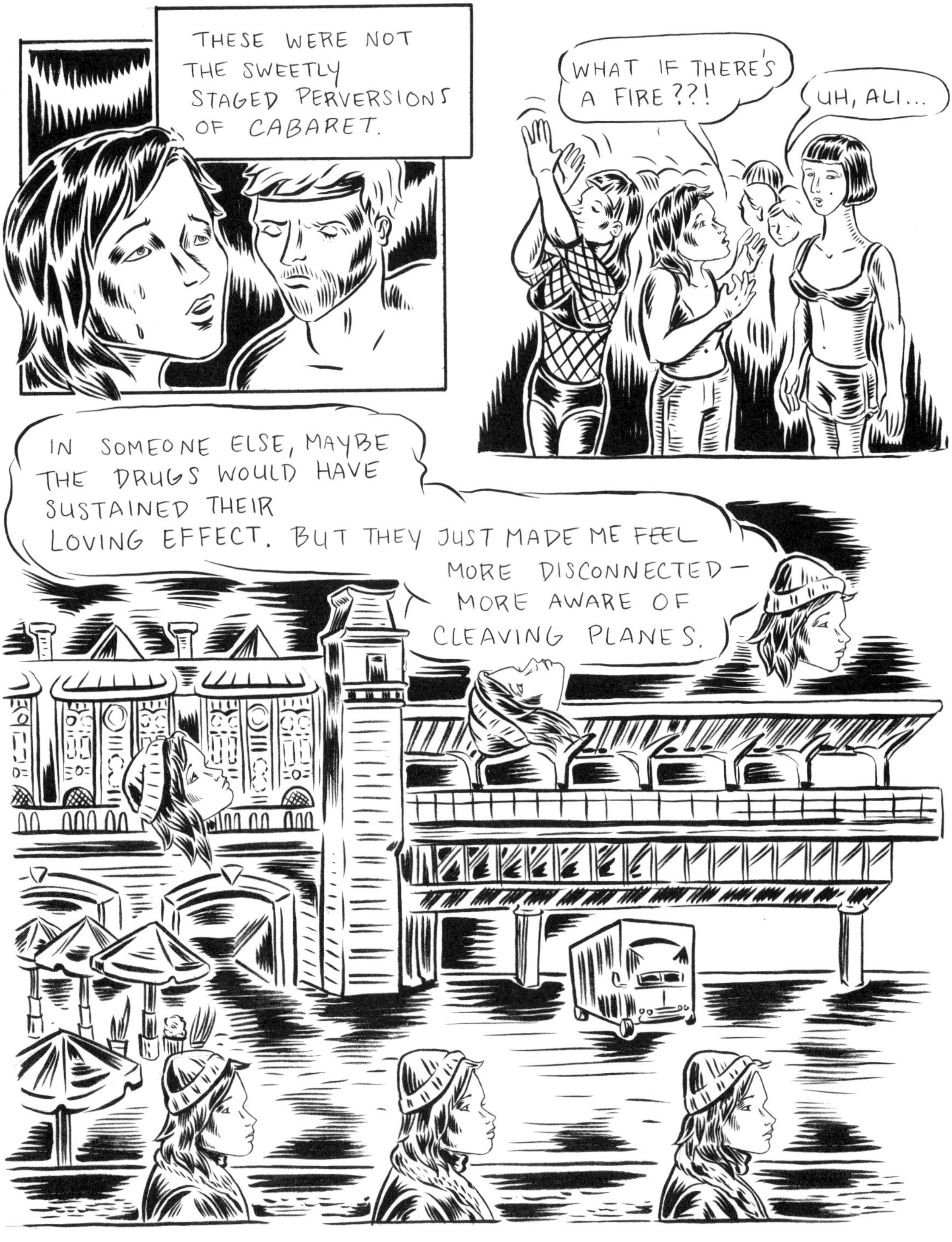
THESE WERE NOT THE SWEETLY STAGED PERVERSIONS OF CABARET.
WHAT IF THERE'S A FIRE??!
UH, ALI...
IN SOMEONE ELSE, MAYBE THE DRUGS WOULD HAVE SUSTAINED THEIR LOVING EFFECT. BUT THEY JUST MADE ME FEEL MORE DISCONNECTED— MORE AWARE OF CLEAVING PLANES.

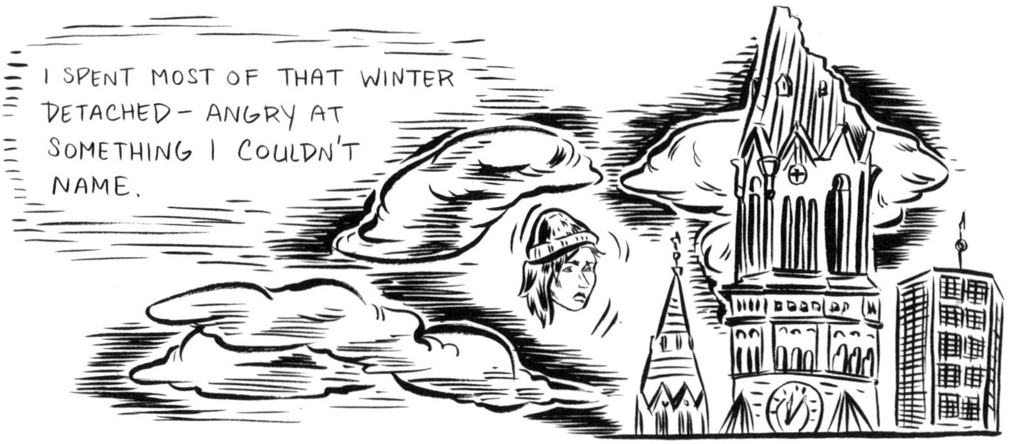
I SPENT MOST OF THAT WINTER DETACHED- ANGRY AT SOMETHING I COULDN'T NAME.

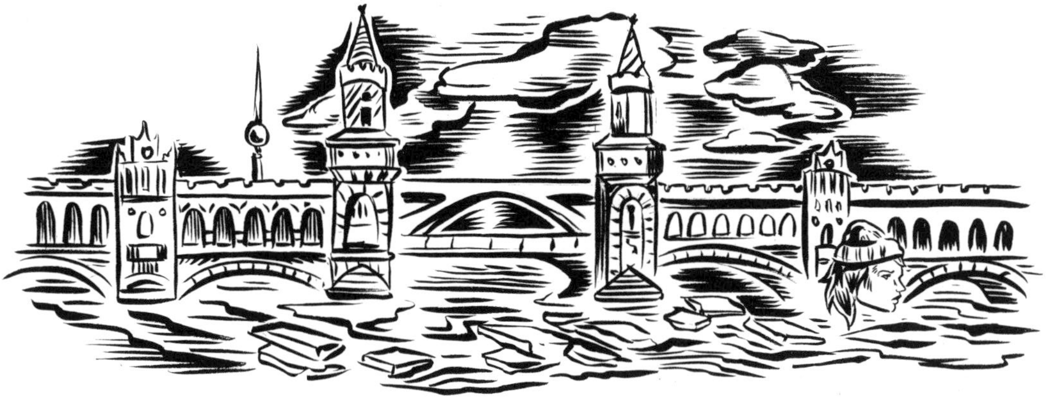

CONVINCED THAT THE WORLD WAS GOVERNED BY BRUTALITY.

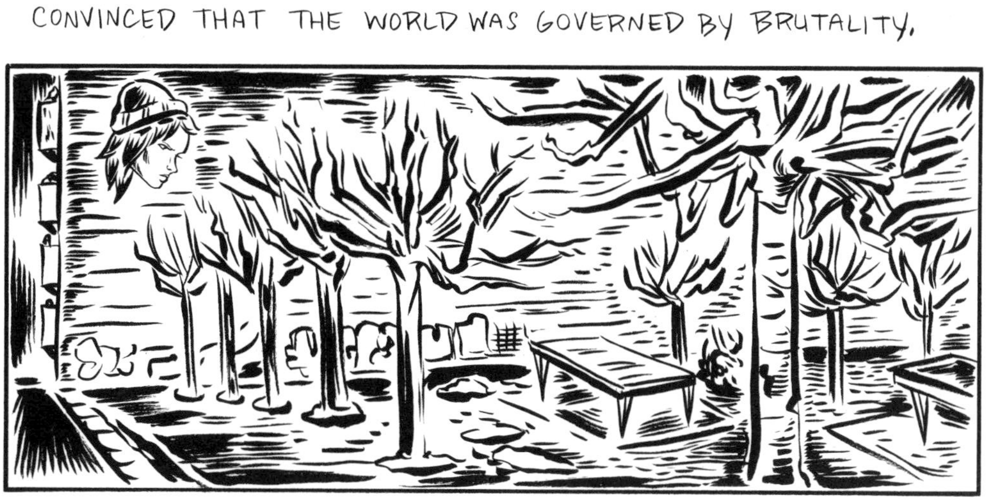

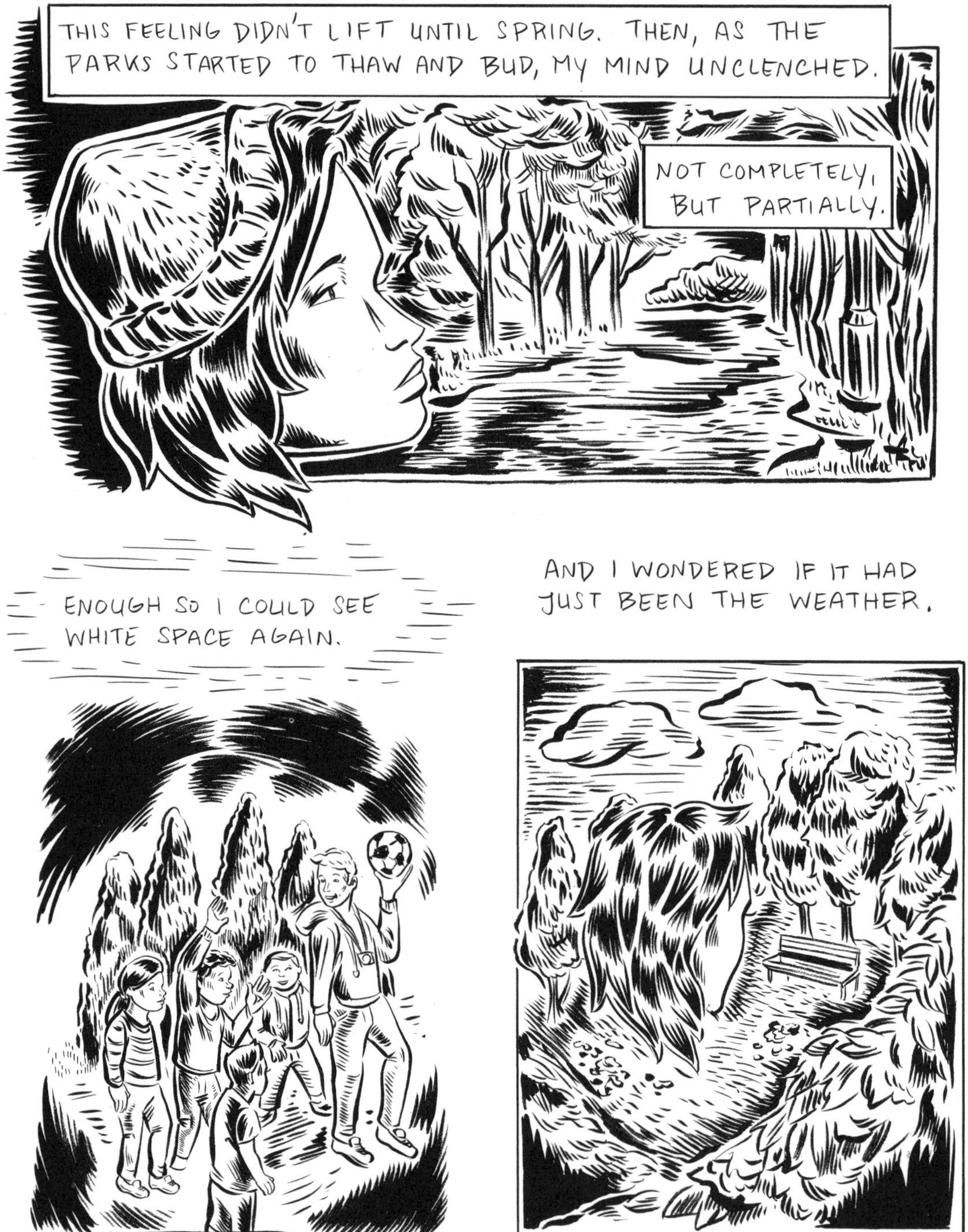
THIS FEELING DIDN'T LIFT UNTIL SPRING. THEN, AS THE PARKS STARTED TO THAW AND BUD, MY MIND UNCLENCHED.
NOT COMPLETELY, BUT PARTIALLY.
ENOUGH SO I COULD SEE WHITE SPACE AGAIN.
AND I WONDERED IF IT HAD JUST BEEN THE WEATHER.

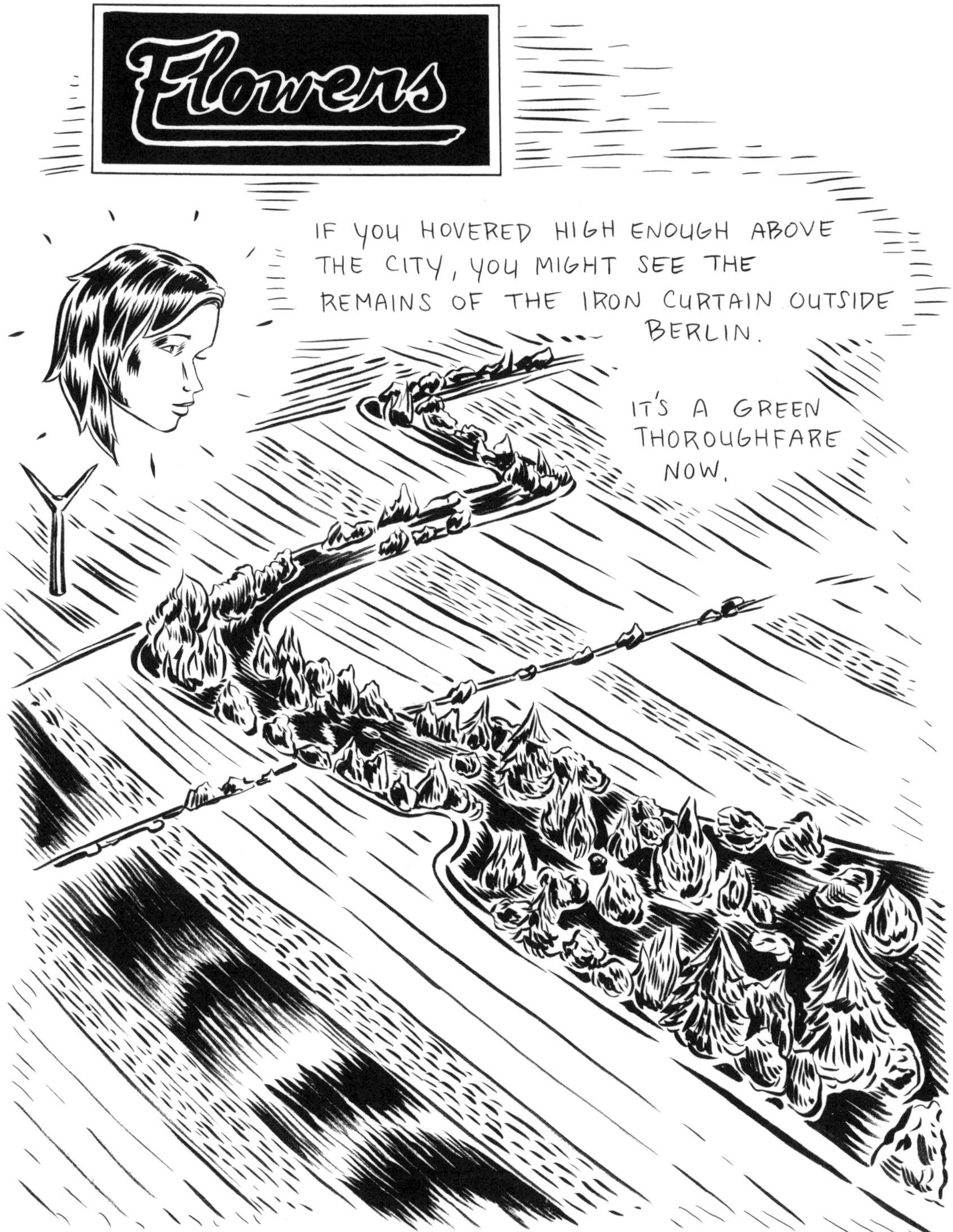
Flowers
IF YOU HOVERED HIGH ENOUGH ABOVE THE CITY, YOU MIGHT SEE THE REMAINS OF THE IRON CURTAIN OUTSIDE BERLIN.
IT'S A GREEN THOROUGHFARE NOW.

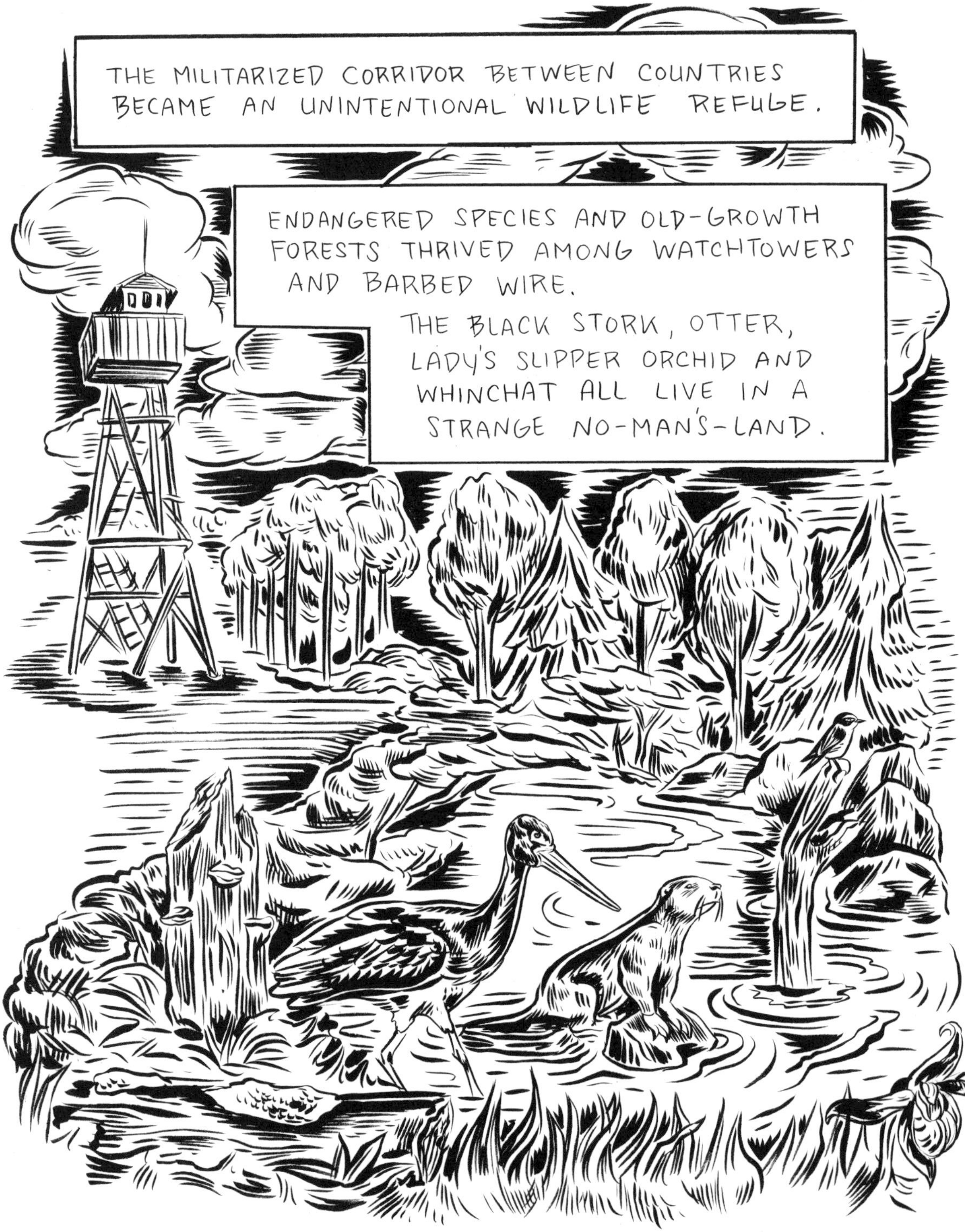
THE MILITARIZED CORRIDOR BETWEEN COUNTRIES BECAME AN UNINTENTIONAL WILDLIFE REFUGE.
ENDANGERED SPECIES AND OLD-GROWTH FORESTS THRIVED AMONG WATCHTOWERS AND BARBED WIRE.
THE BLACK STORK, OTTER, LADY'S SLIPPER ORCHID AND WHINCHAT ALL LIVE IN A STRANGE NO-MAN'S-LAND.

MY OLD APARTMENT WAS ACROSS FROM THE FORMER "DEATH STRIP." EVENTUALLY, ITS WEEDY BADLANDS BECAME A SIEMENS FACTORY.

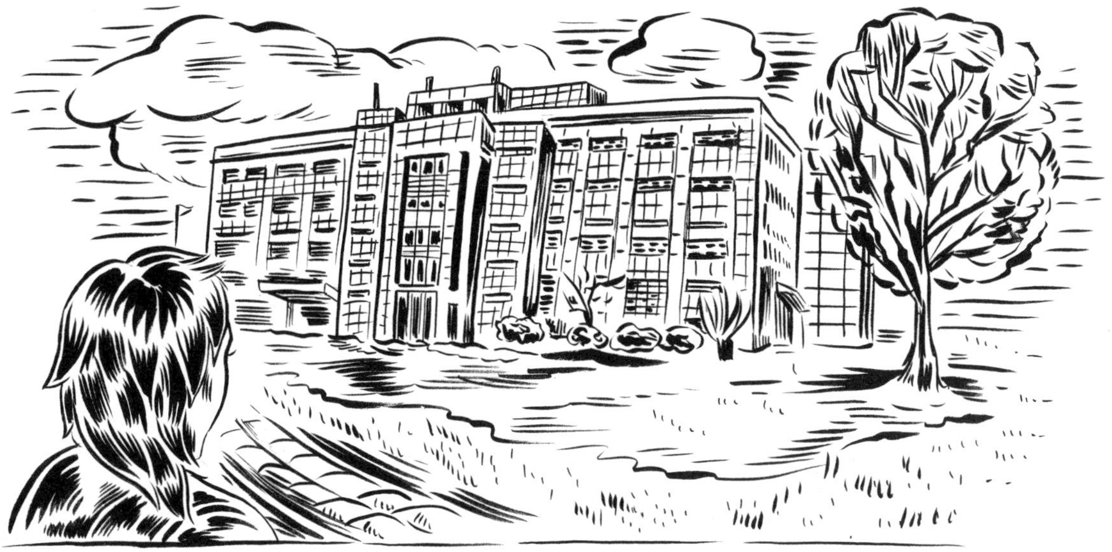

A LOT OF IN-BETWEEN SPACES IN BERLIN HAVE BEEN PAVED OVER. STILL, THE PLANTS GROW EVERYWHERE – THEY ARE RESTLESS AND UNRULY.

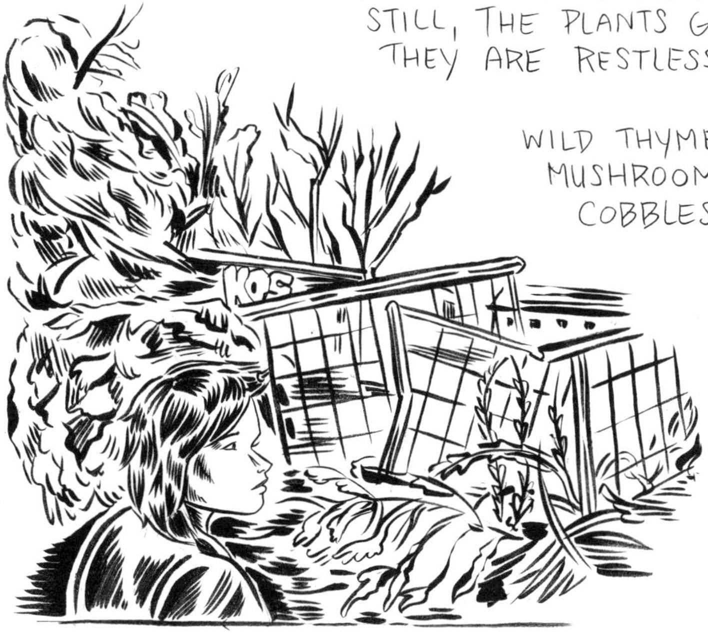
KOS

WILD THYME, BURDOCK AND MUSHROOMS CRAWL BETWEEN COBBLESTONES AND BROKEN CONCRETE.

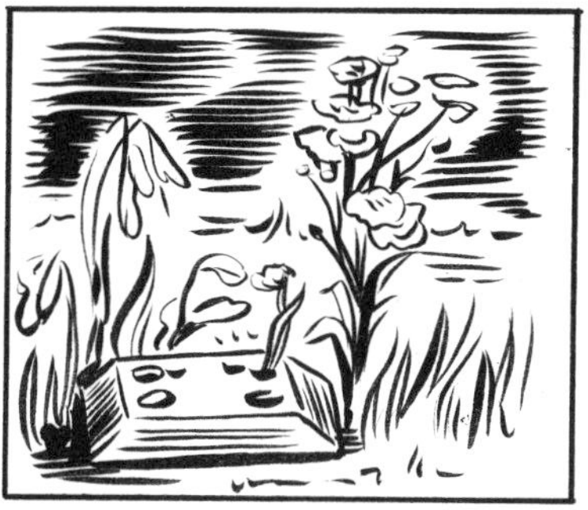

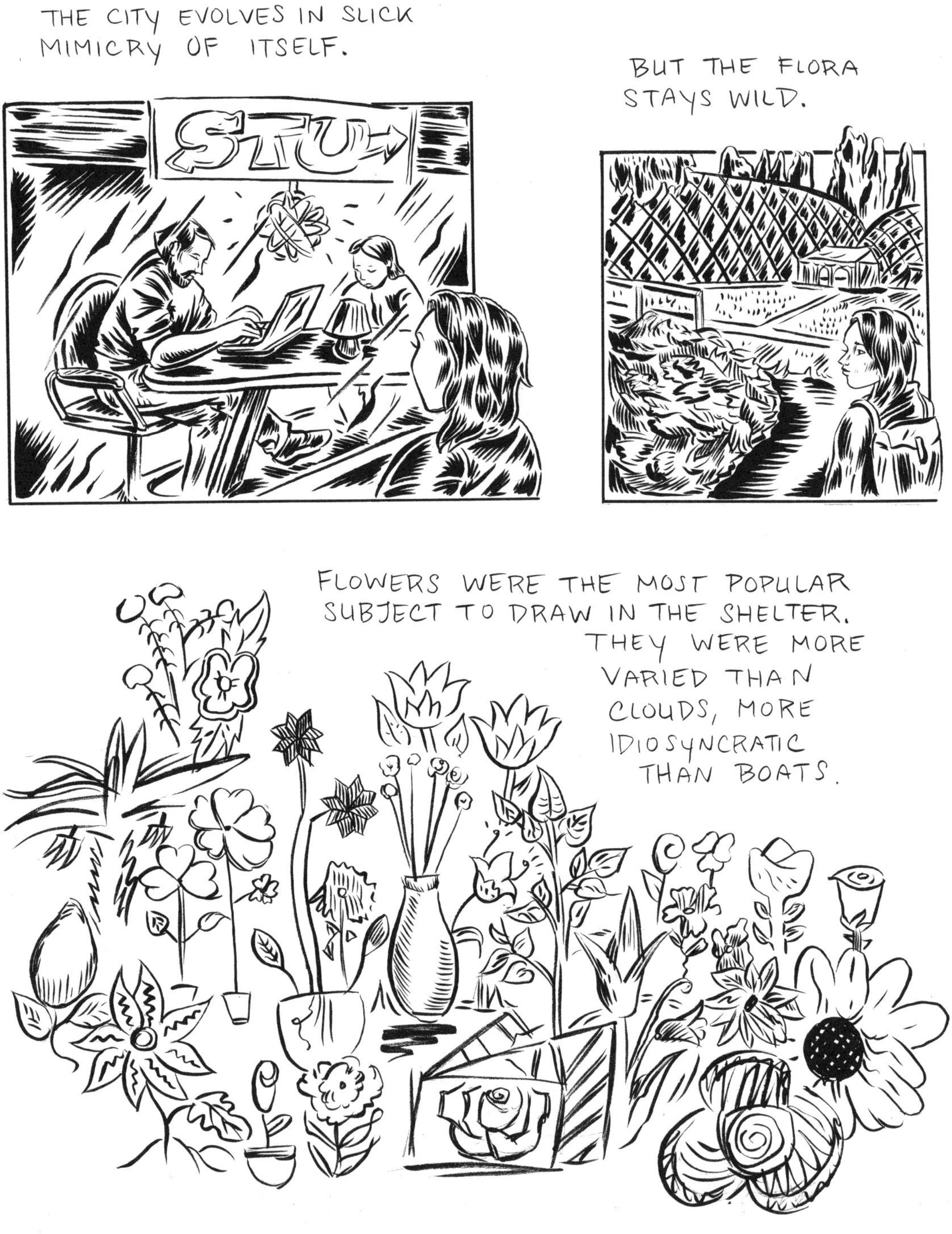
THE CITY EVOLVES IN SLICK MIMICRY OF ITSELF.
STU
BUT THE FLORA STAYS WILD.
FLOWERS WERE THE MOST POPULAR SUBJECT TO DRAW IN THE SHELTER.
THEY WERE MORE VARIED THAN CLOUDS, MORE IDIOSYNCRATIC THAN BOATS.

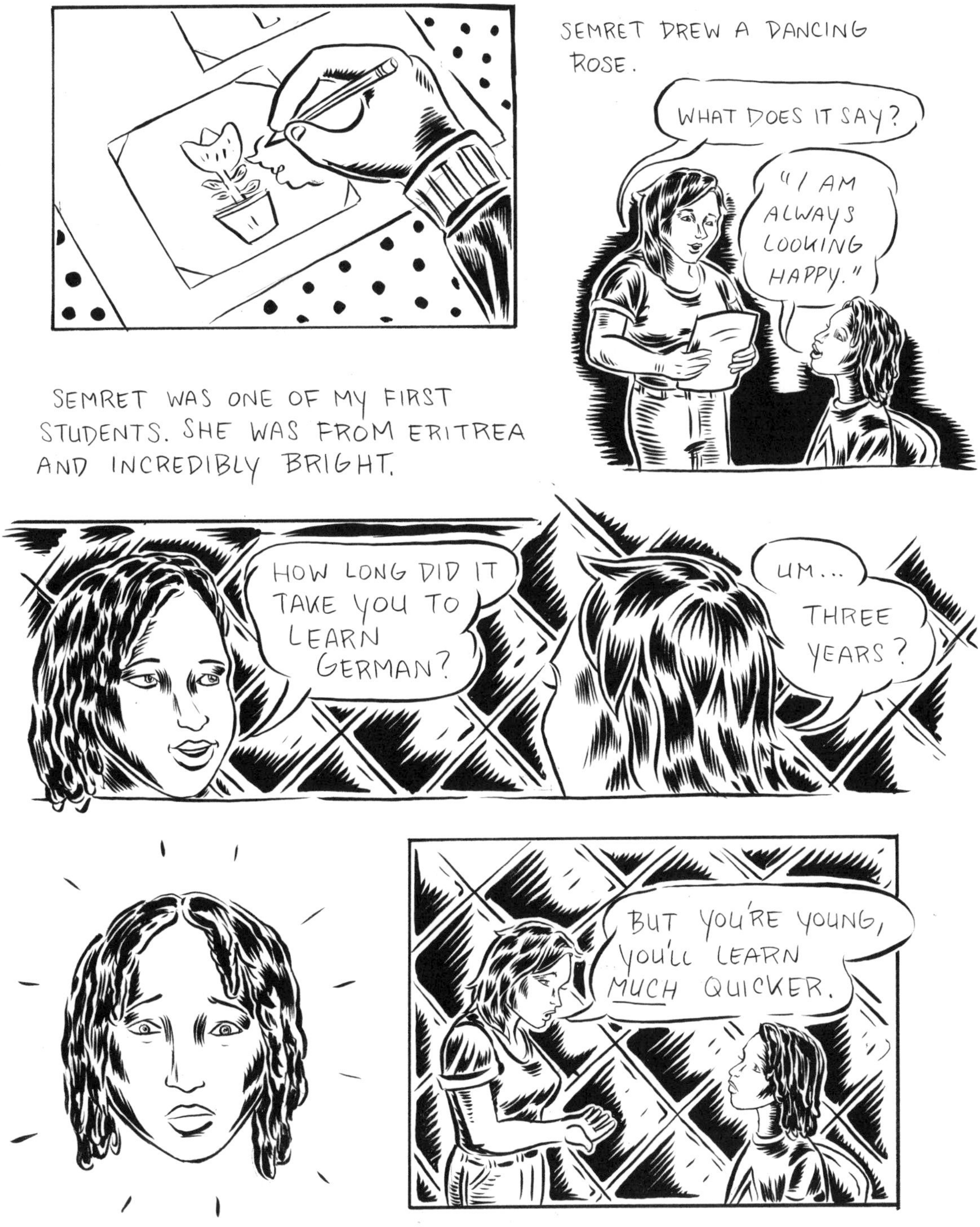
SEMRET DREW A DANCING ROSE.
WHAT DOES IT SAY?
"I AM ALWAYS LOOKING HAPPY."
SEMRET WAS ONE OF MY FIRST STUDENTS. SHE WAS FROM ERITREA AND INCREDIBLY BRIGHT.
HOW LONG DID IT TAKE YOU TO LEARN GERMAN?
UM... THREE YEARS?
BUT YOU'RE YOUNG, YOU'LL LEARN MUCH QUICKER.

SEMRET WAS ALREADY QUITE GOOD AT GERMAN AND MADE COMICS THAT WERE LYNCHIAN AND WEIRD.

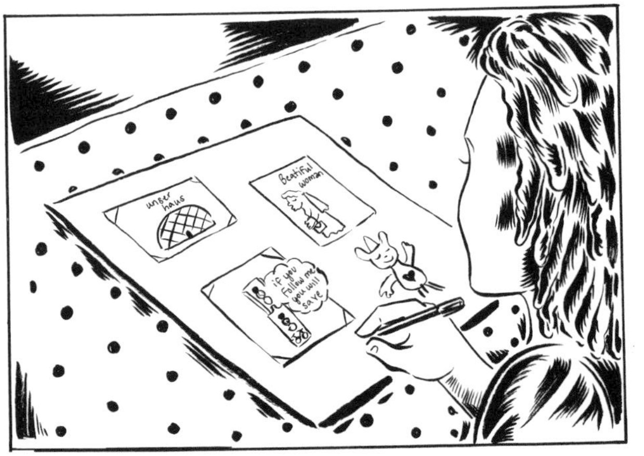
unser haus
Beatiful woman
if you follow me you will save

THERE WERE TALKING STOPLIGHTS AND FLOATING WOMEN.

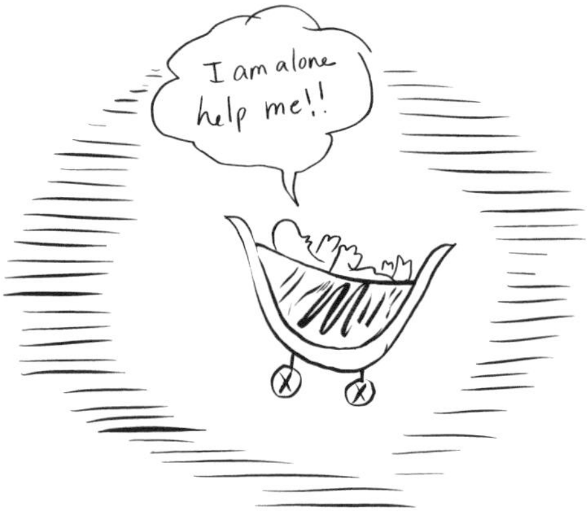
I am alone help me!!

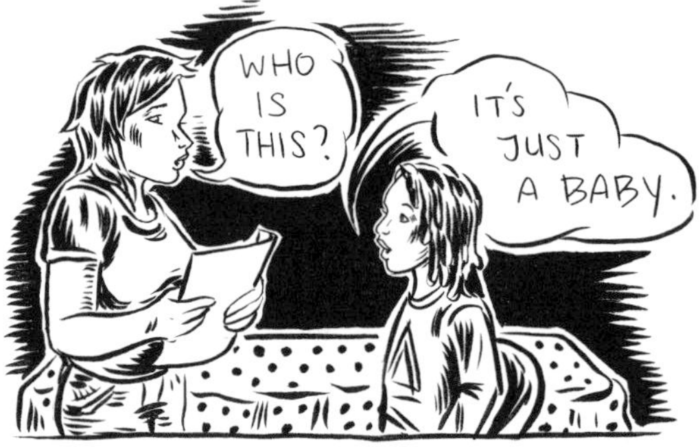
WHO IS THIS?
IT'S JUST A BABY.

AS I WAS CLEANING UP, SHE ASKED CONFIDENTLY:

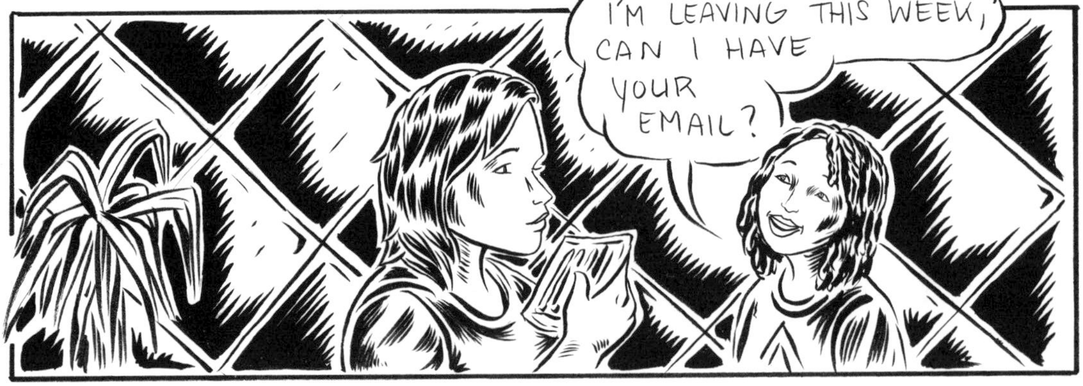
I'M LEAVING THIS WEEK, CAN I HAVE YOUR EMAIL?

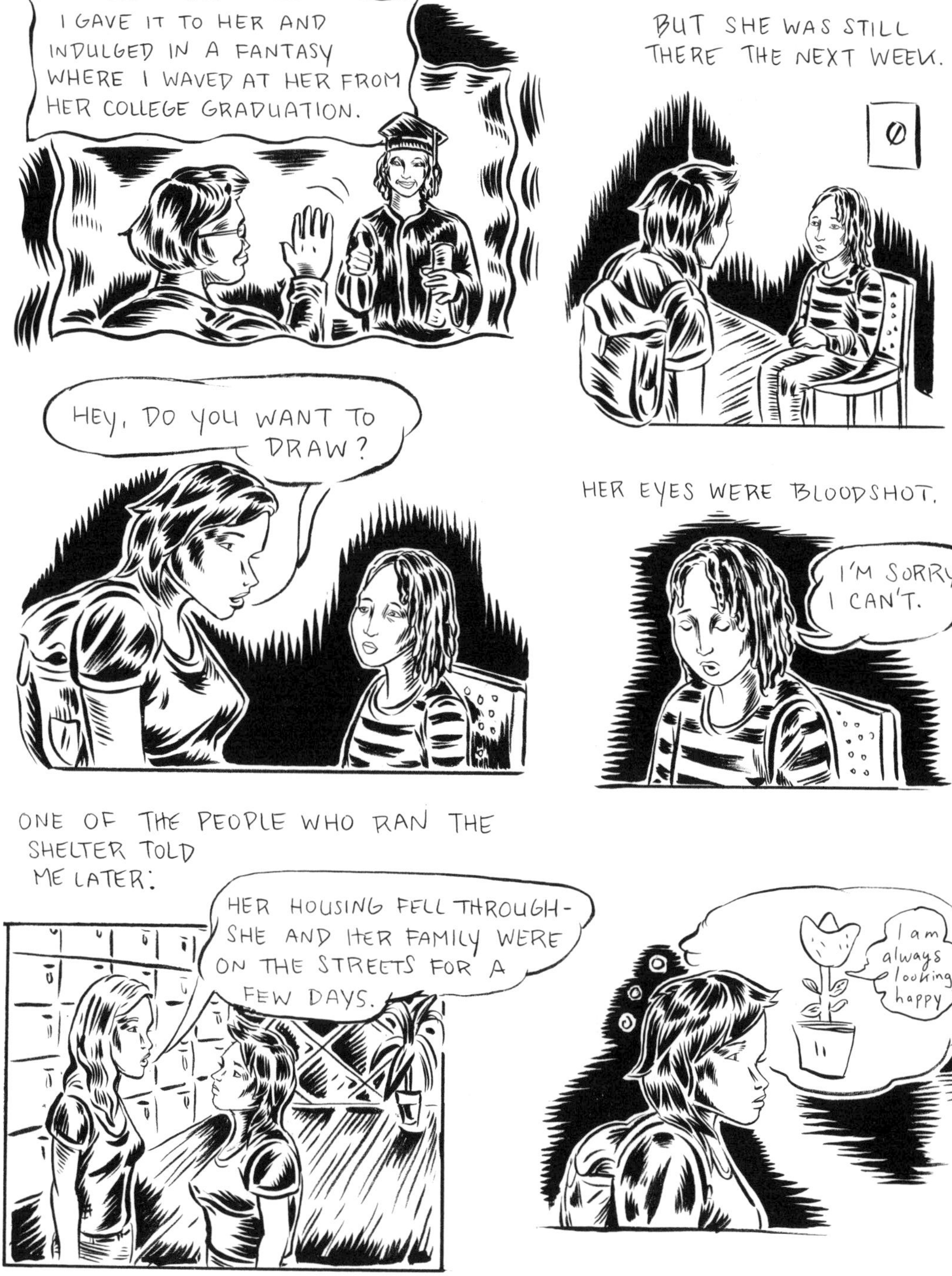
I GAVE IT TO HER AND INDULGED IN A FANTASY WHERE I WAVED AT HER FROM HER COLLEGE GRADUATION.
BUT SHE WAS STILL THERE THE NEXT WEEK.
HEY, DO YOU WANT TO DRAW?
HER EYES WERE BLOODSHOT.
I'M SORRY, I CAN'T.
ONE OF THE PEOPLE WHO RAN THE SHELTER TOLD ME LATER:
HER HOUSING FELL THROUGH- SHE AND HER FAMILY WERE ON THE STREETS FOR A FEW DAYS.
I am always looking happy

MANAN FROM AFGHANISTAN MADE PSYCHEDELIC,
SOLITARY FLOWERS.

ONCE, HE COPIED A PAGE FROM
 WHERE THE WILD THINGS ARE,
BUT MADE IT LUSHER AND GREENER.

HE OFTEN BROUGHT
HIS FRIENDS, WHO
WERE FROM PAKISTAN.

WE HAD NO SHARED LANGUAGE, SO WE COMMUNICATED IN GESTURES.

MANAN SANG AFGHANI FOLK SONGS FOR US.

WE ALL DREW TOGETHER WITHOUT SPEAKING. MANAN'S VOICE WAS OUR QUIVERING SOUNDTRACK AND IT WAS BLISSFUL IN A WAY THAT'S HARD TO DESCRIBE.

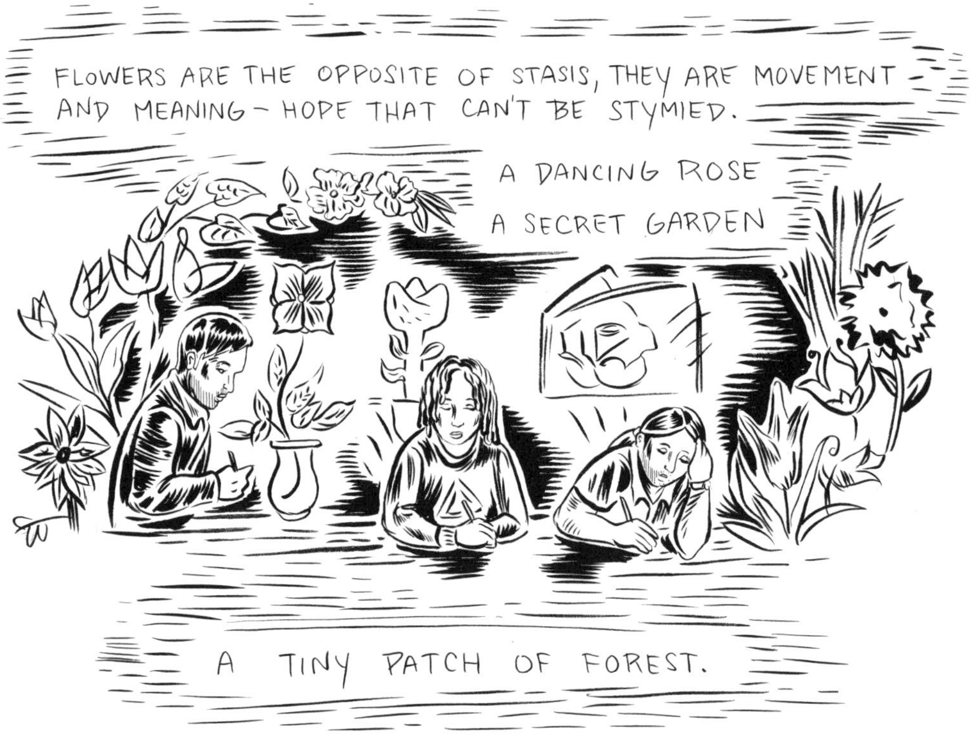
FLOWERS ARE THE OPPOSITE OF STASIS, THEY ARE MOVEMENT AND MEANING – HOPE THAT CAN'T BE STYMIED.
A DANCING ROSE
A SECRET GARDEN
A TINY PATCH OF FOREST.

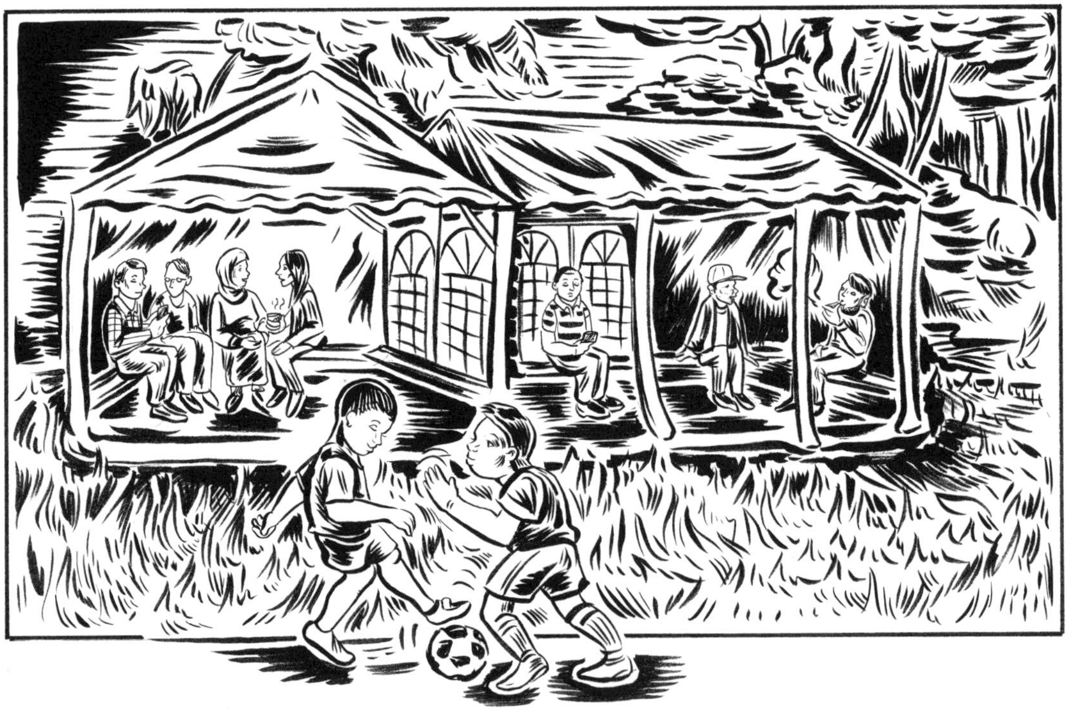

SUMMER

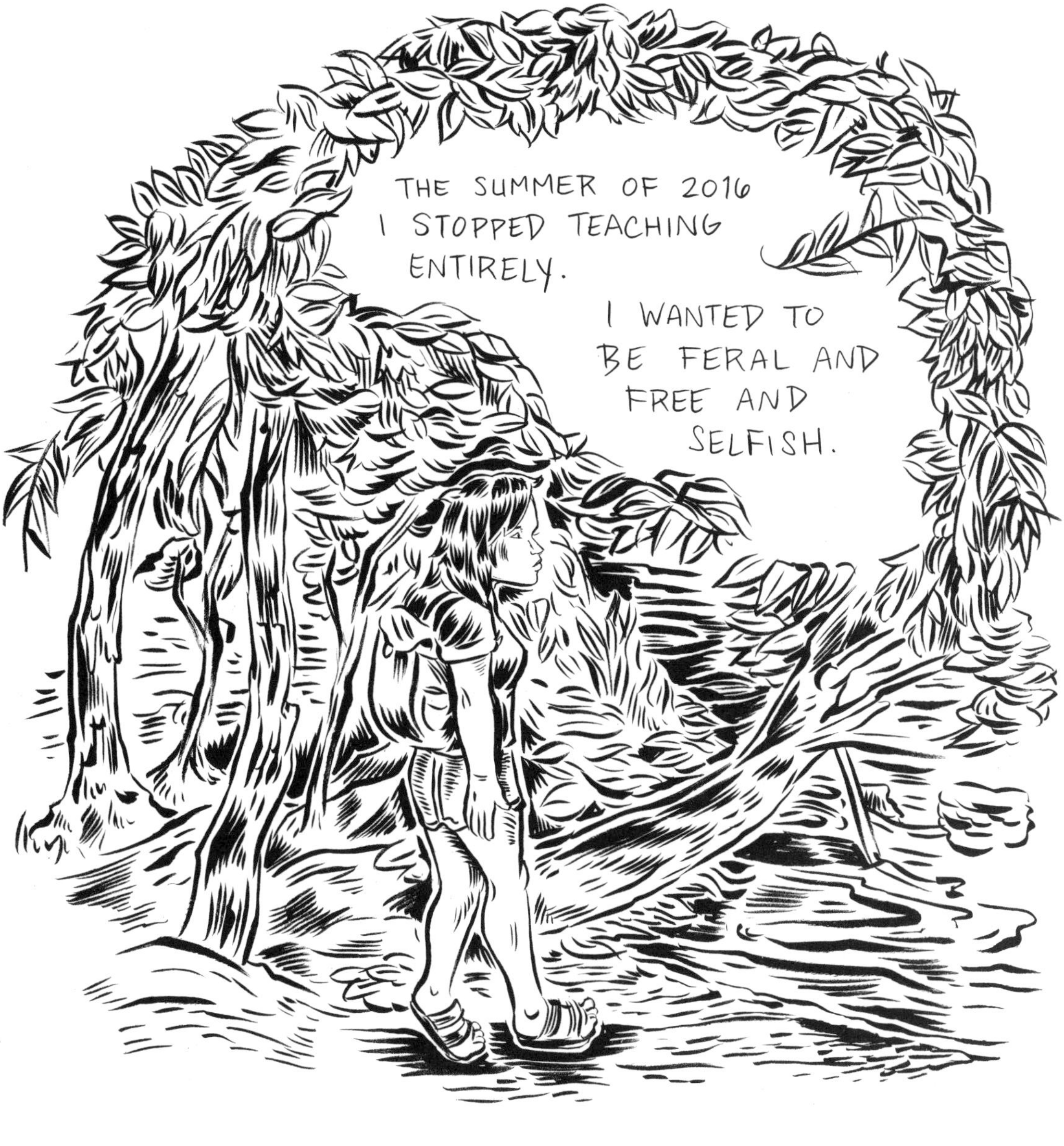
THE SUMMER OF 2016
I STOPPED TEACHING
ENTIRELY.
I WANTED TO
BE FERAL AND
FREE AND
SELFISH.

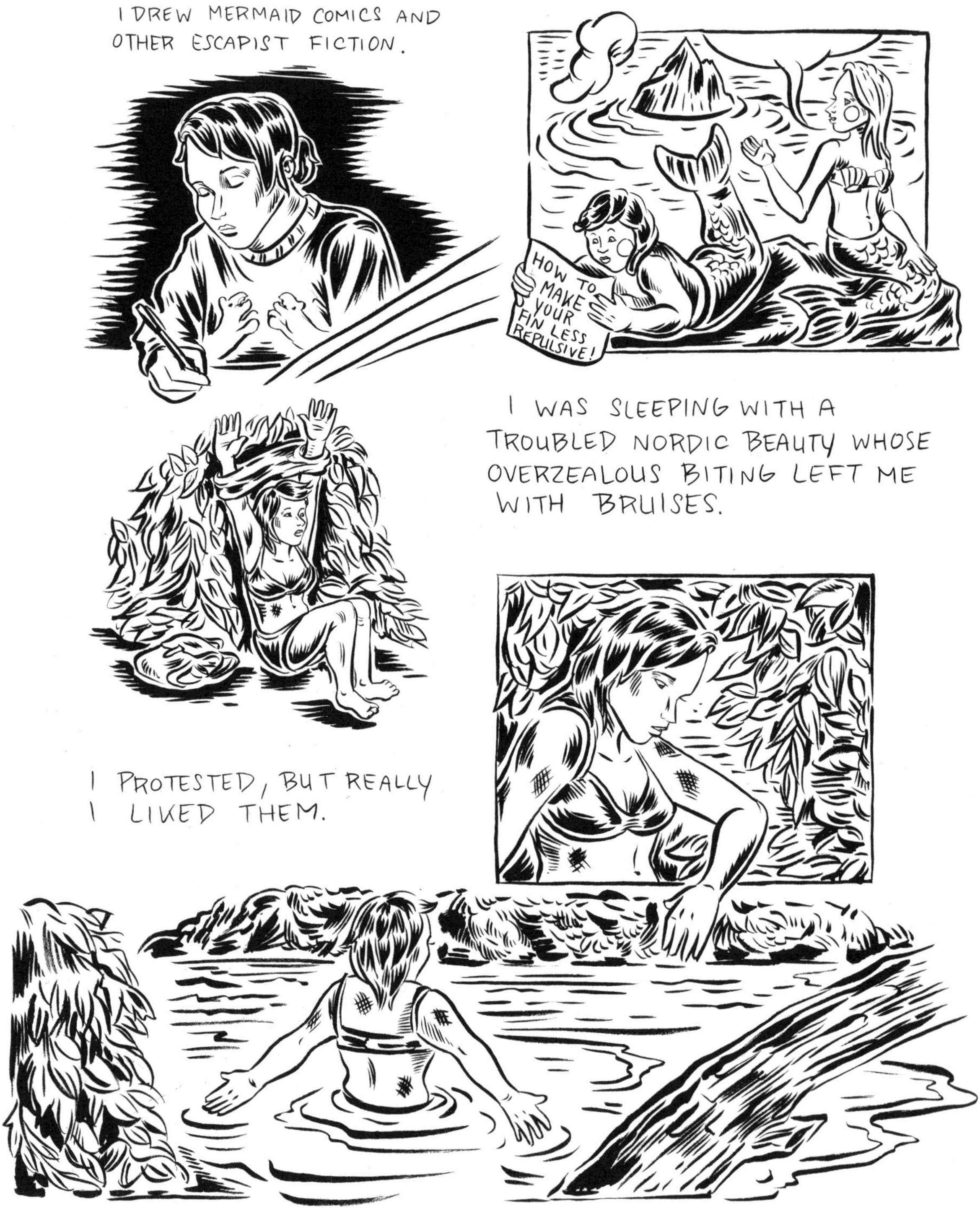
I DREW MERMAID COMICS AND OTHER ESCAPIST FICTION.
HOW TO MAKE YOUR FIN LESS REPULSIVE!
I WAS SLEEPING WITH A TROUBLED NORDIC BEAUTY WHOSE OVERZEALOUS BITING LEFT ME WITH BRUISES.
I PROTESTED, BUT REALLY I LIKED THEM.

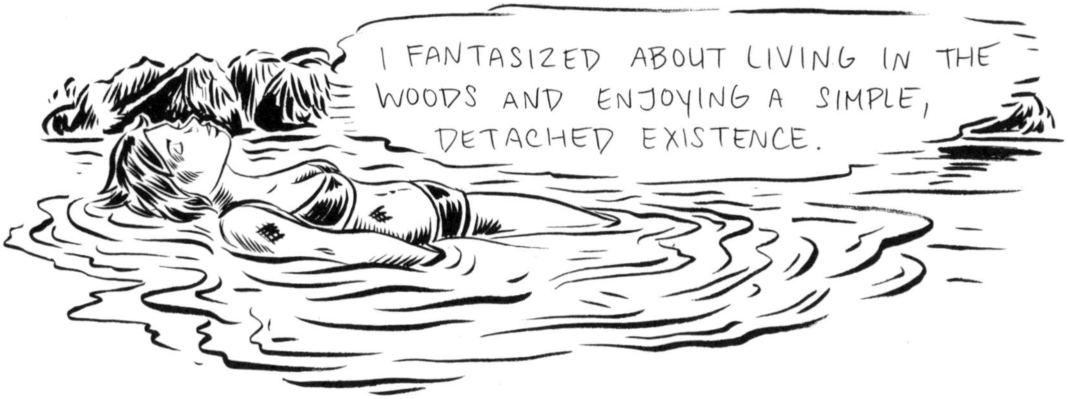
I FANTASIZED ABOUT LIVING IN THE WOODS AND ENJOYING A SIMPLE, DETACHED EXISTENCE.

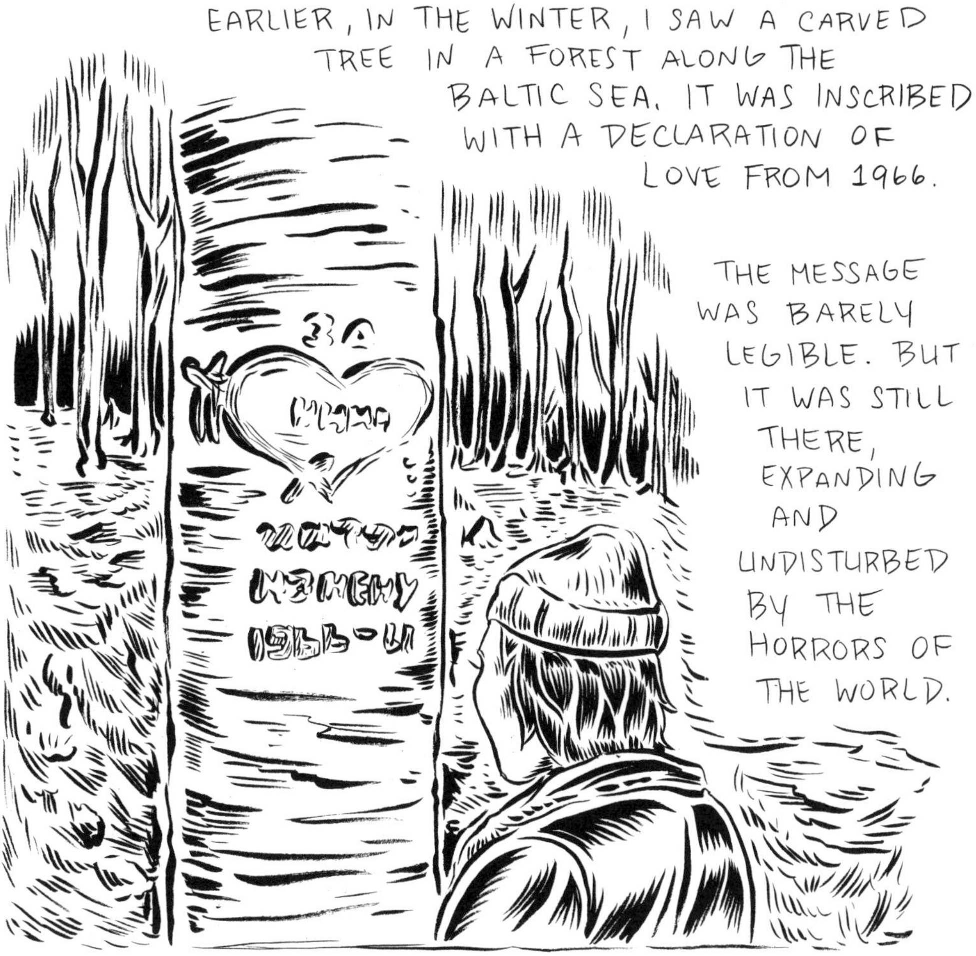
EARLIER, IN THE WINTER, I SAW A CARVED TREE IN A FOREST ALONG THE BALTIC SEA. IT WAS INSCRIBED WITH A DECLARATION OF LOVE FROM 1966.
THE MESSAGE WAS BARELY LEGIBLE. BUT IT WAS STILL THERE, EXPANDING AND UNDISTURBED BY THE HORRORS OF THE WORLD.

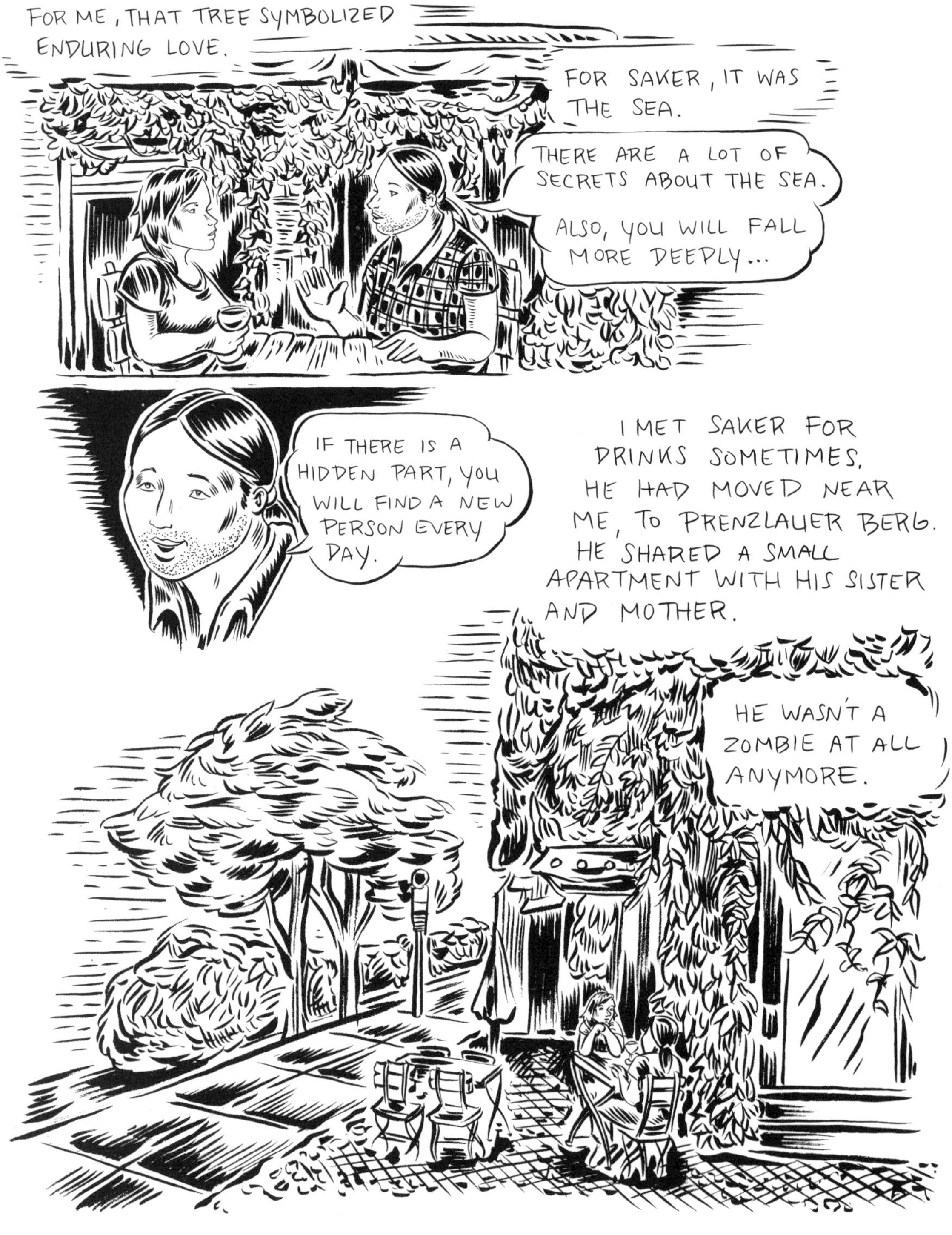
FOR ME, THAT TREE SYMBOLIZED ENDURING LOVE.
FOR SAKER, IT WAS THE SEA.
THERE ARE A LOT OF SECRETS ABOUT THE SEA.
ALSO, YOU WILL FALL MORE DEEPLY...
IF THERE IS A HIDDEN PART, YOU WILL FIND A NEW PERSON EVERY DAY.
I MET SAKER FOR DRINKS SOMETIMES. HE HAD MOVED NEAR ME, TO PRENZLAUER BERG. HE SHARED A SMALL APARTMENT WITH HIS SISTER AND MOTHER.
HE WASN'T A ZOMBIE AT ALL ANYMORE.

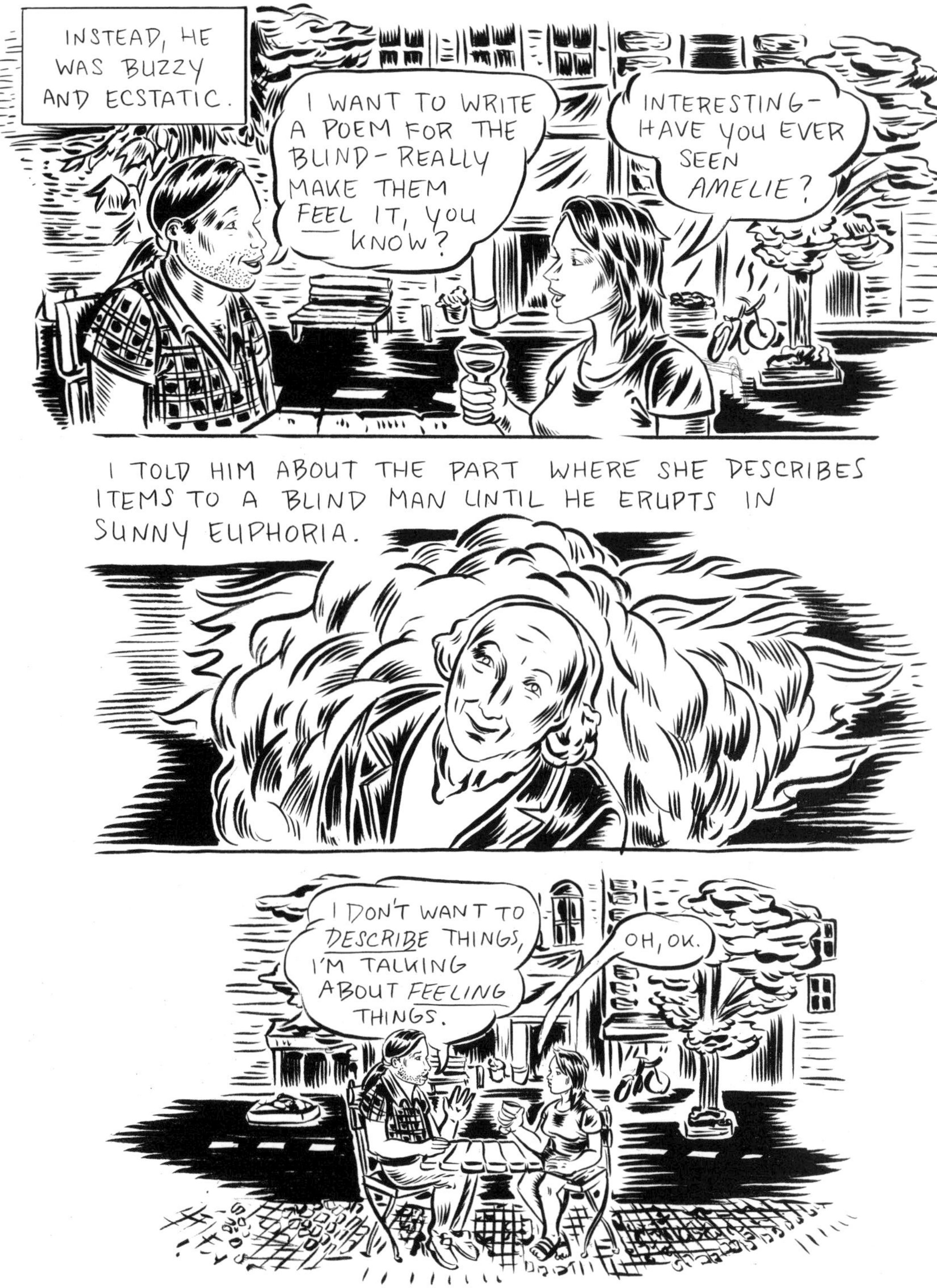
INSTEAD, HE WAS BUZZY AND ECSTATIC.
I WANT TO WRITE A POEM FOR THE BLIND - REALLY MAKE THEM FEEL IT, YOU KNOW?
INTERESTING - HAVE YOU EVER SEEN AMELIE?
I TOLD HIM ABOUT THE PART WHERE SHE DESCRIBES ITEMS TO A BLIND MAN UNTIL HE ERUPTS IN SUNNY EUPHORIA.
I DON'T WANT TO DESCRIBE THINGS, I'M TALKING ABOUT FEELING THINGS.
OH, OK.

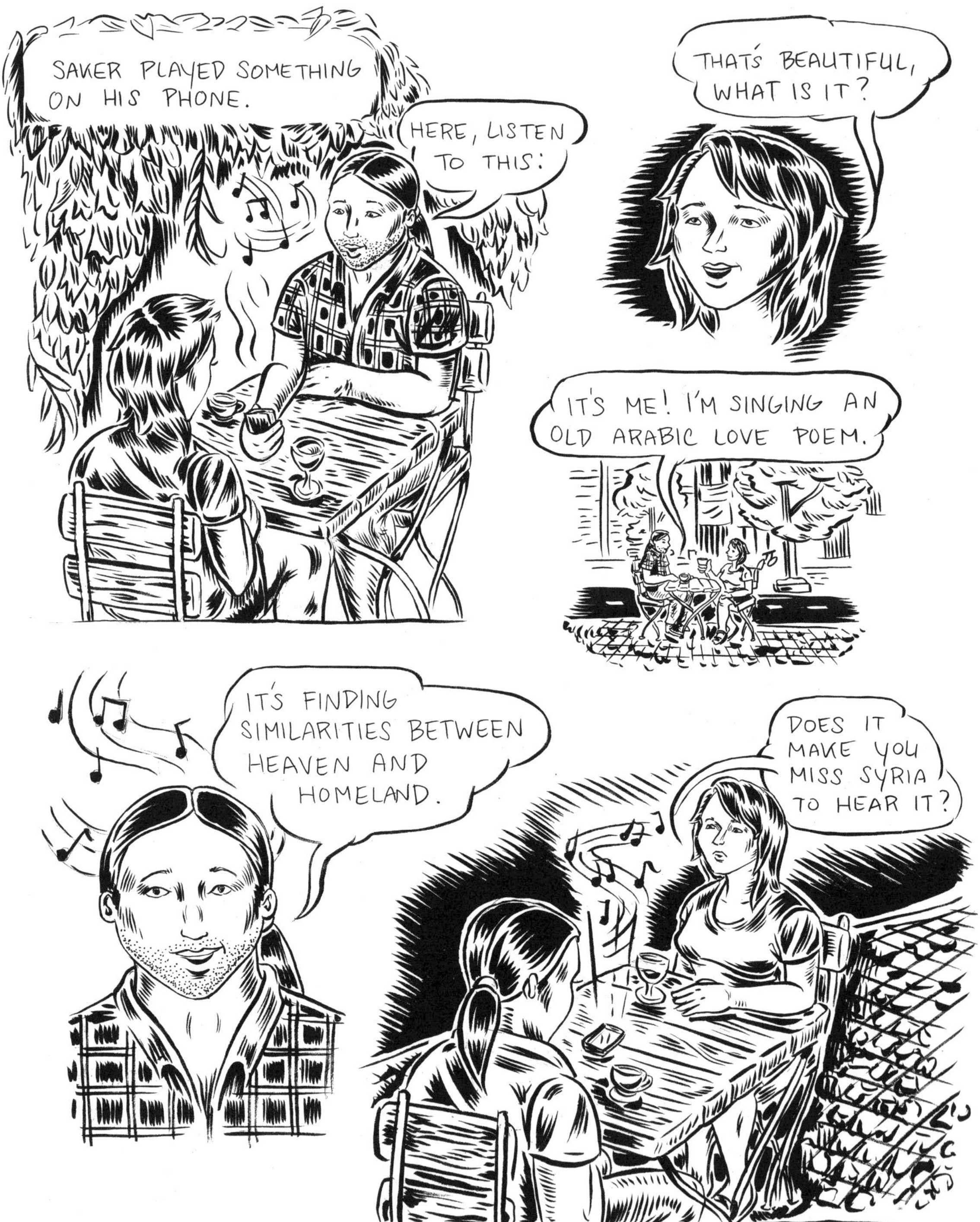
SAKER PLAYED SOMETHING ON HIS PHONE.
HERE, LISTEN TO THIS:
THAT'S BEAUTIFUL, WHAT IS IT?
IT'S ME! I'M SINGING AN OLD ARABIC LOVE POEM.
IT'S FINDING SIMILARITIES BETWEEN HEAVEN AND HOMELAND.
DOES IT MAKE YOU MISS SYRIA TO HEAR IT?

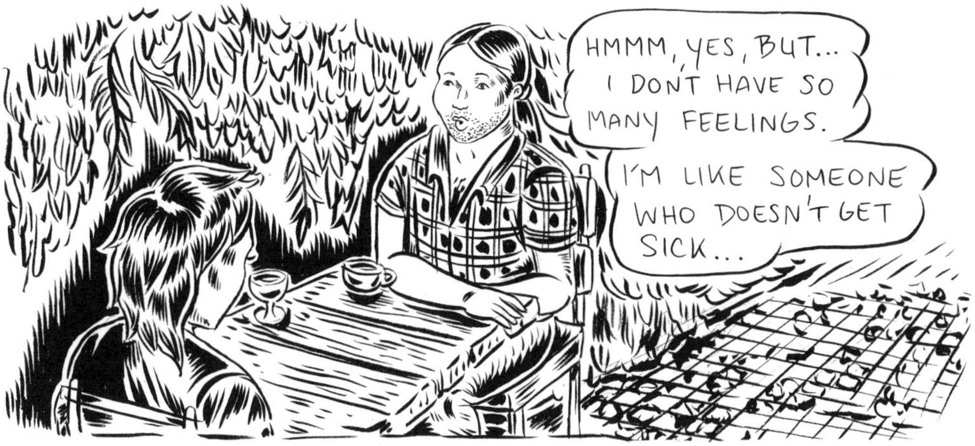
HMMM, YES, BUT... I DON'T HAVE SO MANY FEELINGS.
I'M LIKE SOMEONE WHO DOESN'T GET SICK...

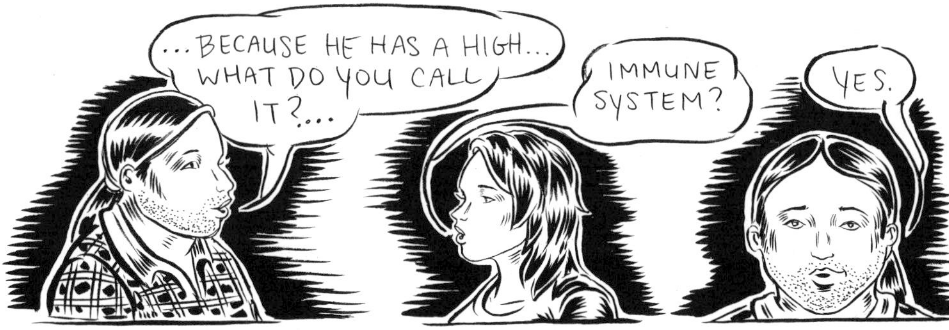
...BECAUSE HE HAS A HIGH... WHAT DO YOU CALL IT?...
IMMUNE SYSTEM?
YES.

SAKER WAS BUSY. HE WAS TAKING GERMAN COURSES IN STEGLITZ AND HE HAD A "*PRAKTIKUM*," OR INTERNSHIP.

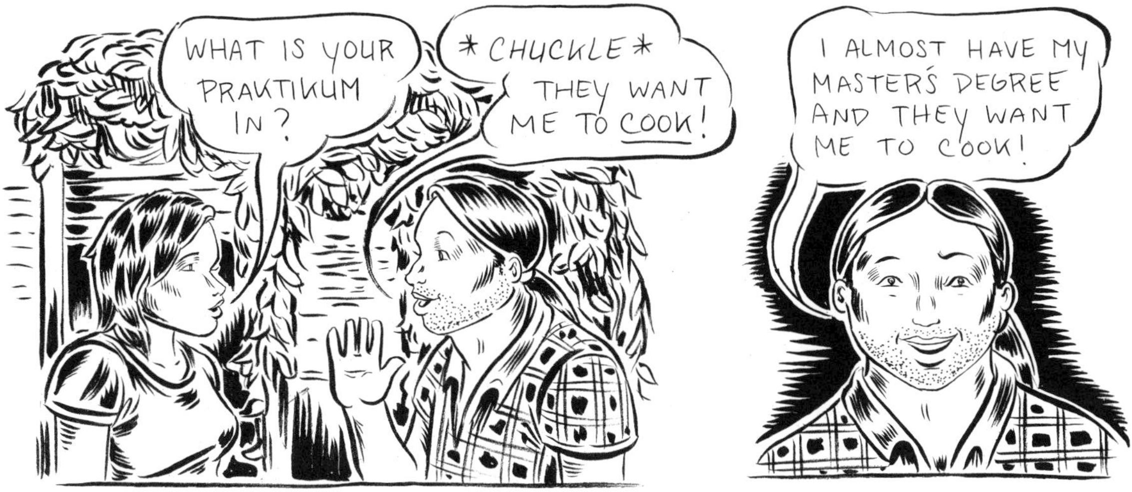
WHAT IS YOUR PRAKTIKUM IN?
CHUCKLE THEY WANT ME TO COOK!
I ALMOST HAVE MY MASTER'S DEGREE AND THEY WANT ME TO COOK!

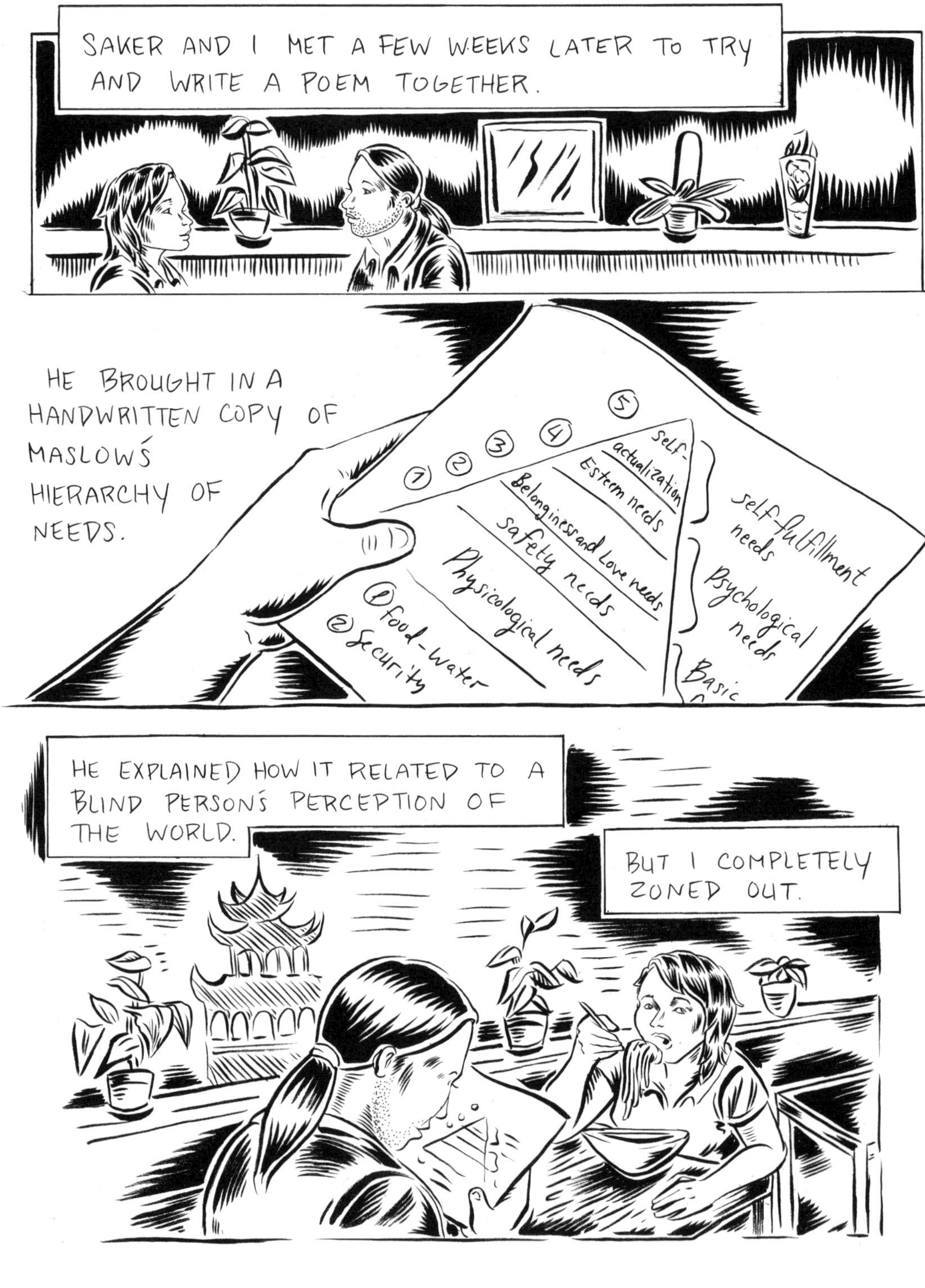
SAKER AND I MET A FEW WEEKS LATER TO TRY AND WRITE A POEM TOGETHER.
HE BROUGHT IN A HANDWRITTEN COPY OF MASLOW'S HIERARCHY OF NEEDS.
self-actualization
Esteem needs
Belonginess and Love needs
safety needs
Physicological needs
self-fulfillment needs
Psychological needs
Basic
① food-water
② Security
HE EXPLAINED HOW IT RELATED TO A BLIND PERSON'S PERCEPTION OF THE WORLD.
BUT I COMPLETELY ZONED OUT.

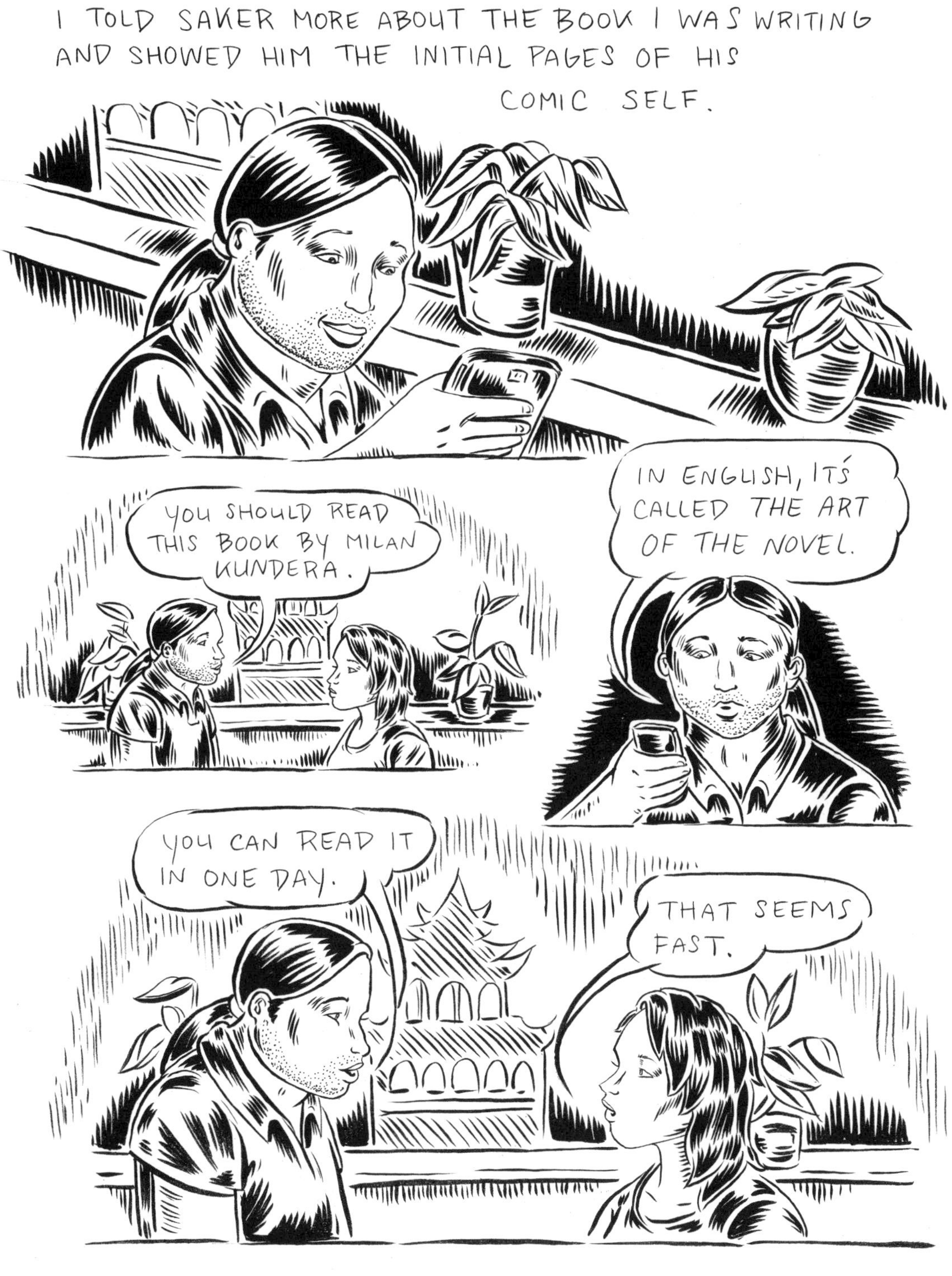
I TOLD SAKER MORE ABOUT THE BOOK I WAS WRITING AND SHOWED HIM THE INITIAL PAGES OF HIS COMIC SELF.
YOU SHOULD READ THIS BOOK BY MILAN KUNDERA.
IN ENGLISH, IT'S CALLED THE ART OF THE NOVEL.
YOU CAN READ IT IN ONE DAY.
THAT SEEMS FAST.

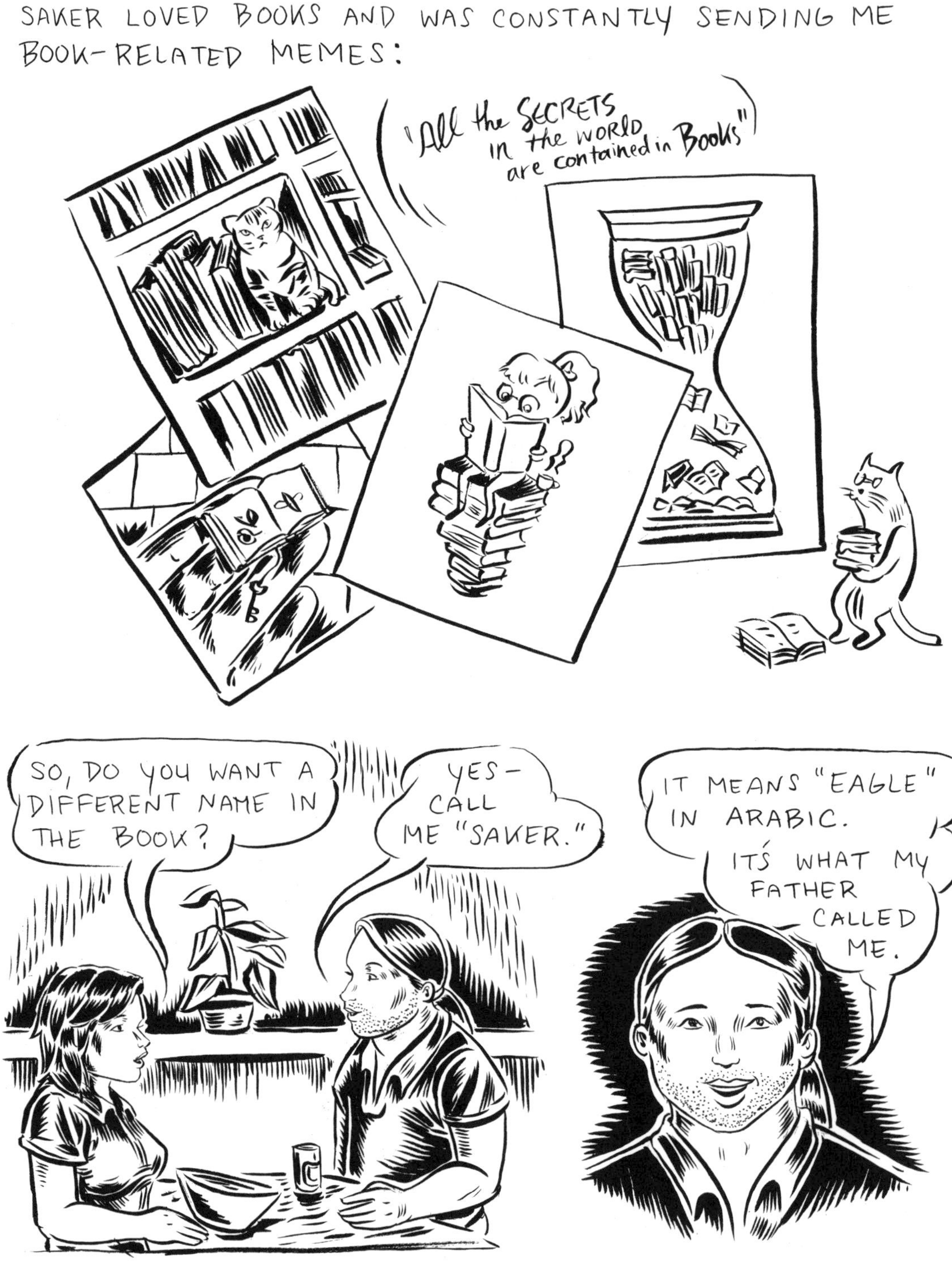
SAKER LOVED BOOKS AND WAS CONSTANTLY SENDING ME BOOK-RELATED MEMES:
"All the SECRETS in the WORLD are contained in Books"
SO, DO YOU WANT A DIFFERENT NAME IN THE BOOK?
YES- CALL ME "SAKER."
IT MEANS "EAGLE" IN ARABIC.
IT'S WHAT MY FATHER CALLED ME.

HANDS

IN THE FALL, I STARTED TEACHING AT AN LGBT REFUGEE SHELTER.

I WAS HAPPY TO RETURN TO THE COMMUNION OF DRAWING.

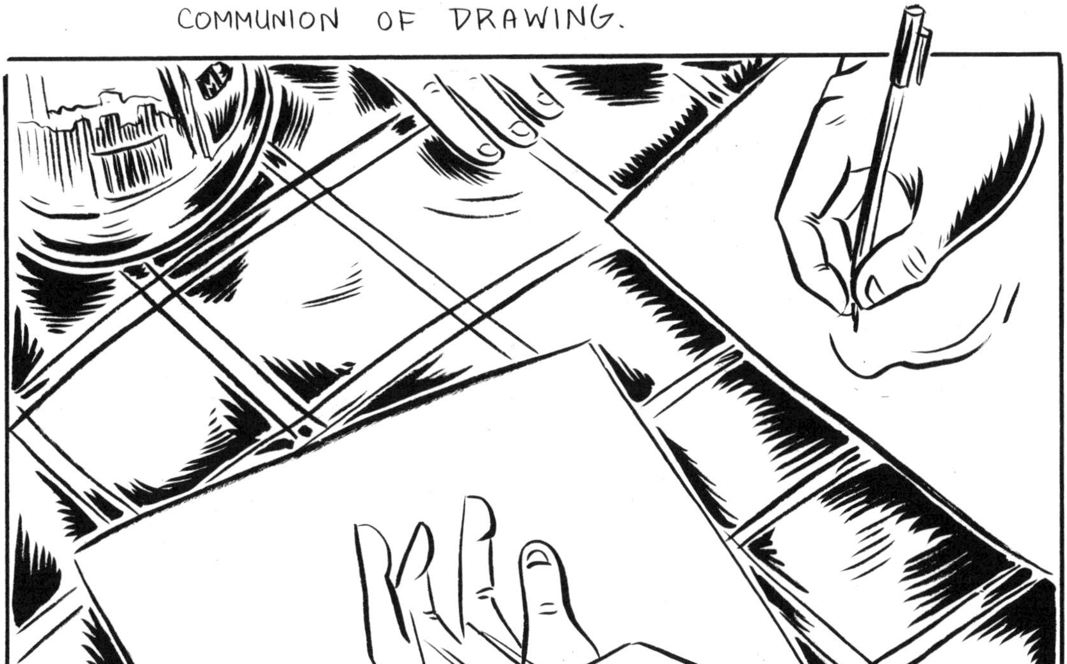

IT WAS SPARE AND WELCOMING, MORE LIKE A
COMMUNITY CENTER WITH ADJOINING APARTMENTS.

PEOPLE CAME FROM SYRIA, BUT ALSO FROM
EGYPT, IRAN AND RUSSIA.

JORAM FROM SYRIA ENTERTAINED US WITH MAGIC TRICKS.

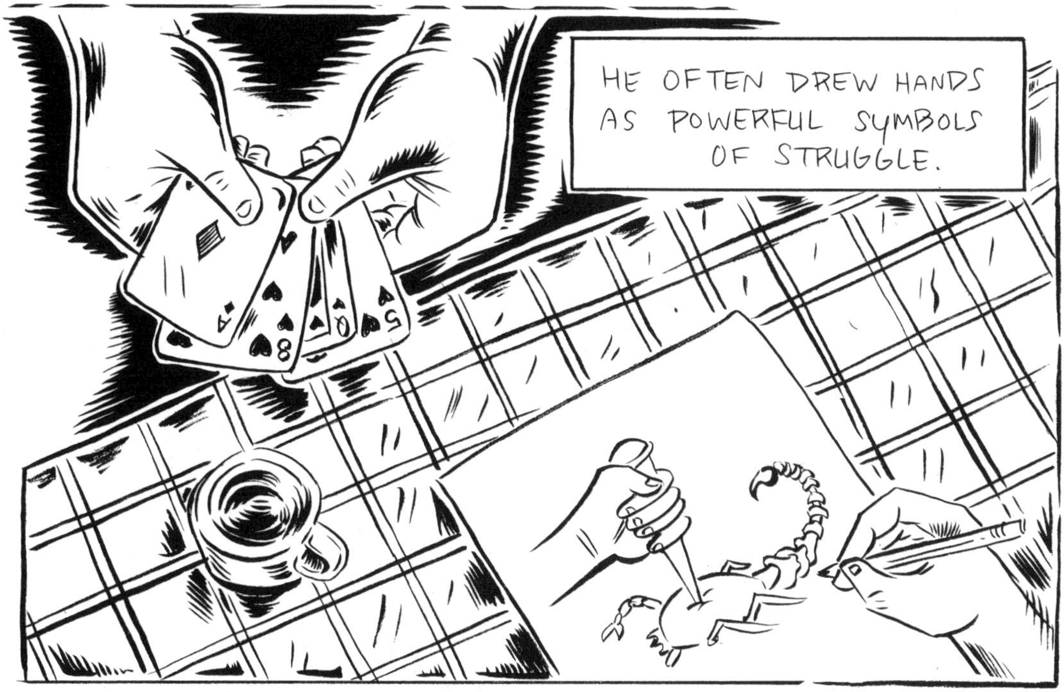
HE OFTEN DREW HANDS AS POWERFUL SYMBOLS OF STRUGGLE.

OCCASIONALLY HE WOULD ALSO DRAW DIRTY NEW-YORKER-STYLE CARTOONS.

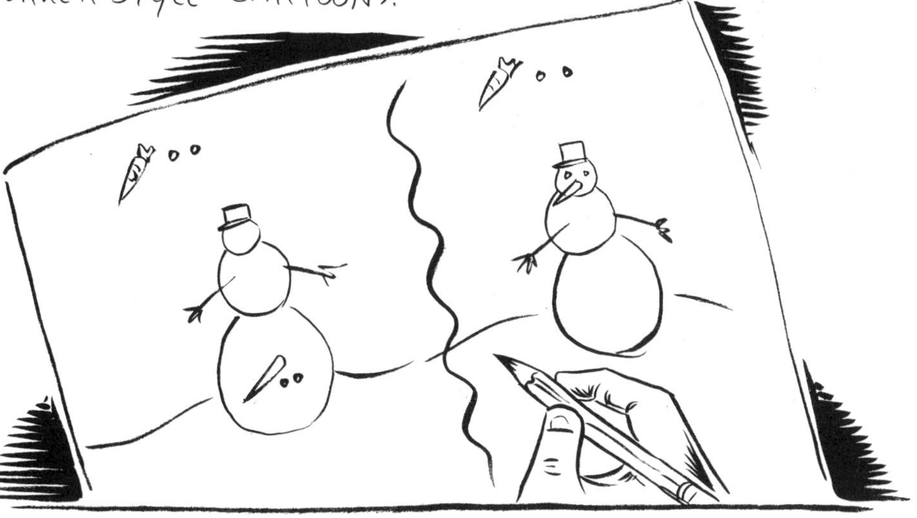

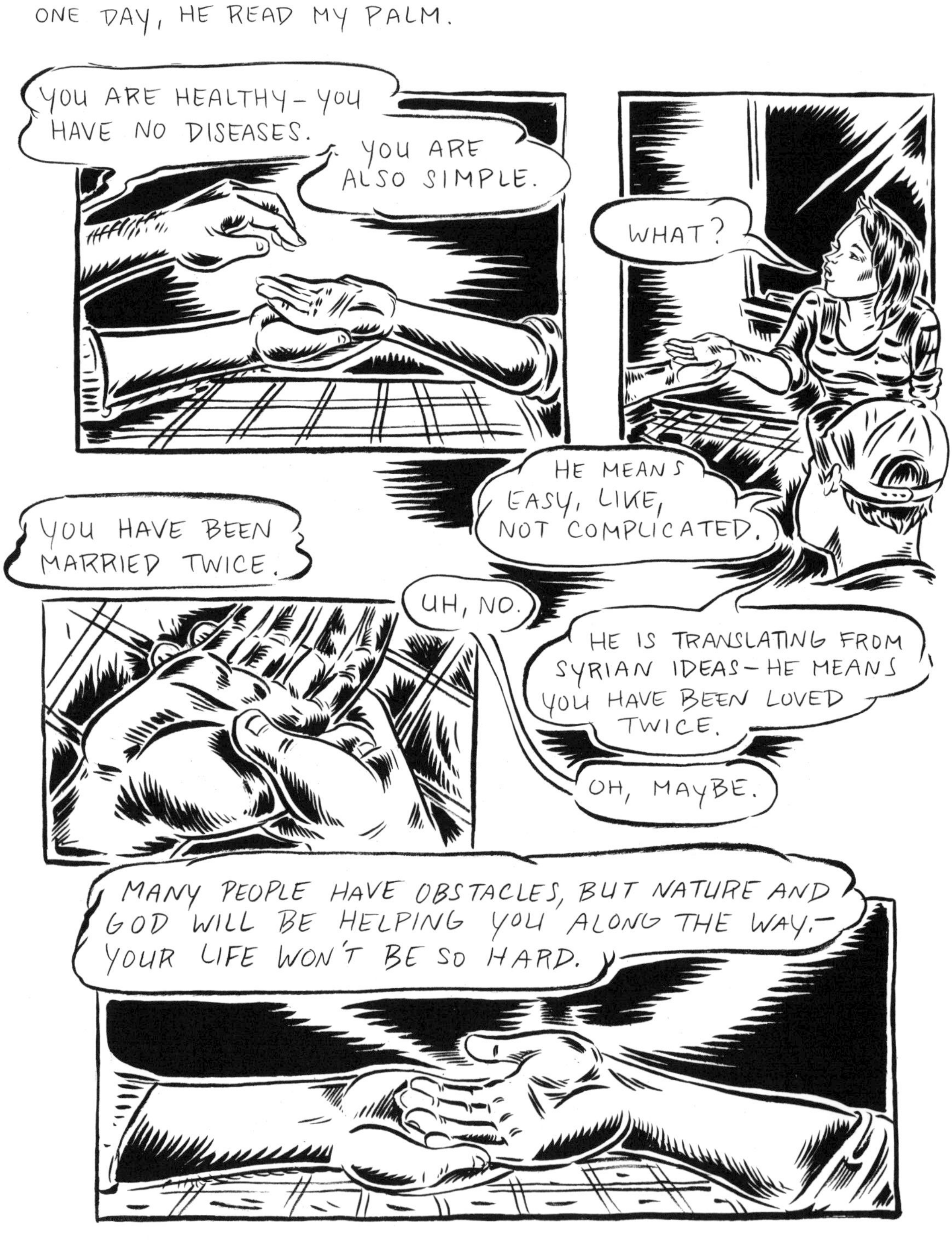
ONE DAY, HE READ MY PALM.
YOU ARE HEALTHY – YOU HAVE NO DISEASES.
YOU ARE ALSO SIMPLE.
WHAT?
HE MEANS EASY, LIKE, NOT COMPLICATED.
YOU HAVE BEEN MARRIED TWICE.
UH, NO.
HE IS TRANSLATING FROM SYRIAN IDEAS – HE MEANS YOU HAVE BEEN LOVED TWICE.
OH, MAYBE.
MANY PEOPLE HAVE OBSTACLES, BUT NATURE AND GOD WILL BE HELPING YOU ALONG THE WAY. – YOUR LIFE WON'T BE SO HARD.

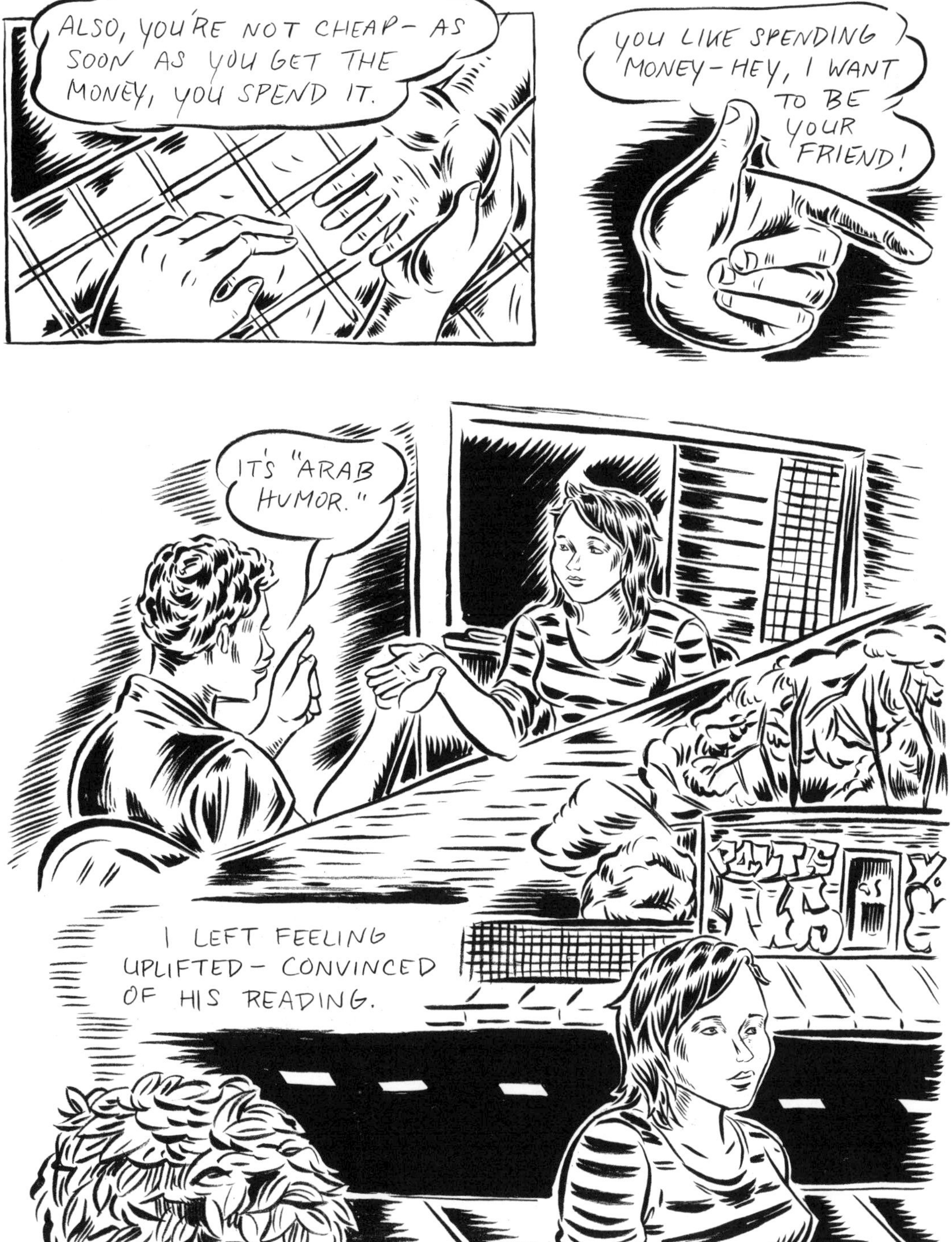
ALSO, YOU'RE NOT CHEAP– AS SOON AS YOU GET THE MONEY, YOU SPEND IT.
YOU LIKE SPENDING MONEY– HEY, I WANT TO BE YOUR FRIEND!
IT'S "ARAB HUMOR."
I LEFT FEELING UPLIFTED– CONVINCED OF HIS READING.

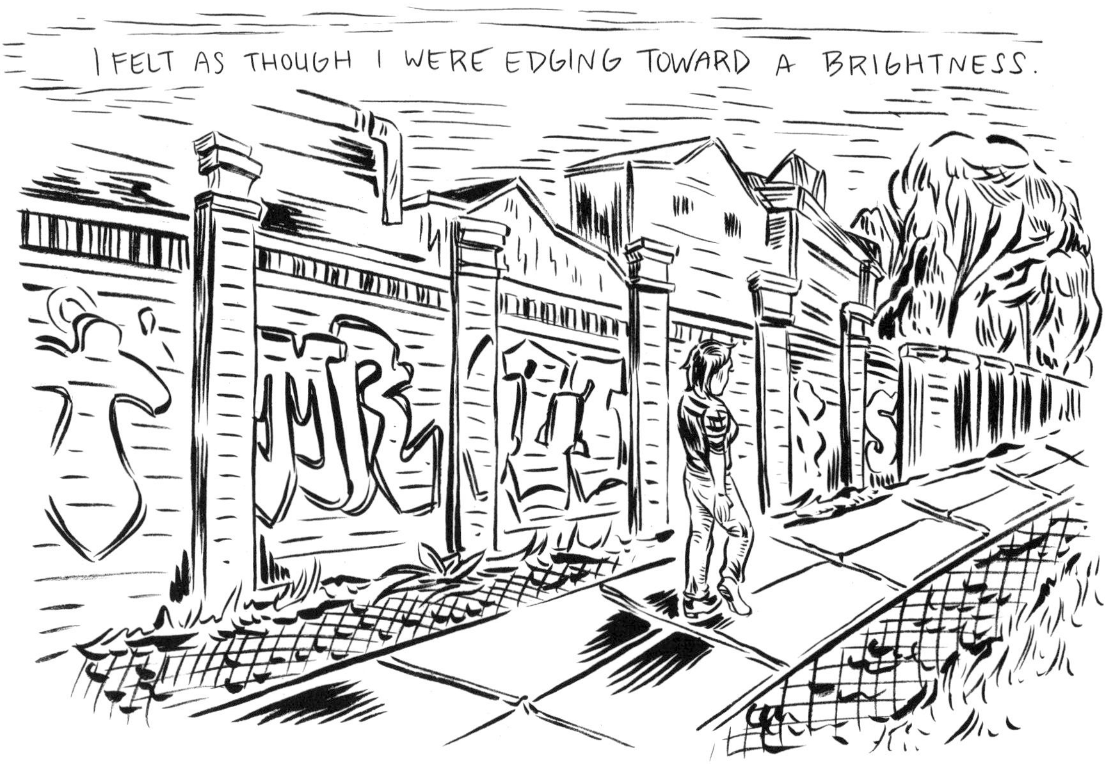
I FELT AS THOUGH I WERE EDGING TOWARD A BRIGHTNESS.

I WAS INSUFFERABLY LUCKY.

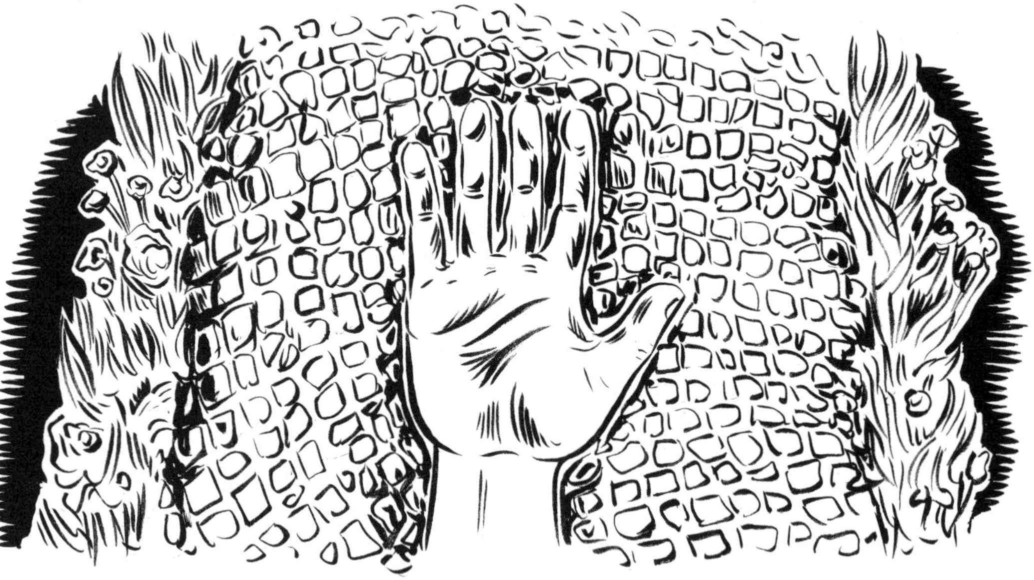

MICHAEL & THE FUTURE

IT TOOK ME A MOMENT TO RECOGNIZE MICHAEL - HE HAD GROWN A FULL BEARD.
DON'T WORRY, I'M STILL NOT SO RELIGIOUS.

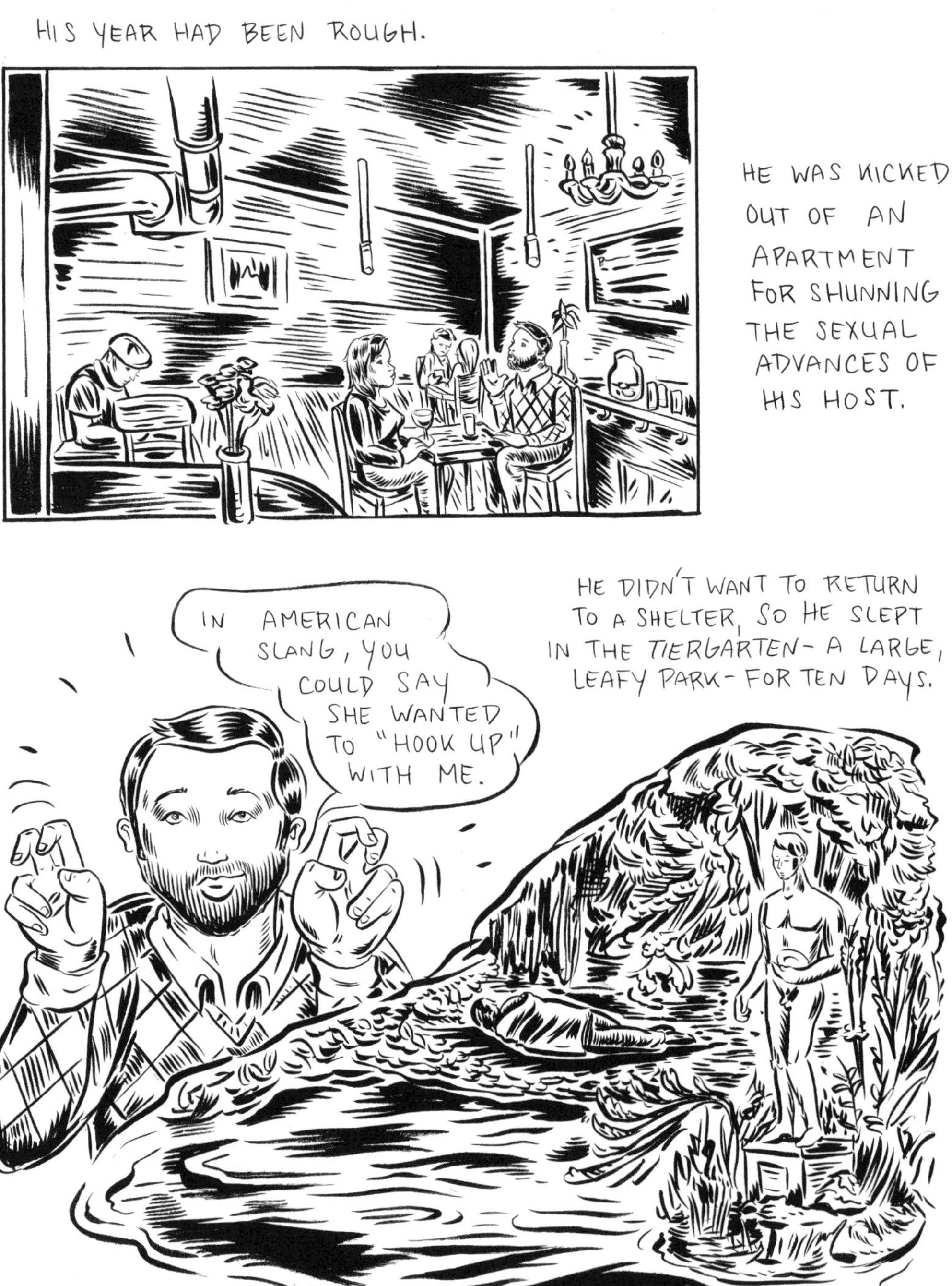
HIS YEAR HAD BEEN ROUGH.
HE WAS KICKED OUT OF AN APARTMENT FOR SHUNNING THE SEXUAL ADVANCES OF HIS HOST.
IN AMERICAN SLANG, YOU COULD SAY SHE WANTED TO "HOOK UP" WITH ME.
HE DIDN'T WANT TO RETURN TO A SHELTER, SO HE SLEPT IN THE *TIERGARTEN*– A LARGE, LEAFY PARK– FOR TEN DAYS.

CHRISTOPHER ISHERWOOD CLAIMED THAT TIERGARTEN WAS BERLIN'S DARK, DAMP HEART. HE DESCRIBED PEASANT BOYS WHO CAME TO THE CITY IN SEARCH OF WORK IN THE 1920s.

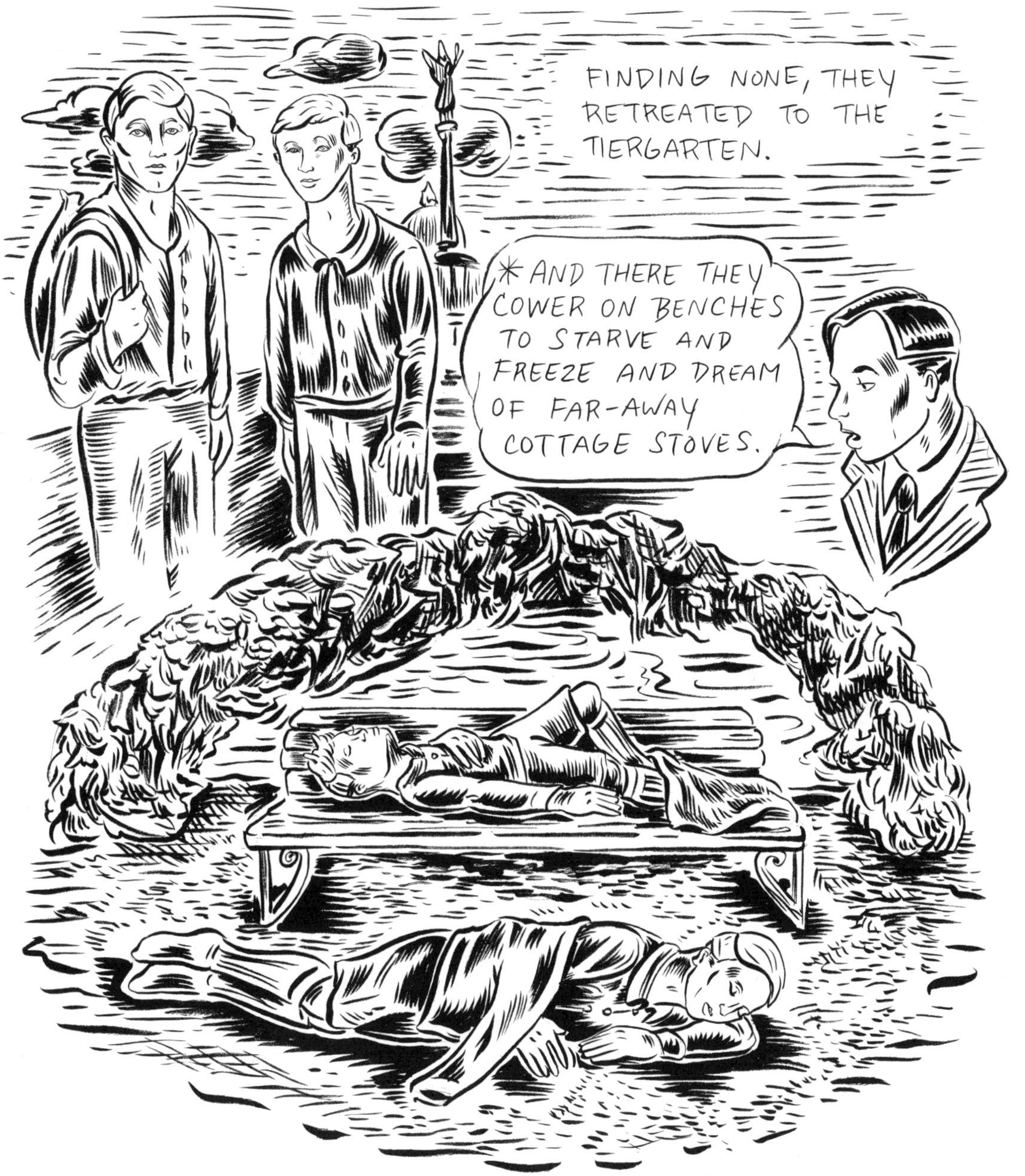
FINDING NONE, THEY RETREATED TO THE TIERGARTEN.
* AND THERE THEY COWER ON BENCHES TO STARVE AND FREEZE AND DREAM OF FAR-AWAY COTTAGE STOVES.

* FROM *THE BERLIN STORIES*

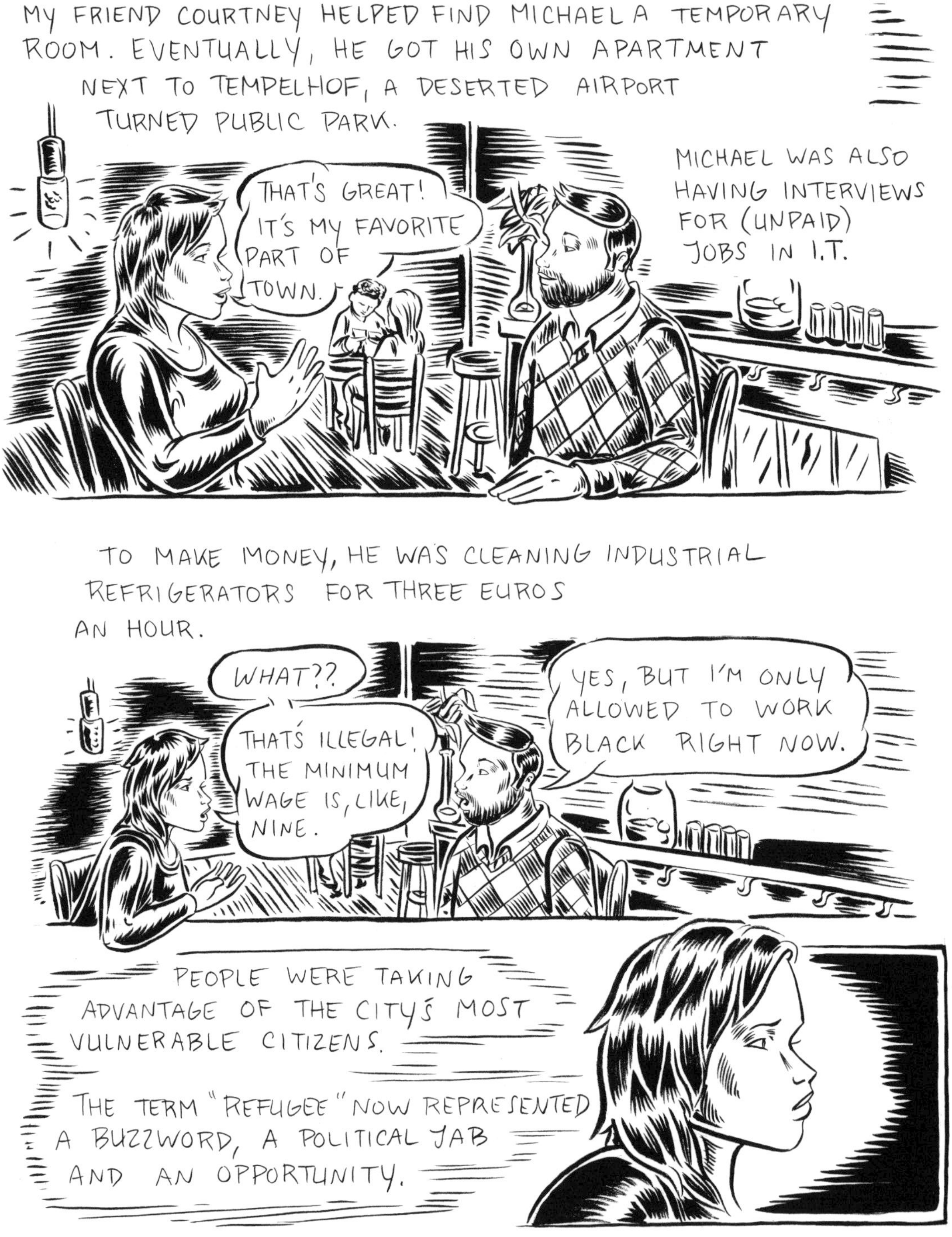
MY FRIEND COURTNEY HELPED FIND MICHAEL A TEMPORARY ROOM. EVENTUALLY, HE GOT HIS OWN APARTMENT NEXT TO TEMPELHOF, A DESERTED AIRPORT TURNED PUBLIC PARK.
THAT'S GREAT! IT'S MY FAVORITE PART OF TOWN.
MICHAEL WAS ALSO HAVING INTERVIEWS FOR (UNPAID) JOBS IN I.T.
TO MAKE MONEY, HE WAS CLEANING INDUSTRIAL REFRIGERATORS FOR THREE EUROS AN HOUR.
WHAT??
THAT'S ILLEGAL! THE MINIMUM WAGE IS, LIKE, NINE.
YES, BUT I'M ONLY ALLOWED TO WORK BLACK RIGHT NOW.
PEOPLE WERE TAKING ADVANTAGE OF THE CITY'S MOST VULNERABLE CITIZENS.
THE TERM "REFUGEE" NOW REPRESENTED A BUZZWORD, A POLITICAL JAB AND AN OPPORTUNITY.

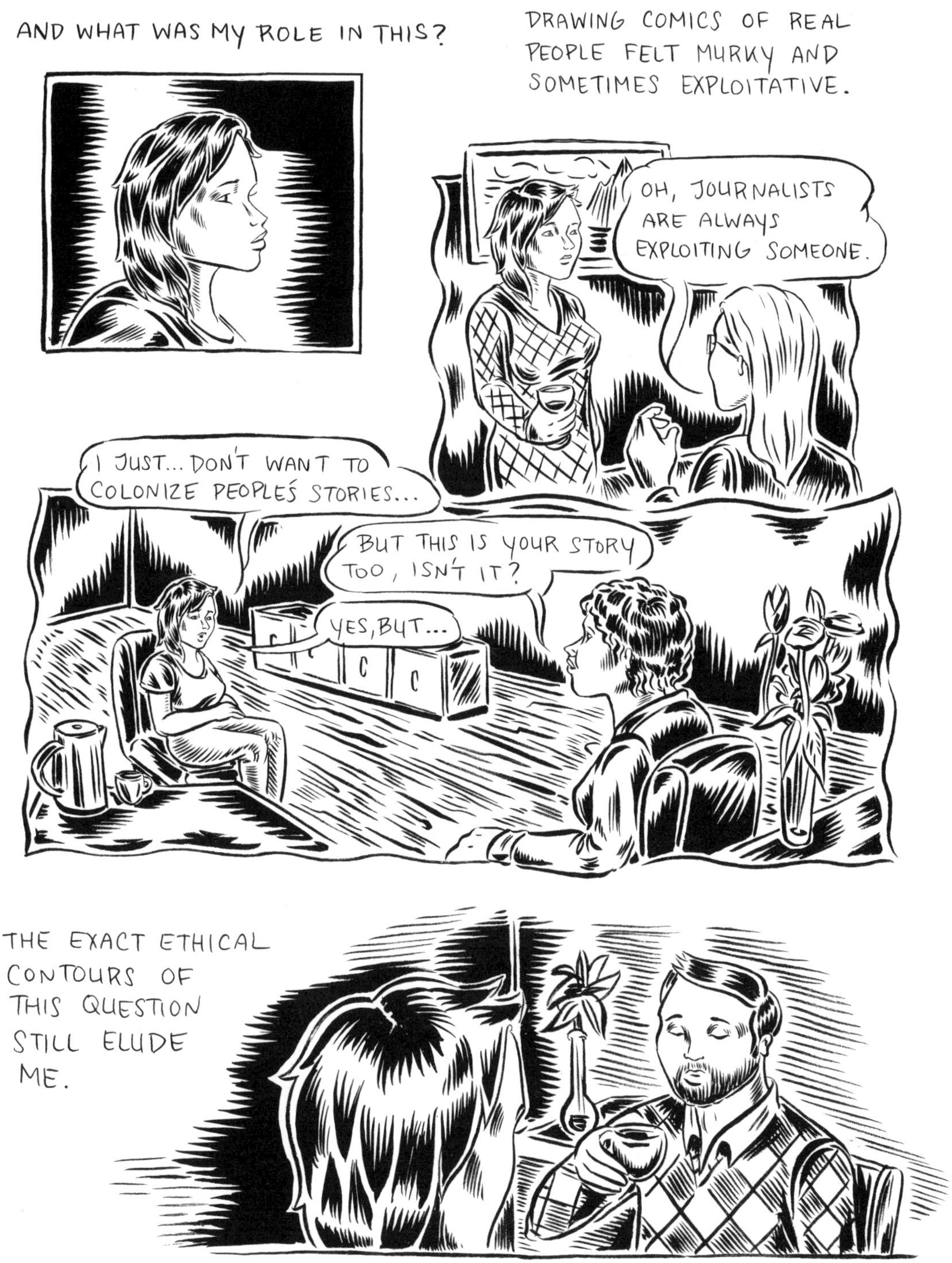
AND WHAT WAS MY ROLE IN THIS?
DRAWING COMICS OF REAL PEOPLE FELT MURKY AND SOMETIMES EXPLOITATIVE.
OH, JOURNALISTS ARE ALWAYS EXPLOITING SOMEONE.
I JUST... DON'T WANT TO COLONIZE PEOPLE'S STORIES...
BUT THIS IS YOUR STORY TOO, ISN'T IT?
YES, BUT...
THE EXACT ETHICAL CONTOURS OF THIS QUESTION STILL ELUDE ME.

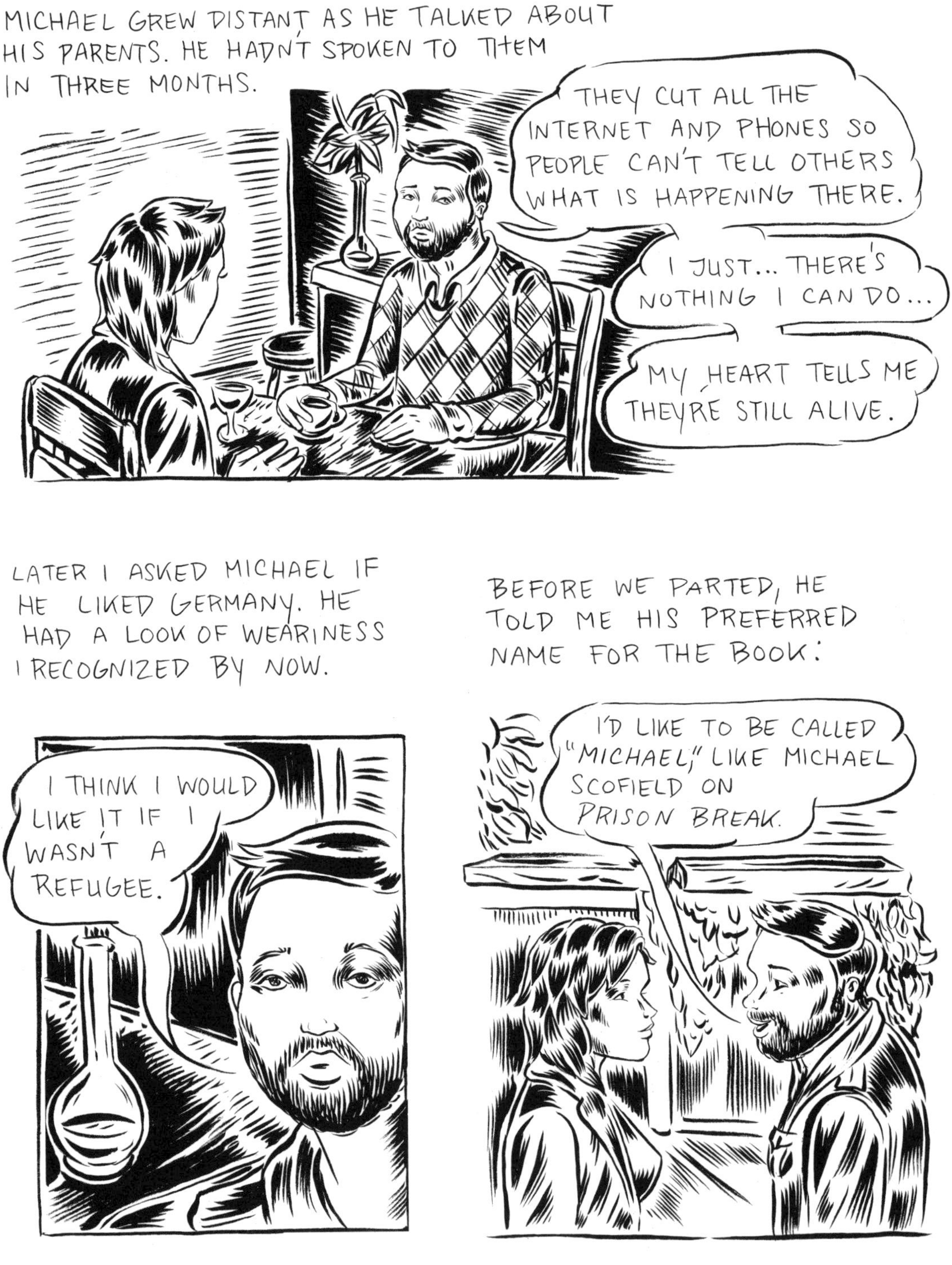
MICHAEL GREW DISTANT AS HE TALKED ABOUT HIS PARENTS. HE HADN'T SPOKEN TO THEM IN THREE MONTHS.
THEY CUT ALL THE INTERNET AND PHONES SO PEOPLE CAN'T TELL OTHERS WHAT IS HAPPENING THERE.
I JUST... THERE'S NOTHING I CAN DO...
MY HEART TELLS ME THEY'RE STILL ALIVE.
LATER I ASKED MICHAEL IF HE LIKED GERMANY. HE HAD A LOOK OF WEARINESS I RECOGNIZED BY NOW.
I THINK I WOULD LIKE IT IF I WASN'T A REFUGEE.
BEFORE WE PARTED, HE TOLD ME HIS PREFERRED NAME FOR THE BOOK:
I'D LIKE TO BE CALLED "MICHAEL," LIKE MICHAEL SCOFIELD ON PRISON BREAK.

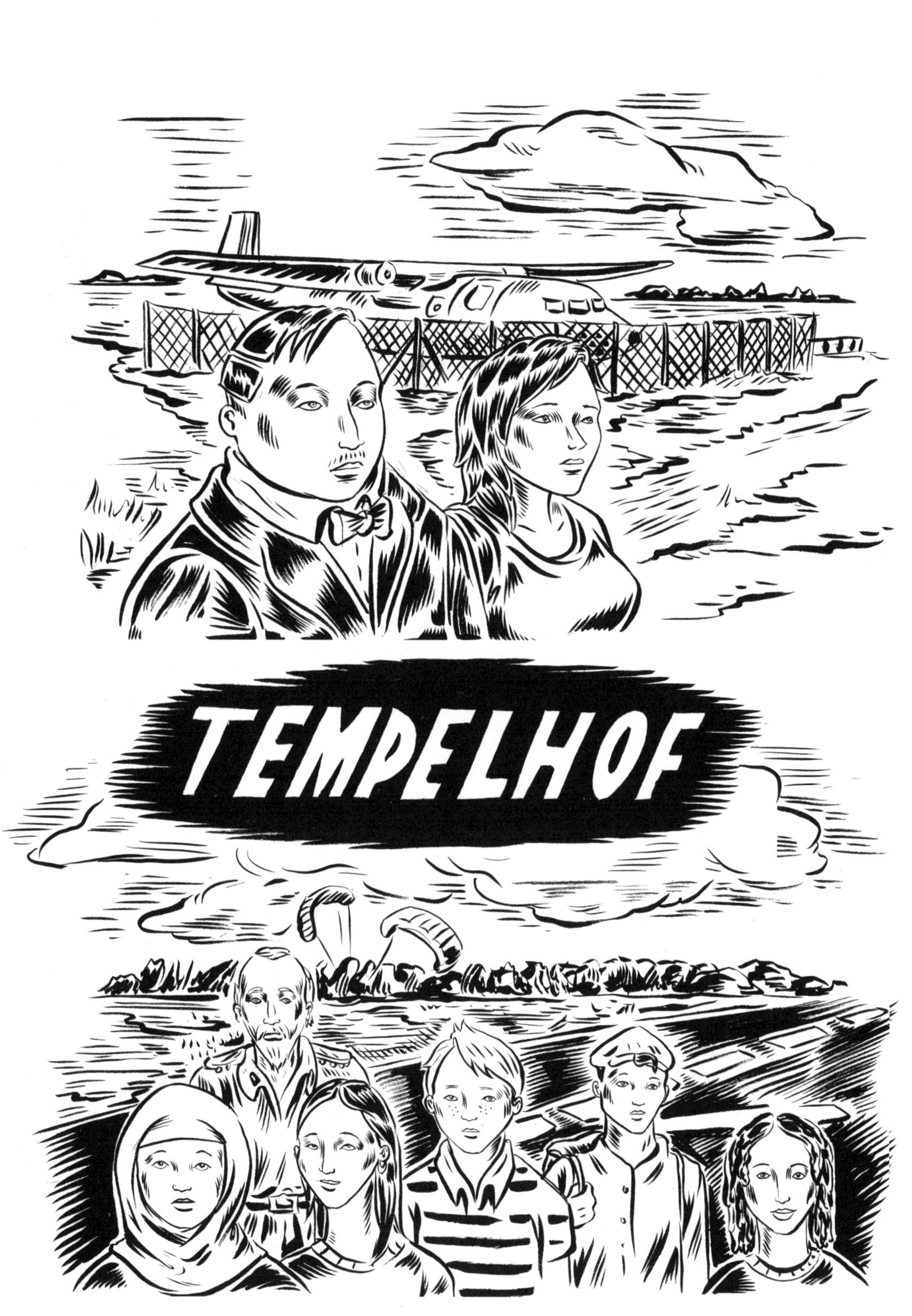
TEMPELHOF

THE DESERTED AIRPORT AT TEMPELHOF
IS SPRAWLING AND OPEN.

THE MAIN, IMPOSING STRUCTURE WAS BUILT BY THE
NAZIS AS A SYMBOL OF HITLER'S *"GERMANIA,"*

IT WAS DESIGNED TO
RESEMBLE AN
EAGLE IN FLIGHT.

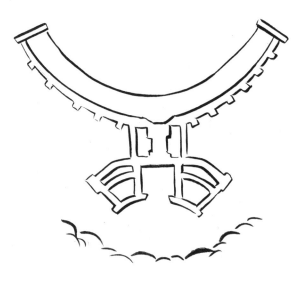

NOW IT'S A MAKESHIFT PARK WHERE THE HORRORS OF WAR ARE REPURPOSED.

THE GRASSY, ONCE BLOODY PLAINS OF "THE BATTLE OF BERLIN" ARE BIRD SANCTUARIES.

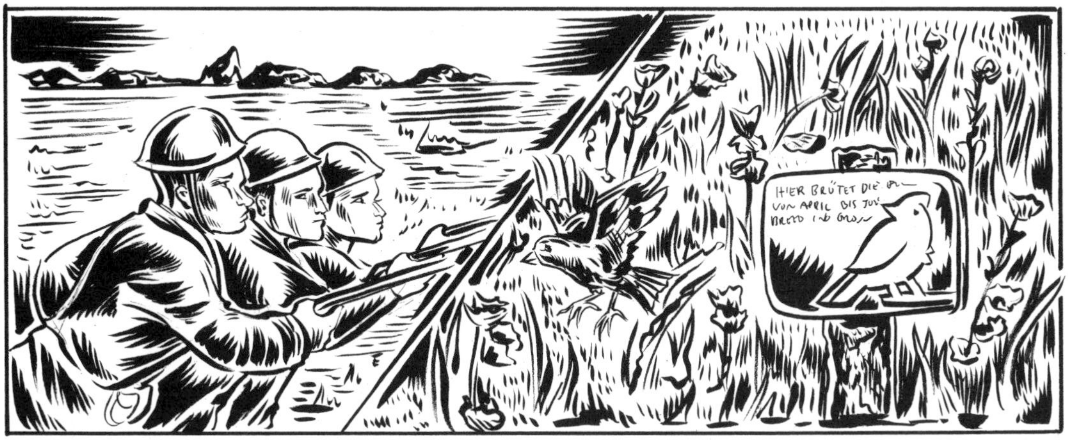
HIER BRÜTET DIE
VON APRIL BIS

THE RUNWAYS WHERE U.S. PLANES TOOK OFF TO FEED STARVING CITIZENS IN THE SOVIET EAST ARE LINED BY COMMUNITY GARDENS.

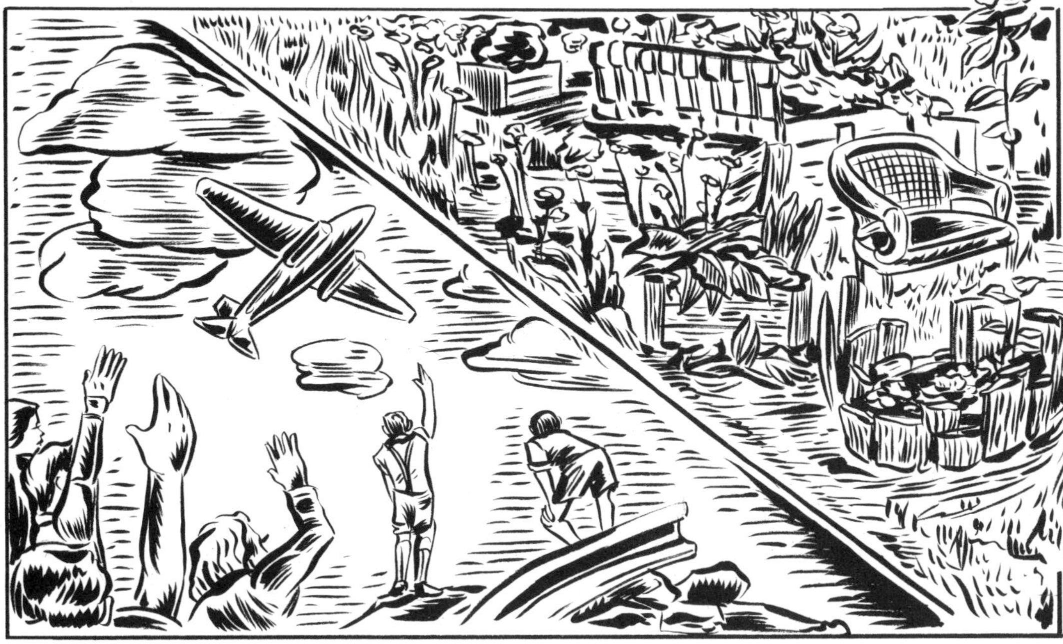

IN 2015, THE GIANT TERMINALS USED TO ASSEMBLE FIGHTER PLANES AND BOMBS WERE CONVERTED INTO BERLIN'S LARGEST REFUGEE SHELTER.

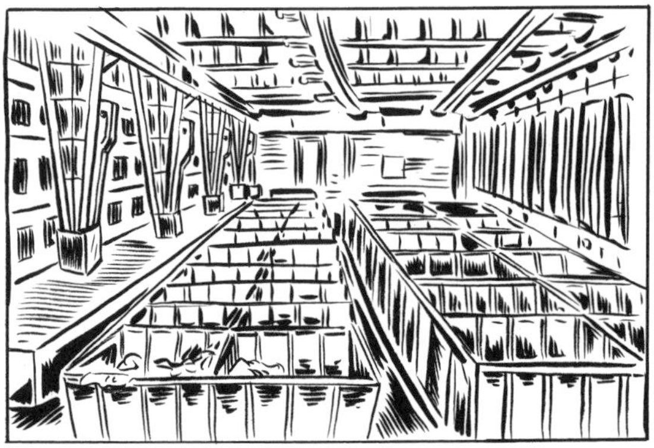

IN 2017, THE VOLKSBÜHNE BEGAN USING HANGAR 5 AS A THEATRE. THE FIRST PIECE, CREATED BY MOHAMMAD AL ATTAR AND OMAR ABUSAADA, STARRED A TROUPE OF YOUNG SYRIAN WOMEN REIMAGINING THE GREEK TRAGEDY "IPHIGENIA."

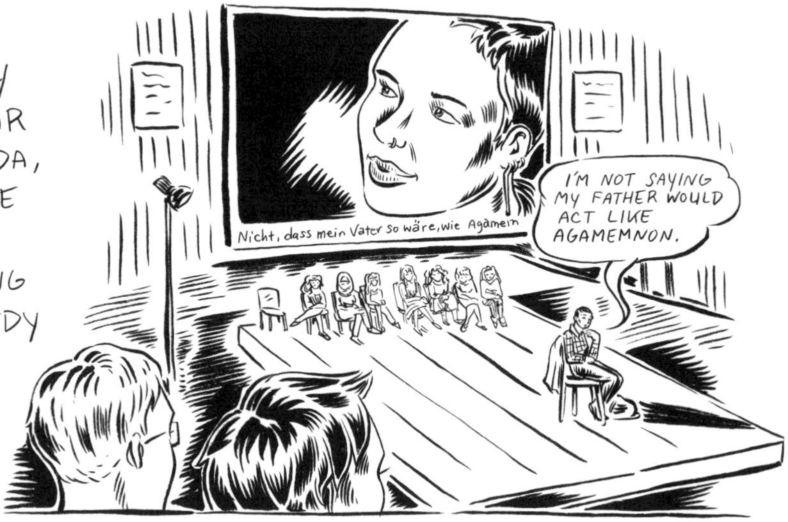
Nicht, dass mein Vater so wäre, wie Agamein
I'M NOT SAYING MY FATHER WOULD ACT LIKE AGAMEMNON.

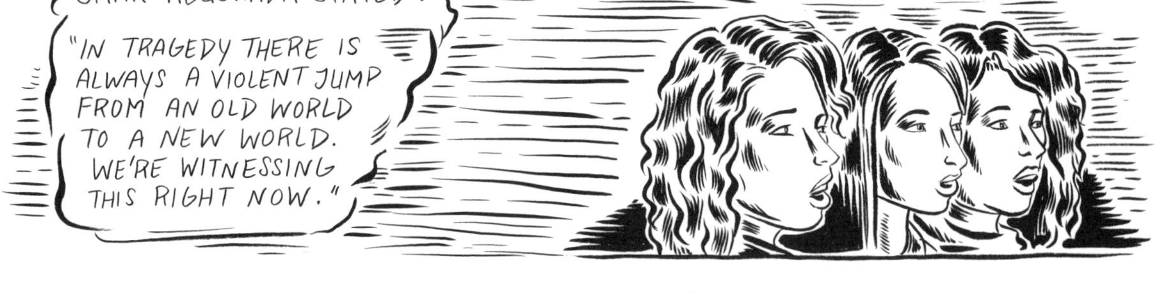
OMAR ABUSAADA STATED:
"IN TRAGEDY THERE IS ALWAYS A VIOLENT JUMP FROM AN OLD WORLD TO A NEW WORLD. WE'RE WITNESSING THIS RIGHT NOW."

EVERY SEPTEMBER, A WELCOME FESTIVAL FOR NEWCOMERS TAKES PLACE ON THE AIRFIELD. IT'S CALLED "SCHÖN, DASS IHR DA SEID!" WHICH ROUGHLY TRANSLATES AS: "IT'S A PLEASURE TO HAVE YOU HERE!"

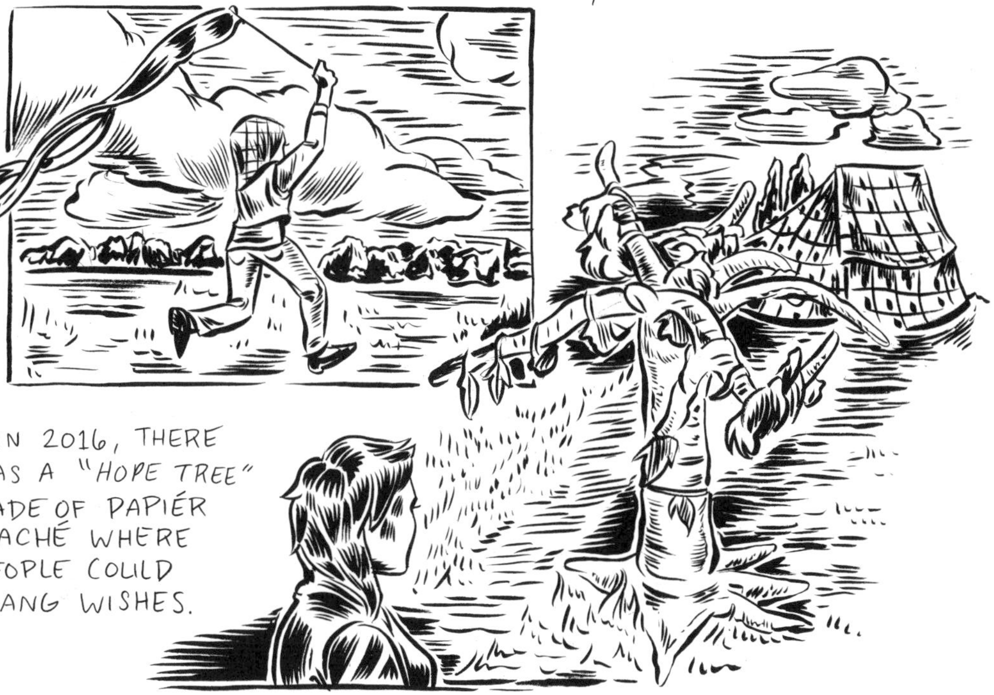

IN 2016, THERE WAS A "HOPE TREE" MADE OF PAPIÉR MACHÉ WHERE PEOPLE COULD HANG WISHES.

THEY WERE SINCERE AND SWEET AND SAD.

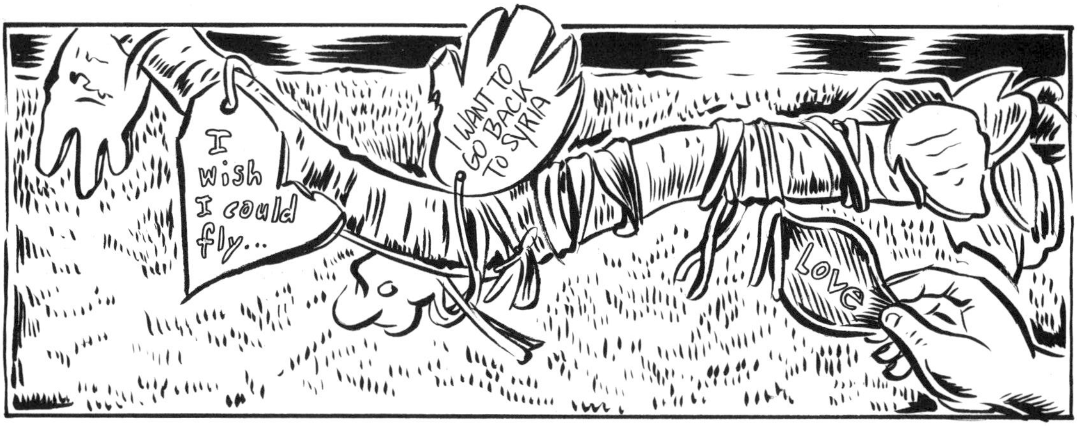
I wish I could fly...
I WANT TO GO BACK TO SYRIA
Love

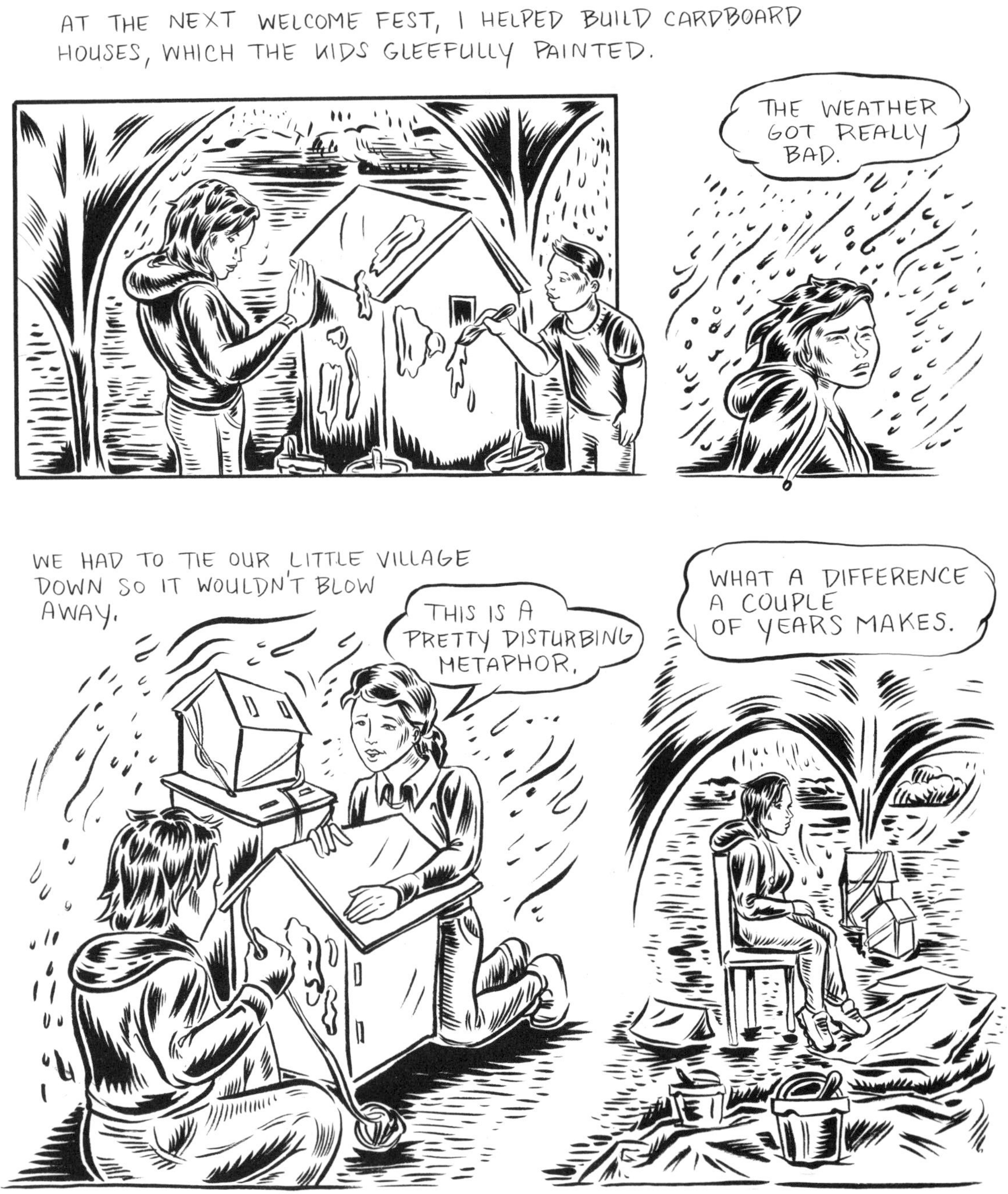
AT THE NEXT WELCOME FEST, I HELPED BUILD CARDBOARD HOUSES, WHICH THE KIDS GLEEFULLY PAINTED.
THE WEATHER GOT REALLY BAD.
WE HAD TO TIE OUR LITTLE VILLAGE DOWN SO IT WOULDN'T BLOW AWAY.
THIS IS A PRETTY DISTURBING METAPHOR.
WHAT A DIFFERENCE A COUPLE OF YEARS MAKES.

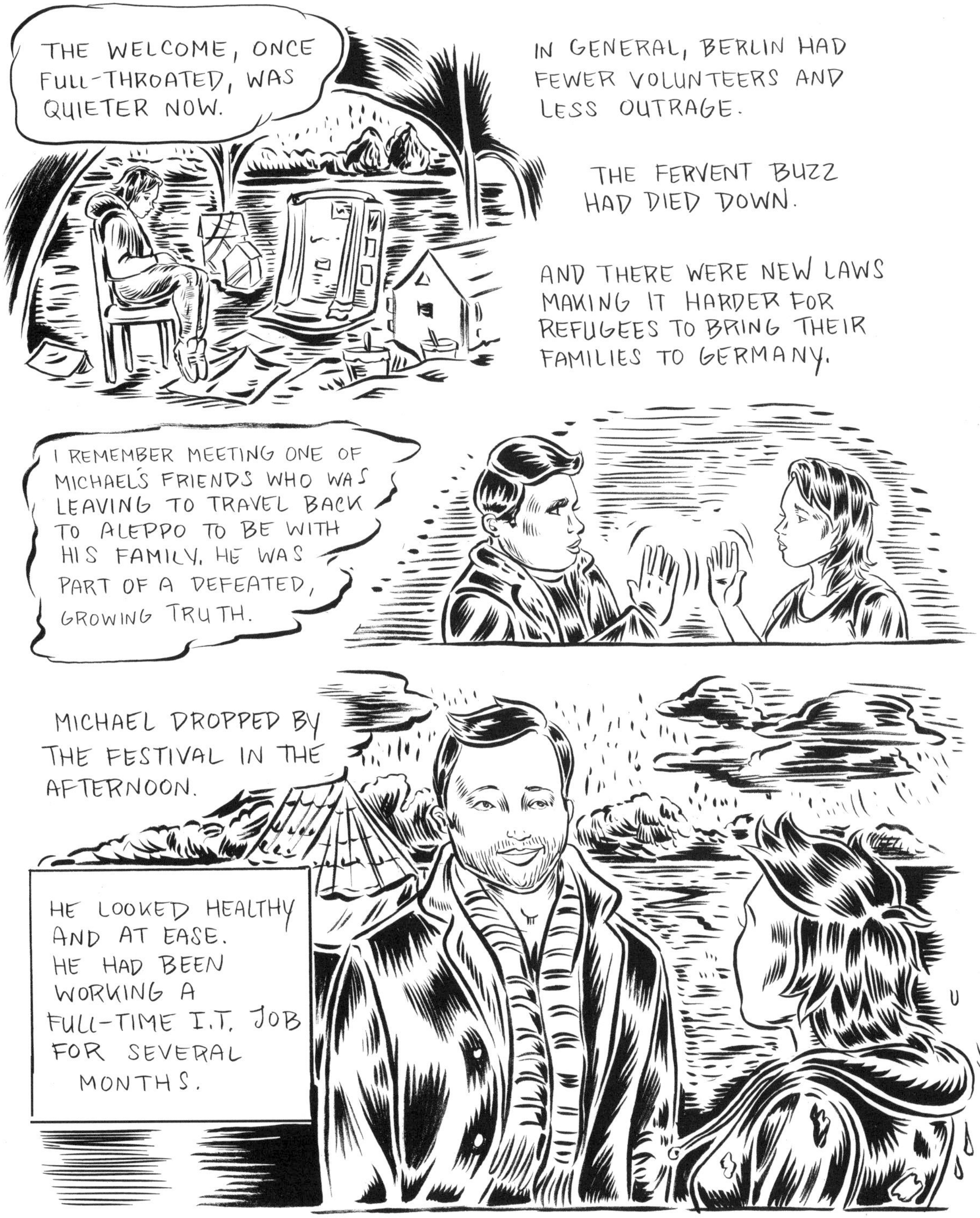
THE WELCOME, ONCE FULL-THROATED, WAS QUIETER NOW.
IN GENERAL, BERLIN HAD FEWER VOLUNTEERS AND LESS OUTRAGE.
THE FERVENT BUZZ HAD DIED DOWN.
AND THERE WERE NEW LAWS MAKING IT HARDER FOR REFUGEES TO BRING THEIR FAMILIES TO GERMANY.
I REMEMBER MEETING ONE OF MICHAEL'S FRIENDS WHO WAS LEAVING TO TRAVEL BACK TO ALEPPO TO BE WITH HIS FAMILY. HE WAS PART OF A DEFEATED, GROWING TRUTH.
MICHAEL DROPPED BY THE FESTIVAL IN THE AFTERNOON.
HE LOOKED HEALTHY AND AT EASE. HE HAD BEEN WORKING A FULL-TIME I.T. JOB FOR SEVERAL MONTHS.

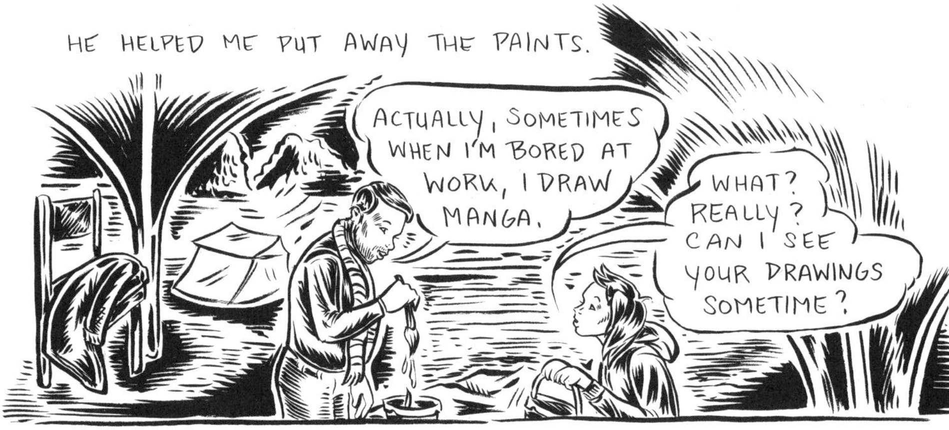
HE HELPED ME PUT AWAY THE PAINTS.
ACTUALLY, SOMETIMES WHEN I'M BORED AT WORK, I DRAW MANGA.
WHAT? REALLY? CAN I SEE YOUR DRAWINGS SOMETIME?

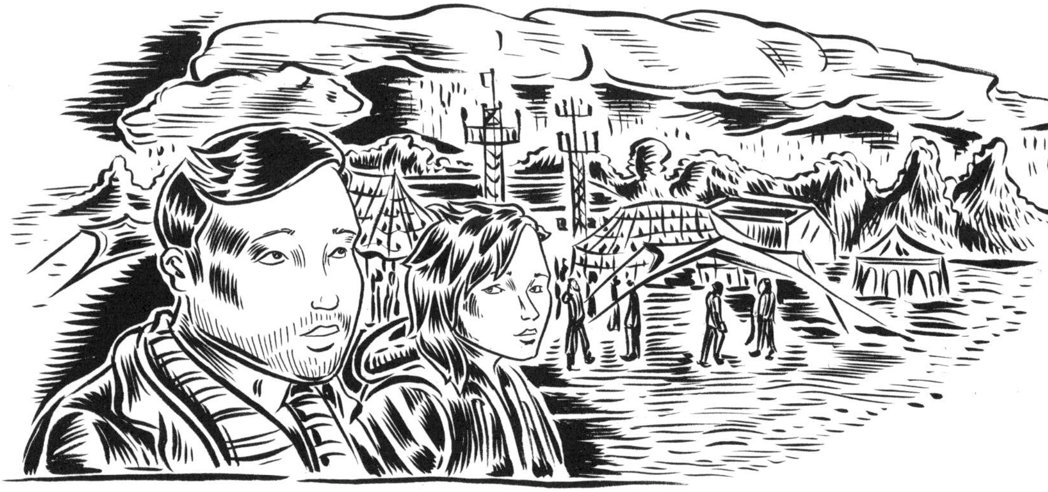

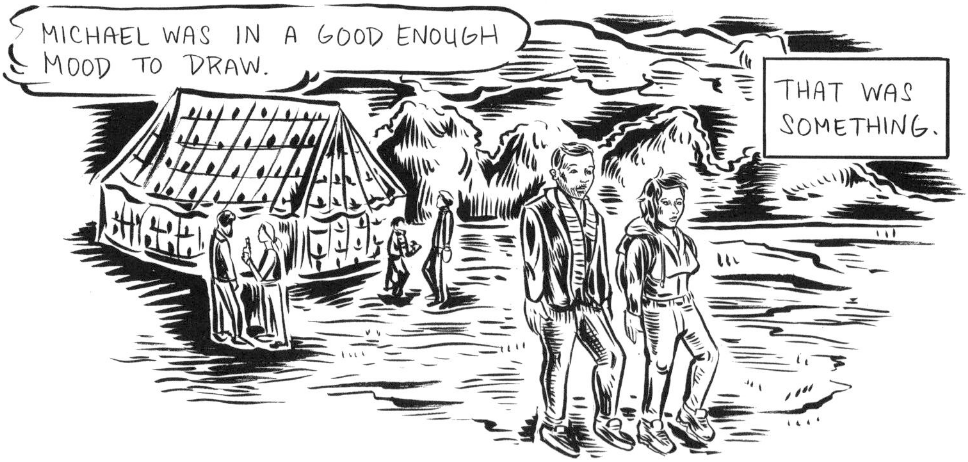
MICHAEL WAS IN A GOOD ENOUGH MOOD TO DRAW.
THAT WAS SOMETHING.

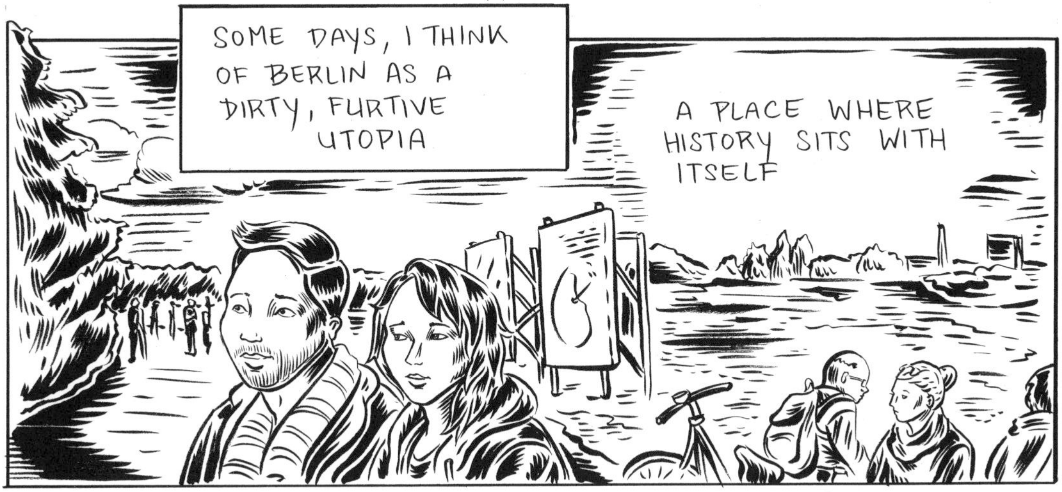
SOME DAYS, I THINK OF BERLIN AS A DIRTY, FURTIVE UTOPIA
A PLACE WHERE HISTORY SITS WITH ITSELF

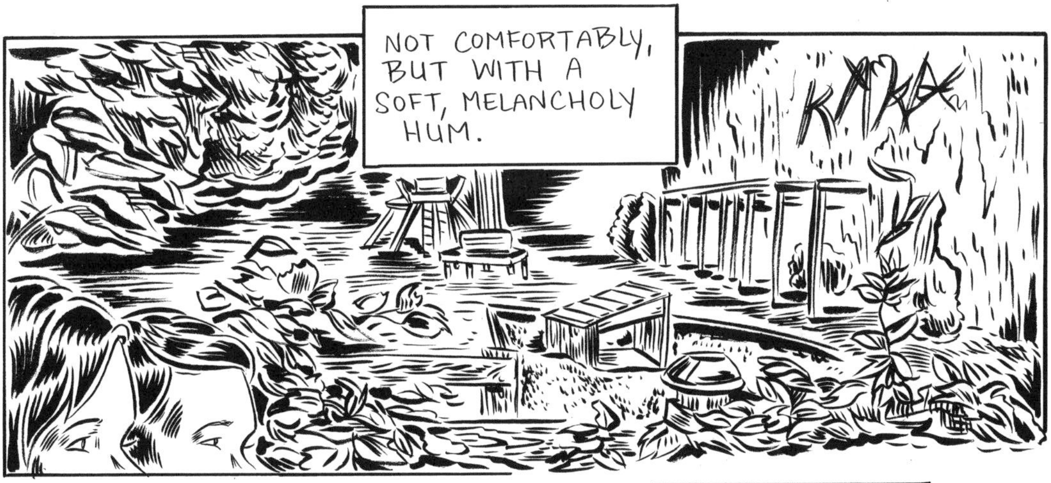
NOT COMFORTABLY, BUT WITH A SOFT, MELANCHOLY HUM.

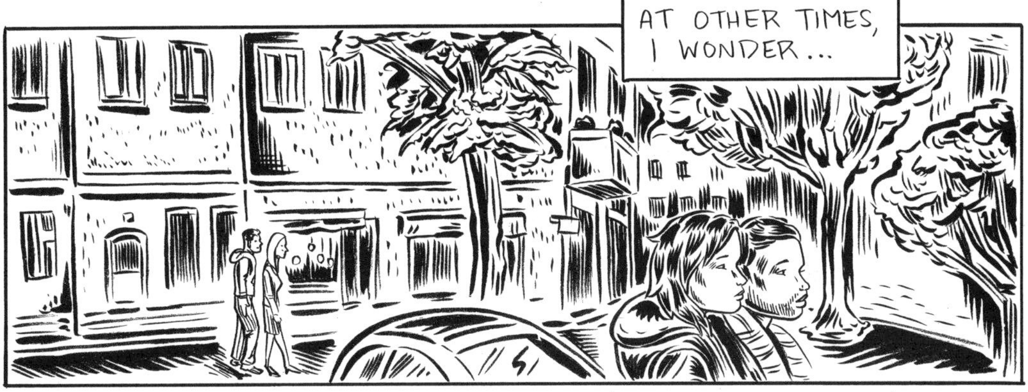
AT OTHER TIMES, I WONDER...

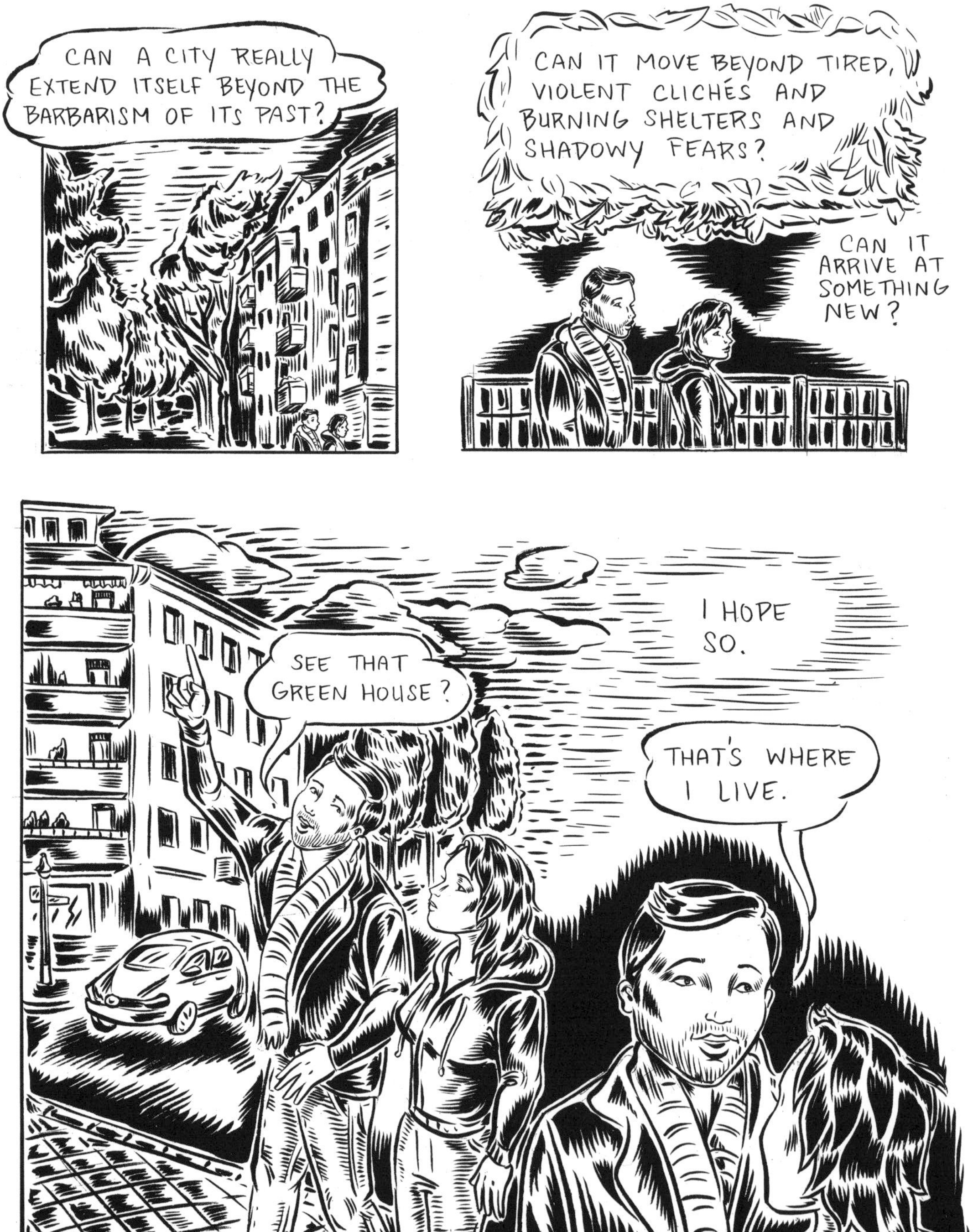
CAN A CITY REALLY EXTEND ITSELF BEYOND THE BARBARISM OF ITS PAST?
CAN IT MOVE BEYOND TIRED, VIOLENT CLICHÉS AND BURNING SHELTERS AND SHADOWY FEARS?
CAN IT ARRIVE AT SOMETHING NEW?
I HOPE SO.
SEE THAT GREEN HOUSE?
THAT'S WHERE I LIVE.

OH — THE WHOLE WORLD THINKS IN SUCH TIRED, WORN, TRADITIONAL CLICHÉS. IT NEVER ASKS THE WANDERER WHERE HE'S GOING. ONLY EVER WHERE HE'S COME FROM. AND WHAT MATTERS TO THE WANDERER IS HIS DESTINATION, NOT HIS POINT OF DEPARTURE.

AUTHOR'S NOTES

ALL OF THE NAMES HAVE BEEN CHANGED IN THIS BOOK: SOME UPON REQUEST AND THE REST AT MY DISCRETION. FOR THE PORTIONS OF THIS BOOK THAT TAKE PLACE IN SHELTERS, I SOUGHT TO RECORD THE PEOPLE AND ENVIRONMENT OF THESE WORKSHOPS FAITHFULLY. TO THAT END, I TRIED TO ONLY USE QUOTATIONS CULLED FROM MY NOTES. I USED SKETCHES AND THE FEW PHOTOGRAPHS I TOOK TO HELP FILL IN MY VISUAL MEMORY. ALTHOUGH THIS BOOK IN MANY WAYS CORRESPONDS TO THE TENETS OF COMIC JOURNALISM, I THINK OF IT AS SURREAL GRAPHIC NONFICTION, A COLLECTION OF ILLUSTRATED OBSERVATIONS, AND/OR AKIN TO MEMOIR — WITH THE SUBJECTIVITY THAT IMPLIES.

I CONSULTED THE FOLLOWING BOOKS/
ARTICLES WHILE RESEARCHING THE
SCHEUNENVIERTEL AND LIFE IN
BERLIN IN THE 1920S :

GEISEL, EIKE. *IM SCHEUNENVIERTEL.*
BERLIN: QUADRIGA GmbH
VERLAGSBUCHHANDLUNG KG, 1981.

ISHERWOOD, CHRISTOPHER. *THE BERLIN
STORIES.* U.K.: NEW DIRECTIONS, 1945.

ROTH, JOSEPH (TRANSLATED BY
MICHAEL HOFMANN). *THE WANDERING
JEWS.* NEW YORK: WW NORTON
& CO, INC., 2001.
—. (TRANSLATED BY MICHAEL
HOFMANN). *WHAT I SAW:
REPORTS FROM BERLIN 1920-1933.*
NEW YORK: WW NORTON COMPANY,
2004.

VAN BENSCHOTEN, ELLEN. "*TRACING
THE SCHEUNENVIERTEL: FORGETTING
AND REMEMBERING SPACES OF
EASTERN EUROPEAN JEWISH
MIGRANTS IN BERLIN-MITTE.*"
DAAD-STIPENDIUM FREIE
UNIVERSITÄT BERLIN, JUNE 2013.

A PORTION OF MY INCOME FROM
THIS BOOK WILL GO TOWARD
SUPPORTING ARTS PROGRAMS FOR
ASYLUM-SEEKERS IN EUROPE.
IF YOU'D LIKE TO VOLUNTEER OR
DONATE, BELOW ARE SOME AID
ORGANIZATIONS:

UNCHR
AMNESTY INTERNATIONAL
WHITE HELMETS

THANKS TO: EVERYONE WHO TOOK
PART IN THE WORKSHOPS, ESPECIALLY
SAKER AND MICHAEL.

THANKS ALSO TO: MATHIAS HAMANN
AND THE STADTMISSION BERLIN AND
VARIOUS SHELTERS FOR PROVIDING
ME WITH THE SPACE TO CONDUCT
THESE WORKSHOPS.

THANKS TO: MY AGENT, ALEX SLATER,
MY EDITOR, KRISTY VALENTI, AND
MY PUBLISHER, GARY GROTH, FOR
ALLOWING ME THE SPACE TO MAKE
THIS BOOK, AND THE CCS CORNISH
RESIDENCY FOR GIVING ME THE
TIME TO FINISH IT.

THANKS TO MY OTHER FAMILY
AND FRIENDS, WHO ARE WONDERFUL
AND SUPPORTIVE.

ALI FITZGERALD is a comic artist and writer living in Berlin. She is a regular contributor to the *New Yorker*. Her comics have also appeared in *New York Magazine*'s *The Cut*, *The New York Times*, *Modern Painters*, the *Huffington Post*, *Bitch*, and other publications. From 2013 to 2016, she wrote and drew the popular webcomic *Hungover Bear and Friends* for *McSweeney's*.

Between 2013 and 2016, Fitzgerald wrote the column *Queer Berlin* for the arts e-magazine *Art21*. In the spring of 2018, she collaborated with the San Francisco Museum of Modern Art on a series of graphic works about Magritte. She has led visual storytelling workshops at the National Library of Germany, the University of Bath, and Shakespeare and Company in Paris.